Beginning iPhone 3 Development
Exploring the iPhone SDK

DAVE MARK
JEFF LAMARCHE

Apress®

Beginning iPhone 3 Development: Exploring the iPhone SDK

Copyright © 2009 by Dave Mark and Jeff LaMarche

ISBN-13 (pbk): 978-1-4302-2459-4

ISBN-13 (electronic): 978-1-4302-2460-0

Printed and bound in the United States of America 9 8 7 6 5 4 3 2 1

Trademarked names may appear in this book. Rather than use a trademark symbol with every occurrence of a trademarked name, we use the names only in an editorial fashion and to the benefit of the trademark owner, with no intention of infringement of the trademark.

Lead Editors: Clay Andres, Douglas Pundick
Technical Reviewer: Mark Dalrymple
Editorial Board: Clay Andres, Steve Anglin, Mark Beckner, Ewan Buckingham, Tony Campbell, Gary Cornell,
    Jonathan Gennick, Michelle Lowman, Matthew Moodie, Jeffrey Pepper, Frank Pohlmann, Ben Renow-Clarke,
    Dominic Shakeshaft, Matt Wade, Tom Welsh
Project Managers: Grace Wong, Beth Christmas
Copy Editors: Kim Wimpsett, Heather Lang
Associate Production Director: Kari Brooks-Copony
Senior Production Editor: Laura Cheu
Compositor: Dina Quan
Proofreader: Nancy Sixsmith
Indexer: BIM Indexing & Proofreading Services
Artist: April Milne
Cover Designer: Kurt Krames
Manufacturing Director: Tom Debolski

Distributed to the book trade worldwide by Springer-Verlag New York, Inc., 233 Spring Street, 6th Floor, New York, NY 10013. Phone 1-800-SPRINGER, fax 201-348-4505, e-mail orders-ny@springer-sbm.com, or visit http://www.springeronline.com.

For information on translations, please contact Apress directly at 2855 Telegraph Avenue, Suite 600, Berkeley, CA 94705. Phone 510-549-5930, fax 510-549-5939, e-mail info@apress.com, or visit http://www.apress.com.

Apress and friends of ED books may be purchased in bulk for academic, corporate, or promotional use. eBook versions and licenses are also available for most titles. For more information, reference our Special Bulk Sales–eBook Licensing web page at http://www.apress.com/info/bulksales.

The source code for this book is available to readers at http://www.apress.com.

To Deneen, you are the light of my life. LFU4FREIH. . .
—Dave

To the most important people in my life, my wife and kids.
—Jeff

Contents at a Glance

Contents

About the Authors

Dave Mark is a longtime Mac developer and author and has written a number of books on Mac development, including *Learn C on the Mac* (Apress, 2009), *The Macintosh Programming Primer* series (Addison-Wesley, 1992), and *Ultimate Mac Programming* (Wiley, 1995). Dave loves the water and spends as much time as possible on it, in it, or near it. He lives with his wife and three children in Virginia.

Jeff LaMarche is a longtime Mac developer and iPhone Developer with more than 20 years of programming experience. He's written on Cocoa and Objective-C for *MacTech Magazine* and has written articles for Apple's Developer Technical Services web site. He has experience working in enterprise software as both a developer for PeopleSoft, starting in the late 1990s, and later as an independent consultant, though he now focuses exclusively on programming for the Mac and iPhone.

About the Technical Reviewer

 **Mark Dalrymple** is a longtime Mac and Unix programmer, working on cross-platform toolkits, Internet publishing tools, high-performance web servers, and end-user desktop applications. He's also the principal author of *Advanced Mac OS X Programming* (Big Nerd Ranch, 2005) and *Learn Objective-C on the Mac* (Apress, 2009). In his spare time, he plays trombone and bassoon and makes balloon animals.

Acknowledgments

This book could not have been written without our mighty, kind, and clever families, friends, and cohorts. First and foremost, eternal thanks to Terry and Deneen for putting up with us and for keeping the rest of the universe at bay while we toiled away on this book. This project saw us tucked away in our writers' cubby for many long hours, and somehow, you didn't complain once. We are lucky men.

This book could not have been written without the fine folks at Apress. More than just a publisher, they became fast friends. Clay Andres brought us to Apress in the first place and carried this book on his back. Dominic Shakeshaft was the brilliant mastermind who dealt with all of our complaints with a smile on his face and somehow found a solution that made sense and made this book better. Our editor, Douglas Pundick, reviewed every single word and made some really helpful suggestions. Laura Esterman, Beth Christmas, and Grace Wong, our wonderful and gracious project managers on the two editions, were the irresistible force to our slowly movable object. They kept the books on the right track and always kept us pointed in the right direction. Heather Lang and Kim Wimpsett, copy editors extraordinaire, you were both such a pleasure to work with; please, please, please copyedit our next book, too! Laura Cheu and the production team took all these pieces and somehow made them whole, and Dina Quan somehow coaxed such beautiful printed pages out of our Word documents. Kari Brooks-Copony pulled together an incredibly yummy interior design. Paul Carlstroem and Pete Aylward assembled the marketing message and got it out to the world. To all the folks at Apress, thank you, thank you, thank you!

A very special shout-out to our incredibly talented technical reviewer, Mark Dalrymple—in addition to providing insightful feedback, Mark tested all the code in this book and helped keep us on the straight and narrow. Thanks, Mark!

Finally, thanks to our children for their patience while their dads were working so hard. This book is for you, Maddie, Gwynnie, Ian, Kai, Daniel, Kelley, and Ryan.

Preface to *Beginning iPhone 3 Development*

What an amazing journey! When we set out to write a book on iPhone development, it was purely a labor of love. We never dreamed our book would end up in so many people's hands. Just imagine, our little book, available around the world. Who'd of thunk it? This wave of interest took us completely by surprise. And, of course, we are delighted by every bit of it.

So, what's new with this edition? Lots! For starters, we've gone through every single line of code and made whatever changes were necessary to bring each project into line with SDK 3. As you'd expect, we've gone through the text, too, so the explanations are all up-to-date. We've also gone through the errata from our Apress web page and the errors reported on our own web site, `http://iphonedevbook.com`, and we've done our best to scrub each and every error from the book. Of course, nothing is perfect, so please do report any errors you do find so we can continue to update the book through each new printing.

Is it worth buying this book if you already own the first edition? This is an excellent question that has spurred many a conversation with Apress and between the two of us. There is a lot of subtle new material, including a new project that introduces Core Data, which is an important persistence technology that has made its way to iPhone. In addition, many of the discussions have been clarified in an attempt to make some of the more complex topics a bit easier to understand.

We've definitely made the book better. If you've already been through the first edition and feel very comfortable with all the material, go ahead and move on to *More iPhone 3 Development*, which takes up where this book leaves off, discussing the amazing new technologies introduced with SDK 3.

If you haven't made it through the entire first edition yet, if you feel a bit fuzzy still, or if you just want to support us as authors, then by all means pick up this second edition. We do appreciate your support. Be sure to check out `http://iphonedevbook.com`, and drop us a line to let us know about your amazing new apps. We look forward to seeing you on the forum. Happy coding!

Dave and Jeff

Preface to *Beginning iPhone 2 Development*

"I haven't been this excited about a programming platform since I first set eyes on the Mac." We've been hearing this sentiment a lot lately, and frankly, we feel exactly the same way. The iPhone is thrilling, a fantastic piece of technology, and a brilliant combination of function and fun. And the things you can do as a programmer!

This world is just beginning to open up. Spend some time browsing through the App Store, and you can't help but be filled with inspiration. And, if designing your own iPhone application just isn't your thing, the opportunities for iPhone development consulting are limitless. Everyone seems to want to port their product to the platform. Our phones have been ringing off the hook.

If you get a few moments, swing by our web site, `http://iphonedevbook.com`, and say "hi." Tell us about your own projects. We'd love to hear from you.

Dave and Jeff

Chapter 1

Welcome to the Jungle

So, you want to write iPhone applications? Well, we can't say that we blame you. iPhone might just be the most interesting new platform to come around in a long time; certainly, it is the most interesting mobile platform to date, especially now that Apple has provided a set of elegant, well-documented tools for developing iPhone applications. And with the recent release of version 3.0 of the iPhone software development kit (SDK), things have only gotten better.

> **NOTE**
>
> This book has been newly revised and updated to work with the latest version of the SDK. In some places, we have chosen to use new functions or methods introduced with version 3.0 that may prove incompatible with earlier versions of the SDK. We'll be sure to point those situations out as they arise in this book.
>
> Be sure to download the latest and greatest source code archives from the book's web site at `http://iphonedevbook.com`.
>
> We've added conditional macros to that code to allow it to build with the latest version of the SDK, as well as with older versions of the SDK. We'll update the code as new versions of the SDK are released, so be sure to check the site periodically.

What This Book Is

This book is a guide to help you get started down the path to creating your own iPhone applications. Our goal is to get you past the initial learning curve to help you understand the way iPhone applications work and how they are built. As you work your way through this book, you will create a number of small applications, each designed to highlight specific iPhone features and show you how to control or interact with those features. If you combine the foundation you'll gain by making your way through this book with your own creativity and determination and then add in the extensive and well-written documentation provided by Apple, you'll have everything you'll need to build your own professional iPhone applications.

NOTE

Dave and Jeff have a forum set up for this book. It's a great place to meet like-minded folks, get your questions answered, and even answer other people's questions. It's at `http://iphonedevbook.com/forum`. Be sure to check it out!

What You Need Before You Can Begin

Before you can begin writing software for iPhone, you'll need a few things. For starters, you'll need an Intel-based Macintosh running Leopard (OS X 10.5.6 or later). Any Macintosh computer—laptop or desktop—released since mid-2006 should work just fine.

You do not need a top-of-the-line model to get started, so a MacBook or Mac Mini will serve admirably. The older and slower the model, the more it will benefit from a RAM upgrade, however.

You'll also need to sign up to become a registered iPhone developer. Apple requires this step before you're allowed to download the iPhone SDK.

To sign up, navigate to `http://developer.apple.com/iphone/`, which will bring you to a page similar to the one shown in Figure 1-1. Somewhere on the page is a link to the latest and greatest iPhone SDK. Click the link, and you'll be brought to a sign-up page with three options.

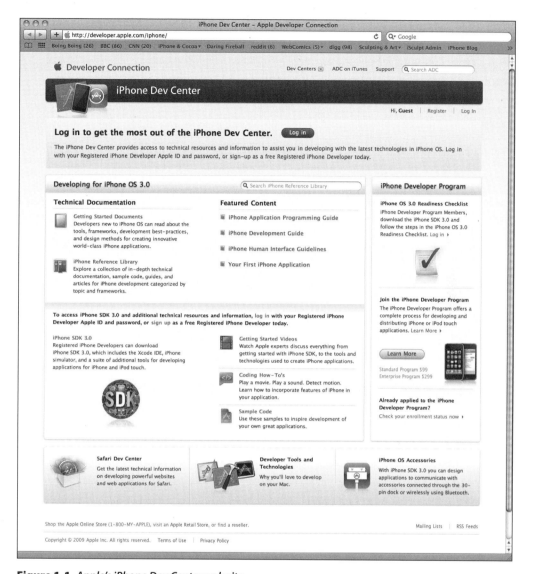

Figure 1-1. *Apple's iPhone Dev Center web site*

The simplest (and free) option is to click the button that reads *Download the Free SDK*. You'll be prompted for your Apple ID. Use your Apple ID to log in. If you don't have an Apple ID, click the *Create Apple ID* button, create one, and then log in. Once you are logged in, you'll be taken to the main iPhone development page. Not only will you find a link to the SDK download, but you'll also find links to a wealth of documentation, videos, sample code, and the like, all dedicated to teaching you the finer points of iPhone application development.

One of the most important elements included with the iPhone SDK is Xcode, Apple's integrated development environment (IDE). Xcode includes tools for creating and debugging source code, compiling applications, and performance tuning the applications you've written. By the time you are finished with this book, you will become an Xcode aficionado!

The free SDK also includes a simulator that will allow you to run most iPhone programs on your Mac. This is perfect for learning how to program your iPhone. The free option will not, however, allow you to download your applications onto your actual iPhone (or iPod touch). It also does not give you the ability to distribute your applications on Apple's iPhone App Store. For that, you'll need one of the other two options, which aren't free.

NOTE

The simulator does *not* support hardware-dependent features, such as iPhone's accelerometer or camera. For those, you'll need the alternate options as well. Just thought you'd like to know!

The Standard program costs $99. It provides a host of development tools and resources, technical support, distribution of your application via Apple's App Store, and, most importantly, the ability to test and debug your code on an iPhone rather than just in the simulator.

The Enterprise program costs $299 and is designed for companies developing proprietary, in-house applications for iPhone and iPod touch and for those developing applications for the Apple's App Store and with more than one developer working on the project.

For more details on these two programs, visit `http://developer.apple.com/iphone/program/`.

Because iPhone is an always-connected mobile device that uses other companies' wireless infrastructure, Apple has had to place far more restrictions on iPhone developers than it ever has on Mac developers, who are able to write and distribute programs with absolutely no oversight or approval from Apple.

Apple has not added restrictions to be mean but rather is trying to minimize the chances of malicious or poorly written programs being distributed that could degrade performance on the shared network. Developing for the iPhone may seem like it presents a lot of hoops to jump through, but Apple has gone through quite an effort to make the process as painless as possible. It should be noted too that $99 is still considerably less than buying, for example, Visual Studio, which is Microsoft's software development IDE.

This may seem obvious, but you'll also need an iPhone or iPod touch. While much of your code can be tested using the iPhone Simulator, not all programs can be, and even those that can really need to be thoroughly tested on an actual iPhone before you ever consider releasing your application to the public.

NOTE

If you are going to sign up for the Standard or Enterprise program, you should go do it right now. The approval process can take a while, and you'll need that approval to be able to run your applications on your iPhone or iPod touch. Don't worry, though, because all the projects in the first several chapters and the majority of the applications in this book will run just fine on the iPhone Simulator.

What You Need to Know Before You Begin

This book assumes that you already have some programming knowledge. It assumes that you understand the fundamentals of object-oriented programming such as what objects, loops, and variables are, for example. It also assumes you are familiar with the Objective-C programming language. Cocoa Touch, the part of the SDK that you will be using through most of this book, uses Objective-C 2.0, but don't worry if you're not familiar with the more recent additions to the Objective-C language. We'll be sure to highlight any of the 2.0 language features we take advantage of and explain how they work and why we are using them.

You should also be familiar with the iPhone itself. Just as you would with any platform for which you wanted to write an application, get to know the iPhone's nuances and quirks, and get familiar with the iPhone interface and with the way Apple's iPhone programs look and feel.

NEW TO OBJECTIVE-C?

If you have not programmed in Objective-C before, here are a few resources to help you get started.

First, check out *Learn Objective-C on the Mac*, an excellent and approachable introduction to Objective-C by Mac programming experts Mark Dalrymple and Scott Knaster (Apress, 2008):

```
http://www.apress.com/book/view/9781430218159
```

Next, navigate over to the Apple iPhone Dev Center, and download a copy of *The Objective-C 2.0 Programming Language*, a very detailed and extensive description of the language and a great reference guide:

```
http://developer.apple.com/iphone/library/ ➡
        documentation/Cocoa/Conceptual/ObjectiveC
```

Note that you'll be asked to log in before you are taken to the start of this document.

What's Different About Coding for iPhone?

If you have never used Cocoa or its predecessor NextSTEP, you may find Cocoa Touch, the application framework you'll be using to write iPhone applications, a little alien; there are some fundamental differences from other common application frameworks such as those used when building .NET or Java applications. Don't worry too much if you feel a little lost at first. Just keep plugging away at the exercises, and it'll all start to fall into place after a while.

If you *have* written programs using Cocoa or NextSTEP, you're going to find a lot in the iPhone SDK that is familiar to you. A great many classes are unchanged from the versions that are used to develop for Mac OS X, and even those that are different tend to follow the same basic principles and use design patterns similar to the ones you are already familiar with. There are, however, several differences between Cocoa and Cocoa Touch.

Regardless of your background, you need to keep in mind some key differences between iPhone development and desktop application development.

Only One Running Application

With the exception of the operating system itself, only one application can be running at any given time on an iPhone. This may change in the future as iPhone gets more memory and more powerful processors, but for the time being, your application will be the only one running while your code is executing. When your application isn't the one the user is interacting with, it won't be able to do anything.

Only One Window

Unlike desktop and laptop operating systems where many running programs coexist, each with the ability to create and control multiple windows, iPhone gives your application just one "window" to work with. All of your application's interaction with the user takes place inside this one window, and its size is fixed at the size of the iPhone screen.

Limited Access

Unlike programs on a computer that pretty much have access to everything the user who launched them does, iPhone seriously restricts what your application can get to. You can read and write files only from the part of iPhone's file system that was created for your application. This area is called your application's **sandbox**, and it is where your application will store documents, preferences, and every other kind of data it may need to store.

Your application is also constrained in some other ways; you will not be able to access low-number network ports on iPhone, for example, or do anything else that would typically require root or administrative access on a desktop computer.

Limited Response Time

Because of the way it is used, iPhone needs to be snappy and expects the same of your application. When your program is launched, you have to get your application open, preferences and data loaded, and the main view shown on the screen as fast as possible—in not more than a few seconds. At any time when your program is running, it may have the rug pulled out from under it. If the user presses the home button, iPhone goes home, and you have to quickly save everything and quit. If you take longer than five seconds to save and give up control, your application process will be killed, regardless of whether you are finished saving.

As a result, you have to carefully craft your iPhone applications to make sure data is not lost when the user quits.

Limited Screen Size

iPhone's screen is really nice. When introduced, it was the highest-resolution screen available on a consumer device, by far. But the iPhone display just isn't all that big, and as a result, you have a lot less room to work with than on modern computers, just 320 × 480 pixels. To give an interesting contrast, at the time of this writing, Apple's least expensive iMac supports 1680 × 1050 pixels, and its least expensive notebook computer, the MacBook, supports 1280 × 800 pixels. On the other end of the spectrum, Apple's largest monitor, the 30-inch Cinema Display, offers a whopping 2560 × 1600 pixels.

Limited System Resources

Any old-time programmers who are reading this are likely laughing at the idea of a machine with at least 128MB of RAM and 4GB of storage being in any way resource constrained, but it is true. Developing for the iPhone is not, perhaps, in exactly the same league as trying to write a complex spreadsheet application on a machine with 48KB of memory, but given the graphical nature of iPhone and all the things it is capable of doing, running out of memory is very, very easy. The versions of iPhone available right now all have either 128MB or 256MB of physical RAM, though that will likely increase over time. Some of that memory is used for the screen buffer and by other system processes. Usually, no more than half of that memory is left for your application to use, and it can be considerably less.

Although that may sound like it leaves a pretty decent amount of memory for such a small computer, there is another factor to consider when it comes to memory on iPhone: modern computer operating systems like Mac OS X will take chunks of memory that aren't being used and write them out to disk in something called a **swap file**, which allows applications to keep running even when they have requested more memory than is actually available on the computer. The iPhone OS, however, will not write volatile memory, such as application data, out to a swap file. As a result, the amount of memory available to your application is constrained by the amount of unused physical memory in the phone.

Cocoa Touch has built-in mechanisms for letting your application know that memory is getting low. When that happens, your application must free up unneeded memory or risk being forced to quit.

No Garbage Collection

We mentioned earlier that Cocoa Touch uses Objective-C 2.0, but one of the key new features of that language is not available on iPhone: Cocoa Touch does not support garbage collection.

Some New Stuff

Since we've mentioned that Cocoa Touch is missing some features that Cocoa has, it seems only fair to mention that the iPhone SDK contains some new functionality that is not currently present in Cocoa or, at least, is not available on every Mac. The iPhone SDK provides a way for your application to determine the phone's current geographic coordinates using Core Location. iPhone also has a built-in camera and photo library, and the SDK provides mechanisms that allow your application to access both. iPhone also has a built-in accelerometer that lets you detect how your iPhone is being held and moved.

A Different Approach

Two things iPhone doesn't have are a physical keyboard and a mouse, which means you have a fundamentally different way of interacting with the user than you do when programming for a general-purpose computer. Fortunately, most of that interaction is handled for you. If you add a text field to your application, iPhone knows to bring up a keyboard when the user clicks in that field, for example, without you having to write any extra code.

What's in This Book

Here is a very brief overview of the remaining chapters in this book.

Chapter 2

In this chapter, we'll learn how to use Xcode's partner in crime, Interface Builder, to create a simple interface, placing some text on the iPhone screen.

Chapter 3

In Chapter 3, we'll start interacting with the user, building a simple application that dynamically updates displayed text at runtime based on buttons the user presses.

Chapter 4

Chapter 4 will build on Chapter 3 by introducing you to several more of iPhone's standard user interface controls. We'll also look at how to use alerts and sheets to prompt users to make a decision or to inform them that something out of the ordinary has occurred.

Chapter 5

In Chapter 5, we'll look at handling autorotation, the mechanism that allows iPhone applications to be used in both portrait and landscape modes.

Chapter 6

We'll move into more advanced user interfaces in Chapter 6 and look at creating multiview interfaces. We'll change which view is being shown to the user at runtime, allowing you to create more complex user interfaces.

Chapter 7

Toolbar controllers are one of the standard iPhone user interfaces; in Chapter 7, we'll look at how to implement this kind of interface.

Chapter 8

In Chapter 8, we'll look at table views, the primary way of providing lists of data to the user and the foundation of hierarchical navigation-based applications and also see how to let the user search in your application data.

Chapter 9

One of the most common iPhone application interfaces is the hierarchical list that lets you drill down to see more data or more details. In Chapter 9, you'll see what's involved in implementing this standard type of interface.

Chapter 10

In Chapter 10, we'll look at implementing application settings, which is iPhone's mechanism for letting users set their application-level preferences.

Chapter 11

Chapter 11 looks at data management on iPhone. We'll talk about creating objects to hold application data and see how that data can be persisted to iPhone's file system. We'll also see the basics of using something called Core Data, which allows you to save and retrieve data easily.

Chapter 12

Everybody loves to draw, so we'll look at doing some custom drawing in Chapter 12, using basic drawing functions in Quartz and OpenGL ES.

Chapter 13

iPhone's multitouch screen can accept a wide variety of gestural inputs from the user. In Chapter 13, you'll learn all about detecting basic gestures such as the pinch and swipe. We'll also look at the process of defining new gestures and talk about when new gestures are appropriate.

Chapter 14

iPhone is capable of determining its latitude and longitude thanks to Core Location. We'll build some code that makes use of Core Location to figure out where in the world your iPhone is and use that information in our quest for world dominance.

Chapter 15

In Chapter 15, we'll look at interfacing with iPhone's accelerometer, which is how your iPhone knows which way it's being held. We'll look at some of the fun things your application can do with that information.

Chapter 16

Each iPhone has a camera and a library of pictures, both of which are available to your application, if you ask nicely! In Chapter 16, we'll show you how to ask nicely.

Chapter 17

iPhone is currently available in 80 countries. In Chapter 17, we'll show you how to write your applications in such a way that all parts of your application can be easily translated into other languages to expand the potential audience for your applications.

Chapter 18

At this point in the book, you'll have mastered the fundamental building blocks for creating iPhone applications. But where do you go from here? In Chapter 18, we'll explore the logical next steps for you to take on your journey to master the iPhone SDK.

What's New in This Update?

Since the first edition of this book hit the bookstores, lots has been happening in the iPhone development universe. The growth of the iPhone development community has been phenomenal. The SDK has continually evolved, with Apple releasing a steady stream of updates to SDK 2. In March 2009, Apple announced a major release, SDK 3.0. Apple's iPhone team sure has been busy.

Well, we've been busy, too! The second we found out about SDK 3.0, we immediately went to work, updating every single project to ensure not only that the code for each one compiles under the new version of the SDK but also that each one takes advantage of the latest and greatest features offered by Cocoa Touch. We reshot a boatload of screenshots; tweaked the prose throughout the book; and, in Chapter 11, added a brief introduction to Core Data, one of the most exciting new parts of iPhone SDK 3.

Are You Ready?

iPhone is an incredible computing platform and an exciting new frontier for your development pleasure. Programming your iPhone is going to be a new experience, different from that of any platform you've worked with before. For everything that looks familiar, there will be something alien, but as you work through the book's code, the concepts should all come together and start to make sense.

You should keep in mind that the exercises in this book are not simply a checklist that, when completed, magically grants you iPhone developer guru status. Make sure you understand what you did, and why, before moving on to the next project. Don't be afraid to make changes to the code; experimenting and observing the results is one of the best ways you can wrap your head around the complexities of coding in an environment like Cocoa Touch.

That said, if you've got your iPhone SDK installed, turn the page. If not, get to it! Got it? Good. Then let's go!

Chapter 2

Appeasing the Tiki Gods

*a*s you're probably well aware, it has become something of a tradition to call the first project in any book on programming "Hello, World!" We considered breaking this tradition but were scared that the tiki gods would inflict some painful retribution on us for such a gross breach of etiquette. So, let's do it by the book, shall we?

In this chapter, we're going use Xcode and Interface Builder to create a small iPhone application to display the text "Hello, World!" on its screen. We'll look at what's involved in creating an iPhone application project in Xcode, work through the specifics of using Interface Builder to design our application's user interface, and then run our application on the iPhone simulator. After that, we'll give our application an icon and a unique identifier to make it feel more like a real iPhone application.

We've got a lot to do here, so let's get going.

Setting Up Your Project in Xcode

By now, you should have Xcode and the iPhone SDK installed on your machine. You should also download the book projects archive from the book web site. Here's a link:

```
http://www.iphonedevbook.com/forum/
```

The book forums are a great place to download the latest book source code, get your questions answered, and meet up with like-minded people.

As to the book project archive, even though you have the complete set of project files at your disposal, we think you'll get more out of the book if you create each project by hand instead of simply running the version you downloaded. The biggest reason for this is the familiarity and expertise you'll gain in working with the various tools we use throughout the book if you roll your own projects. There's just no substitute for actually clicking and dragging out buttons and sliders and scrolling through source code to make changes as we move from one version of a program to another.

That said, our first project is in the *02 Hello World* folder. If you'll be creating your own projects, create a new *02 Hello World* folder and follow along.

Launch Xcode, which is located in */Developer/Applications*. If this is your first time using Xcode, don't worry; we'll walk you through the process of creating a new project. If you're already an old hand, just skim ahead.

When you first launch Xcode, you'll be presented with a welcome screen like the one shown in Figure 2-1. The welcome screen contains useful links to iPhone and Mac OS X technical documentation, tutorial videos, news, sample code, and lots more. All of this information is available on Apple's developer web site and within Xcode's documentation browser, so if you'd rather not see this screen in the future, just uncheck the *Show at launch* checkbox before closing it. If you feel like poking through the information here for a few minutes, by all means, go right ahead. When you're done, close the window, and we'll proceed.

Figure 2-1. *The Xcode welcome screen*

NOTE

If you have an iPhone or iPod touch connected to your machine, you might see a message when you first launch Xcode asking whether you want to use that device for development. Alternatively, a window titled *Organizer*, designed to list the devices you'll be working with, might appear. For now, click the *Ignore* button or, in the case of the *Organizer* window, close the window. If you choose to join the paid iPhone Developer Program, you will gain access to a program portal that will tell you how to use your iPhone or iPod touch for development and testing.

Create a new project by selecting **New Project...** from the **File** menu, or by pressing ⇧⌘N, which will bring up the New Project assistant (see Figure 2-2).

Figure 2-2. *The New Project assistant, which lets you select from various file templates when creating a new file*

As you can see in Figure 2-2, the pane on the left side of the window is divided into two main sections: *iPhone OS* and *Mac OS X*. You'll notice that there are a number of project template categories available for Mac OS X, but only one category (at least at the time of this writing) for the iPhone: *Application*.

As we did in Figure 2-2, select *Application* from under the iPhone heading, and you'll be shown a number of icons in the upper-right pane, each of which represents a separate **project template** that can be used as a starting point for your iPhone applications. The icon labeled *View-based Application* is the simplest template and the one we'll be using for the first several chapters. The others provide you with additional code and/or resources needed to create common iPhone application interfaces and contain stuff we're not ready to look at yet, but don't worry, we'll get to them later.

For this first project, click the *View-based Application* icon (that icon is selected in Figure 2-2) and then click the button labeled *Choose.*

Once you've selected your project template, you'll be asked to save your new project using the standard save sheet (see Figure 2-3). Type *Hello World* for the project name, and save it wherever you want it stored. The *Document* folder is not a bad place, but you might want to create a dedicated folder for your Xcode projects.

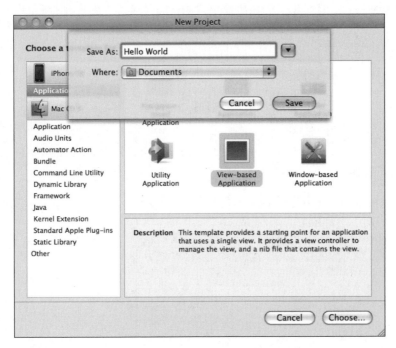

Figure 2-3. *Selecting the name and location for your project*

The Xcode Project Window

After you dismiss the save sheet, Xcode will create and then open your project, and a new project window will appear that looks like Figure 2-4. We find that the project window, when first created, is a little small for our tastes, so we usually expand the window to take up more of the screen. There's a lot of information crammed into this window, and it's where you will be spending a lot of your iPhone development time.

Figure 2-4. *The Hello World project in Xcode*

Your project window features a toolbar across the top, which gives you ready access to a lot of commonly used commands. Below the toolbar, the window is divided into three main sections, or panes.

The pane that runs down the left side of the window is called the *Groups & Files* pane. All of the resources that make up your project are grouped here, as are a number of relevant project settings. Just as in the Finder, clicking the little triangle to the left of an item expands that item to show available subitems. Click the triangle again to hide the subitems.

The top-right pane is called the *Detail View* (or just *Detail* pane) and shows you detailed information about items selected in the *Groups & Files* pane. The lower-right pane is called the *Editor* pane. If you select a single file in either the *Groups & Files* or *Detail* pane and Xcode knows how to display that kind of file, the contents of the file will be displayed in the *Editor* pane. Editable files, such as source code, can also be edited here. In fact, this is where you will be writing and editing your application's source code.

Now that we have the terminology out of the way, take a look at the *Groups & Files* pane. The first item in the list should bear the same name as your project, in this case, *Hello World*. This item is the gathering point for the source code and the other resources specific to your project. For the time being, don't worry about the items in the *Groups & Files* pane except those under *Hello World*.

Take a look at Figure 2-4. Note that the disclosure triangle to the left of *Hello World* is open, and there are five subfolders: *Classes*, *Other Sources*, *Resources*, *Frameworks*, and *Products*. Let's briefly talk about what each subfolder is used for:

- *Classes* is where you will spend much of your time. This is where most of the code that you write will go, since this is where all Objective-C classes rightfully belong. You are free to create subfolders under the *Classes* folder to help organize your code. We'll be using this folder starting in the next chapter.

- *Other Sources* contains source code files that aren't Objective-C classes. Typically, you won't spend a lot of time in the *Other Sources* folder. When you create a new iPhone application project, there are two files in this folder:

  - *Hello_World_Prefix.pch*: The extension *.pch* stands for "precompiled header." This is a list of header files from external frameworks that are used by our project. Xcode will precompile the headers contained in this file, which will reduce the amount of time it takes to compile your project whenever you select **Build** or **Build and Go**. It will be a while before you have to worry about this, because the most commonly used header files are already included for you.

  - *main.m*: This is where your application's `main()` method is. You normally won't need to edit or change this file.

- *Resources* contains noncode files that will be included as part of your application. This is where you will include files such as your application's icon image and other images, sound files, movie files, text files, or property lists that your program may need while it's running. Remember, since your application runs in its own sandbox, you will have to include any files you need here, because you won't be able to access files located elsewhere on the iPhone except through sanctioned APIs, such as the ones that provide access to the iPhone's photo library and address book. There should be three items in this folder:

  - *Hello_WorldViewController.xib*: This file contains information used by the program Interface Builder, which we'll take for a spin a bit later in this chapter.

  - *MainWindow.xib*: This is your application's main Interface Builder (or "nib") file. In a simple application like the one we're building in this chapter, there's often no need to touch this file. In later chapters, when we design more complex interfaces, we will work with this file and look at it in more depth.

  - *Hello_World-Info.plist*: This is a property list that contains information about our application. We'll look at this file a little bit later in the chapter too.

- *Frameworks* are a special kind of library that can contain code as well as resources such as image and sound files. Any framework or library that you add to this folder will be linked in to your application, and your code will be able to use objects, functions, and resources contained in that framework or library. The most commonly needed frameworks and libraries are linked in to our project by default, so most of the time, we will not need to do anything with this folder. Less commonly used libraries and frameworks, however, are not included by default, and you will see how to link to them into an application later in this book.

- *Products* contains the application that this project produces when it is compiled. If you expand *Products*, you'll see an item called *Hello World.app*. This is the application that this particular project creates. *Hello World.app* is this project's only product. Right now, *Hello World.app* is listed in red, which means that the file cannot be found, which makes sense, since we haven't compiled our project yet! Highlighting a file's name in red is Xcode's way of telling us that it can't find the underlying physical file.

NOTE

The "folders" in the *Groups & Files* pane do not necessarily correspond to folders in your Mac's file system. These are logical groupings within Xcode to help you keep everything organized and to make it faster and easier to find what you're looking for while working on your application. If you look into your project's folder on your hard drive, you'll notice that while there is a *Classes* folder, there is no folder called *Other Sources* or *Resources*. Often, the items contained in those two project folders are stored right in the project's root directory, but you can store them anywhere, even outside of your project folder if you want. The hierarchy inside Xcode is completely independent of the file system hierarchy. Moving a file out of the *Classes* folder in Xcode, for example, will not change the file's location on your hard drive.

Introducing Interface Builder

Now that you're familiar with the basics of Xcode, let's take a look at the other half of the dynamic duo used in iPhone software development: Interface Builder, commonly referred to as IB.

In your project window's *Groups & Files* list, expand the *Resources* group, and then double-click the file *Hello_WorldViewController.xib*. This will open that file in Interface Builder. If this is your first time using Interface Builder, a window grouping similar to that shown in Figure 2-5 should appear. If you've used Interface Builder before, the windows will be where you left them the last time you used it.

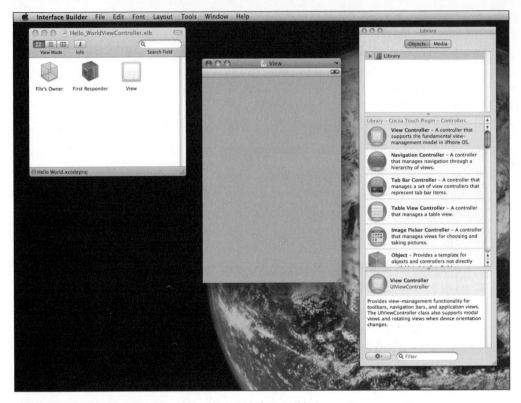

Figure 2-5. *Hello_WorldViewController.xib in Interface Builder*

NOTE

Interface Builder has a long history; it has been around since 1988 and has been used to develop applications for NextSTEP, OpenSTEP, Mac OS X, and now iPhone. Interface Builder supports two file types: an older format that uses the extension *.nib* and a newer format that utilizes the extension *.xib*. The iPhone project templates all use *.xib* files by default, but until very recently, all Interface Builder files had the extension *.nib*, and as a result, most developers took to calling Interface Builder files **nib files**. Interface Builder files are commonly called nib files regardless of whether the extension actually used for the file is *.xib* or *.nib*. In fact, Apple actually uses the terms **nib** and **nib file** throughout its documentation.

The window labeled *Hello_WorldViewController.xib* (the upper-left window in Figure 2-5) is the nib's main window. It is your home base and starting point in this particular nib file. With the exception of the first two icons (*File's Owner* and *First Responder*), every icon in this window represents a single instance of an Objective-C class that will be created automatically for you when this nib file is loaded.

Want to create an instance of a button? You could, of course, create the button by writing code. But more commonly, you will use Interface Builder to create the button and specify its attributes (shape, size, label, etc.).

The *Hello_WorldViewController.xib* file we are looking at right now gets loaded automatically when your application launches—for the moment, don't worry about how—so it is an excellent place to create the objects that make up your user interface.

For example, to add a button to your application, you'll need to instantiate an object of type `UIButton`. You can do this in code by typing a line like this:

```
UIButton *myButton = [[UIButton alloc] initWithFrame:aRect];
```

In Interface Builder, you can accomplish the same exact thing by dragging a button from a palette of interface objects onto your application's main window. Interface Builder makes it easy to set the button's attributes, and since the button will be saved in the nib file, the button will be automatically instantiated when your application starts up. You'll see how this works in a minute.

What's in the Nib File?

Take a look at Figure 2-5. As we mentioned earlier, the window labeled *Hello_WorldViewController.xib* (the upper-left window) is the nib file's main window. Every nib file starts off with the same two icons, *File's Owner* and *First Responder*. They are created automatically and cannot be deleted. From that, you can probably guess that they are important, and they are.

File's Owner will always be the first icon in any nib file and represents the object that loaded the nib file from disk. In other words, *File's Owner* is the object that "owns" this copy of the nib file. If this is a bit confusing, don't worry; it's not important at the moment. When it does become important later, we'll go over it again.

The second icon in this and any other nib file is called *First Responder*. We'll talk more about responders later in the book, but in very basic terms, the first responder is the object with which the user is currently interacting. If, for example, the user is currently entering data into a text field, that field is the current first responder. The first responder changes as the user interacts with the interface, and the *First Responder* icon gives you a convenient way to communicate with whatever control or view is the current first responder without having to write code to determine which control or view that might be. Again, we'll talk about this much more later, so don't worry if this concept is a bit fuzzy right now.

Every other icon in this window, other than these first two special cases, represents an object instance that will be created when the nib file loads. In our case, as you can see in Figure 2-5, there is a third icon called *View*.

The *View* icon represents an instance of the UIView class. A UIView object is an area that a user can see and interact with. In this application, we will have only one view, so this icon represents everything that the user can see in our application. Later, we'll build more complex applications that have more than one view, but for now, just think of this as what the users can see when they're using your application.

NOTE

> Technically speaking, our application will actually have more than one view. All user interface elements that can be displayed on the screen, including buttons, text fields, and labels, are all subclasses of UIView. When you see the term **view** used in this book, however, we will generally be referring only to actual instances of UIView, and this application has only one of those.

If you go back to Figure 2-5, you'll notice two other windows open besides the main window. Look at the window that has the word *View* in the title bar. That window is the graphical representation of that third icon in the nib's main window. If you close this window and then double-click the *View* icon in the nib file's main window, this window will open again. This is where you can design your user interface graphically. Let's do that now.

Adding a Label to the View

The rightmost window shown in Figure 2-5 is the **library**, which you can see in more detail in Figure 2-6. This is where you will find all the stock Cocoa Touch objects that Interface Builder supports. Dragging an item from the library to a nib file window will add an instance of that class to your application. If you close the library window, you can get it to reappear by selecting **Tools ➤ Library** or by pressing ⇧L⌘. The items on this palette are primarily from the iPhone UIKit, which is a framework of objects used to create an application's user interface.

Figure 2-6. *The Library palette, where you'll find stock objects from the UIKit that are available for use in Interface Builder*

UIKit fulfills the same role in Cocoa Touch as AppKit does in Cocoa. The two frameworks are similar conceptually, but because of differences in the platforms, there are obviously many differences between them. On the other hand, the Foundation framework classes, such as NSString and NSArray, are shared between Cocoa and Cocoa Touch.

Scroll through the list of objects in the library until you find one called *Label* (see Figure 2-7).

A label represents a bit of text that can be displayed on the iPhone's screen but can't be directly edited by the user. In a moment, we're going to add a label to our view.

Because user interface objects are hierarchical, we'll be adding our label as a **subview** to our main view (the view named *View*). Interface Builder is smart. If an object does not accept subviews, you will not be able to drag other objects onto it.

Dragging a label from the library to the view called *View* will add an instance of UILabel as a subview of our application's main view. Got that?

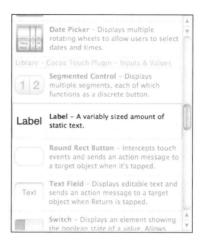

Figure 2-7. *Label object in the Library palette*

TIP

Having trouble finding the Label in that long list of library objects? No problem! Click in the search field at the bottom of the library (or, as a shortcut, press ⇧L⌘L to get there), and type the word *label*. As you type, the list of objects is reduced to match your search term. Be sure to empty the search window when you are done so you can see the full list again.

Drag a *Label* from the library into the *View* window. The view should look something like Figure 2-8 when you're done.

Let's edit the label so it says something profound. Double-click the label you just created, and type the text *Hello, World!*. Next, drag the label to wherever you want it to appear on the screen.

Figure 2-8. *Adding a label to your application's View window*

Guess what? Once we save, we're finished. Select **File ➤ Save**, and go back to Xcode so we can build and run our application.

In Xcode, select **Build ➤ Build and Run** (or press ⌘R). Xcode will compile our application and launch it in the iPhone simulator, as shown in Figure 2.9.

When you are finished admiring your handiwork, be sure to quit the simulator. Xcode, Interface Builder, and the simulator are all separate applications.

CAUTION

If your iPhone is connected to your Mac when you build and run, things might not go quite as planned. In a nutshell, in order to be able to build and run your applications on your iPhone, you have to sign up and pay for one of Apple's iPhone developer programs and then go through the process of configuring Xcode appropriately. When you join the program, Apple will send you the information you'll need to get this done. In the meantime, most of the programs in this book will run just fine using the iPhone simulator. If your iPhone is plugged in, before you select **Build and Run**, select **Project ➤ Set Active SDK ➤ Simulator—iPhone OS 3.0**.

Figure 2-9. *Here's the Hello World program in its full iPhone glory!*

Wait a second! That's it? But, we didn't write any code.

That's right. Pretty neat, huh?

But what if we had wanted to change some of the properties of the label, like the text size or color? We'd have to write code to do that, right?

Nope.

Head back to Interface Builder and single-click the *Hello World* label so that it is selected. Now press ⌘1 or select **Tools ➤ Inspector**. This will open a window called the **inspector**, where you can set the attributes of the currently selected item (see Figure 2-10).

From the inspector, you can change things like the font size, color, and drop shadow—just lots of stuff. The inspector is context sensitive. If you select a text field, you will be shown the editable attributes of a text field. If you select a button, you will be shown the editable attributes of a button, and so on.

Go ahead and change the label's appearance to your heart's delight, and then save, go back to Xcode, and select **Build and Run** again. The changes you made should show up in your application, once again without writing any code. By letting you design your interface graphically, Interface Builder frees you up to spend time writing the code that is specific to your application instead of spending time writing tedious code to construct your user interface.

NOTE

Most modern application development environments have some tool that lets you build your user interface graphically. One distinction between Interface Builder and many of these other tools is that Interface Builder does not generate any code that has to be maintained. Instead, Interface Builder creates Objective-C objects, just as you would do in code, and then serializes those objects into the nib file so that they can be loaded directly into memory at runtime. This avoids many of the problems associated with code generation and is, overall, a more powerful approach.

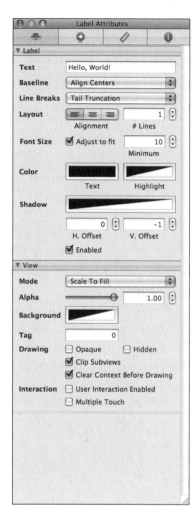

Figure 2-10. *The inspector showing our label's attributes*

Some iPhone Polish—Finishing Touches

Before we leave this chapter, let's just put a last little bit of spit and polish on our application to make it feel a little more like an authentic iPhone application. First, run your project. When the simulator window appears, click the iPhone's home button, the black button with the white square at the very bottom of the window. That will bring you back to the iPhone home screen (see Figure 2-11). Notice anything a bit, well, boring?

Take a look at the Hello World icon at the top of the screen. Yeah, that icon will never do, will it? To fix it, you need to create an icon and save it as a portable network graphic (*.png*) file. It needs to be 57 × 57 pixels in size. Do not try to match the style of the buttons that are already on the phone; your iPhone will automatically round the edges and give it that nice glassy appearance. Just create a normal flat, square image. We have provided an icon image in the project's archive (within the *02 Hello World* folder) that you can use if you don't want to create your own.

NOTE

For your application's icon, you have to use a *.png* image, but you should actually use this format for all images you add to your iPhone projects. Even though most common image formats will display correctly, you should use *.png* files unless you have a compelling reason to use another format. Xcode automatically optimizes *.png* images at build time to make them the fastest and most efficient image type for use in iPhone applications.

After you've designed your application icon, drag the *.png* file from the Finder to the *Resources* folder in Xcode, as shown in Figure 2-12, or select the *Resources* folder in Xcode, choose **Project ➤ Add to Project...**, and navigate to your icon image file.

Figure 2-11. *That leftmost application icon is just plain boring.*

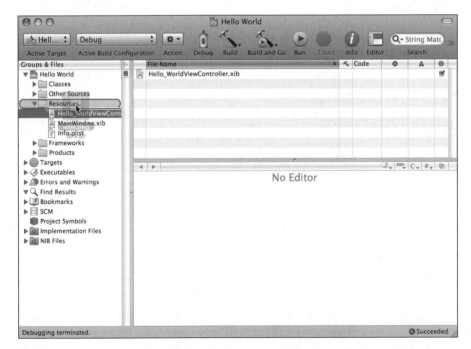

Figure 2-12. *Dragging an icon file into the Resources folder of your Xcode project*

Once you've done this, Xcode will prompt you for some specifics (see Figure 2-13). You can choose to have Xcode copy the file into your project directory, or you can just add it to your project as a reference to the original file. Generally, it's a good idea to copy resources into your Xcode project unless the file is shared with other projects.

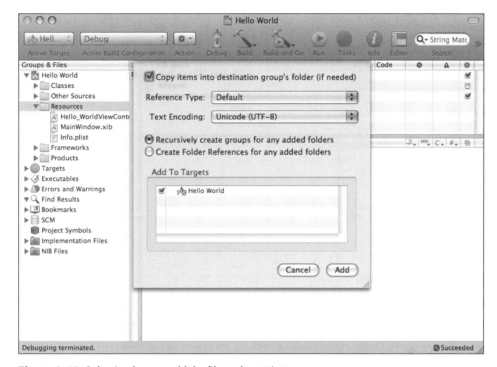

Figure 2-13. *Selecting how to add the file to the project*

When you add any common kind of file to your project, Xcode knows what to do with it, and as a result, this image file will now get compiled into our application automatically without doing anything further.

What we've done so far is incorporate the *icon.png* image into the project, which will result in the image getting built into our application bundle. The next thing we need to do is to specify that this particular image should be used as our application's icon.

In your Xcode project window's *Groups & Files* pane, expand the *Resources* folder, if it isn't already, and then single-click the *Hello_World-Info.plist* file. This is a **property list** file that contains some general information about our application including, among other things, the name of the icon file.

When you select *Hello_World-Info.plist*, the property list will appear in the editing pane (see Figure 2-14). Within the property list, find a row with the label *Icon file* in the left column. The corresponding right column in that same row should be empty. Double-click the empty cell, and type in the name of the *.png* file you just added to your project.

NOTE

If you ignored the *Icon file* entry in the plist, your icon will likely show up anyway. Huh? Why's that? By default, if no icon file name is provided, the SDK looks for a resource named *icon.png* and uses that. Just thought you'd like to know!

Key	Value
▼ Information Property List	(12 items)
Localization native development re	en
Bundle display name	${PRODUCT_NAME}
Executable file	${EXECUTABLE_NAME}
Icon file	
Bundle identifier	com.yourcompany.${PRODUCT_NAME:identifier}
InfoDictionary version	6.0
Bundle name	${PRODUCT_NAME}
Bundle OS Type code	APPL
Bundle creator OS Type code	????
Bundle version	1.0
LSRequiresIPhoneOS	☑
Main nib file base name	MainWindow

Figure 2-14. *Specifying the icon file*

Ready to Compile and Run

Before we compile and run, take a look at the other rows in *Hello_World-Info.plist*. While most of these settings are fine as they are, one in particular requires our attention, the setting named *Bundle identifier*. This is a unique identifier for your application and should always be set. If you're just going to run your application on the iPhone simulator, the standard naming convention for bundle identifiers is to use one of the top-level Internet domains such as *com* or *org* followed by a period, then the name of your company or organization followed by another period, and finally the name of your application. If you want to run your application on an actual iPhone, creating your application's bundle identifier is a little more involved process that you can read about in the iPhone Program Portal if you choose to pay to join the iPhone SDK Program. Since we're here, why don't we double-click the word *yourcompany* in the existing bundle identifier and change that to *apress*. The value at the end of the string is a special code that will get replaced with your application's name when your application is built. This allows you to tie your application's bundle identifier to its name.

Once that change is made, compile and run. When the simulator has finished launching, press the button with the white square to go home, and check out your snazzy new icon. Ours is shown in Figure 2-15.

NOTE

If you want to clear out old applications from the
iPhone simulator's home screen, you can simply delete
the folder called *iPhone Simulator* from the *Application Support* folder contained in your home directory's
Library folder.

Figure 2-15. *Your application
now has a snazzy icon!*

Bring It on Home

Pat yourself on the back. Although it may not seem like
you accomplished all that much in this chapter, we actually covered a lot of ground. You learned about the iPhone
project templates, created an application, saw how to use
Interface Builder, and learned how to set your application
icon and bundle identifier.

Hello World, however, is a strictly one-way application: we
show some information to the user, but we never get any
input from them. When you're ready to see how we go about getting input from the user of
an iPhone and taking actions based on that input, take a deep breath and turn the page.

Chapter 3

Handling Basic Interaction

Our Hello World application was a good introduction to iPhone development using Cocoa Touch, but it was missing a crucial capability: the ability to inter-act with the user. Without that, our application is severely limited in terms of what it can accomplish.

In this chapter, we're going to write a slightly more complex application, one with two buttons as well as a label (see Figure 3-1). When the user taps either of the buttons, the label's text changes. This may seem like a rather simplistic example, but it dem-onstrates the key concepts you'll need to master the use of controls in your iPhone applications.

The Model-View-Controller Paradigm

Before diving in, a tiny bit of theory is in order. The designers of Cocoa Touch were guided by a concept called **Model-View-Controller** (or MVC), which is a very logical way of dividing up the code that makes up a GUI-based application. These days, almost

Figure 3-1. *The simple two-button application we will be building in this chapter*

all object-oriented frameworks pay a certain amount of homage to MVC, but few are as true to the MVC model as Cocoa Touch.

The MVC model divides up all functionality into three distinct categories:

- *Model*: The classes that hold your application's data

- *View*: Made up of the windows, controls, and other elements that the user can see and interact with

- *Controller*: Binds the model and view together and is the application logic that decides how to handle the user's inputs

The goal in MVC is to make the objects that implement these three types of code as distinct from one another as possible. Any object you write should be readily identifiable as belonging in one of the three categories, with little or no functionality within it that could be classified within either of the other two. An object that implements a button, for example, shouldn't contain code to process data when that button is tapped, and code that implements a bank account shouldn't contain code to draw a table to display its transactions.

MVC helps ensure maximum reusability. A class that implements a generic button can be used in any application. A class that implements a button that does some particular calculation when it is clicked can be used only in the application for which it was originally written.

When you write Cocoa Touch applications, you will primarily create your view components using Interface Builder, although you will sometimes also modify your interface from code, or you might subclass existing views and controls.

Your model will be created by crafting Objective-C classes designed to hold your application's data or by building a data model using Core Data, which you'll learn about in Chapter 11. We won't be creating any model objects in this chapter's application because we have no need to store or preserve data, but we will introduce model objects as our applications get more complex in future chapters.

Your controller component will typically be composed of classes that you create and that are specific to your application. Controllers can be completely custom classes (`NSObject` subclasses), but more often, they will be subclasses of one of several existing generic controller classes from the UIKit framework such as `UIViewController`, which you'll see in a moment. By subclassing one of these existing classes, you will get a lot of functionality for free and won't have to spend time recoding the wheel, so to speak.

As we get deeper into Cocoa Touch, you will quickly start to see how the classes of the UIKit framework follow the principles of MVC. If you keep this concept in the back of your head as you develop, you will end up creating cleaner, more easily maintained code.

Creating Our Project

It's time to create our Xcode project. We're going to use the same template that we used in the previous chapter: View-based Application. We'll start using some of the other templates before too long, but by starting with the simple template again, it'll be easier for you to see how the view and controller objects work together in an iPhone application. Go ahead and create your project, saving it under the name *Button Fun*. If you have any trouble creating your project, refer to the preceding chapter for the proper steps.

You probably remember that the project template created some classes for us. You'll find those same classes in your new project, although the names will be a little different because some class names are based on the project name.

Creating the View Controller

A little later in this chapter, we're going to design a view (or user interface) for our application using Interface Builder, just as we did in the previous chapter. Before we do that, we're going to look at and make some changes to the source code files that were created for us. Yes, Virginia, we're actually going to write some code in this chapter.

Before we make any changes, let's look at the files that were created for us. In the project window, expand the *Classes* folder to reveal the four files within (see Figure 3-2).

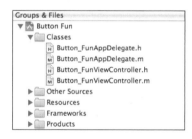

These four files implement two classes, each of which contains a *.m* and *.h* file. The application we are creating in this chapter has only one view, and the controller class that is responsible for managing that one view is called `Button_FunViewController`. The `Button_Fun` part of the name comes from our project name, and

Figure 3-2. *The class files that were created for us by the project template*

the `ViewController` part of the name means this class is, well, a view controller. Click *Button_FunViewController.h* in the *Groups & Files* pane, and take a look at the contents of the file:

```
#import <UIKit/UIKit.h>

@interface Button_FunViewController : UIViewController {
}

@end
```

Not much to it, is there? This is a subclass of `UIViewController`, which is one of those generic controller classes we mentioned earlier. It is part of the UIKit and gives us a bunch of functionality for free. Xcode doesn't know what our application-specific functionality is going to be, but it does know we're going to have some, so it has created this class to hold that functionality.

Take a look back at Figure 3-1. Our program consists of two buttons and a text label that reflects which button was tapped. We'll create all three of these elements in Interface Builder. Since we're also going to be writing code, there must be some way for our code to interact with the elements we create in Interface Builder, right?

Absolutely right. Our controller class can refer to objects in the nib by using a special kind of instance variable called an **outlet**. Think of an outlet as a pointer that points to an object within the nib. For example, suppose you created a text label in Interface Builder and wanted to change the label's text from within your code. By declaring an outlet and connecting that outlet to the label object, you could use the outlet from within your code to change the text displayed by the label. You'll see how to do just that in a bit.

Going in the opposite direction, interface objects in our nib file can be set up to trigger special methods in our controller class. These special methods are known as **action** methods. For example, you can tell Interface Builder that when the user touches up (pulls a finger off the screen) within a button, a specific action method within your code should be called.

As we've already said, Button Fun will feature two buttons and a label.

In our code, we'll create an outlet that points to the label, and this outlet will allow us to change the text of that label. We'll also create a method named `buttonPressed:` that will fire whenever one of the two buttons is tapped. `buttonPressed:` will set the label's text to let the user know which button was tapped.

We'll use Interface Builder to create the buttons and label, and then we'll do some clicking and dragging to connect the label to our label outlet and our buttons to our `buttonPressed:` action.

But before we get to our code, here's a bit more detail on outlets and actions.

Outlets

Outlets are instance variables that are declared using the keyword `IBOutlet`. A declaration of an outlet in your controller's header file might look like this:

```
@property (nonatomic, retain) IBOutlet UIButton *myButton;
```

The IBOutlet keyword is defined like this:

```
#ifndef IBOutlet
#define IBOutlet
#endif
```

Confused? IBOutlet does absolutely nothing as far as the compiler is concerned. Its sole purpose is to act as a hint to tell Interface Builder that this is an instance variable that we're going to connect to an object in a nib. Any instance variable that you create and want to connect to an object in a nib file must be preceded by the IBOutlet keyword. When you open Interface Builder, it will scan your project header files for occurrences of this keyword and will allow you to make connections from your code to the nib based on these (and only these) variables. In a few minutes, you'll see how to actually make the connection between an outlet and a user interface object in Interface Builder.

OUTLET CHANGES

In the first version of the book, we placed the IBOutlet keyword before the instance variable declaration, like this:

```
IBOutlet UIButton *myButton;
```

Since that time, Apple's sample code has been moving toward placing the IBOutlet keyword in the property declaration, like this:

```
@property (nonatomic, retain) IBOutlet UIButton *myButton;
```

Both mechanisms are supported, and for the most part, there is no difference in the way things work based on where you put the keyword. There is one exception to that, however. If you declare a property with a different name than its underlying instance variable (which can be done in the @synthesize directive), then you have to put the IBOutlet keyword in the property declaration, and not before the instance variable declaration, in order for it to work correctly. If you are a bit fuzzy on the property concept, we'll talk you through it in just a bit.

Although both approaches work, we've followed Apple's lead and have moved the IBOutlet keyword to the property declaration in all of our code.

You can read more about the new Objective-C properties in the second edition of *Learn Objective-C on the Mac*, by Mark Dalrymple and Scott Knaster (Apress 2008), and in *The Objective-C 2.0 Programming Language* available from Apple's developer web site:

```
http://developer.apple.com/documentation/Cocoa/Conceptual/ObjectiveC/
ObjC.pdf
```

Actions

Actions are methods that are part of your controller class. They are also declared with a special keyword, IBAction, which tells Interface Builder that this method is an action and can be triggered by a control. Typically, the declaration for an action method will look like this:

```
- (IBAction)doSomething:(id)sender;
```

The actual name of the method can be anything you want, but it must have a return type of IBAction, which is the same as declaring a return type of void. This is another way of saying that action methods do not return a value. Usually, the action method will take one argument, and it's typically defined as id and given a name of sender. The control that triggers your action will use the sender argument to pass a reference to itself. So, for example, if your action method was called as the result of a button tap, the argument sender would contain a reference to the specific button that was tapped.

As you'll see in a bit, our program will use that sender argument to set the label to the text "left" or "right," depending on which button was tapped. If you don't need to know which control called your method, you can also define action methods without a sender parameter. This would look like so:

```
- (IBAction)doSomething;
```

It won't hurt anything if you declare an action method with a sender argument and then ignore sender. You will likely see a lot of sample code that does just that, because historically action methods in Cocoa had to accept sender whether they used it or not.

Adding Actions and Outlets to the View Controller

Now that you know what outlets and actions are, let's go ahead and add one of each to our controller class. We need an outlet so we can change the label's text. Since we won't be changing the buttons, we don't need an outlet for them.

We'll also declare a single action method that will be called by both buttons. While many action methods are specific to a single control, it's possible to use a single action to handle input from multiple controls, which is what we're going to do here. Our action will grab the button's name from its sender argument and use the label outlet to embed that button name in the label's text. You'll see how this is done in a moment.

Go ahead and add the following code to *Button_FunViewController.h*:

```
#import <UIKit/UIKit.h>

@interface Button_FunViewController : UIViewController {
    UILabel    *statusText;
}
@property (nonatomic, retain) IBOutlet UILabel *statusText;
- (IBAction)buttonPressed:(id)sender;
@end
```

If you have worked with Objective-C 2.0, you're probably familiar with the `@property` declaration, but if you aren't, that line of code might look a little intimidating. Fear not: Objective-C properties are really quite simple. Let's take a quick detour to talk about them, since they are relatively new and we will use them extensively in this book. Even if you are already a master of the property, please do read on, because there is a bit of Cocoa Touch–specific information that you'll definitely find useful.

Objective-C Properties

Before the property was added to Objective-C, programmers traditionally defined pairs of methods to set and retrieve the values for each of a class's instance variables. These methods are called **accessors** and **mutators** (or, if you prefer, **getters** and **setters**) and might look something like this:

```
- (id) foo {
    return foo;
}
- (void) setFoo: (id) aFoo {
    if (aFoo != foo) {
        [aFoo retain];
        [foo release];
        foo = aFoo;
    }
}
```

Although this approach is still perfectly valid, the @property declaration allows you to say goodbye to the tedious process of creating accessor and mutator methods, if you want. The @property declarations we just typed, combined with another declaration in the implementation file (@synthesize), which you'll see in a moment, will tell the compiler to create the getter and setter methods at compile time. You do still have to declare the underlying instance variables as we did here, but you do not need to define the accessor or mutator.

In our declaration, the @property keyword is followed by some optional attributes, wrapped in parentheses. These further define how the accessors and mutators will be created by the compiler. The two you see here will be used often when defining properties in iPhone applications:

```
@property (nonatomic, retain) UILabel *statusText;
```

The first of these attributes, retain, tells the compiler to send a retain message to any object that we assign to this property. This will keep the instance variable underlying our property from being flushed from memory while we're still using it. This is necessary because the default behavior (assign) is intended for use with garbage collection, a feature of Objective-C 2.0 that isn't currently available on iPhone. As a result, if you define a property that is an object (as opposed to a raw datatype like int), you should generally specify retain in the optional attributes. When declaring a property for an int, float, or other raw datatype, you do not need to specify any optional attributes.

The second of our optional attributes, nonatomic, changes the way that the accessor and mutator methods are generated. Without getting too technical, let's just say that, by default, these methods are created with some additional code that is helpful when writing multi-threaded programs. That additional overhead, though small, is unnecessary when declaring a pointer to a user interface object, so we declare nonatomic to save a bit of overhead. There will be times where you don't want to specify nonatomic for a property, but as a general rule, most of the time you will specify nonatomic when writing iPhone applications.

Objective-C 2.0 has another nice feature that we'll be using along with properties. It introduced the use of **dot notation** to the language. Traditionally, to use an accessor method, you would send a message to the object, like this:

```
myVar = [someObject foo];
```

This approach still works just fine. But when you've defined a property, you also have the option of using dot notation, similar to that used in Java, C++, and C#, like so:

```
myVar = someObject.foo;
```

Those two statements are identical as far as the compiler is concerned; use whichever one makes you happy. Dot notation also works with mutators. The statement shown here:

```
someObject.foo = myVar;
```

is functionally identical to the following:

```
[someObject setFoo:myVar];
```

Declaring the Action Method

After the property declaration, we added another line of code:

```
- (IBAction)buttonPressed:(id)sender;
```

This is our action method declaration. By placing this declaration here, we are informing other classes, and Interface Builder, that our class has an action method called button-Pressed:.

Adding Actions and Outlets to the Implementation File

We are done with our controller class header file for the time being, so save it and single-click the class's implementation file, *Button_FunViewController.m*. The file should look like this:

```
#import "Button_FunViewController.h"

@implementation Button_FunViewController

/*
// The designated initializer. Override to perform setup
// that is required before the view is loaded.
- (id)initWithNibName:(NSString *)nibNameOrNil bundle:
        (NSBundle *)nibBundleOrNil {
    if (self=[super initWithNibName:nibNameOrNil bundle:nibBundleOrNil]) {
        // Custom initialization
    }
    return self;
}
*/

/*
// Implement loadView to create a view hierarchy programmatically,
// without using a nib.
- (void)loadView {
}
*/

/*
// Implement viewDidLoad to do additional setup after loading the view,
```

```
// typically from a nib.
- (void)viewDidLoad {
    [super viewDidLoad];
}
*/


/*
// Override to allow orientations other than the default portrait
// orientation.
- (BOOL)shouldAutorotateToInterfaceOrientation:
        (UIInterfaceOrientation)interfaceOrientation {
    // Return YES for supported orientations
    return (interfaceOrientation == UIInterfaceOrientationPortrait);
}
*/


- (void)didReceiveMemoryWarning {
    // Releases the view if it doesn't have a superview.
    [super didReceiveMemoryWarning];

    // Release any cached data, images, etc that aren't in use.
}


- (void)viewDidUnload {
    // Release any retained subviews of the main view.
    // e.g. self.myOutlet = nil;
}


- (void)dealloc {
    [super dealloc];
}

@end
```

Apple has anticipated some of the methods that we are likely to override and has included method stubs in the implementation file. Some of them are commented out and can be either uncommented or deleted as appropriate. The ones that aren't commented out are either used by the template or are so commonly used that they were included to save us time. We won't need any of the commented-out methods for this application, so go ahead and delete them, which will shorten up the code and make it easier to follow as we insert new code into this file.

Once you've deleted the commented-out methods, add the following code. When you're done, meet us back here, and we'll talk about what we did:

```
#import "Button_FunViewController.h"

@implementation Button_FunViewController
@synthesize statusText;

- (IBAction)buttonPressed:(id)sender {
    NSString *title = [sender titleForState:UIControlStateNormal];
    NSString *newText = [[NSString alloc] initWithFormat:
                            @"%@ button pressed.", title];
    statusText.text = newText;
    [newText release];
}
- (void)didReceiveMemoryWarning {
    [super didReceiveMemoryWarning]; // Releases the view if it
    // doesn't have a superview
    // Release anything that's not essential, such as cached data
}
- (void)viewDidUnload {
    // Release any retained subviews of the main view.
    // e.g. self.myOutlet = nil;
    self.statusText = nil;
}
- (void)dealloc {
    [statusText release];
    [super dealloc];
}


@end
```

OK, let's look at the newly added code. First, we added this:

```
@synthesize statusText;
```

This is how we tell the compiler to automatically create the accessor and mutator methods for us. By virtue of this line of code, there are now two "invisible" methods in our class: statusText and setStatusText:. We didn't write them, but they are there nonetheless, waiting for us to use them.

The next bit of newly added code is the implementation of our action method that will get called when either button is tapped:

```
-(IBAction)buttonPressed: (id)sender {
    NSString *title = [sender titleForState:UIControlStateNormal];
    NSString *newText = [[NSString alloc] initWithFormat:
                            @"%@ button pressed.", title];
```

```
    statusText.text = newText;
    [newText release];
}
```

Remember that the parameter passed into an action method is the control or object that invoked it. So, in our application, `sender` will always point to the button that was tapped. This is a very handy mechanism, because it allows us to have one action method handle the input from multiple controls, which is exactly what we're doing here: both buttons call this method, and we tell them apart by looking at sender. The first line of code in this method grabs the tapped button's title from `sender`.

```
NSString *title = [sender titleForState:UIControlStateNormal];
```

NOTE

We had to provide a **control state** when we requested the button's title. The four possible states are **normal**, which represents the control when it's active but not currently being used; **highlighted**, which represents the control when it is in the process of being tapped or otherwise used; **disabled**, which is the state of a button that is not enabled and can't be used; and **selected**, which is a state that only certain controls have and which indicates that the control is currently selected. `UIControlStateNormal` represents a control's normal state and is the one you will use the vast majority of the time. If values for the other states are not specified, those states will have the same value as the normal state.

The next thing we do is create a new string based on that title:

```
NSString *newText = [[NSString alloc] initWithFormat:
                     @"%@ button pressed.", title];
```

This new string will append the text "button pressed." to the name of the button. So if we tapped a button with a title of "Left," this new string would equal "Left button pressed."

Finally, we set the text of our label to this new string:

```
statusText.text = newText;
```

We're using dot notation here to set the label's text, but we could have also used `[statusText setText:newText];` instead. Finally, we release the string:

```
[newText release];
```

The importance of releasing objects when you're done with them cannot be overstated. iPhone is a very resource-constrained device, and even a small number of memory leaks can cause your program to crash. It's also worth pointing out that we *didn't* do this:

```
NSString *newText = [NSString stringWithFormat:
                      @"%@ button pressed.", title];
```

This code would work exactly the same as the code we used. Class methods like this one are called **convenience** or **factory** methods, and they return an autoreleased object. Following the general memory rule that "if you didn't allocate it or retain it, don't release it," these autoreleased objects don't have to be released unless you specifically retain them, and using them often results in code that's a little shorter and more readable.

But, there is a cost associated with these convenience methods because they use the autorelease pool. The memory allocated for an autoreleased object will stay allocated for some period of time after we're done with it. On Mac OS X, with swap files and relatively large amounts of physical memory, the cost of using autoreleased objects is nominal, but on iPhone, these objects can have a detrimental effect on your application's memory footprint. It is OK to use autorelease, but try to use it only when you really need to, not just to save typing a line or two of code.

Next, we added a single line of code to the existing `viewDidUnload:` method:

```
self.statusText = nil;
```

Don't worry too much about this line of code for now; we'll explain why this line of code is needed in the next chapter. For now, just remember that you need to set any outlets your class has to `nil` in `viewDidUnload`.

TIP

> If you're a bit fuzzy on objective-C memory management, you really should review the memory management "contract" at `http://developer.apple.com/documentation/Cocoa/Conceptual/MemoryMgmt/Articles/mmRules.html`. Even a small number of memory leaks can wreak havoc in an iPhone application.

The last thing we did was to release the outlet in our `dealloc` method:

```
[statusText release];
```

Releasing this item might seem strange. You might be thinking, since we didn't instantiate it, we shouldn't be responsible for releasing it. If you have worked with older versions of Cocoa and Objective-C, you're probably thinking this is just plain wrong. However, because we implemented properties for each of these outlets and specified `retain` in that property's attributes, releasing it is correct and necessary. Interface Builder will use our generated mutator method when assigning the outlets, and that mutator will retain the object that is assigned to it, so it's important to release the outlet here to avoid leaking memory.

Before moving on, make sure you've saved this file, and then go ahead and build the project by pressing ⌘B to make sure you didn't make any mistakes while typing. If it doesn't compile, go back and compare your code to the code in this book.

MESSAGE NESTING

Objective-C messages are often nested by some developers. You may come across code like this in your travels:

```
statusText.text = [NSString stringWithFormat:@"%@ button pressed.",
    [sender titleForState:UIControlStateNormal]];
```

This one line of code will function exactly the same as the four lines of code that make up our `button-Pressed:` method. For sake of clarity, we won't generally nest Objective-C messages in the code examples in this book, with the exception of calls to `alloc` and `init`, which, by longstanding convention, are almost always nested.

Using the Application Delegate

The other two files under the *Classes* folder implement our **application delegate**. Cocoa Touch makes extensive use of **delegates**, which are classes that take responsibility for doing certain things on behalf of another object. The application delegate lets us do things at certain predefined times on behalf of the UIApplication class. Every iPhone application has one and only one instance of UIApplication, which is responsible for the application's run loop and handles application-level functionality such as routing input to the appropriate controller class.

UIApplication is a standard part of the UIKit, and it does its job mostly behind the scenes, so you don't have to worry about it for the most part. At certain well-defined times during an application's execution, however, UIApplication will call specific delegate methods, if there is a delegate and if it implements that method. For example, if you have code that needs to fire just before your program quits, you would implement the method applicationWill-Terminate: in your application delegate and put your termination code there. This type of delegation allows our application to implement common application-wide behavior without having to subclass UIApplication or, indeed, to even know anything about its inner workings.

Click *Button_FunAppDelegate.h* in the *Groups & Files* pane, and look at the application delegate's header file. It should look like this:

```
#import <UIKit/UIKit.h>

@class Button_FunViewController;

@interface Button_FunAppDelegate : NSObject <UIApplicationDelegate> {
    UIWindow *window;
    Button_FunViewController *viewController;
}

@property (nonatomic, retain) IBOutlet UIWindow *window;
@property (nonatomic, retain) IBOutlet Button_FunViewController
    *viewController;

@end
```

We don't need to make any changes to this file, and after implementing our controller class, most everything here should look familiar to you. One thing worth pointing out is this line of code:

```
@interface Button_FunAppDelegate : NSObject <UIApplicationDelegate> {
```

Do you see that value between the angle brackets? This indicates that this class conforms to a protocol called `UIApplicationDelegate`. Hold down the option key, and move your cursor so that it is over the word `UIApplicationDelegate`. Your cursor should turn into crosshairs; when it does, double-click. This will open the documentation browser and show you the documentation for the `UIApplicationDelegate` protocol (see Figure 3-3). This same trick works with class, protocol, and category names, as well as method names displayed in the editor pane. Just option–double-click a word, and it will search for that word in the documentation browser.

Knowing how to quickly look up things in the documentation is definitely worthwhile, but looking at the definition of this protocol is perhaps more important. Here's where you'll find what methods the application delegate can implement and when those methods will get called. It's probably worth your time to read over the descriptions of these methods.

NOTE

If you've worked with Objective-C before but not with Objective-C 2.0, you should be aware that protocols can now specify optional methods. `UIApplicationDelegate` contains many optional methods, and you do not need to implement any of the optional methods in your application delegate unless you have a reason.

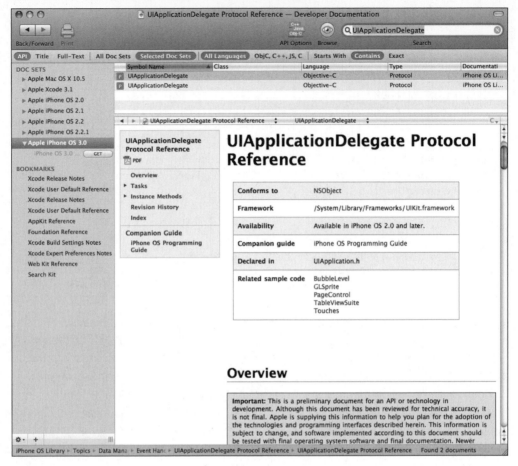

Figure 3-3. *Looking at the UIApplicationDelegate documentation using the documentation browser*

Click *Button_FunAppDelegate.m,* and look at the implementation of the application delegate. It should look like this:

```
#import "Button_FunAppDelegate.h"
#import "Button_FunViewController.h"

@implementation Button_FunAppDelegate

@synthesize window;
@synthesize viewController;


- (void)applicationDidFinishLaunching:(UIApplication *)application {
```

```
    // Override point for customization after app launch
    [window addSubview:viewController.view];
    [window makeKeyAndVisible];
}


- (void)dealloc {
    [viewController release];
    [window release];
    [super dealloc];
}


@end
```

Right in the middle of the file, you can see that our application delegate has implemented one of the protocol's methods: `applicationDidFinishLaunching:`, which, as you can probably guess, fires as soon as the application has finished all the setup work and is ready to start interacting with the user.

Our delegate version of `applicationDidFinishLaunching:` adds our view controller's view as a subview to the application's main window and makes the window visible, which is how the view we are going to design gets shown to the user. You don't need to do anything to make this happen; it's all part of the code generated by the template we used to build this project.

We just wanted to give you a bit of background on application delegates and see how this all ties together.

Editing MainWindow.xib

So far, we've looked at the four files in our project's *Classes* tab (two `.m` files, two `.h` files). In previous chapters, we've had experience with two of the three files in our project's Resources tab. We looked at the equivalent of *Button_Fun-Info.plist* when we added our icon to the project, and we looked at the equivalent of `Button_FunViewController.xib` when we added our "Hello, World!" label.

There's one other file in the *Resources* tab that we want to talk about. The file *MainWindow. xib* is what causes your application's delegate, main window, and view controller instances to get created at runtime. Remember, this file is provided as part of the project template. You don't need to change or do anything here. This is just a chance to see what's going on behind the scenes, to get a glimpse of the big picture.

Expand the *Resources* folder in Xcode's *Groups & Files* pane, and double-click *MainWindow.xib*. Once Interface Builder opens, take a look at the nib's main window—the one labeled *MainWindow.xib*, which should look like Figure 3-4.

You should recognize the first two icons in this window from Chapter 2. As a reminder, every icon in a nib window after the first two represents an object that will get instantiated when the nib file loads. Let's take a look at the third, fourth, and fifth icons.

Figure 3-4. *Our application's MainWindow.xib as it appears in Interface Builder*

NOTE

Long names get truncated in the nib file's main window in the default view, as you can see in Figure 3-4. If you hold your cursor over one of these icons for a few seconds, a tooltip will pop up to show you the full name of the item. Note also that the names shown in the main window do not necessarily indicate the underlying class of the object. The default name for a new instance usually will clue you in to the underlying class, but these names can be, and often are, changed.

The third icon is an instance of `Button_FunAppDelegate`. The fourth icon is an instance of `Button_FunViewController`. And, finally, the fifth icon is our application's one and only window (an instance of `UIWindow`). These three icons indicate that once the nib file is loaded, our application will have one instance of the application delegate, `Button_FunAppDelegate`; one instance of our view controller, `Button_FunViewController`; and one instance of `UIWindow` (the class that represents the application's one and only window). As you can see, Interface Builder can do much more than just create interface elements. It allows you to create instances of other classes as well. This is an incredibly powerful feature. Every line of code that you don't write is a line of code you don't have to debug or maintain. Right here, we're creating three object instances at launch time without having to write a single line of code.

OK, that's all there is to see here, folks; move along. Be sure to close this nib file on the way out. And if you are prompted to save, just say "no," because you shouldn't have changed anything.

Editing Button_FunViewController.xib

Now that you have a handle on the files that make up our project and the concepts that bring them all together, let's turn our attention to Interface Builder and the process of constructing our interface.

Creating the View in Interface Builder

In Xcode, double-click *Button_FunViewController.xib* in the *Groups & Files* pane. The nib file should open in Interface Builder. Make sure the library is visible. If it's not, you can show it by selecting **Library** from the **Tools** menu. You also need to make sure that the nib's *View* window is open. If it's not, double-click the icon called *View* in the nib's main window (see Figure 3-5).

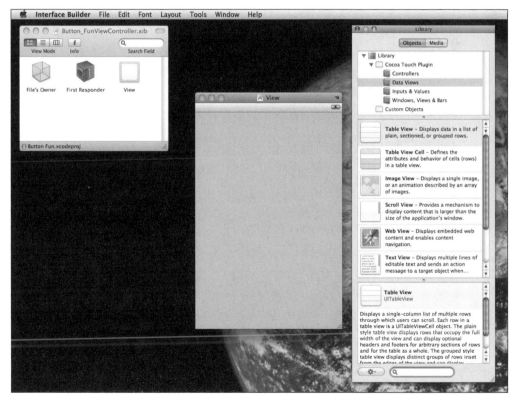

Figure 3-5. *Button_FunViewController.xib open in Interface Builder*

Now we're ready to design our interface. Drag a label from the library over to the view window, just as you did in the previous chapter. Place the label toward the bottom of the view, so the label lines up with the left and bottom blue guidelines (see Figure 3-6). Next, expand the label so the right side lines up with the guideline on the right side of the window.

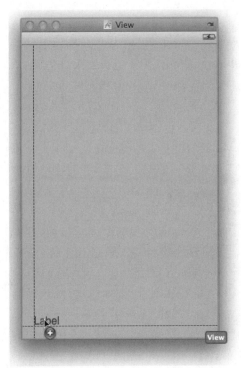

Figure 3-6. *Using the blue guidelines to place objects*

NOTE

The little blue guidelines are there to help you stick to the *Apple Human Interface Guidelines* (usually referred to as "the HIG"). Yep, just like it does for Mac OS X, Apple provides the *iPhone Human Interface Guidelines* for designing iPhone applications. The HIG tells you how you should—and shouldn't—design your user interface. You really should read it, because it contains valuable information that every iPhone developer needs to know. You'll find it at `http://developer.apple.com/iphone/library/documentation/UserExperience/Conceptual/MobileHIG/`.

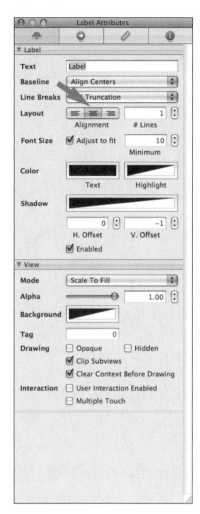

Figure 3-7. *The inspector's text alignment buttons*

After you've placed the label at the bottom of the view, click it to select it, and press ⌘1 to bring up the inspector. Change the text alignment to centered by using the text alignment buttons on the inspector (see Figure 3-7).

Now, double-click the label, and delete the existing text. We don't want any text to display until a button has been tapped.

Next, we're going to drag two *Round Rect Buttons* from the library (see Figure 3-8) to our view.

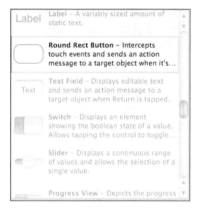

Figure 3-8. *The Round Rect Button as it appears in the library*

Place the two buttons next to each other, roughly in the middle of the view. The exact placement doesn't matter. Double-click the button that you placed on the left. Doing this will allow the button's title to be edited, so go ahead and change its text to read "Left." Next, double-click the button on the right, and change its text to read "Right." When you're done, your view should look something like the one shown in Figure 3-9.

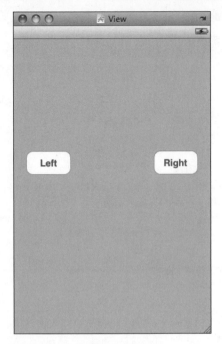

Figure 3-9. *The finished view*

Connecting Everything

We now have all the pieces of our interface. All that's left is to make the various connections that will allow these pieces to work together.

The first step is to make a connection from *File's Owner* to the label in the *View* window. Why *File's Owner*?

When an instance of `UIViewController` or one of its subclasses is instantiated, it can be told to initialize itself from a nib. In the template we've used, the `Button_FunViewController` class will be loaded from the nib file *Button_FunViewController.xib*. We don't have to do anything to make that happen; it's part of the project template we chose. In future chapters, you'll see exactly how that process works. Since the *MainWindow.xib* file contains an icon that represents *Button_FunViewController*, an instance of `Button_FunViewController` will get created automagically when our application launches. When that happens, that instance will automatically load *Button_FunViewController.xib* into memory and become its file's owner.

Earlier in the chapter, we added an outlet to `Button_FunViewController`, which is this nib's owner. We can now make a connection between that outlet and the label using the *File's Owner* icon. Let's look at how we do that.

Connecting Outlets

Hold down the control key; click the *File's Owner* icon in the main nib window; and keep the mouse button down. Drag away from the *File's Owner* icon toward the *View* window. A blue guideline should appear. Keep dragging until your cursor is over the label in the *View* window. Even though you won't be able to see the label, it will magically appear once you are over it (see Figure 3-10).

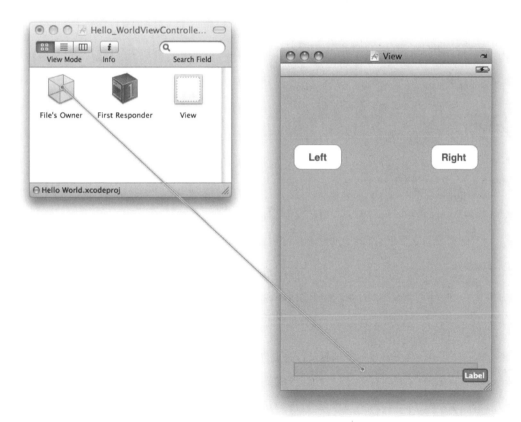

Figure 3-10. *Control-dragging to connect outlets*

With the cursor still over the label, let go of the mouse button, and a small gray menu like the one shown in Figure 3-11 should pop up.

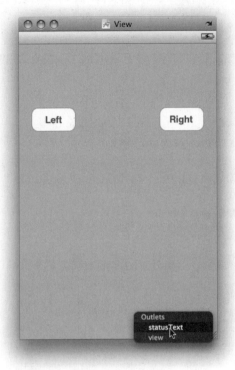

Figure 3-11. *Outlet selection menu*

Select *statusText* from the gray menu.

By control-dragging from *File's Owner* to an interface object, you are telling Interface Builder that you want to connect one of the *File's Owner's* outlets to this object when the nib file is loaded. In this case, the file's owner is the class `Button_FunViewController`, and the `Button_FunViewController` outlet we are interested in is `statusText`. When we control-dragged from *File's Owner* to the label object and selected `statusText` from the pop-up menu that appeared, we told Interface Builder to have `Button_FunViewController`'s `sta-tusText` outlet point to the label, so any time we refer to `statusText` in our code, we will be dealing with this label. Cool, eh?

Specifying Actions

The only thing left to do is to identify which actions these buttons trigger and under what circumstances they trigger them. If you're familiar with Cocoa programming for Mac OS X, you're probably getting ready to control-drag from the buttons over to the *File's Owner* icon. And, to be honest, that will work, but it's not the best way to do it.

iPhone is different from Mac OS X, and here's one of the places where that difference becomes apparent. On the Mac, a control can be associated with just one action, and that action is typically triggered when that control is used. There are some exceptions to this, but by and large, a control triggers its corresponding action method when the mouse button is released if the cursor is still inside the bounds of that control.

Controls in Cocoa Touch offer a lot more possibilities, so instead of click-dragging from the control, it's best to get in the habit of using the connections inspector, which we can get to by pressing ⌘2 or selecting **Connection Inspector** from the **Tools** menu. Click the *Left* button, and then bring up the connections inspector. It should look like Figure 3-12.

Under the heading *Events*, you'll see a whole list of events that can potentially trigger an action. If you like, you can associate different actions with different events. For example, you might use *Touch Up Inside* to trigger one action, while *Touch Drag Inside* triggers a different action. Our situation is relatively simple and straightforward. When the user taps our button, we want it to call our `buttonPressed:` method. The first question is which of the events in Figure 3-12 do we use?

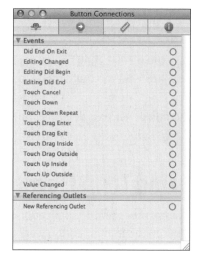

Figure 3-12. *The connections inspector showing our button's available events*

The answer, which may not be obvious at first, is *Touch Up Inside*. When the user's finger lifts up from the screen, if the last place it touched before lifting was inside the button, the user triggers a touch up inside. Think about what happens in most of your iPhone applications if you touch the screen and change your mind. You move your finger off the button before lifting up, right? We should give our users the same ability. If our user's finger is still on the button when it's lifted off the screen, then we can safely assume that the button tap is intended.

Now that we know the event we want to trigger our action, how do we associate the event with a specific action method?

See that little circle in the inspector to the right of *Touch Up Inside*? Click in that circle and drag away with the mouse button still pressed; there's no need to hold down the control key this time. You should get a gray connection line, just as you did when we were connecting outlets earlier. Drag this line over to the *File's Owner* icon, and when the little gray menu pops up, select *buttonPressed:*. Remember, the *File's Owner* icon represents the class whose nib we are editing. In this case, *File's Owner* represents our application's sole instance of the `Button_FunViewController` class. When we drag from the button's event to the *File's*

Owner icon, we are telling Interface Builder to call the selected method when the specified event occurs. So when the user touches up inside the button, the `Button_FunViewController` class's `buttonPressed:` method will be called.

Do this same sequence with the other button and then save. Now, any time the user taps one of these buttons, our `buttonPressed:` method will get called.

Trying It Out

Save the nib file; then head back to Xcode and take your application for a spin. Select **Build and Run** from the **Build** menu. Your code should compile, and your application should come up in the iPhone Simulator. When you tap the left button, the text "Left button pressed." should appear, as it does in Figure 3-1. If you then tap the right button, the label will change to say "Right button pressed."

Bring It on Home

This chapter's simple application introduced you to MVC, creating and connecting outlets and actions, implementing view controllers, and using application delegates. You learned how to trigger action methods when a button is tapped and saw how to change the text of a label at runtime. Although a simple application, the basic concepts we used to build it are the same concepts that underlie the use of all controls on the iPhone, not just buttons. In fact, the way we used buttons and labels in this chapter is pretty much the way that we will implement and interact with most of the standard controls on the iPhone.

It's very important that you understand everything we did in this chapter and why we did it. If you don't, go back and redo the parts that you don't fully understand. This is important stuff! If you don't make sure you understand everything now, you will only get more confused as we get into creating more complex interfaces later on in this book.

In the next chapter, we'll take a look at some of the other standard iPhone controls. You'll also learn how to use alerts to notify the user of important happenings and how to indicate that the user needs to make a choice before proceeding by using action sheets. When you feel you're ready to proceed, give yourself a pat on the back for being such an awesome student, and head on over to the next chapter.

Chapter 4

More User Interface Fun

*i*n Chapter 3, we discussed the Model-View-Controller concept and built an application that brought that idea to life. You learned about outlets and actions and used them to tie a button control to a text label. In this chapter, we're going to build an application that will take your knowledge of controls to a whole new level.

We'll implement an image view, a slider, two different text fields, a segmented control, a couple of switches, and an iPhone button that looks more like, well, an iPhone button. You'll learn how to use the view hierarchy to group multiple items under a common parent view and make manipulating the interface at runtime easier. You'll see how to set and retrieve the values of various controls, both by using outlets and by using the sender argument of our action methods. After that, we'll look at using action sheets to force the user to make a choice and alerts to give the user important feedback. We'll also learn about control states and the use of stretchable images to make buttons look the way they should.

Because this chapter's application uses so many different user interface items, we're going to work a little differently than we did in the previous two chapters. We're going to break our application into pieces, implementing one piece at a time and bouncing back and forth between Xcode, Interface Builder, and the iPhone simulator and testing each piece before we move on to the next. Breaking the process of building a complex interface into smaller chunks will make it much less intimidating and will make it more closely resemble the actual process you'll go through when building your own applications. This code-compile-debug cycle makes up a large part of a software developer's typical day.

A Screen Full of Controls

As we mentioned, the application we're going to build in this chapter is a bit more complex than was the case in Chapter 3. We're still going to use only a single view and controller, but as you can see in Figure 4-1, there's quite a bit more going on in this one view.

The logo at the top of the iPhone screen is an **image view**, and in this application, it does nothing more than display a static image. Below the logo, there are two text fields, one that allows the entry of alphanumeric text and one that allows only numbers. Below the text fields is a **slider**. As the user changes the slider, the value of the label next to it will change so that it always reflects the slider's value.

Below the slider is a segmented control and two switches. The **segmented control** will toggle between two different types of controls in the space below it. When the application first launches, there will be two switches below the segmented control. Changing the value of either switch will cause the other one to change its value to match. Now, this isn't something you would likely do in a real application,

Figure 4-1. *The Control Fun application, featuring text fields, labels, a slider, and several other stock iPhone controls*

but it will let us show you how to change the value of a control programmatically and how Cocoa Touch animates certain actions for you without you having to do any work.

Figure 4-2 shows what happens when the user taps the segmented control. The switches disappear and are replaced by a button.

When the *Do Something* button is pressed, an action sheet will pop up and ask the user if they really meant to tap the button (see Figure 4-3). This is the standard way of responding to input that is potentially dangerous or that could have significant repercussions and gives the user a chance to stop potential badness from happening.

If *Yes, I'm Sure!* is selected, the application will put up an alert, letting the user know that everything is OK (see Figure 4-4).

Figure 4-2. *Tapping the segmented controller on the left side cause a pair of switches to be displayed. Tapping the right side causes a button to be displayed.*

Figure 4-3. *Our application uses an action sheet to solicit a response from the user.*

Figure 4-4. *Alerts are used to notify the user when important things happen. We use one here to confirm that everything went OK.*

Active, Static, and Passive Controls

User interface controls come in three basic forms: active, static (or inactive), and passive. The buttons that we used in the previous chapter are classic examples of active controls. You push them, and something happens—usually, a piece of code fires. Although many of the controls that you will use will directly trigger action methods, not all controls will.

The label that you used in the previous chapter is a good example of a static control. You added it to your interface and even changed it programmatically, but the user could not do anything with it. Labels and images are both controls that are often used in this manner, though both are subclasses of UIControl and can be made to fire code if you need them to do so.

Some controls can work in a passive manner, simply holding on to a value that the user has entered until you're ready for it. These controls don't trigger action methods, but the user can interact with them and change their values.

A classic example of a passive control is a text field on a web page. Although there can be validation code that fires when you tab out of a field, the vast majority of web page text fields are simply containers for data that get submitted to the server when you click the submit button. The text fields themselves don't actually trigger any code to fire, but when the submit button is clicked, the text field's data goes along for the ride.

On an iPhone, many of the available controls can be used in all three ways, and most can function in more than one, depending on your needs. All iPhone controls are subclasses of UIControl and, because of that, are capable of triggering action methods. Most controls can also be used passively, and all of them can be made inactive when they are created or changed from active to inactive, and vice versa, at runtime. For example, using one control could trigger another inactive control to become active. However, some controls, such as buttons, really don't serve much purpose unless they are used in an active manner to trigger code.

As you might expect, there are some behavioral differences between controls on the iPhone and those on your Mac. Here are a few examples. Because of the multitouch interface, all iPhone controls can trigger multiple actions depending on how they are touched: your user might trigger a different action with a finger swipe across the control than with just a touch. You could also have one action fire when the user presses down on a button and a separate action fire when the finger is lifted off the button. Conversely, you could also have a single control call multiple action methods on a single event. You could have two different action methods fire on the touch up inside event, meaning that both methods would get called when the user's finger is lifted after touching that button.

Another major difference between the iPhone and the Mac stems from the fact that the iPhone has no physical keyboard. The iPhone keyboard is actually just a view filled with a series of button controls. Your code will likely never directly interact with the iPhone keyboard, but as you'll see later in the chapter, sometimes you have to write code to make the keyboard behave in exactly the manner you want.

Creating the Application

Fire up Xcode if it's not already open, and create a new project called Control Fun. We're going to use the *View-based Application* template option again, so create your project just as you did in the previous two chapters.

Importing the Image

Now that you've created your project, let's go get the image we'll use in our image view. The image has to be imported into Xcode before it will be available for use inside Interface Builder, so let's import it now. You can find a suitable *.png* image in the project archives in the *04 Control Fun* directory, or you can use an image of your own choosing—make sure that the image you select is a *.png* image sized correctly for the space available. It should be fewer than 100 pixels tall and not more than 300 pixels wide so that it can comfortably fit at the top of the view without being resized.

Add the image to the *Resources* folder of your project, just as we did in Chapter 2, by either dragging the image from the Finder to the *Resources* folder or by selecting **Add to** from the **Project** menu.

Implementing the Image View and Text Fields

With the image added to your project, your next step is to implement the five interface elements at the top of the application's screen, with the image view, the two text fields, and the two labels (see Figure 4-5).

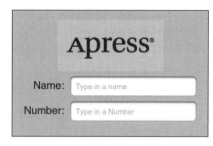

Figure 4-5. *The image view, labels, and text fields we will implement first*

Determining Outlets

Before we hop over to Interface Builder, we need to figure out which of these objects requires an outlet. Remember, outlets have to be defined in your controller class's header file before you can connect them to anything in Interface Builder.

The image view is just a static image. We're going to designate the image to be displayed right in Interface Builder, and that image won't change while our application is running. As a result, it does not require an outlet. If we *did* want to change the image or change any of its characteristics at runtime, we *would* need an outlet. That is not the case here.

The same is true for the two labels. They are there to display text but won't be changed at runtime, and the user won't interact with them, so we don't need outlets for them either.

On the other hand, the two text fields aren't really much use if we can't get to the data they contain. The way to access the data held by a passive control is to use an outlet, so we need to define an outlet for each of these text fields. This is old hat for you by now, so why don't you add two outlets and their corresponding properties to your *Control_FunViewController.h* class file using the names `nameField` and `numberField`? When you're done, it should look something like this:

```
#import <UIKit/UIKit.h>

@interface Control_FunViewController : UIViewController {
    UITextField     *nameField;
    UITextField     *numberField;
}
```

```
@property (nonatomic, retain) IBOutlet UITextField *nameField;
@property (nonatomic, retain) IBOutlet UITextField *numberField;
@end
```

Before we move on to Interface Builder, let's also add our @synthesize directives to *Control_FunViewController.m*:

```
#import "Control_FunViewController.h"

@implementation Control_FunViewController
@synthesize nameField;
@synthesize numberField;
...
```

NOTE

See the ellipsis (...) at the end of that code listing? We'll use that symbol to indicate that there is existing code beyond what we've shown in the listing that does not require any changes. We'll be adding all of our code to the top of the implementation file in this chapter, so by using the ellipsis, we can avoid having to show the whole file every time we have you add a line or two of code.

We also need to make sure that we're careful about memory, so since we declared the nameField and numberField properties with the retain keyword, we need to release them both in our dealloc method. Scroll down to the bottom of the file, and add the following two lines to the existing dealloc method:

```
- (void)dealloc {
    [nameField release];
    [numberField release];
    [super dealloc];
}
```

Determining Actions

Take a look at the five objects in Figure 4-5 again. Do you see the need to declare any actions? The image views and the labels do not have user interaction enabled and can't receive touches, so there's no reason to have actions for them, right? Right.

What about the two text fields? Text fields are the classic passive control. The vast majority of the time, all they do is hold onto values until you're ready for them. We're not doing any validation on these fields, other than limiting the input of the number field by showing only the number pad instead of the full keyboard (which we can do entirely in Interface Builder), so we don't need an action for these either, right? Well, hold that thought. Let's build and test the first part of our user interface.

Building the Interface

Make sure both of those files are saved, expand the *Resources* folder in the *Groups & Files* pane, and double-click *Control_FunViewController.xib* to launch Interface Builder. If the window titled *View* is not open, double-click the *View* icon in the nib file's main window.

Now, turn your attention to the library. If it's not open, select **Library** from the **Tools** menu. Scroll about one-fourth of the way through the list until you find *Image View* (see Figure 4-6).

Figure 4-6. *The Image View element in Interface Builder's library*

Adding the Image View

Drag an image view onto the window called *View*. Because this is the first item you're putting on your view, Interface Builder is going to automatically resize the image view so that it's the same size as the view. Since we don't want our image view to take the entire space, use the drag handles to resize the image view to the approximate size of the image you imported into Xcode. Don't worry about getting it exactly right yet. It'll be easier to do that in a moment.

By the way, sometimes an object will get deselected and can be very hard to select again because it is behind another object, takes up the entire view, or has no drawn border. In those cases, don't despair! There is a way to select the object again. In the nib's main window, you'll see three buttons labeled *View Mode*. Click the middle one, and you'll get a hierarchical view of the nib, which will let you drill down into subviews, as shown in Figure 4-7. Double-clicking any item in this view will also cause the same item to become selected in the *View* window.

Figure 4-7. *Putting the nib's main window in hierarchical view and drilling down to subviews*

With the image view selected, bring up the inspector by pressing ⌘1, and you should see the editable options of the UIImageView class, as shown in Figure 4-8.

The most important setting for our image view is the topmost item in the inspector, labeled *Image*. If you click the little arrow to the right of the field, a menu will pop up with the available images, which should include any images that you added to your Xcode project. Select the image you added a minute ago. Your image should now appear in your image view.

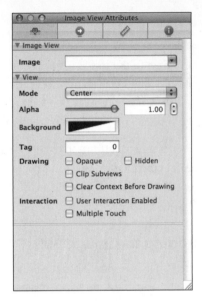

Figure 4-8. *The image view inspector*

Resize the Image View

Now, resize your image view so that it is exactly the same size as your image. We'll talk about why in a moment. An easy way to resize the view so that it's the same size as the selected image is to press ⌘= or to select **Size to Fit** from the **Layout** menu, which will automatically resize any view to the exact size needed to contain its contents. You'll also want to move the resized image so that it's centered and the top is aligned with the blue guidelines. You can easily center an item in the view by choosing **Align Horizontal Center in Container** from the **Layout** menu's **Alignment** submenu.

TIP

Dragging and resizing views in Interface Builder can be tricky. Don't forget about the hierarchical *View Mode* button in the main nib window. It will help you find and select (double-click) the image view. When it comes to resizing, hold down the option key. Interface Builder will draw some helpful red lines on the screen that make it much easier to get a sense of the image view's size. This trick won't work for dragging, but if you select **Show Bounds Rectangles** from the **Layout** Menu, it will draw a line around all of your interface items, making them easier to see. You can turn those lines off by selecting **Show Bounds Rectangles** a second time.

The Mode Attribute

The next option down in the image view inspector is a pop-up menu labeled *Mode*. The *Mode* menu defines how the image will be aligned inside the view and whether it will be scaled to fit. You can feel free to play with the various options, but the default value of *Center* is probably best for our needs. Keep in mind that choosing any option that causes the image to scale will potentially add processing overhead, so it's best to avoid those and size your images correctly before you import them. If you want to display the same image at multiple sizes, generally it's better to have multiple copies of the image at different sizes in your project rather than force the iPhone to do scaling at runtime.

The Alpha Slider

The next item in the inspector is *Alpha*, and this is one you need to be very careful with. Alpha defines how transparent your image is: how much of what's beneath it shows through. If you have any value less than 1.0, your iPhone will draw this view as transparent so that any objects underneath it show through. With a value less than 1.0, even if there's nothing actually underneath your image, you will cause your application to spend processor cycles calculating transparency, so don't set this to anything other than 1.0 unless you have a very good reason for doing so.

Ignore the Background

You can ignore the next item down, called *Background*. This is a property inherited from UIView, but it doesn't impact the appearance of an image view.

The Tag Attribute

The next item down—*Tag*—is worth mentioning, though we won't be using it in this chapter. All subclasses of UIView, including all views and controls, have a property called *tag*, which is just a numeric value that you can set that will tag along with your image view. The tag is designed for your use; the system will never set or change its value. If you assign a tag value to a control or view, you can be sure that the tag will always have that value unless you change it.

Tags provide an easy, language-independent way of identifying objects on your interface. Let's say you had five different buttons, each with a different label, and you wanted to use a single action method to handle all five buttons. In that case, you would probably need some way to differentiate among the buttons when your action method was called. Sure, you could look at the button's title, but code that does that probably won't work when your application is translated into Swahili or Sanskrit. Unlike labels, tags will never change, so if you set a tag value here in Interface Builder, you can then use that as a fast and reliable way to check which control was passed into an action method in the sender argument.

The Drawing Checkboxes

Below *Tag* are a series of *Drawing* checkboxes. The first one is labeled *Opaque*. Select it. This tells the iPhone OS that nothing behind your view should be drawn and allows iPhone's drawing methods to do some optimizations that speed up drawing.

You might be wondering why we need to select the Opaque checkbox, when we've already set the value of *Alpha* to 1.0 to indicate no transparency. The reason is that the alpha value applies to the parts of the image to be drawn, but if an image doesn't completely fill the image view, or there are holes in the image thanks to an alpha channel or clipping path, the objects below will still show through regardless of the value set in *Alpha*. By selecting *Opaque*, we are telling iPhone that nothing below this view ever needs to be drawn no matter what, so it needn't waste processing time with anything below our object. We can safely select the Opaque checkbox, because we earlier selected *Size to Fit*, which caused the image view to match the size of the image it contains.

The *Hidden* checkbox does exactly what you think it does. If it's checked, the user can't see this control. Hiding the control can be useful at times, including later in this chapter when we hide the switches and button, but the vast majority of the time you want this to remain unchecked. We can leave this at the default value.

The next checkbox, called *Clear Context Before Drawing*, will rarely need to be checked. When it is checked, iPhone will draw the entire area covered by the control in transparent black before it actually draws the control. Again, it is turned off for the sake of performance and because it's rarely needed.

Clip Subviews is an interesting option. If your view has subviews, and those subviews are not completely contained within the bounds of its parent view, this checkbox determines how the subviews will be drawn. If *Clip Subviews* is checked, only the portions of subviews that lie within the bounds of the parent will be drawn. If *Clip Subviews* is unchecked, subviews will be drawn completely even if they lie outside of the bounds of the parent. If that seems confusing, you can see an illustration of the concept in Figure 4-9.

It might seem that the default behavior should be the opposite of what it actually is: that *Clip Subviews* should be enabled by default. As with many other things on the iPhone, this has to do with performance. Calculating the clipping area and displaying only part of the subviews is a somewhat costly operation, mathematically speaking, and the vast majority of the time subview won't lay outside the bounds of the superview. You can turn on *Clip Subviews* if you really need it for some reason, but it is off by default for the sake of performance.

The final checkbox in this section, *Autoresize Subviews*, tells iPhone to resize any subviews if this view is resized. Leave this checked. Since we don't allow the view to be resized, this setting does not really matter.

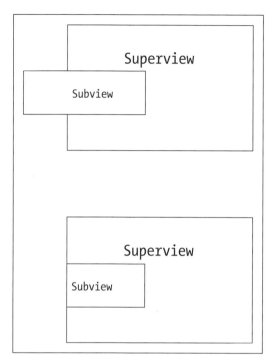

Figure 4-9. *Clip subviews in action: The top view is the default setting, with Clip Subviews turned off. The bottom shows what happens when you turn on Clip Subviews.*

The Interaction Checkboxes

The last two checkboxes have to do with user interaction. The first checkbox, *User Interaction Enabled*, specifies whether the user can do anything at all with this object. For most controls, this box will be checked, because if it's not, the control will never be able to trigger action methods. However, labels and image views default to unchecked, because they are very often used just for the display of static information. Since all we're doing here is displaying a picture on the screen, there is no need to turn this on.

The last checkbox is *Multiple Touch*, and it determines whether this control is capable of receiving multitouch events. Multitouch events allows complex gestures like the pinch gesture used to zoom in many iPhone applications. We'll talk more about gestures and multitouch events in Chapter 13. Since this image view doesn't accept user interaction at all, there's no reason to turn on multitouch events, so leave it at the default value.

Adding the Text Fields

Once you have your image view all finished, grab a text field from the library, and drag it over to the *View* window. Place it underneath the image view, using the blue guides to align it with the right margin (see Figure 4-10). A horizontal blue guideline will appear just above the text field when you move it very close to the bottom of your image. That guideline tells you when you are as close as you should possibly be to another object. You can leave your text field there for now, but to give it a balanced appearance, consider moving the text field just a little further down. Remember, you can always come back to Interface Builder and change the position and size of interface elements without having to change code or reestablish connections.

After you drop the text field, grab a label from the library, and drag that over so it is aligned with the left margin of the view and aligned vertically with the text field you placed earlier. Note that multiple blue guidelines will pop up as you move the label around, making it easy to align the label to the text field using the top, bottom, middle, or text baseline. We're going to align the label and the text field using the text baseline guide, which will draw a line from the bottom of the label's text going through the text field, as shown in Figure 4-11. If the blue guideline is being drawn through the middle of the label's text, you're on the center guideline, not the text baseline guide. Using the text baseline guide will cause the label's text label and the text that the user will type into the text field to be at the same vertical position on the screen.

Figure 4-10. *Placing the text field. Notice the blue guideline just above the text field that tells you not to move the text field any closer to the image.*

Figure 4-11. *Aligning the label and text field using the baseline guide*

Double-click the label you just dropped, change it to read *Name:* instead of *Label*, and press the return key to commit your changes. Next, drag another text field from the library to the view, and use the guidelines to place it below the first text field (see Figure 4-12).

Once you've placed the second text field, grab another label from the library, and place it on the left side, below the existing label. Use the blue text baseline guide again to align it with the second text field. Double-click the new label, and change it to read *Number:*.

Now, let's expand the size of the bottom text field to the left. Single-click the bottom text field, and drag the left resize dot to the left until a blue guideline appears to tell you that you are as close as you should ever be to the label (see Figure 4-13).

Now expand the top text field the same way so that it matches the bottom one in size. Note that we did the bottom one first because the bottom label is the larger of the two labels.

We're basically done with the text fields except for one small detail. Look back at Figure 4-5. See how the *Name:* and *Number:* are right-aligned? Right now, ours are both against the left margin. To align the right sides of the two labels, click the *Name:* label, hold down the shift key, and click the *Number:* label so both labels are selected. From the **Alignment** submenu of the **Layout** menu, select **Align Right Edges**.

Figure 4-12. *Adding the second text field*

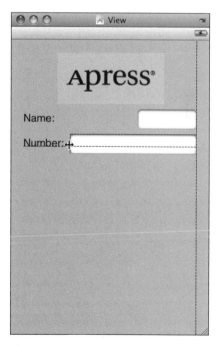

Figure 4-13. *Expanding the size of the bottom text field*

When you are done, the interface should look very much like the one shown in Figure 4-5. The only difference is the light gray text in each text field. We'll add that now.

Click somewhere where there's no control to deselect the two labels, then select the top text field and press ⌘1 to bring up the inspector (see Figure 4-14).

The Text Field Inspector Settings

Text fields are one of the most complex controls on the iPhone as well as being one of the most commonly used. Let's look at the topmost section of the inspector first. In the first field, *Text*, you can set a default value for this field. Whatever you type in this field will show up in the text field when your application launches.

The second field, *Placeholder*, allows you to specify a bit of text that will be displayed in gray inside the text field, but only when the field has no value. You can use a placeholder instead of a label if space is tight, or you can use it to clarify what the user should type into this field.

Type in the text *Type in a name* as the placeholder for this text field.

The next two fields are used only if you need to customize the appearance of your text field, which is completely unnecessary and actually ill-advised the vast majority of the time. Users expect text fields to look a certain way. As a result, we're going to skip right over the *Background* and *Disabled* fields and leave them blank.

Below these fields are three buttons for controlling the alignment of the text displayed in the field. We'll leave this field at the default value of left-aligned (the leftmost button). Next to that is a field that lets us specify the color of the text field's text. Again, we'll leave it at the default value of black.

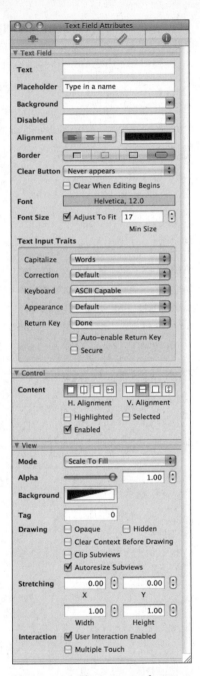

Figure 4-14. *The inspector for a text field showing the default values*

Next are four buttons labeled *Border*. These allow you to change the way the text field's edge will be drawn. You can feel free to try all four different styles, but the default value is the rightmost button, and it creates the text field style that users are most accustomed to seeing for normal text fields in an iPhone application, so when you're done playing, set it back to that one.

The *Clear When Editing Begins* checkbox specifies what happens when the user touches this field. If this box is checked, any value that was previously in this field will get deleted, and the user will start with an empty field. If this box is unchecked, the previous value will stay in the field, and the user will be able to edit it. Uncheck this checkbox.

The *Adjust to Fit* checkbox specifies whether the size of the text should shrink if the text field is reduced in size. Adjusting to fit will keep the entire text visible in the view even if the text would normally be too big to fit in the allotted space. To the right of the checkbox is a text field that allows you to specify a minimum text size. No matter the size of the field, the text will not be resized below that minimum size. Specifying a minimum size will allow you to make sure that the text doesn't get too small to be readable.

Text Input Traits

The next section defines how the keyboard will look and behave when this text field is being used. Since we're expecting a name, let's change the *Capitalize* drop-down to *Words*, which will cause every word to be automatically capitalized, which is what you typically want with names. Let's also change the value of the *Return Key* pop-up to *Done* and leave all the other text input traits at their default values. The *Return Key* is the key on the lower right of the keyboard, and its label changes based on what you're doing. If you are entering text into Safari's search field, for example, then it says *Google*. In an application like this, where there text fields share the screen with other controls, *Done* is the right choice.

If the *Auto-enable Return Key* checkbox is checked, the return key is disabled until at least one character is typed into the text field. Leave this unchecked because we want to allow the text field to remain empty if the user so chooses.

The *Secure* checkbox specifies whether the characters being typed are displayed in the text field. You'd check this checkbox if this text field was being used as a password field. Leave it unchecked.

And the Rest . . .

The next section allows you to set general control attributes inherited from `UIControl`, but these generally don't apply to text fields and, with the exception of the *Enabled* checkbox, won't affect the field's appearance. We want to leave these text fields enabled so that the user can interact with them, so just leave everything here as is.

The last section on the inspector should look familiar to you. It's identical to the section of the same name on the image view inspector we looked at a few minutes ago. These are attributes inherited from the UIView class, and since all controls are subclasses of UIView, they all share this section of attributes. Note that for a text field, you do *not* want to check *Opaque*, because doing so will make the entered text unreadable. In fact, you can leave all the values in this section exactly as they are.

Set the Attributes for the Second Text Field

Next, single-click the second text field in the *View* window, and return to the inspector. In the *Placeholder* field, type *Type in a number*, and uncheck *Clear When Editing Begins*. In the section called *Text Input Traits*, click the *Keyboard Type* pop-up menu. Since we want the user to enter numbers only, not letters, go ahead and select *Number Pad*. By doing this, the users will be presented with a keyboard containing only numbers, meaning they won't be able to enter alphabetical characters, symbols, or anything besides numbers. We don't have to set the *Return Key* value for the numeric keypad, because that style of keyboard doesn't have a return key, so everything else on the inspector can stay at the default values.

Connecting Outlets

OK, for this first part of the interface, all that's left is hooking up our outlets. Control-drag from *File's Owner* to each of the text fields, and connect them to their corresponding outlets. Save the nib file once you've connected both text fields to their corresponding outlets, and then go back to Xcode.

Build and Run

Let's see how it works, shall we? Select **Build and Run** from Xcode's **Build** menu. Your application should come up in the iPhone simulator. Click the *Name* text field. The keyboard should appear (see Figure 4-15). Now click the *Number* field, and the keyboard should change to the number pad. Cocoa Touch gives us all this functionality for free just by adding text fields to our interface.

Woo-hoo! But, there's a little problem. How do you get the keyboard to go away? Go ahead and try; we'll wait right here while you do.

Figure 4-15. *The keyboard comes up automatically when you touch the text field.*

Making the Keyboard Go Away When Done Is Tapped

Because the keyboard is software based, rather than being a physical keyboard, we need to take a few extra steps to make sure the keyboard goes away when the user is done with it. When the user taps the *Done* button, a *Did End On Exit* event will be generated, and at that time, we need to tell the text field to give up control so that the keyboard will go away. In order to do that, we need to add an action method to our controller class, so add the following line of code to *Control_FunViewController.h*:

```
#import <UIKit/UIKit.h>

@interface Control_FunViewController : UIViewController {
    UITextField    *nameField;
    UITextField    *numberField;
}
@property (nonatomic, retain) IBOutlet UITextField *nameField;
@property (nonatomic, retain) IBOutlet UITextField *numberField;
- (IBAction)textFieldDoneEditing:(id)sender;
@end
```

Now switch over to *Control_FunViewController.m*, and we'll implement this method. Only one line of code is needed in this new action method to make it work. Add the following method to *Control_FunViewController.m*:

```
- (IBAction)textFieldDoneEditing:(id)sender{
    [sender resignFirstResponder];
}
```

We mentioned the concept of a first responder earlier and said that it's the control that the user is currently interacting with. Here, we tell any control that triggers this action to give up first responder status. When a text field yields first responder status, the keyboard associated with it goes away.

Save both of the files you just edited. Let's just hop back over to Interface Builder and trigger this action from both of our text fields.

Once you're back in Interface Builder, single-click the *Name* text field, and press ⌘**2** to bring up the connections inspector. This time, we don't want the *Touch Up Inside* event that we used in the previous chapter. Instead, we want *Did End On Exit* since that is the event that will fire when the user taps the *Done* button on iPhone's keyboard. Drag from the circle next to *Did End On Exit* to the *File's Owner* icon, and connect it to the `textFieldDoneEditing:` action. Repeat with the other text field, and save. Let's go back to Xcode to build and run again.

TIP

If you drag from *Did End On Exit* but the *File's Owner* icon does not highlight, signifying you can complete the drag, chances are that you did not save your source code before you switched over to Interface Builder. Go back to Xcode, save, and try again. If it still doesn't work, try quitting Interface Builder and Xcode and relaunching both. That should do the trick!

When the simulator appears, click the name field, type in something, and then tap the *Done* button. Sure enough, the keyboard drops away, just as you expect it to. All right! What about the number field, though? Um, where's the *Done* button on that one (see Figure 4-16)?

Well, crud! Not all keyboard layouts feature a *Done* button. We could force the user to tap the name field and then tap *Done*, but that's not very user friendly, is it? And we most definitely want our application to be user friendly.

Can you recall what Apple's iPhone applications do in this situation? Well, in most places where there are text fields, tapping anywhere in the view where there's no active control will cause the keyboard to go away. How do we do that?

The answer is probably going to surprise you because of its simplicity. Our view controller has a property called `view` that it inherited from `UIViewController`. This `view` property corresponds to the view icon in the nib file. This property points to an instance of `UIView` in the nib that acts as a container for all the items in our user interface. It has

Figure 4-16. *The numeric keypad doesn't have a Done button*

no appearance in the user interface, but it covers the entire iPhone window, sits "below" all of the other user interface objects, and is sometimes referred to as a nib's **container view** because its main purpose is to simply hold other views and controls. For all intents and purposes, the container view is the background of our user interface.

In Interface Builder, we can change the class of the object that `view` points to so that its underlying class is `UIControl` instead of `UIView`. Because `UIControl` is a subclass of `UIView`, it is perfectly appropriate for us to connect our `view` property to an instance of `UIControl`. Remember when a class subclasses another object, it is just a more specific version of that class, so a `UIControl` *is* a `UIView`. If we simply change the instance that gets created from `UIView` to `UIControl`, we gain the ability to trigger action methods.

Before we do that, though, we have to create an action method that will be called when the background is tapped.

Touching the Background to Close the Keyboard

Go to Xcode if you're not already there. We need to add one more action to our controller class. Add the following line to your *Control_FunViewController.h* file:

```
#import <UIKit/UIKit.h>

@interface Control_FunViewController : UIViewController {
    UITextField    *nameField;
    UITextField    *numberField;
}
@property (nonatomic, retain) IBOutlet UITextField *nameField;
@property (nonatomic, retain) IBOutlet UITextField *numberField;
- (IBAction)textFieldDoneEditing:(id)sender;
- (IBAction)backgroundTap:(id)sender;
@end
```

Save the header file; switch over to the implementation file, and add this code, which simply tells both text fields to yield first responder status if they have it. It is perfectly safe to call `resignFirstResponder` on a control that is not the first responder, so we can safely call it on both text fields without having to check whether either is the first responder.

```
- (IBAction)backgroundTap:(id)sender {
    [nameField resignFirstResponder];
    [numberField resignFirstResponder];
}
```

TIP

> You'll be switching between header and implementation files a lot as you code. Fortunately, Xcode has a key combination that will switch you between these files quickly. The default key combination is ⌥⌘⇧ (option-command-up arrow), although you can change it to anything you want using Xcode's preferences.

Save this file, and go back to Interface Builder. We now need to change the underlying class of our nib's view. If you look at the nib's main window (Figure 4-17), you'll see that there are three icons in that view. The third one, called View, is our nib's main view that holds all the other controls and views as subviews.

Single-click the icon called *View*, which represents our nib's container view. Press ⌘**4** to bring up the **identity inspector** (Figure 4-18). This is where we can change the underlying class of any object instance in Interface Builder.

Figure 4-17. *The nib's main window has three icons. The third one, labeled View, is our nib's content view.*

Figure 4-18. *The identity inspector allows you to change the underlying class of any object instance in a nib.*

The field labeled *Class* currently says *UIView*. Change it to read *UIControl*. All controls that are capable of triggering action methods are subclasses of `UIControl`, so by changing the underlying class, we have just given this view the ability to trigger action methods. You can verify this by pressing ⌘2 to bring up the connections inspector (Figure 4-19). You should now see all the events that you saw before when you were connecting buttons to actions in the previous chapter.

Drag from the *Touch Down* event to the *File's Owner* icon, and choose the `backgroundTap:` action. Now, touches anywhere in the view without an active control will trigger our new action method, which will cause the keyboard to retract.

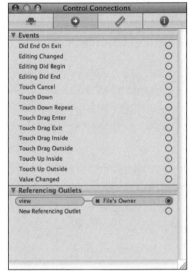

Figure 4-19. *By changing the class of our view from UIView to UIControl, we gain the ability to trigger action methods on any of the standard events.*

NOTE

You might be wondering why we selected Touch Down instead of Touch Up Inside, like we did in the previous chapter. The answer is that the background isn't a button. It's not a control in the eyes of the user, so it wouldn't occur to most users to try to drag their finger somewhere to cancel the action.

Save the nib, and let's go back and try it. Compile and run your application again. This time, the keyboard should disappear not only when the *Done* button is tapped but also when you click anywhere that's not an active control, which is the behavior that your user will expect.

Excellent! Now that we have this section all squared away, are you ready to move onto the next group of controls?

Implementing the Slider and Label

Now that we have the text fields done, let's implement the slider. Remember, as the user moves the slider, the label will change to reflect the slider's value.

Determining Outlets

We're going to add two more items to the interface: a slider and a label that will show the current value of the slider. Want to take a stab at figuring out how many outlets we'll need? Well, the label will need to be changed programmatically when the slider changes, so we're going to need an outlet for it. What about the slider?

The slider will trigger an action, and when it does, that action method will receive a pointer to the slider in the `sender` argument. We'll be able to retrieve the slider's value from `sender`, so we won't need an outlet to get the slider's value. So do we need an outlet for the slider at all? In other words, do we need access to the slider's value outside of the action method it will call?

In a real application, you very often would. Here, since we have another control that will have the same value as the slider and already has an outlet, there's really no reason to have one for the slider itself. Remember that you want to get in the habit of being memory cautious when programming for iPhone. Even though a pointer is a minimal amount of memory, why use it if we don't need it, and why clutter up our code with extra stuff we aren't going to use?

Determining Actions

Figuring out the actions for this pair of controls is straightforward. We need one for the slider to call when it is changed. The label is static, and the user can't do anything with it directly, so it won't need to trigger any actions.

Adding Outlets and Actions

Let's declare one more outlet and one more action in our *Control_FunViewController.h* file, like so:

```objc
#import <UIKit/UIKit.h>

@interface Control_FunViewController : UIViewController {
    UITextField *nameField;
    UITextField *numberField;
    UILabel     *sliderLabel;
}
@property (nonatomic, retain) IBOutlet UITextField *nameField;
@property (nonatomic, retain) IBOutlet UITextField *numberField;
@property (nonatomic, retain) IBOutlet UILabel *sliderLabel;
- (IBAction)textFieldDoneEditing:(id)sender;
- (IBAction)backgroundTap:(id)sender;
- (IBAction)sliderChanged:(id)sender;
@end
```

Since we know exactly what our method needs to do, let's switch to *Control_FunViewController.m* to add our property synthesizer and write our `sliderChanged:` method:

```objc
#import "Control_FunViewController.h"

@implementation Control_FunViewController
@synthesize nameField;
@synthesize numberField;
@synthesize sliderLabel;
- (IBAction)sliderChanged:(id)sender {
    UISlider *slider = (UISlider *)sender;
    int progressAsInt = (int)(slider.value + 0.5f);
    NSString *newText = [[NSString alloc] initWithFormat:@"%d",
    progressAsInt];
    sliderLabel.text = newText;
    [newText release];
}
- (IBAction)backgroundTap:(id)sender {
...
```

Let's talk for a second about what's going on in the sliderChanged: method. The first thing we do is cast sender to a UISlider *. This simply makes our code more readable and lets us avoid having to typecast sender every time we use it. After that, we get the value of the slider as an int, add 0.5 in order to round it to the nearest integer, and use that integer to create a new string that we use to set the label's text. Since we allocated newText, we are responsible for releasing it, so we do that in the last line of code in the method. Simple enough, right?

Speaking of being responsible for memory, since we added the sliderLabel property with the retain keyword, we have to make sure we release it. To do that, add the following line of code to your dealloc method:

```
- (void)dealloc {
    [nameField release];
    [numberField release];
    [sliderLabel release];
    [super dealloc];
}
```

We're done here, so let's go add the objects to our interface. Save your changes, and move on.

Adding the Slider and Label

You know the routine by now. Double-click *Control_FunViewController.xib*, or if it's already open, just go back to Interface Builder.

Before we add the slider, let's add a little bit of breathing room to our design. The blue guidelines we used to determine the spacing between the top text field and the image above it are really suggestions for minimum proximity. In other words, the blue guidelines tell you, "don't get any closer than this." Drag the two text fields and their labels down a bit, using Figure 4-1 as a guide. Now let's add the slider.

From the library, bring over a slider and arrange it below the number text field taking up most but not all of the horizontal space. Leave a little room to the left for the label. Again, use Figure 4-1 as a guide. Single-click the newly added slider to select it, and then press ⌘1 to go back to the inspector if it's not already visible. The inspector should look like the one shown in Figure 4-20.

A slider lets you choose a number in a given range, and here, we can set the range and the initial value in Interface Builder. Put in a minimum value of *1*, a maximum value of *100*, and an initial value of *50*. That's all we need to worry about for now.

Bring over a label and place it next to the slider, using the blue guidelines to align it vertically with the slider and to align its left edge with the left margin of the view (see Figure 4-21).

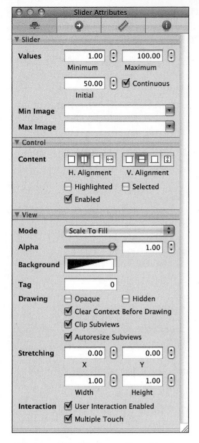

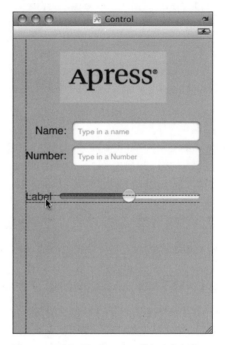

Figure 4-20. *The inspector showing default attributes for a slider*

Figure 4-21. *Placing the slider's label*

Double-click the newly placed label, and change its text from *Label* to *100*. This is the largest value that the slider can hold, and we can use that to determine the correct width of the slider. Since "100" is shorter than "Label," you should resize the label by grabbing the right-middle resize dot and dragging to the left. Make sure you stop resizing before the text starts to get smaller. If it does start to get smaller, bring the resize dot back to the right until it returns to its original size. You can also use the size-to-fit option we discussed earlier by pressing ⌘= or selecting **Size to Fit** from the **Layout** Menu. Next, resize the slider by single-clicking the slider to select it and dragging the left resize dot to the left until the blue guides indicate that you should stop.

Now double-click the label again, and change its value to *50*. That is the starting value of the slider, and we need to change it back to make sure that the interface looks correct at launch time; once the slider is used, the code we just wrote will make sure the label continues to show the correct value.

Connecting the Actions and Outlets

All that's left to do with these two controls is to connect the outlet and action. Well, what are you waiting for? You know how to do that. Well, in case you've forgotten, control-drag from the *File's Owner* icon to the label you just added, and select sliderLabel. Next, single-click the slider, press ⌘2 to bring up the connections inspector, and drag from—hmm, we don't want *Touch Up Inside*, this time, do we? How about *Value Changed*? That sounds like a good one, huh? Yep, go ahead and drag from that one to *File's Owner*, and select sliderChanged.

Save the nib; go back to Xcode; and try out the slider. As you move it, you should see the label's text change in real time. Another piece falls into place. Now, let's look at implementing the switches.

Implementing the Switches, Button, and Segmented Control

Back to Xcode we go once again. Getting dizzy yet? This back and forth may seem a bit strange, but it's fairly common to bounce around among Interface Builder, Xcode, and the iPhone simulator while you're developing.

Our application is going to have two switches, which are small controls that can only have two states: on and off. We'll also add a segmented control to hide and show the switches. Let's implement those next.

Determining Outlets

We won't need an outlet for the segmented control, since we won't be changing its attributes or doing anything with it outside of the action method it calls. We will need some outlets for the switches, however. Since changing the value of either switch will trigger a change in the value of the other switch, we'll need to change the value of the switch that didn't trigger the action method, so we won't be able to rely on using sender. We also need another outlet. We need one for another view that we're going to add. Remember that we're going to hide and show these switches and their labels whenever the segmented control is touched.

We could hide each of the items individually, but the easiest way to group multiple controls to hide and unhide them together is to use a UIView as a common parent for the items that need to be hidden or shown together. You'll see how that works in Interface Builder in a moment, but first, we need to create the outlet for the parent view in addition to the outlets for the two switches.

Determining Actions

The segmented control is going to need to trigger an action method that will hide or show the view containing the switches and their labels. We're also going to need an action that will fire when either switch is tapped. We'll have both switches call the same action method, just as we did with the two buttons in Chapter 3. In *Control_FunViewController.h*, go ahead and add three outlets and two actions, like so:

```
#import <UIKit/UIKit.h>
#define kSwitchesSegmentIndex     0
@interface Control_FunViewController : UIViewController {
    UITextField    *nameField;
    UITextField    *numberField;
    UILabel        *sliderLabel;
    UISwitch       *leftSwitch;
    UISwitch       *rightSwitch;
    UIButton       *doSomethingButton;
}
@property (nonatomic, retain) IBOutlet UITextField *nameField;
@property (nonatomic, retain) IBOutlet UITextField *numberField;
@property (nonatomic, retain) IBOutlet UILabel *sliderLabel;
@property (nonatomic, retain) IBOutlet UISwitch *leftSwitch;
@property (nonatomic, retain) IBOutlet UISwitch *rightSwitch;
@property (nonatomic, retain) IBOutlet UIButton *doSomethingButton;
- (IBAction)textFieldDoneEditing:(id)sender;
- (IBAction)backgroundTap:(id)sender;
- (IBAction)sliderChanged:(id)sender;
- (IBAction)toggleControls:(id)sender;
- (IBAction)switchChanged:(id)sender;
- (IBAction)buttonPressed;
@end
```

In the code we'll be writing in a minute, we're going to refer to a UISegmentedControl property named selectedSegmentIndex, which tells us which segment is currently selected. That property is an integer number. The *Switches* segment will have an index of 0. Rather than stick that 0 in our code, the meaning of which we might not remember a few months from now, we define the constant kSwitchesSegmentIndex to use instead, which will make our code more readable.

Switch over to *Control_FunViewController.m*, and add the following code:

```
#import "Control_FunViewController.h"

@implementation Control_FunViewController
@synthesize nameField;
@synthesize numberField;
@synthesize sliderLabel;
```

```objc
@synthesize leftSwitch;
@synthesize rightSwitch;
@synthesize doSomethingButton;
- (IBAction)toggleControls:(id)sender {
    if ([sender selectedSegmentIndex] == kSwitchesSegmentIndex)
    {
        leftSwitch.hidden = NO;
        rightSwitch.hidden = NO;
        doSomethingButton.hidden = YES;
    }
    else
    {
        leftSwitch.hidden = YES;
        rightSwitch.hidden = YES;
        doSomethingButton.hidden = NO;
    }
}
- (IBAction)switchChanged:(id)sender {
    UISwitch *whichSwitch = (UISwitch *)sender;
    BOOL setting = whichSwitch.isOn;
    [leftSwitch setOn:setting animated:YES];
    [rightSwitch setOn:setting animated:YES];
}
- (IBAction)buttonPressed {
    // TODO: Implement Action Sheet and Alert
}
- (IBAction)sliderChanged:(id)sender {
...
```

The first method, toggleControls:, is called whenever the segmented control is tapped. In this method, we look at the selected segment, and either hide the switches and show the button, or show the switches and hide the button, as appropriate.

The second method we just added, switchChanged:, gets called whenever one of the two switches is tapped. In this method, we simply grab the value of sender, which represents the switch that was pressed, and use that value to set both switches. Now, sender is always going to be either leftSwitch or rightSwitch, so you might be wondering why we're setting them both. It's less work to just set the value of both switches every time than to determine which switch called us and only set the other one. Whichever switch called this method will already be set to the correct value, and setting it again to that same value won't have any affect.

Notice that when we change the value of the switch, we pass a parameter called animated. This lets us specify whether the button should slide over slowly, just as if somebody had pressed it, or if it should just be moved instantly to the new position. We specified YES because having the switches slide over looks cool, and iPhone users have come to expect that kind of visual feedback. You can try specifying NO if you want to see the difference, but unless you have good reason, it's generally a good idea to animate changes made programmatically to the user interface so the user is aware of them.

The third new method, buttonPressed, gets called when the button is pressed. We're not going to implement this method quite yet, so we added a special comment here to remind ourselves to come back to this method. After typing this special comment, if you select the function method at the top of the editor pane (Figure 4-22), you'll see that we now have a reminder every time we use the function pop-up that we need to come back here and finish this.

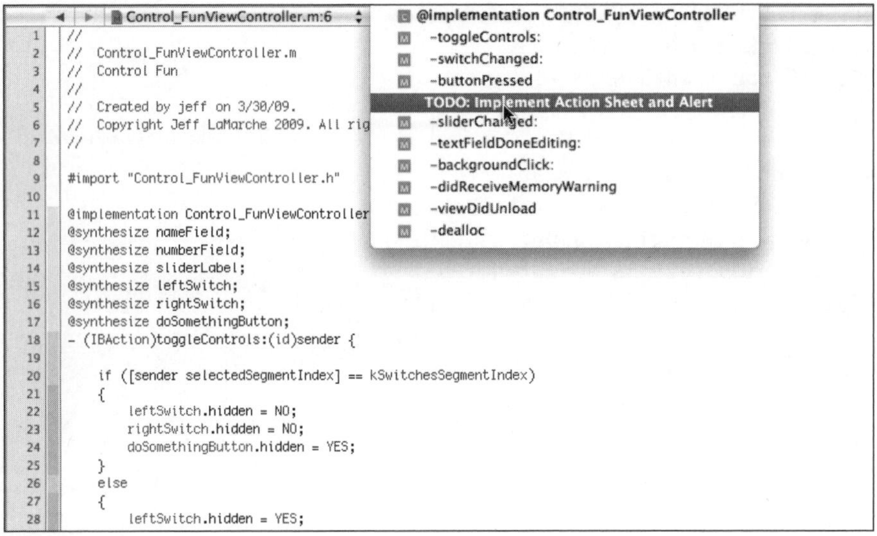

Figure 4-22. *Comments that begin with // TODO: will show up on the function pop-up menu at the top of the Editor pane.*

Releasing the Outlets

Since we declared three new outlets, we need to release those outlets in our dealloc method. Add the following three lines to the existing dealloc method in *Control_FunViewController.m*:

```
- (void)dealloc {
    [nameField release];
    [numberField release];
    [sliderLabel release];
    [leftSwitch release];
    [rightSwitch release];
    [doSomethingButton release];
    [super dealloc];
}
```

Adding the Switches, Button, and Segmented Control

Next, we're going to tackle the segmented control and the switches and button that it toggles between. Back in Interface Buidler, drag a segmented control from the library (see Figure 4-23) and place it on the *View* window, a little below the slider.

Expand the width of the segmented control so that it stretches from the view's left margin to its right margin, as it does in Figure 4-24. Place your cursor over the word *First* on the segmented control and double-click. This should cause the segment's title to become editable, so change it from *First* to *Switches*, as shown in Figure 4-24. After doing that, repeat the process with the *Second* segment; rename it *Button*.

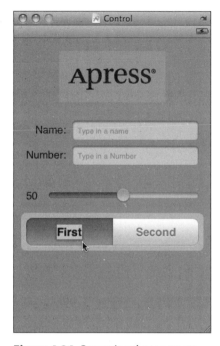

Figure 4-23. *The Segmented Control option in the library*

Figure 4-24. *Renaming the segments*

Adding Two Labeled Switches

Grab a switch from the library, and place it on the view. Place it below the segmented control, against the left margin (Figure 4-25). Drag a second switch and place it against the right margin, aligned vertically with the first switch.

TIP

> Holding down the option key and dragging an object in Interface Builder will create a copy of that item. When you have many instances of the same object to create, it can be faster to drag only one object from the library and then option-drag as many copies as you need.

Connecting the Switch Outlets and Actions

Before we add the button, we're going to connect the switches to the `leftSwitch` and `right-Switch` outlets. The button that we'll be adding in a moment will actually sit on top of the switches, making it harder to control-drag to and from them, so we want to do the switches' connections before we add the button. Since the button and the switches will never be visible at the same time, having them in the same physical location won't be a problem.

Control-drag from *File's Owner* to each of the switches, and connect them to the appropriate `leftSwitch` or `rightSwitch` outlet.

Now select the left switch again by single-clicking it, and press ⌘2 to bring up the connections inspector. Drag from the *Value Changed* event to the *File's Owner* icon, and select the `switch-Changed:` action. Repeat with the other switch.

Single-click the segmented control, and look for the *Value Changed* event on the connections inspector. Drag from the circle next to it to the *File's Owner* icon, and select the `toggleControls:` action method.

Adding the Button

Next, drag a Round Rect Button from the library to your view. Add this one right on top of the left-most button, aligning it with the left margin and vertically aligning its center with the two switches (Figure 4-26).

Now grab the right center resize handle and drag all the way to the right until you reach the blue guideline that indicates the right margin. The button should completely cover the two switches (Figure 4-27).

Figure 4-25. *Adding the switches to the view*

Figure 4-26. *Adding a round rect button on top of the existing switches*

Double-click the button and give it a label of *Do Something*. Because the segmented control will start with the *Switches* segment selected, we need to hide this button. Press ⌘1 to bring up the attribute inspector and click the *Hidden* checkbox down in the bottommost section.

Connecting the Buttons Outlets and Actions

Control-drag from *File's Owner* to the new button, and select the *doSomethingButton* outlet. Then, press ⌘2 to go back to the connections inspector. Drag from the circle next to the *Touch Up Inside* event to *File's Owner,* and select the *buttonPressed* action. Now your button is all wired up.

Save your work.

Go back to Xcode, and take the application for a test drive. The segmented control should now be live. When you tap the *Switches* segment, the pair of switches should appear. Tap one of the switches,

Figure 4-27. *The round rect button, once placed and resized, will completely obscure the two switches.*

and both switches should toggle. Tap the *Button* segment, and the switches should be be hidden, replaced by the *Do Something* button. Tapping the button doesn't do anything yet, because we haven't implemented that particular method. Let's do that now.

Implementing the Action Sheet and Alert

Action sheets and **alerts** are both used to provide the user with feedback.

Action sheets are used to force the user to make a choice between two or more items. The action sheet comes up from the bottom of the screen and displays a series of buttons for the user to select from (Figure 4-3). The user is unable to continue using the application until they have tapped one of the buttons. Action sheets are often used to confirm a potentially dangerous or irreversible action such as deleting an object.

NOTE

A view that forces the user to make a choice before they are allowed to continue using their application is known as a **modal** view.

Alerts appear as a blue rounded rectangle in the middle of the screen (shown earlier in Figure 4-4). Just like action sheets, alerts force users to respond before they are allowed to continue using their application. Alerts are used more to inform the user that something important or out of the ordinary has occurred and, unlike action sheets, alerts may be presented with only a single button, though you have the option of presenting multiple buttons if more than one response is appropriate.

Conforming to the Action Sheet Delegate Method

Remember back in Chapter 2 when we talked about the application delegate? Well, UIApplication is not the only class in Cocoa Touch that uses delegates. In fact, delegation is a very common design pattern in Cocoa Touch. Action sheets and alerts both use delegates so that they know what object to notifiy when they're done being displayed. In our application, we're going to need to get notified when the action sheet is dismissed. We don't need to know when the alert gets dismissed because we're just using it to notify the user of something, not to actually solicit a choice.

In order for our controller class to act as the delegate for an action sheet, it needs to conform to a protocol called UIActionSheetDelegate. We do that by adding the name of the protocol in angle backets after the superclass in our class declaration. Do that by adding the following code to *Control_FunViewController.h*:

```
#import <UIKit/UIKit.h>
#define kSwitchesSegmentIndex     0
@interface Control_FunViewController : UIViewController
        <UIActionSheetDelegate> {
    UITextField *nameField;
    UITextField *numberField;
    UILabel     *sliderLabel;
...
```

Showing the Action Sheet

Let's switch over to *Control_FunViewController.m* and implement the button's action method. We actually need to implement another method in addition to our existing action method because, as we discussed a moment ago, we need to implement the UIActionSheetDelegate method that the action sheet will use to notify us that it has been dismissed.

Here are the changes you need to make to the buttonPressed method in *Control_ FunViewController.m*. Type it in, and then we'll talk about what's going on:

```
- (IBAction)buttonPressed {

    // TODO: Implement Action Sheet and Alert
    UIActionSheet *actionSheet = [[UIActionSheet alloc]
                                  initWithTitle:@"Are you sure?"
                                  delegate:self
                                  cancelButtonTitle:@"No Way!"
                                  destructiveButtonTitle:@"Yes, I'm Sure!"
                                  otherButtonTitles:nil];
    [actionSheet showInView:self.view];
    [actionSheet release];
}
```

Next, add this method to *Control_FunViewController.m*, just below the `buttonPressed`
method:

```
- (void)actionSheet:(UIActionSheet *)actionSheet
didDismissWithButtonIndex:(NSInteger)buttonIndex
{
    if (buttonIndex != [actionSheet cancelButtonIndex])
    {
        NSString *msg = nil;

        if (nameField.text.length > 0)
            msg = [[NSString alloc] initWithFormat:
                    @"You can breathe easy, %@, everything went OK.",
                    nameField.text];
        else
            msg = @"You can breathe easy, everything went OK.";

        UIAlertView *alert = [[UIAlertView alloc]
                              initWithTitle:@"Something was done"
                              message:msg
                              delegate:self
                              cancelButtonTitle:@"Phew!"
                              otherButtonTitles:nil];
        [alert show];
        [alert release];
        [msg release];
    }
}
```

What, exactly, did we do there? Well, first, in the action method we allocated and initialized
a `UIActionSheet` object, which is the object that represents an action sheet (in case you
couldn't puzzle that one out for yourself):

```
UIActionSheet *actionSheet = [[UIActionSheet alloc]
        initWithTitle:@"Are you sure?"
        delegate:self
        cancelButtonTitle:@"No Way!"
        destructiveButtonTitle:@"Yes, I'm Sure!"
        otherButtonTitles:nil];
```

The initializer method took a number of parameters. Let's look at each of them in turn. The first parameter is the title to be displayed. If you look at Figure 4-3, you can see how the title we're supplying will be displayed at the top of the action sheet.

The next argument is the delegate for the action sheet. The action sheet's delegate will be notified when a button on that sheet has been tapped. More specifically, the delegate's `actionSheet:didDismissWithButtonIndex:` method will be called. By passing `self` as the delegate parameter, we ensure that our version of `actionSheet:didDismissWithButton Index:` will be called.

Next, we pass in the title for the button that users will tap to indicate they do not want to proceed. All action sheets should have a cancel button, though you can give it any title that is appropriate to your situation. You do not want to use an action sheet if there is no choice to be made. In situations where you want to notify the user without giving a choice of options, an alert sheet is more appropriate. We'll see how to use alert sheets in a bit.

The next parameter is the destructive button, and you can think of this as the "yes, please go ahead" button, though once again, you can assign any title to it that is appropriate to your situation.

The last parameter allows us to specify any number of other buttons that we may want shown on the sheet. This final argument can take a variable number of values, which is one of the nice features of the Objective-C language. If we had wanted two more buttons on our action sheet, we could have done it like this:

```
UIActionSheet *actionSheet = [[UIActionSheet alloc]
        initWithTitle:@"Are you sure?"
        delegate:self
        cancelButtonTitle:@"No Way!"
        destructiveButtonTitle:@"Yes, I'm Sure!"
        otherButtonTitles:@"Foo", @"Bar", nil];
```

This code would have resulted in an action sheet with four buttons. You can pass as many arguments as you want in the `otherButtonTitles` parameter, as long as you pass `nil` as the last one, but there is, of course, a practical limitation on how many buttons you can have based on the amount of screen space available.

After we create the action sheet, we tell it to show itself:

```
[actionSheet showInView:self.view];
```

On an iPhone, action sheets always have a parent, which must be a view that is currently visible to the user. In our case, we want the view that we designed in Interface Builder to be the parent, so we use self.view. Note the use of Objective-C dot notation. self.view is equivalent to saying [self view], using the accessor to return the value of our view property.

Why didn't we just use view, instead of self.view? view is a private instance variable and must be accessed via the accessor.

Finally, when we're all done, we release the action sheet. Don't worry; it will stick around until the user has tapped a button.

The Action Sheet Delegate and Creating an Alert

Well, that wasn't so hard, was it? In just a few lines of code, we showed an action sheet and required the user to make a decision. iPhone will even animate the sheet for us without requiring us to do any additional work. Now, we just need to find out which button the user tapped. The other method that we just implemented, actionSheet:didDismissWith ButtonIndex, is one of the UIActionSheetDelegate methods, and since we specified self as our action sheet's delegate, this method will automatically get called by the alert sheet when a button is tapped.

The argument buttonIndex will tell us which button was actually tapped. But, how do we know which button index refers to the cancel button and which one refers to the destructive button? Well, fortunately, the delegate method receives a pointer to the UIActionSheet object that represents the sheet, and that action sheet object knows which button is the cancel button. We just need look at one of its properties, cancelButtonIndex:

```
if (buttonIndex != [actionSheet cancelButtonIndex])
```

This line of code makes sure the user didn't tap the cancel button. Since we only gave the user two options, we know that if they didn't tap the cancel button, they must have tapped the destructive button, so it's OK to proceed. Once we know the user didn't cancel, the first thing we do is create a new string that will be displayed to the user. In a real application, here you would do whatever processing the user requested. We're just going to pretend we did something, and notify the user using an alert.

If the user has entered a name in the top text field, we'll grab that, and we'll use it in the message that we're going to display in the alert. Otherwise, we'll just craft a generic message to show:

```
NSString *msg = nil;

if (nameField.text.length > 0)
    msg = [[NSString alloc] initWithFormat:
        @"You can breathe easy, %@, everything went OK.",
        nameField.text];
else
    msg = @"You can breathe easy, everything went OK.";
```

The next lines of code are going to look kind of familiar. Alerts and actions sheets are created and used in a very similar manner:

```
UIAlertView *alert = [[UIAlertView alloc]
        initWithTitle:@"Something was done"
        message:msg
        delegate:nil
        cancelButtonTitle:@"Phew!"
        otherButtonTitles:nil];
```

Again, we pass a title to be displayed, this time along with a more detailed message, which is that string we just created. Alerts have delegates too, and if we needed to know when the user had dismissed the alert or which button was tapped, we could specify self as the delegate here just as we did with the action sheet. If we had done that, we would now have to go conform our class to the UIAlertViewDelegate protocol also and implement one or more of the methods from that protocol. In this case, we're just informing the user of something and only giving the user one button. We don't really care when the button is tapped, and we already know which button will be tapped, so we just specify nil here to indicate that we don't need to be pinged when the user is done with the alert.

Alerts, unlike action sheets, are not tied to a particular view, so we just tell the alert to show itself without specifying a parent view. After that, it's just a matter of some memory cleanup and we're done. Go ahead and save, and then build, run, and try out the completed application.

Spiffing Up the Button

If you compare your running application to Figure 4-2, you might notice an interesting difference. Your *Do Something* button doesn't look like ours, and it doesn't look like the button on the action sheet or those in other iPhone applications, does it? That default *Round Rect Button* doesn't really look that spiffy, so let's take care of that before we finish up the chapter.

Most of the buttons you see on your iPhone are drawn using images. Don't worry; you don't have to create images in an image editor for every button. All you have to do is specify a kind of template image that the iPhone will use when drawing your buttons.

It's important to keep in mind that your application is sandboxed. You can't get to the template images that are used in other applications on your iPhone or the ones used by the iPhone OS, so you have to make sure that any images you need are in your application's bundle. So, where can we get these image templates?

Fortunately, Apple has provided a bunch for you. You can get them from the iPhone sample application called UICatalog, available at:

http://developer.apple.com/iphone/library/samplecode/UICatalog/index.html

Alternatively, you can simply copy them out of the *04 Control Fun* folder from this book's project archive. Yes, it is OK to use these images in your own applications; Apple's sample code license specifically allows you to use and distribute them.

So, from either the *04 Control Fun* folder or the *Images* subfolder of the UICatalog project's folder, add the two images named *blueButton.png* and *whiteButton.png* to your Xcode project.

If you open one of these two images in *Preview.app* or in an image editing program, you'll see that there's not very much to them, and there's a trick to using them for your buttons.

Go back to Interface Builder, single-click the *Do Something* button, and press ⌘1 to open the attributes inspector. In the inspector, use the first pop-up menu to change the type from *Rounded Rect* to *Custom*. You'll see in the inspector that you can specify an image for your button, but we're not going to do that, because these image templates need to be handled a little differently. Save the nib, and go back to Xcode.

The viewDidLoad Method

UIViewController, our controller's superclass, has a method called viewDidLoad that we can override if we need to modify any of the objects that were created from our nib. Because we can't do what we want completely in Interface Builder, we're going to take advantage of viewDidLoad. Go ahead and add the following method to your *Control_FunViewController.m* file. When you're done, we'll talk about what the method does.

```
- (void)viewDidLoad
{
    UIImage *buttonImageNormal = [UIImage imageNamed:@"whiteButton.png"];
    UIImage *stretchableButtonImageNormal = [buttonImageNormal
        stretchableImageWithLeftCapWidth:12 topCapHeight:0];
    [doSomethingButton setBackgroundImage:stretchableButtonImageNormal
        forState:UIControlStateNormal];

    UIImage *buttonImagePressed = [UIImage imageNamed:@"blueButton.png"];
    UIImage *stretchableButtonImagePressed = [buttonImagePressed
        stretchableImageWithLeftCapWidth:12 topCapHeight:0];
```

```
[doSomethingButton setBackgroundImage:stretchableButtonImagePressed
    forState:UIControlStateHighlighted];

}
```

This code sets the background image for the button based on those template images we added to our project. It specifies that, while being touched, the button should change from using the white image to the blue image. This short method introduces two new concepts: **control states**, and **stretchable images**. Let's look at each of them in turn.

Control States

Every iPhone control has four possible control states and is always in one and only one of those states at any given moment. The most common state is the **normal** control state, which is the default state. It's the state that controls are in when not in any of the other states. The **highlighted** state is the state a control is in when it's currently being used. For a button, this would be while the user has a finger on the button. The **disabled** state is what controls are in when they've been turned off, which can be done by unchecking the *Enabled* checkbox in Interface Builder or setting the control's enabled property to NO. The final state is **selected**, which only some controls support, and it is usually used to indicate that this control is turned on or selected. Selected is similar to highlighted, but controls can continue to be selected when the user is no longer directly using that control.

Certain iPhone controls have attributes that can take on different values depending on their state. For example, by specifying one image for UIControlStateNormal and a different image for UIControlStateHighlighted, we are telling the iPhone to use one image when the user has a finger on the button and a different image the rest of the time.

Stretchable Images

Stretchable images are an interesting concept. A stretchable image is a resizable image that knows how to resize itself intelligently so that it maintains the correct appearance. For these button templates, we don't want the edges to stretch evenly with the rest of the image. **End caps** are the parts of an image, measured in pixels, that should not be resized. We want the bevel around the edges to stay the same no matter what size we make the button, so we specify a left end cap size of 12.

Because we pass in the new stretchable image into our button rather than the image template, the iPhone knows how to draw the button properly at any size. We could now go in and change the size of the button in Interface Builder, and it would still be drawn correctly. If we had specified the button image right in Interface Builder, it would resize the entire image evenly, and our button would look weird at most sizes.

TIP

How did we know what value to use for the end caps? It's simple really: we copied them from Apple's sample code.

Being a Good Memory Citizen

Before we take our new button for a spin, there's one more topic we'd like to discuss. With the release of iPhone SDK 3.0, Apple introduced a new method in `UIViewController`, which is the class from which all view controllers in Cocoa Touch descend, including `Control_FunViewController`. This new method is called `viewDidUnload`, and it's an important method in terms of keeping memory overhead down

In Chapter 6, we'll start talking about applications with multiple views. When you have multiple views, the iPhone OS will load and unload nib files to preserve memory. We'll look at this process in-depth in Chapter 6 and throughout the rest of the book, and we don't want you to worry too much about multiple views yet, but we do want to show you the correct way of implementing a view controller class. When a view gets unloaded, any object that your controller class has an outlet to can't be flushed from memory because you have retained that object by specifying the `retain` keyword in the outlet's property.

Therefore, when your controller gets notified that its view has been unloaded, it is important to set all the controller's outlet properties to `nil` so that memory can get freed up. Cocoa Touch will automatically re-connect your outlets when the nib file gets re-loaded, so there's no danger with doing this, and by doing it, you will be a good memory citizen by not hogging memory you don't need.

Our Control Fun application is a single-view application, so `viewDidUnload` will never be called while the program is running. But, just because an application starts as a single-view application doesn't mean it will always be one, so you should be a good memory citizen even when you know you can get away with not being one. Let's be good memory citizens by adding the following method to *Control_FunViewController.m* to free up our outlets when our view gets unloaded:

```
- (void)viewDidUnload {
    self.nameField = nil;
    self.numberField = nil;
    self.sliderLabel = nil;
    self.leftSwitch = nil;
    self.rightSwitch = nil;
    self.doSomethingButton = nil;
    [super viewDidUnload];
}
```

Note the use of Objective-C dot notation once again. This time, since it is used as the left side of an assignment, the dot notation is equivalent to calling our mutator. For example, this line of code:

```
self.nameField = nil;
```

is equivalent to this line of code:

```
[self setNameField:nil];
```

Think about what happens when our mutator does its thing. Remember, we synthesized our mutators using the `retain` keyword. First, our mutator retains the new object, then it releases the old object, and then it assigns the new object to its instance variable. In this case, the mutator retains `nil`, which doesn't do anything. Next, the old object is released, which is exactly what we want to do, since that old object was retained when it was originally connected. And, finally, `nil` is assigned to `nameField`. Pretty cool, eh?

Once you've added that method, why don't you save and go try it out? Everything should work exactly as it did earlier, but that button should look a lot more iPhone-like. You won't see any difference in the way the application behaves as a result of adding the `viewDidUnload` method, but you can sleep soundly at night knowing you did the right thing. Good job, citizen!

Crossing the Finish Line

This was a big chapter. Conceptually, we didn't hit you with too much new stuff, but we took you through the use of a good number of controls and showed you a lot of different implementation details. You got a lot more practice with outlets and actions and saw how to use the hierarchical nature of views to your advantage. You learned about control states and stretchable images, and you also learned to use both action sheets and alerts.

There's a lot going on in this little application. Feel free to go back and play with it. Change values, experiment by adding and modifying code, and see what different settings in Interface Builder do. There's no way we could take you through every permutation of every control available on an iPhone, but the application you just put together is a good starting point and covers a lot of the basics.

In the next chapter, we're going to look at what happens when the user rotates the iPhone from portrait to landscape or vice versa. You're probably well aware that many iPhone applications change their displays based on the way the user is holding the iPhone, and we're going to show you how to do that in your own applications.

Chapter 5

Autorotation and Autosizing

*t*he iPhone is an amazing piece of engineering. Apple engineers found all kinds of ways to squeeze maximum functionality into a pocket-sized package. One example is the mechanism that allows applications to be used in either portrait (tall and skinny) or landscape (short and wide) mode and to change that orientation at runtime if the phone is rotated. A prime example of this behavior, which is called **autorotation**, can be seen in iPhone's web browser, Mobile Safari (see Figure 5-1).

Figure 5-1. *Like many iPhone applications, Mobile Safari changes its display based on how it is held, making the most of the available screen space.*

Autorotation might not be right for every application. Several of Apple's iPhone applications support only a single orientation. Movies can be watched only in landscape mode, for example, and contacts can be edited only in portrait mode. Bottom line, if autorotation enhances the user experience, add it to your application.

Fortunately, Apple did a great job of hiding the complexities of autorotation in the iPhone OS and in the UIKit, so implementing this behavior in your own iPhone applications is actually quite easy.

Autorotation is specified in the view controller, so if the user rotates the phone, the active view controller will be asked if it's OK to rotate to the new orientation (something you'll see how to do in this chapter). If the view controller responds in the affirmative, the application's window and views will be rotated, and the window and view will get resized to fit the new orientation.

A view that starts in portrait mode will be 320 pixels wide and 460 pixels tall or 480 pixels tall if there's no **status bar**. The status bar is the 20-pixel strip at the top of the screen (see Figure 5-1) that shows things like signal strength, time, and battery charge. When the phone is switched to landscape mode, the view rotates, along with the application's window, and gets resized to fit the new orientation, so that it is 480 pixels wide by 300 pixels tall (320 pixels if there's no status bar).

Most of the work in actually moving the pixels around the screen is managed by the iPhone OS. Your application's main job in all this is making sure everything fits nicely and looks proper in the resized window.

Your application can take three general approaches when managing rotation. Which one you use depends on the complexity of your interface, and we'll look at all three approaches in this chapter. With simpler interfaces, you can simply specify the correct **autosize** attributes for all of the objects that make up your interface. Autosize attributes tell the iPhone how your controls should behave when their enclosing view gets resized. If you've worked with Cocoa on Mac OS X, you're already familiar with the basic process, because it is the same one used to specify how Cocoa controls behave when the user resizes the window in which they are contained. You'll see this concept in action in just a bit.

Autosize is quick and easy but not appropriate for all applications. More complex interfaces have to handle autorotation in a different manner. For more complex views, you have two basic approaches. One approach is to manually reposition the objects in your view when notified that your view is rotating. The second approach is to actually design two different versions of your view in Interface Builder, one for portrait mode and a separate one for landscape mode. In both cases, you will need to override methods from UIViewController in your view's controller class.

Let's get started, shall we? We'll look at autosizing first.

Handling Rotation Using Autosize Attributes

Start a new project in Xcode, and call it Autosize. We're going to stick with the same view-based application template for this application. Before we design our view in Interface Builder, we need to tell the iPhone that our view supports autorotation. We do that by modifying the view controller class.

Specifying Rotation Support

Once your project is open in Xcode, expand the *Classes* folder, and single-click *AutoSizeViewController.m*. If you look at the code that's already there, you'll see that a method called shouldAutorotateToInterfaceOrientation: is already provided for you, courtesy of the template, but it's commented out. Uncomment it now by deleting the comment beginning and ending:

```
...
/*
// Override to allow orientations other than the default portrait
//    orientation.
- (BOOL)shouldAutorotateToInterfaceOrientation:(UIInterfaceOrientation)➥
interfaceOrientation {
    // Return YES for supported orientations
    return (interfaceOrientation == UIInterfaceOrientationPortrait);
}
*/
...
```

This method is the system's way of asking your view controller if it's OK to rotate to a specific orientation. Four defined orientations correspond to the four general ways that the iPhone can be held:

- UIInterfaceOrientationPortrait

- UIInterfaceOrientationPortraitUpsideDown

- UIInterfaceOrientationLandscapeLeft

- UIInterfaceOrientationLandscapeRight

When the phone is changed to a new orientation, this method is called on the active view controller. The parameter interfaceOrientation will contain one of the four values in the preceding list, and this method needs to return either YES or NO to signify whether the application's window should be rotated to match the new orientation. Because every view controller subclass can implement this differently, it is possible for one application to support autorotation with some of its views but not with others.

TIP

Have you noticed that the defined system constants on iPhone are always designed so that values that work together start with the same letters? One reason why `UIInterfaceOrientationPortrait`, `UIInterfaceOrientationPortraitUpsideDown`, `UIInterfaceOrientation-LandscapeLeft`, and `UIInterfaceOrientationLandscapeRight` all begin with `UIInterfaceOrientation` is to let you take advantage of Xcode's Code Sense feature. You've probably noticed that as you type Xcode frequently tries to complete the word you are typing. That's Code Sense in action. Developers cannot possibly remember all the various defined constants in the system, but you can remember the common beginning for the groups you use frequently. When you need to specify an orientation, simply type *UIInterfaceOrientation* (or even *UIInterf*) and then press the escape key to bring up a list of all matches (in Xcode's preferences, you can change that matching key from escape to something else). You can use the arrow keys to navigate the list that appears and make a selection by pressing the tab or return key. This is much faster than having to go look the values up in the documentation or header files.

The default implementation of this method looks at `interfaceOrientation` and returns YES only if it is equal to `UIInterfaceOrientationPortrait`, which limits this application to one orientation, effectively disabling autorotation.

If we wanted to enable rotation to any orientation, we'd simply change the method to return YES for any value passed in, like so:

```
- (BOOL)shouldAutorotateToInterfaceOrientation:
    (UIInterfaceOrientation)interfaceOrientation {
    return YES;
}
```

In order to support some but not all orientations, we have to look at the value of `interfaceOrientation` and return YES for those that we want to support and NO for those we don't. For example, to support portrait mode and landscape mode in both directions but not rotation to the upside down portrait mode, we could do this:

```
- (BOOL)shouldAutorotateToInterfaceOrientation:
    (UIInterfaceOrientation)interfaceOrientation {
    return (interfaceOrientation !=
        UIInterfaceOrientationPortraitUpsideDown);
}
```

Go ahead and change the `shouldAutorotateToInterfaceOrientation:` method to match the preceding version. As a general rule, `UIInterfaceOrientationPortraitUpsideDown` is discouraged by Apple, because if the phone rings while it is being held upside down, the phone is likely to remain upside down when it's answered.

Save, and then we'll look at setting autosize attributes in Interface Builder.

Designing an Interface with Autosize Attributes

In Xcode, expand the *Resources* folder, and double-click *AutosizeViewController.xib* to open the file in Interface Builder. One nice thing about using autosize attributes is that they require very little code. We do have to specify which orientations we support, as we just did in our view controller, but everything else we need to do in order to imple-ment this technique will be done right here in Interface Builder.

To see how this works, drag six *Round Rect Buttons* from the library over to your view, and place them as we've done in Figure 5-2. Double-click each but-ton, and assign a title to each one so we can tell them apart later. We've numbered ours from 1 to 6.

Save, and go back to Xcode. Let's see what happens now that we've specified that we support autorota-tion but haven't set any autosize attributes. Build and run. Once the iPhone simulator comes up, select **Rotate Left** from the **Hardware** menu, which will simulate turning the iPhone into landscape mode. Take a look at Figure 5-3. Oh, dear.

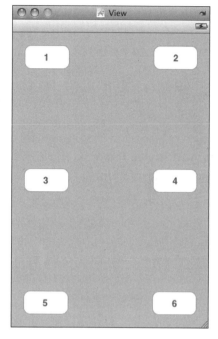

Figure 5-2. *Adding six numbered but-tons to the interface*

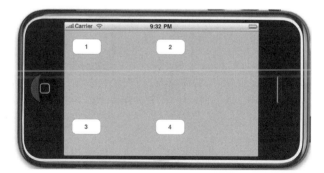

Figure 5-3. *Well, that's not very useful, is it?*

Most controls default to a setting that has them stay where they are in relation to the left side and top of the screen. There are some controls for which this would be appropriate. The top-left button, number 1, for example, is probably right where we want it—the rest of them, however, not so much.

Quit the simulator, and go back to Interface Builder.

Autosize Attributes

Single-click the top-left button on your view, and then press ⌘3 to bring up the size inspector, which should look like Figure 5-4.

The **size inspector** allows you to set an object's **autosize attributes**. Figure 5-5 shows the part of the size inspector that controls an object's autosize attributes.

The box on the left in Figure 5-5 is where we actually set the attributes; the box on the right is a little animation that will show us how the object will behave during a resize. In the box on the left, the inner square represents the current object. If a button is selected, the inner square represents that button.

The red arrows inside the inner square represent the horizontal and vertical space inside the selected object. Clicking either arrow will change it from solid to dashed or from dashed back to solid. If the horizontal arrow is solid, the width of the object is free to change as the window resizes; if the horizontal arrow is dashed, the iPhone will try to keep the width of the object at its original value if possible. The same is true for the height of the object and the vertical arrow.

The four red "I" shapes outside the inner box represent the distance between the edge of the selected object and the same edge of the view that contains it. If the "I" is dashed, the space is flexible, and if it's solid red, the amount of space should be kept constant if possible.

Huh?

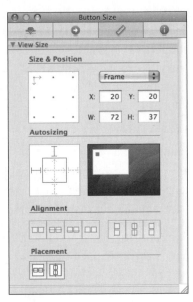

Figure 5-4. *The size inspector allows you to set an object's autosize attributes.*

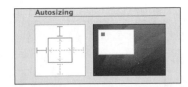

Figure 5-5. *The Autosizing section of the size inspector*

Perhaps this concept will make a little more sense if you actually see it in action. Take a look back at Figure 5-5, which represents the default autosize settings. These default settings specify that the object's size will remain constant as its superview is resized and that the distance from the left and top edges should also stay constant. If you look at the animation next to the autosize control, you can see how it will behave during a resize. Notice that the inner box stays in the same place relative to the left and top edges of the parent view as the parent view changes in size.

Try this experiment. Click both of the solid red "I" shapes (to the top and left of the inner box) so they become dashed and look like the ones shown in Figure 5-6.

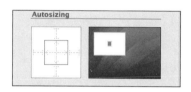

With all the lines set to dashed, the size of the object will be kept the same, and it will float in the middle of the superview as the superview is resized.

Figure 5-6. *With all dashed lines, your control floats in the parent and keeps its size.*

Now, click the vertical arrow inside the box and the "I" shape both above and below the box so that your auto-size attributes look like the ones shown in Figure 5-7.

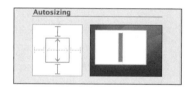

With this configuration, we are indicating that the vertical size of our object can change and that the distance from the top of our object to the top of the window and the distance from the bottom of our object to the bottom of the window should stay constant. With this configuration, the width of the object wouldn't change, but its height

Figure 5-7. *This configuration allows the vertical size of our object to change.*

would. Change the autosize attributes a few more times and watch the animation until you grok how different settings will impact the behavior when the view is rotated and resized.

Setting the Buttons' Autosize Attributes

Now, let's set the autosize attributes for our six buttons. Go ahead and see if you can figure them out. If you get stumped, take a look at Figure 5-8, which shows you the autosize attributes needed for each button in order to keep them on the screen when the phone is rotated.

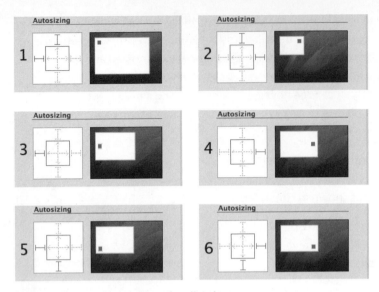

Figure 5-8. *Autosize attributes for all six buttons*

Once you have the attributes set the same as Figure 5-8, save the nib, go back to Xcode, and build and run. This time, when the iPhone simulator comes up, you should be able to select **Rotate Left** or **Rotate Right** from the **Hardware** menu and have all the buttons stay on the screen (see Figure 5-9). If you rotate back, they should return to their original position. This technique will work for a great many applications.

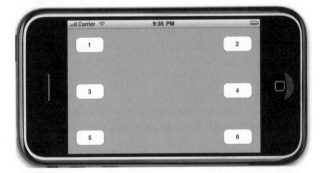

Figure 5-9. *The buttons in their new positions after rotating*

In this example, we kept our buttons the same size, so now all of our buttons are visible and usable, but there is an awful lot of unused white space on the screen. Perhaps it would be better if we allowed the width or height of our buttons to change so that there will be less empty space on the interface? Feel free to experiment with the autosize attributes of these six buttons, and add some other buttons if you want. Play around until you feel comfortable with the way autosize works.

In the course of your experimentation, you're bound to notice that, sometimes, no combination of autosize attributes will give you exactly what you want. Sometimes, you are going to need to rearrange your interface more drastically than can be handled with this technique. For those situations, a little more code is in order. Let's take a look at that, shall we?

Restructuring a View When Rotated

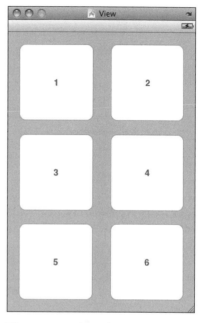

In Interface Builder, single-click each of the buttons, and use the size inspector to change the *w* and *h* field to *125*, which will set the width and height of the button to 125 pixels. When you are done, rearrange your buttons using the blue guidelines so that your view looks like Figure 5-10.

Can you guess what's going to happen this time when we rotate the screen? Well, assuming that you returned the buttons' autosize attributes back to those shown in Figure 5-8, what will happen isn't likely what we want to happen. The buttons are going to overlap and look like Figure 5-11, because there simply isn't enough height on the screen in landscape mode to accommodate three buttons that are 125 pixels tall.

Figure 5-10. *View after resizing all the buttons*

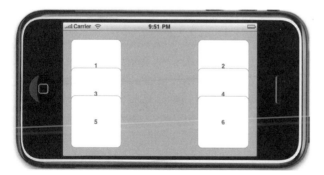

Figure 5-11. *Not exactly what we want*

We could accommodate this scenario using the autosize attributes by allowing the height of the buttons to change, but that's not going to make the best use of our screen real estate because it's going to leave a large gap in the middle of the screen. If there was room for six square buttons when the interface was in portrait mode, there should still be room for six square buttons in landscape mode, we just need to shuffle them around a bit. One way we can handle this is to specify new positions for each of the buttons when the view is rotated.

Declaring and Connecting Outlets

To change a control's attributes, we need an outlet that points to the object we want to change. As a result, we need to declare an outlet for each of the six buttons in order to rearrange them. Add the following code to *AutosizeViewController.h*:

```
#import <UIKit/UIKit.h>

@interface AutosizeViewController : UIViewController {
    UIButton *button1;
    UIButton *button2;
    UIButton *button3;
    UIButton *button4;
    UIButton *button5;
    UIButton *button6;
}
@property (nonatomic, retain) IBOutlet UIButton *button1;
@property (nonatomic, retain) IBOutlet UIButton *button2;
@property (nonatomic, retain) IBOutlet UIButton *button3;
@property (nonatomic, retain) IBOutlet UIButton *button4;
@property (nonatomic, retain) IBOutlet UIButton *button5;
@property (nonatomic, retain) IBOutlet UIButton *button6;
@end
```

Save this file, and go back to Interface Builder. Control-drag from the *File's Owner* icon to each of the six buttons, and connect them to the corresponding outlet. Once you've connected all six, save the nib, and pop back over to Xcode.

Moving the Buttons on Rotation

To move these buttons to make the best use of space, we need to override the method `willAnimateRotationToInterfaceOrientation:duration:` in *AutosizeViewController.m*. This method gets called automatically after a rotation has occurred but before the final rotation animations have occurred.

NOTE

> The method `willAnimateRotationToInterfaceOrientation:duration:` is new with 3.0. In previous versions of the SDK, the method `willAnimateSecondHalfOfRotationFrom InterfaceOrientation:duration:` can be used; however, the two-part animation used prior to 3.0 is considerably slower than the method we're using here, so you should avoid those methods unless you absolutely need to support older versions of the iPhone OS in your application.

Add the following code, and then we'll talk about what it's doing:

```
#import "AutosizeViewController.h"

@implementation AutosizeViewController
@synthesize button1;
@synthesize button2;
@synthesize button3;
@synthesize button4;
@synthesize button5;
@synthesize button6;

- (void)willAnimateRotationToInterfaceOrientation:(UIInterfaceOrientation)
    interfaceOrientation duration:(NSTimeInterval)duration {

    if (interfaceOrientation == UIInterfaceOrientationPortrait
        || interfaceOrientation ==
            UIInterfaceOrientationPortraitUpsideDown) {
        button1.frame = CGRectMake(20, 20, 125, 125);
        button2.frame = CGRectMake(175, 20, 125, 125);
        button3.frame = CGRectMake(20, 168, 125, 125);
        button4.frame = CGRectMake(175, 168, 125, 125);
        button5.frame = CGRectMake(20, 315, 125, 125);
        button6.frame = CGRectMake(175, 315, 125, 125);
    }
    else {
        button1.frame = CGRectMake(20, 20, 125, 125);
        button2.frame = CGRectMake(20, 155, 125, 125);
        button3.frame = CGRectMake(177, 20, 125, 125);
        button4.frame = CGRectMake(177, 155, 125, 125);
        button5.frame = CGRectMake(328, 20, 125, 125);
        button6.frame = CGRectMake(328, 155, 125, 125);
    }
}
- (BOOL)shouldAutorotateToInterfaceOrientation:
    (UIInterfaceOrientation)interfaceOrientation {
    return (interfaceOrientation !=
        UIInterfaceOrientationPortraitUpsideDown);
}
- (void)didReceiveMemoryWarning {
    [super didReceiveMemoryWarning];
    // Releases the view if it doesn't have a superview
    // Release anything that's not essential, such as cached data
}
- (void)viewDidUnload {
    // Release any retained subviews of the main view.
    // e.g. self.myOutlet = nil;
    self.button1 = nil;
```

```
        self.button2 = nil;
        self.button3 = nil;
        self.button4 = nil;
        self.button5 = nil;
        self.button6 = nil;
        [super viewDidUnload];
    }
    - (void)dealloc {
        [button1 release];
        [button2 release];
        [button3 release];
        [button4 release];
        [button5 release];
        [button6 release];
        [super dealloc];
    }
```

The size and position of all views, including controls such as buttons, are specified in a property called frame, which is a struct of type CGRect. CGRectMake is a function provided by Apple that lets you easily create a CGRect by specifying the x and y positions along with the width and height.

NOTE

The function CGRect() begins with the letters "CG," indicating that it comes from the Core Graphics framework. As its name implies, the Core Graphics framework contains code related to graphics and drawing. In earlier versions of the iPhone SDK, the Core Graphics framework was not included in Xcode iPhone project templates and had to be added manually. That step is no longer necessary, since the Core Graphics framework is automatically included when you use any of the iPhone Xcode templates.

Save this code. Now build and run to see it in action. Try rotating, and watch how the buttons end up in their new positions.

Swapping Views

There is one other way of handling autorotation, and it's an option you'll likely use only in the case of very complex interfaces. Moving controls to different locations, as we did in the previous section, can be a very tedious process, especially with a complex interface. Wouldn't it be nice if we could just design the landscape and portrait views separately and then swap them out when the phone is rotated?

Well, we can. But it's a moderately complex option. While controls on both views can trigger the same actions, we will have to have two completely distinct sets of outlets, one for each of the views, and that will add a certain complexity to our code. It is, by no means, an insurmountable amount of complexity, and there are times when this option is the best one. Let's try it out.

Create a new project in Xcode using the view-based application template again; we'll start working with other templates next chapter. Call this project *Swap*. The interface we'll be building in this application won't actually be complex enough to really justify the technique we're using. However, we want to make sure the process is clear, so we're going to use a fairly simple interface. When this application we're writing starts up, it will be in portrait mode. There will be two buttons, one on top of the other (see Figure 5-12).

Figure 5-12. *The Swap application at launch*

When you rotate the phone, we'll swap in a completely different view to be shown for the landscape orientation. It will also feature two buttons with the exact same labels (see Figure 5-13), so the user won't know they're looking at two different views.

Figure 5-13. *Similar but not the same*

When the buttons are tapped, they will become hidden. This gives us a chance to show you some of the nuances of dealing with two sets of outlets. In a real application, there may be times when you want to hide or disable a button like this. As an example, you might create a button that kicked off a lengthy process and you didn't want the user tapping the same button again until that process had finished.

Determining Outlets

Because there are two buttons on each view that we're going to build and because an outlet can't point to more than one object, we need to declare four outlets, two for the landscape view buttons and two for the portrait view buttons. When using this technique, it becomes very important to put some thought into your outlet names to keep your code from becoming confusing to read.

But, oho! Is that somebody in the back saying, "Do we really need outlets for all these buttons? Since we're deactivating the button that was tapped, can't we just use sender instead?" And in a single-view scenario, that would be exactly the right way to go about it.

Think about this. What if the user taps the *Foo* button and then rotates the phone? The *Foo* button on the other view is a completely different button, and it will still be active, which isn't the behavior we want. We don't really want to advertise to the users that the object they're dealing with now isn't the same one they were dealing with a moment ago.

In addition to the outlets for the buttons, we need two more outlets to point to the two different versions of our view. When working with a single view only, our parent class's view property was all we needed. But, since we're going to be changing the value of view at runtime, we need to make sure we have a way to get to both views, hence the need for two UIView outlets.

Determining Actions

Our buttons need to trigger an action, so we're definitely going to need at least one action method. We're going to design a single action method to handle the pressing of any of the buttons, so we'll just declare a single buttonPressed: action in our view controller class.

Declaring Actions and Outlets

Add the following code to *SwapViewController.h* to create the outlets we'll need when we go to Interface Builder.

```
#import <UIKit/UIKit.h>
#define degreesToRadians(x) (M_PI * (x) / 180.0)
@interface SwapViewController : UIViewController {
    UIView     *landscape;
    UIView     *portrait;

    // Foo
    UIButton *landscapeFooButton;
    UIButton *portraitFooButton;

    // Bar
    UIButton *landscapeBarButton;
```

```
    UIButton *portraitBarButton;
}
@property (nonatomic, retain) IBOutlet UIView *landscape;
@property (nonatomic, retain) IBOutlet UIView *portrait;
@property (nonatomic, retain) IBOutlet UIButton *landscapeFooButton;
@property (nonatomic, retain) IBOutlet UIButton *portraitFooButton;
@property (nonatomic, retain) IBOutlet UIButton *landscapeBarButton;
@property (nonatomic, retain) IBOutlet UIButton *portraitBarButton;

-(IBAction)buttonPressed:(id)sender;
@end
```

This line of code:

```
#define degreesToRadians(x) (M_PI  * (x) / 180.0)
```

is simply a macro to convert between degrees and radians. We'll use that in a few minutes when calling a function that requires radians as an input. Most people, including us, don't think in radians, so this macro will make our code much more readable by letting us specify angles in degrees instead of radians.

Everything else in this header should be familiar to you, so now that we have our outlets implemented, let's go to Interface Builder and build the two views we need. Double-click *SwapViewController.xib* in the *Resources* folder of the *Groups & Files* pane to open the file in Interface Builder.

Designing the Two Views

Ideally, what you're seeing in Interface Builder right now should feel very familiar to you. We'll need two views in our nib. We don't want to use the existing view that was provided as part of the template because its size can't be changed. Instead, we'll delete the default view and create two new ones.

Single-click the *View* icon, and press the *Delete* button. Next, drag over two *Views* from the library. After doing that, you'll have two icons labeled *View*. That might get a little confusing, so let's rename them to make it obvious what each one does.

To rename an icon in the nib's main window, you have to single-click the view to select it, wait a second or two, and then click the name of the icon. After another second, the name will become editable, and you can type the new name. Note that this trick works only in the icon view mode. Name one view *Portrait* and the other *Landscape*.

Now, control-drag from the *File's Owner* icon to the *Portrait* icon, and when the gray menu pops up, select the *portrait* outlet. Then, control-drag from *File's Owner* to the *Landscape* icon, and select the *landscape* outlet. Now control-drag a third time from *File's Owner* to *Portrait*, and select the *view* outlet to indicate which view should be shown at launch time.

Double-click the icon called *Landscape*, and press ⌘3 to bring up the size inspector. Right now, the size of this view should be 320 pixels wide by 460 pixels tall. Change the values so that it is 480 pixels wide by 300 pixels tall, or you can press the little arrow icon in the right side of the view's title bar, which will automatically change the view's proportions to landscape. Now drag two *Round Rect Button*s over from the library onto the *Landscape* view. The exact size and placement doesn't matter, but we made them nice and big at 125 pixels wide and 125 pixels tall. Double-click the left button, and give it a title of *Foo*; then double-click the right one, and give it a title of *Bar*.

Control-drag from the *File's Owner* icon to the *Foo* button, and assign it to the landscape FooButton outlet; then do the same thing to assign the *Bar* button to the landscapeBar Button outlet. Now, single-click the *Foo* button, and switch to the connections inspector by pressing ⌘2. Drag from the circle that represents the *Touch Up Inside* event to the *File's Owner* icon, and select the *buttonPressed:* action. Repeat with the *Bar* button so that both buttons trigger the buttonPressed: action method. You can now close the *Landscape* window.

Double-click the *Portrait* icon to open that view for editing. Drag two more *Round Rect Button*s from the library, placing them one above the other this time. Again, make the size of each button 125 pixels wide and 125 pixels tall. Double-click the top button, and give it a title of *Foo*. Then, double-click the bottom button, and assign it a title of *Bar*. Control-drag from the *File's Owner* icon to the *Foo* button, and assign it to the portraitFooButton outlet. Control-drag from the *File's Owner* icon once again to the *Bar* button, and assign it to the portraitBarButton outlet. Click the *Foo* button, and drag from the *Touch Up Inside* event on the connections inspector over to the *File's Owner* icon, and select the *buttonPressed:* action. Repeat this connection with the *Bar* button.

Save the nib, and go back to Xcode.

Implementing the Swap and the Action

We're almost done now; we just need to put the code in place to handle the swap and the button taps. Add the code that follows to your *SwapViewController.m* file.

NOTE

> This code listing does not show commented-out methods provided by the stub. Feel free to delete the commented-out methods that were already in your controller class.

```
#import "SwapViewController.h"

@implementation SwapViewController
@synthesize landscape;
```

```objc
@synthesize portrait;
@synthesize landscapeFooButton;
@synthesize portraitFooButton;
@synthesize landscapeBarButton;
@synthesize portraitBarButton;

- (void)willAnimateRotationToInterfaceOrientation:(UIInterfaceOrientation)
    interfaceOrientation duration:(NSTimeInterval)duration {
    if (interfaceOrientation == UIInterfaceOrientationPortrait) {
        self.view = self.portrait;
        self.view.transform = CGAffineTransformIdentity;
        self.view.transform =
            CGAffineTransformMakeRotation(degreesToRadians(0));
        self.view.bounds = CGRectMake(0.0, 0.0, 300.0, 480.0);
    }
    else if (interfaceOrientation == UIInterfaceOrientationLandscapeLeft) {
        self.view = self.landscape;
        self.view.transform = CGAffineTransformIdentity;
        self.view.transform =
        CGAffineTransformMakeRotation(degreesToRadians(-90));
        self.view.bounds = CGRectMake(0.0, 0.0, 460.0, 320.0);
    }
    else if (interfaceOrientation ==
            UIInterfaceOrientationPortraitUpsideDown) {
        self.view = self.portrait;
        self.view.transform = CGAffineTransformIdentity;
        self.view.transform =
            CGAffineTransformMakeRotation(degreesToRadians(180));
        self.view.bounds = CGRectMake(0.0, 0.0, 300.0, 480.0);
    }
    else if (interfaceOrientation ==
            UIInterfaceOrientationLandscapeRight) {
        self.view = self.landscape;
        self.view.transform = CGAffineTransformIdentity;
        self.view.transform =
            CGAffineTransformMakeRotation(degreesToRadians(90));
        self.view.bounds = CGRectMake(0.0, 0.0, 460.0, 320.0);
    }
}
-(IBAction)buttonPressed:(id)sender {

    if (sender == portraitFooButton || sender == landscapeFooButton) {
        portraitFooButton.hidden = YES;
        landscapeFooButton.hidden = YES;
    } else {
        portraitBarButton.hidden = YES;
        landscapeBarButton.hidden = YES;
```

```
        }
    }
    - (BOOL)shouldAutorotateToInterfaceOrientation:(UIInterfaceOrientation)
        interfaceOrientation {
        return YES;
    }
    - (void)didReceiveMemoryWarning {
        [super didReceiveMemoryWarning];
        // Releases the view if it doesn't have a superview
        // Release anything that's not essential, such as cached data
    }
    - (void)viewDidUnload {
        // Release any retained subviews of the main view.
        // e.g. self.myOutlet = nil;
        self.landscape = nil;
        self.portrait = nil;
        self.landscapeFooButton = nil;
        self.landscapeBarButton = nil;
        self.portraitFooButton = nil;
        self.portraitBarButton = nil;
        [super viewDidUnload];
    }
    - (void)dealloc {
        [landscape release];

        [portrait release];
        [landscapeFooButton release];
        [portraitFooButton release];
        [landscapeBarButton release];
        [portraitBarButton release];

        [super dealloc];
    }

@end
```

The first method in our new code is called willAnimateRotationToInterfaceOrientation:
duration:. This is a method from our superclass that we've overridden that gets called as
the rotation begins but before the rotation actually happens. Actions that we take in this
method will be animated as part of the first half of the rotation animation.

In this method, we look at the orientation that we're rotating to and set the view property
to either landscape or portrait, as appropriate for the new orientation. We then call
CGAffineTransformMakeRotation, part of the Core Graphics framework, to create a **rotation transformation**. A **transformation** is a mathematical description of changes to an
object's size, position, or angle. Ordinarily, iPhone takes care of setting the transform value
automatically when the phone is rotated. However, when we swap in our new view here, we

have to make sure that we give it the correct value so as not to confuse the iPhone. That's what `willAnimateRotationToInterfaceOrientation:duration:` is doing each time it sets the view's `transform` property. Once the view has been rotated, we adjust its frame so that it fits snugly into the window at the current orientation.

Next up is our `buttonPressed:` method, and there shouldn't be anything too surprising there. We look at the button that was tapped, hide it, and then hide the corresponding button on the other view.

You should be comfortable with everything else we wrote in this class. The new `shouldAutorotateToInterfaceOrientation:` method simply returns YES to tell the iPhone that we support rotation to any orientation, and the code added to the `dealloc` method is simple memory cleanup.

Now, we're ready to compile it and try it. Note that if you accidentally clicked both buttons, the only way to bring them back is to quit the simulator and rerun the project. Don't use this approach in your own applications.

Rotating Out of Here

In this chapter, you got to try out three completely different approaches to supporting autorotation in your applications. You learned about autosizing attributes and how to restructure your views, in code, when the phone rotates. You saw how to swap between two completely different views when the phone rotates, and you learned how to link new frameworks into your project.

In this chapter, you also got your first taste of using multiple views in an application by swapping between two views from the same nib. In the next chapter, we're going to start looking at true multiview applications. Every application we've written so far has used a single view controller and all except the last used a single content view. A lot of complex iPhone applications such as Mail and Contacts, however, are only made possible by the use of multiple views and view controllers, and we're going to look at exactly how that works in Chapter 6.

Multiview Applications

U p until this point, we've written applications with a single view controller. While there certainly is a lot you can do with a single view, the real power of the iPhone platform emerges when you can switch out views based on user input. Multiview applications come in several different flavors, but the underlying mechanism is the same, regardless of how it may appear on the screen.

Strictly speaking, we have worked with multiple views in our previous applications, since buttons, labels, and other controls are all subclasses of UIView and can all go into the view hierarchy. But when Apple uses the term "view" in documentation, it is generally referring to a UIView or one of its subclasses that have a corresponding view controller. These types of views are also sometimes referred to as **content views**, because they are the primary container for the content of our application.

The simplest example of a multiview application is a utility application. A utility application focuses primarily on a single view but offers a second view that can be used to configure the application or to provide more detail than the primary view. The Stocks application that ships with iPhone is a good example (see Figure 6-1). If you click the little *i* icon in the lower-right corner, the view flips over to let you configure the list of stocks tracked by the application.

Figure 6-1. *The Stocks application that ships with iPhone has two views, one to display the data and another to configure the stock list.*

There are also several **tab bar applications** that ship with the iPhone, such as the Phone application (see Figure 6-2) and the Clock application. A tab bar application is a multiview application that displays a row of buttons, the **tab bar**, at the bottom of the screen. Tapping one of the buttons causes a new view controller to become active and a new view to be shown. In the Phone application, for example, tapping *Contacts* shows a different view than the one shown when you tap *Keypad*.

NOTE

Tab bars and toolbars can be confusing. A **tab bar** is used for selecting one and only one option from among two or more. A **toolbar** can hold buttons and certain other controls, but those items are not mutually exclusive. Figure 6-3 shows a toolbar at the bottom of the iPhone screen. Figure 6-4 shows a tab bar at the bottom of the iPhone screen. In practical application, the tab bar is almost always used to select between two or more content views, while the toolbar is usually used to display buttons for doing common tasks.

Another common kind of multiview iPhone application is the navigation-based application, which uses a navigation controller to present hierarchical information to the user. The Mail application is a good example (see Figure 6-3). In Mail, the first view you get is a list of your mail accounts. Touching one of those takes you into a list of your folders. Touching a folder shows you the e-mail messages in that folder, and touching the e-mail message shows you the content of the message. A navigation-based application is useful when you want to present a hierarchy of views.

Because views are themselves hierarchical in nature, it's even possible to combine different mechanisms for swapping views within a single application. For example, the iPhone's iPod application uses a tab bar to switch between different methods of organizing your music and a navigation controller and its associated navigation bar to allow you to browse your music based on that selection. In Figure 6-4, the tab bar is at the bottom of the screen, and the navigation bar is at the top of the screen.

Each of these types of multiview application uses a specific controller class from the UIKit. Tab bar interfaces are implemented using the class `UITabBarController` and navigation interfaces using `UINavigationController`. In this chapter, we're going to focus on the structure of multiview applications and the basics of swapping content views by building our own multiview application from scratch. We will write our own custom controller class that switches between two different content views, which will give you a strong foundation for taking advantage of the various multiview controllers that Apple provides.

Figure 6-2. *The Phone application is an example of a multiview application using a tab bar.*

Figure 6-3. *The iPhone Mail application is an example of a multiview application using a navigation bar.*

Figure 6-4. *The iPod application uses both a navigation bar and a tab bar.*

The View Switcher Application

The application we're going to build in this chapter, View Switcher, is fairly simple in appearance, but in terms of the code we're going to write, it's by far the most complex application we've tackled. View Switcher will consist of three different controllers, three nibs, and an application delegate.

When first launched, View Switcher will look like Figure 6-5, with a toolbar at the bottom containing a single button. The rest of the view will contain a blue background and a button yearning to be pressed.

When the *Switch Views* button is pressed, the background will turn yellow, and the button's title will change (see Figure 6-6).

If either the *Press Me* or *Press Me, Too* button is pressed, an alert will pop up indicating which view's button was pressed (see Figure 6-7).

Although we could achieve this same functionality by writing a single-view application, we're taking this more complex approach to demonstrate the mechanics of a multiview application. There are actually three view controllers interacting in this simple application: one that controls the blue view, one that controls the yellow view, and a third special controller that swaps the other two in and out when the *Switch Views* button is pressed.

Figure 6-5. *View Switcher at launch*

Figure 6-6. *After pressing the Switch Views button*

Figure 6-7. *Pressing the center button shows an alert.*

The Architecture of a Multiview Application

Before we start building our application, let's talk a little bit about the way iPhone multiview applications are put together. Nearly all multiview applications use the same basic pattern.

The nib file is a key player here. In a bit, when you create the *View Switcher* project, you'll find the file *MainWindow.xib* in your project window's *Resources* folder. Inside the file, you'll find the application delegate and the application's main window, along with the *File's Owner* and *First Responder* icons. We'll add an instance of a controller class that is responsible for managing which other view is currently being shown to the user. We call this controller the **root controller** because it is the first controller the user sees and the controller that is loaded when the application loads. This root controller is often an instance of UINavigationController or UITabBarController, though it can also be a custom subclass of UIViewController. In a multiview application, the job of the root controller is to take two or more other views and present them to the user as appropriate, based on the user's input. A tab bar controller, for example, will swap in different views and view controllers based on which tab bar item was last tapped. A navigation controller will do the same thing as the user drills down and backs up through hierarchical data.

NOTE

> The root controller is the primary view controller for the application and, as such, is the view that specifies whether it is OK to automatically rotate to a new orientation, though the root controller can pass responsibility for things like that to the currently active controller.

In multiview applications, most of the screen will be taken up by a content view, and each content view will have its own controller with its own outlets and actions. In a tab bar application, for example, taps on the tab bar will go to the tab bar controller, but taps anywhere else on the screen will go to the controller that corresponds to the content view currently being displayed.

Anatomy of a Content View

In a multiview application, each view controller controls a content view, and these content views are where the bulk of your application's user interface gets built. Each content view generally consists of up to three pieces: the view controller, the nib and a subclass of UIView. Unless you are doing something really unusual, your content view will always have an associated view controller, will usually have a nib, and will sometimes subclass UIView. Although you can create your interface in code rather than using a nib file, few people choose that route because it is more time consuming and more difficult to maintain.

In this chapter, we'll only be creating a nib and a controller class for each content view.

In the *View Switcher* project, our root controller controls a content view that consists of a toolbar that occupies the bottom of the screen. The root controller then loads a blue view controller, placing the blue content view as a subview to the root controller view. When the root controller's switch views button is pressed (the button is in the toolbar), the root controller swaps out the blue view controller and swaps in a yellow view controller, instantiating it if it needs to do so. Confused? Don't worry, because this will become clearer as you walk through the code.

Building View Switcher

Enough theory! Let's go ahead and build our project. Select **New Project…** from the **File** menu, or press ⇧⌘N. When the assistant opens, select *Window-based Application* (see Figure 6-8), and make sure the checkbox labeled *Use Core Data for Storage* is unchecked. Type in a project name of *View Switcher*.

Figure 6-8. *Selecting a new project template*

The template we just selected is actually even simpler than the one we've been using up to now. This template will give us a window, an application delegate, and nothing else—no views, no controllers, no nothing. You won't use this template very often when you're creating applications, but by starting from nothing, you'll really get a feel for the way multiview applications are put together.

Take a second to expand the *Resources* and *Classes* folders in the *Groups & Files* pane and
look at what's there. You'll find a single nib file, *MainWindow.xib*; the *View_Switcher-Info.plist*
file; and the two files in the class folder that implement the application delegate. Everything
else we need for our application, we will have to create.

Creating Our View Controller and Nib Files

One of the more daunting aspects of creating a multiview application from scratch is that
we have to create several interconnected objects. We're going to create all the files that will
make up our application before we do anything in Interface Builder and before we write any
code. By creating all the files first, we'll be able to use Xcode's Code Sense to write our code
faster. If a class hasn't been declared, Code Sense has no way to know about it, so we would
have to type it in full every time, which takes longer and is more error prone.

Fortunately, in addition to project templates, Xcode also provides file templates for many
standard file types, which makes creating the basic skeleton of our application fairly easy.
Single-click the *Classes* folder in the *Groups & Files* pane, and then press ⌘N or select **New
File...** from the **File** menu. Take a look at the window that opens (see Figure 6-9).

Figure 6-9. *Creating a new view controller class*

If you select *Cocoa Touch Class* from the left-hand pane, you will be given templates for a
number of common Cocoa Touch classes. Select *UIViewController subclass*. In the lower-right
pane, you'll see a checkbox labeled *With XIB for user interface*. If that box is checked, click it to
uncheck it. If you select that option, Xcode will also create a nib file that corresponds to this

controller class. We will start using that option in the next chapter, but for now, we want you to see how the different parts of the puzzle fit together by creating them all individually.

Click *Next*. Then type in the name *SwitchViewController.m*, and make sure that *Also create "SwitchViewController.h"* is checked before clicking the *Finish* button. Xcode should add two files to your *Classes* folder; the `SwitchViewController` class will be your root controller that swaps the other views in and out. Repeat the same steps two more times to create *BlueViewController.m* and *YellowViewController.m*, making sure to also create the corresponding header files for both. These are the two content views that will get swapped in and out by `SwitchViewController`.

We also need two more nib files, one for each of the two content views we just created. To create these, single-click the *Resources* folder in the *Groups & Files* pane so that we create them in the correct place, and then press ⌘N or select **New File...** from the **File** menu again. This time, when the assistant window comes up, select *User Interfaces* under the *iPhone OS* heading in the left pane (see Figure 6-10).

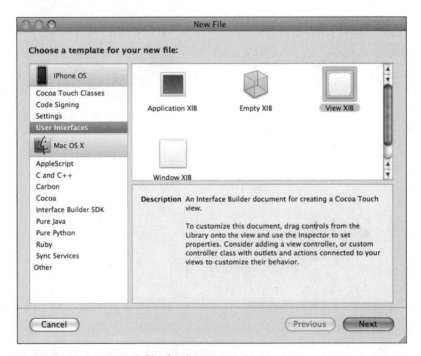

Figure 6-10. *Creating nib files for the content views*

Select the icon for the *View XIB* template, which will create a nib with a content view, and then click the *Next* button. When prompted for a filename, type *BlueView.xib*. Repeat the steps to create a second nib file called *YellowView.xib*. Once you've done that, you have all the files you need. It's time to start hooking everything together.

Modifying the App Delegate

Our first stop on the multiview express is the application delegate. Single-click the file *View_ SwitcherAppDelegate.h* in the Groups & Files pane, and make the following changes to that file:

```
#import <UIKit/UIKit.h>
@class SwitchViewController;
@interface View_SwitcherAppDelegate : NSObject <UIApplicationDelegate> {
    UIWindow *window;
    SwitchViewController *switchViewController;
}

@property (nonatomic, retain) IBOutlet UIWindow *window;
@property (nonatomic, retain) IBOutlet SwitchViewController
    *switchViewController;
@end
```

The IBOutlet declaration you just typed is an outlet that will point to our application's root controller. We need this outlet because we are about to write code that will add the root controller's view to our application's main window when the application launches. By doing that, when we go to Interface Builder and add an instance of the SwitchViewController class to *MainWindow.xib*, we'll already have an outlet to connect it to.

Now, we need to add the root controller's view to our application's main window. Click *View_ SwitcherAppDelegate.m*, and add the following code:

```
#import "View_SwitcherAppDelegate.h"
#import "SwitchViewController.h"
@implementation View_SwitcherAppDelegate

@synthesize window;
@synthesize switchViewController;

- (void)applicationDidFinishLaunching:(UIApplication *)application {
    // Override point for customization after application launch
    [window addSubview:switchViewController.view];
    [window makeKeyAndVisible];
}

- (void)dealloc {
    [window release];
    [switchViewController release];
    [super dealloc];
}
@end
```

Besides implementing the `switchViewController` outlet, we are adding the root controller's view to the window. Remember, the window is the only gateway to the user, so anything that needs to be displayed to the user has to get added as a subview of the application's window.

SwitchViewController.h

Because we're going to be adding an instance of `SwitchViewController` to *MainWindow.xib*, now is the time to add any needed outlets or actions to the *SwitchViewController.h* header file.

We'll need one action method to toggle between the two views. We won't need any outlets, but we will need two other pointers, one to each of the view controllers that we're going to be swapping in and out. These don't need to be outlets, because we're going to create them in code rather than in a nib. Add the following code to *SwitchViewController.h*:

```
#import <UIKit/UIKit.h>

@class BlueViewController;
@class YellowViewController;

@interface SwitchViewController : UIViewController {
    YellowViewController *yellowViewController;
    BlueViewController *blueViewController;
}
@property (retain, nonatomic) YellowViewController *yellowViewController;
@property (retain, nonatomic) BlueViewController *blueViewController;

-(IBAction)switchViews:(id)sender;
@end
```

Now that we've declared the action we need, we can add an instance of this class to *MainWindow.xib*.

Modifying MainWindow.xib

Save your source code, and double-click *MainWindow.xib* to open it in Interface Builder. Four icons should appear in the nib's main window: *File's Owner*, *First Responder*, *View_SwitcherAppDelegate*, and *Window* (see Figure 6-11). We need to add one more icon that will represent an instance of our root controller. Since Interface Builder's library doesn't have a `SwitchViewController`, we'll have to add a view controller and change its class to `SwitchViewController`.

Since the class we need to add is a subclass of `UIViewController`, look in the library for *View Controller* (see Figure 6-12), and drag one to the nib's main window (the window with the icons and the title *MainWindow.xib*).

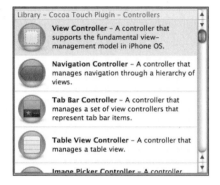

Figure 6-11. *MainWindow.xib*   **Figure 6-12.** *View Controller in the library*

Once you do this, your nib's main window will now have five icons, and a new window containing a dashed, gray, rounded rectangle labeled *View* should appear (see Figure 6-13).

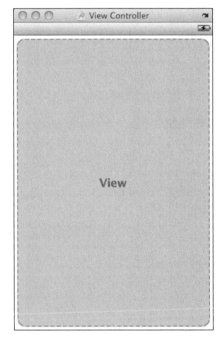

Figure 6-13. *The window representing your view controller in Interface Builder*

We just added an instance of UIViewController, but we actually need an instance of SwitchViewController, so let's change our view controller's class to SwitchViewController. Single-click the *View Controller* icon in the nib's main window, and press ⌘4 to open the identity inspector (see Figure 6-14).

The identity inspector allows you to specify the class of the currently selected object. Our view controller is currently specified as a `UIViewController`, and it has no actions defined. Click inside the combo box labeled *Class*, the one at the top of the inspector that currently reads *UIViewController*. Change the *Class* to *SwitchViewController*. Once you make that change, the `switchViews:` action method should appear in the section labeled *Class Actions* (see Figure 6-15). You should also notice that in the nib's main window, the name of that new icon has switched from *View Controller* to *Switch View Controller*.

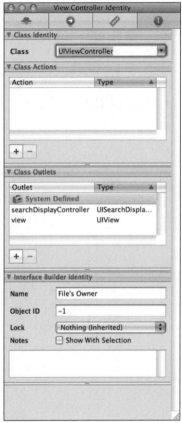

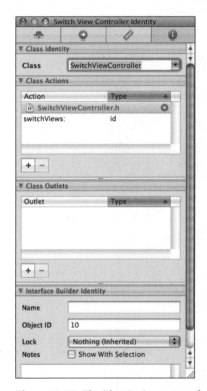

Figure 6-14. *The identity inspector*

Figure 6-15. *The identity inspector after changing the class to SwitchViewController*

We now need to build our root controller's view. The root controller's content view will consist of a toolbar that occupies the bottom of the screen.

Remember that new window that appeared when we dragged the generic view controller onto the main nib window (see Figure 6-13)? We'll build the view for our root controller, `SwitchViewController`, in that window.

As a reminder, SwitchViewController's job is to switch between the blue view and the yellow view. To do that, it will need a way for the user to change the views, and for that, we're going to use a toolbar with a button. Let's build the toolbar view now.

Drag a *View* from the library onto the window shown in Figure 6-13. Hint: it's the one with a gray background that says *View*. The gray background should be replaced by this new view.

Now grab a toolbar from the library, drag it onto your view, and place it at the bottom, so that it looks like Figure 6-16.

The toolbar features a single button. Let's use that button to let the user switch between the different content views. Double-click the button, and change its title to *Switch Views*. Press the return key to commit your change.

Now, we can link the toolbar button to our action method. Before we do that, though, we should warn you: toolbar buttons aren't like other iPhone controls. They support only a single target action, and they trigger that action only at one well-defined moment, the equivalent of a *Touch Up Inside* event on other iPhone controls.

Instead of using the connections inspector to connect this button to our action, single-click the *Switch Views* button, wait a second or two to avoid a double-click, and then single-click the button again

Figure 6-16. *Adding a toolbar to the view controller's view*

to select it. You can confirm you have the button selected by looking at the title bar of the attributes inspector (⌘1) and making sure it says *Bar Button Item*.

Once you have the *Switch Views* button selected, control-drag from it over to the *Switch View Controller* icon, and select the *switchViews:* action. If the *switchViews:* action doesn't pop up and instead you see an outlet called *delegate*, you've most likely control-dragged from the toolbar rather than the button. To fix it, just make sure you've got the button and not the toolbar selected and redo your control-drag.

Earlier, we created an outlet in *View_SwitcherAppDelegate.h* so our application could get to our instance of SwitchViewController and add its view to the main application window. Now, we need to connect the instance of SwitchViewController in our nib to that outlet. Control-drag from the *View_Switcher App Delegate* icon to the *Switch View Controller* icon, and select the *switchViewController* outlet. You may see a second outlet with a similar name called *viewController*. If you do, make sure you connect to *switchViewController* and not *viewController*.

That's all we need to do here, so save your nib file, and head back to Xcode so that we can implement `SwitchViewController`.

Writing SwitchViewController.m

It's time to write our root view controller. Its job is to switch between the yellow view and the blue view whenever the user clicks the *Switch Views* button.

Making the following changes to *SwitchViewController.m*. You can feel free to delete the commented-out methods provided by the template if you want.

```
#import "SwitchViewController.h"
#import "BlueViewController.h"
#import "YellowViewController.h"

@implementation SwitchViewController
@synthesize yellowViewController;
@synthesize blueViewController;

- (void)viewDidLoad
{
    BlueViewController *blueController = [[BlueViewController alloc]
            initWithNibName:@"BlueView" bundle:nil];
    self.blueViewController = blueController;
    [self.view insertSubview:blueController.view atIndex:0];
    [blueController release];
    [super viewDidLoad];
}

- (IBAction)switchViews:(id)sender
{
    if (self.yellowViewController.view.superview == nil)
    {
        if (self.yellowViewController == nil)
        {
            YellowViewController *yellowController =
            [[YellowViewController alloc] initWithNibName:@"YellowView"
                                                  bundle:nil];
            self.yellowViewController = yellowController;
            [yellowController release];
        }

        [blueViewController.view removeFromSuperview];
        [self.view insertSubview:yellowViewController.view atIndex:0];
    }
```

```
    else
    {
        if (self.blueViewController == nil)
        {
            BlueViewController *blueController =
            [[BlueViewController alloc] initWithNibName:@"BlueView"
                                                bundle:nil];
            self.blueViewController = blueController;
            [blueController release];
        }
        [yellowViewController.view removeFromSuperview];
        [self.view insertSubview:blueViewController.view atIndex:0];

    }
}
...
```

Also, add the following code to the existing didReceiveMemoryWarning method:

```
- (void)didReceiveMemoryWarning {
    // Releases the view if it doesn't have a superview
    [super didReceiveMemoryWarning];

    // Release anything that's not essential, such as cached data
    if (self.blueViewController.view.superview == nil)
        self.blueViewController = nil;
    else
        self.yellowViewController = nil;
}
```

and add the following two statements to the dealloc method:

```
- (void)dealloc {
    [yellowViewController release];
    [blueViewController release];
    [super dealloc];
}
@end
```

The first method we added, viewDidLoad, overrides a UIViewController method that gets called when the nib is loaded. How could we tell? Option–double-click the method name, and take a look at the document that appears. The method is defined in our superclass and is intended to be overridden by classes that need to get notified when the view has finished loading.

We override viewDidLoad to create an instance of BlueViewController. We use the initWithNibName method to load the BlueViewController instance from the nib file

BlueView.xib. Note that the filename provided to `initWithNibName` does not include the
.xib extension. Once the `BlueViewController` is created, we assign this new instance to our
`blueViewController` property.

```
BlueViewController *blueController = [[BlueViewController alloc]
        initWithNibName:@"BlueView" bundle:nil];
self.blueViewController = blueController;
```

Next, we insert the blue view as a subview of the root view. We insert it at index zero, which
tells iPhone to put this view behind everything else. Sending the view to the back ensures
that the toolbar we created in Interface Builder a moment ago will always be visible on the
screen, since we're inserting the content views behind it.

```
[self.view insertSubview:blueController.view atIndex:0];
```

Now, why didn't we load the yellow view here also? We're going to need to load it at some
point, so why not do it now? Good question. The answer is that the user may never tap the
Switch Views button. The user might come in, use the view that's visible when the application launches, and then quit. In that case, why use resources to load the yellow view and its
controller?

Instead, we'll load the yellow view the first time we actually need it. This is called **lazy
loading**, and it's a standard way of keeping memory overhead down. The actual loading
of the yellow view happens in the `switchViews:` method, so let's take a look at that.

`switchViews:` first checks which view is being swapped in by checking to see whether
`yellowViewController`'s `view`'s superview is `nil`. This will return YES if one of two things
are true. First, if `yellowViewController` exists but its view is not being shown to the user,
that view will have no superview because it's not presently in the view hierarchy and the
equation will evaluate to YES. Second, if `yellowViewController` doesn't exist because it
hasn't been created yet or was flushed from memory, it will also return YES.

```
if (self.yellowViewController.view.superview == nil)
{
```

We then check to see whether `yellowViewController` is `nil`. If it is, that means there is no
instance of `yellowViewController`, and we need to create one. This could happen because
it's the first time the button has been pressed or because the system ran low on memory and
it was flushed. In this case, we need to create an instance of `YellowViewController` as we
did for the `BlueViewController` in the `viewDidLoad` method:

```
if (self.yellowViewController == nil)
{
    YellowViewController *yellowController =
    [[YellowViewController alloc] initWithNibName:@"YellowView"
                                    bundle:nil];
```

```
            self.yellowViewController = yellowController;
            [yellowController release];
        }
```

At this point, we know that we have a `yellowViewController` instance, because either we already had one or we just created it. Then, we remove `blueViewController`'s view from the view hierarchy and add `yellowViewController`'s:

```
        [blueViewController.view removeFromSuperview];
        [self.view insertSubview:yellowViewController.view atIndex:0];
    }
```

If `self.yellowViewController.view.superview` is not `nil`, then we have to do the same thing, but for `blueViewController`. Although we create an instance of `blueViewController` in `viewDidLoad`, it is still possible that the instance has been flushed because memory got low. Now, in this application, the chances of memory running out are slim, but we're still going to be good memory citizens and make sure we have an instance before proceeding:

```
    else
    {
        if (self.blueViewController == nil)
        {
            BlueViewController *blueController =
            [[BlueViewController alloc] initWithNibName:@"BlueView"
                                              bundle:nil];
            self.blueViewController = blueController;
            [blueController release];
        }
        [yellowViewController.view removeFromSuperview];
        [self.view insertSubview:blueViewController.view atIndex:0];

    }
}
```

In addition to not using resources for the yellow view and controller if the *Switch Views* button is never tapped, lazy loading also gives us the ability to release whichever view is not being shown to free up its memory. iPhone OS will call the `UIViewController` method `didReceiveMemoryWarning`, which is inherited by every view controller, when memory drops below a system-determined level.

Since we know that either view will get reloaded the next time it gets shown to the user, we can safely release either controller, something we do by adding a few lines to the existing `didReceiveMemoryWarning` method:

```
- (void)didReceiveMemoryWarning {
    [super didReceiveMemoryWarning]; // Releases the view if it
                                     // doesn't have a superview
```

```
    // Release anything that's not essential, such as cached data
    if (self.blueViewController.view.superview == nil)
        self.blueViewController = nil;
    else
        self.yellowViewController = nil;
}
```

This newly added code checks to see which view is currently being shown to the user and releases the controller for the other view by assigning nil to its property. This will cause the controller, along with the view it controls, to be deallocated, freeing up its memory. Lazy loading is a key component of resource management on iPhone and should be implemented anywhere you can. In a complex, multiview application, being responsible and flushing unused objects from memory can be the difference between an application that works well and one that crashes periodically because it ran out of memory.

Implementing the Content Views

The two content views that we are creating in this application are extremely simple. They each have one action method that is triggered by a button, and neither one needs any outlets. The two views are also nearly identical. In fact, they are so similar that they could have been represented by the same class. We chose to make them two separate classes, because that's how most multiview applications are constructed. Let's declare an action method in each of the header files. First, in *BlueViewController.h*, add the following declaration:

```
#import <UIKit/UIKit.h>
@interface BlueViewController : UIViewController {

}
-(IBAction)blueButtonPressed;
@end
```

Save it, and then add the following line to *YellowViewController.h*:

```
#import <UIKit/UIKit.h>

@interface YellowViewController : UIViewController {

}
- (IBAction)yellowButtonPressed;
@end
```

Save this one as well, and then double-click *BlueView.xib* to open it in Interface Builder so we can make a few changes. First, we have to tell it that the class that will load this nib from disk is BlueViewController, so single-click the *File's Owner* icon and press ⌘4 to bring up the identity inspector. *File's Owner* defaults to *NSObject*; change it to *BlueViewController*.

Single-click the icon called *View* and then press ⌘1 to bring up the attribute inspector. Click the color well that's labeled *Background*, and change the background color of this view to a nice shade of blue.

Next, we'll change the size of the view in the nib. In the attribute inspector, the top section is labeled *Simulated User Interface Elements*. If we set these drop-downs to reflect which top and bottom elements are used in our application, Interface Builder will automatically calculate the size of the remaining space. The status bar is already specified. If you select the *Bottom Bar* pop-up, you can select *Toolbar* to indicate that the enclosing view has a toolbar. By setting this, Interface Builder will automatically calculate the correct size for our view so that you know how much space you have to work with. You can press ⌘3 to bring up the size inspector to confirm this. After making the change, the height of the window should now be 416, and the width should still be 320.

Drag a *Round Rect Button* from the library over to the window. Double-click the button, and change its title to *Press Me*. You can place the button anywhere that looks good to you. Next, switch to the connections inspector (by pressing ⌘2), drag from the *Touch Up Inside* event to the *File's Owner* icon, and connect to the *blueButtonPressed* action method.

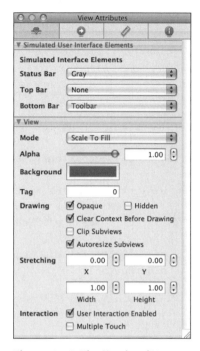

Figure 6-17. *The Simulated User Interface Elements section of the View's attributes inspector*

We have one more thing to do in this nib, which is to connect the `BlueViewController`'s `view` outlet to the view in the nib. The `view` outlet is inherited from the parent class, `UIViewController`, and gives the controller access to the view it controls. When we changed the underlying class of the file's owner, the existing outlet connections were broken. As a result, we need to reestablish the connection from the controller to its view. Control-drag from the *File's Owner* icon to the *View* icon, and select the view outlet to do that.

Save the nib, go back to Xcode, and double-click *YellowView.xib*. We're going to make almost the same exact changes to this nib file. We need to change the file's owner from *NSObject* to *YellowViewController* using the identity inspector, change the view's height to 416 pixels using the size inspector, and change the view's background to a nice yellow color using the attributes inspector. You'll also need to add a round rectangular button to this view, give it a label of *Press Me, Too*, and connect that button's *Touch Up Inside* event to the *yellowButtonPressed* action method in *File's Owner*. Finally, control-drag from the *File's Owner* icon to the *View* icon, and connect to the view outlet.

Once all that is done, save the nib, and go back to Xcode.

The two action methods we're going to implement do nothing more than show an alert, something you already know how to do, so go ahead and add the following code to *BlueViewController.m*:

```
#import "BlueViewController.h"

@implementation BlueViewController

- (IBAction)blueButtonPressed
{
    UIAlertView *alert = [[UIAlertView alloc]
        initWithTitle:@"Blue View Button Pressed"
            message:@"You pressed the button on the blue view"
            delegate:nil
    cancelButtonTitle:@"Yep, I did."
    otherButtonTitles:nil];
    [alert show];
    [alert release];
}

...
```

Save, switch over to *YellowViewController.m*, and add this very similar code to that file:

```
#import "YellowViewController.h"

@implementation YellowViewController
-(IBAction)yellowButtonPressed
{
    UIAlertView *alert = [[UIAlertView alloc]
        initWithTitle:@"Yellow View Button Pressed"
            message:@"You pressed the button on the yellow view"
            delegate:nil
    cancelButtonTitle:@"Yep, I did."
    otherButtonTitles:nil];
    [alert show];
    [alert release];
}

...
```

Save it, and we're ready to try it. When our application launches, it'll show the view we built in *BlueView.xib*, and when you tap the *Switch Views* button, it will change to show us the view that we built in *YellowView.xib*. Tap it again, and it goes back to the view we built in *BlueView.xib*. Whether you tap the button on the blue or yellow view, you'll get an alert view with a message indicating which button was pressed. This alert shows us that the correct controller class is getting called for the view that is being shown.

The transition between the two views is kind of abrupt, though. Gosh, if only there were some way to make the transition look nicer.

Animating the Transition

Of course, there is a way to make the transition look nicer! We can animate the transition in order to give the user visual feedback of the change. UIView has several class methods we can call to indicate that the transition should be animated, to indicate the type of transition that should be used, and to specify how long the transition should take.

Go back to *SwitchViewController.m*, and replace your switchViews: method with this new version:

```
- (IBAction)switchViews:(id)sender
{
    [UIView beginAnimations:@"View Flip" context:nil];
    [UIView setAnimationDuration:1.25];
    [UIView setAnimationCurve:UIViewAnimationCurveEaseInOut];

    if (self.yellowViewController.view.superview == nil)
    {
        if (self.yellowViewController == nil)
        {
            YellowViewController *yellowController =
            [[YellowViewController alloc] initWithNibName:@"YellowView"
                                                   bundle:nil];
            self.yellowViewController = yellowController;
            [yellowController release];
        }
        [UIView setAnimationTransition:
         UIViewAnimationTransitionFlipFromRight
                               forView:self.view cache:YES];

        [blueViewController viewWillAppear:YES];
        [yellowViewController viewWillDisappear:YES];

        [blueViewController.view removeFromSuperview];
        [self.view insertSubview:yellowViewController.view atIndex:0];
        [yellowViewController viewDidDisappear:YES];
        [blueViewController viewDidAppear:YES];
```

```
        }
    else
    {
        if (self.blueViewController == nil)
        {
            BlueViewController *blueController =
            [[BlueViewController alloc] initWithNibName:@"BlueView"
                                                bundle:nil];
            self.blueViewController = blueController;
            [blueController release];
        }
        [UIView setAnimationTransition:
         UIViewAnimationTransitionFlipFromLeft
                            forView:self.view cache:YES];

        [yellowViewController viewWillAppear:YES];
        [blueViewController viewWillDisappear:YES];

        [yellowViewController.view removeFromSuperview];
        [self.view insertSubview:blueViewController.view atIndex:0];
        [blueViewController viewDidDisappear:YES];
        [yellowViewController viewDidAppear:YES];


    }
    [UIView commitAnimations];
}
```

Compile this new version, and run your application. When you tap the *Switch Views* button, instead of the new view just appearing, the view will flip over, as shown in Figure 6-18.

In order to tell iPhone that we want a change animated, we need to declare an **animation block** and specify how long the animation should take. Animation blocks are declared by using the UIView class method beginAnimations:context:, like so:

```
[UIView beginAnimations:@"View Flip" context:nil];
[UIView setAnimationDuration:1.25];
```

beginAnimations:context: takes two parameters. The first is an animation block title. This title comes into play only if you take more direct advantage of Core Animation, the framework behind this animation. For our purposes, we could have used nil. The second parameter is a (void *) that allows you to specify an object whose pointer you'd like associated with this animation block. We used nil here, since we don't have any need to do that.

Figure 6-18. *The view transition animated using the flip style*

After that, we set the **animation curve**, which determines the timing of the animation. The default, which is a linear curve, causes the animation to happen at a constant speed. The option we set here indicates that it should change the speed so that it is slow at the beginning and end of the transition but faster in the middle. This gives the animation a more natural, less mechanical appearance.

```
[UIView setAnimationCurve:UIViewAnimationCurveEaseInOut];
```

Next, we have to specify the transition to use. At the time of this writing, four view transitions are available on the iPhone:

- UIViewAnimationTransitionFlipFromLeft

- UIViewAnimationTransitionFlipFromRight

- UIViewAnimationTransitionCurlUp

- UIViewAnimationTransitionCurlDown

We chose to use two different effects, depending on which view was being swapped in. Using a left flip for one transition and a right flip for the other will make the view seem to flip back and forth. The cache option speeds up drawing by taking a snapshot of the view when the animation begins and using that image rather than redrawing the view at each step of the animation. You should always have it cache the animation unless the appearance of the view may need to change during the animation.

```
[UIView setAnimationTransition:UIViewAnimationTransitionFlipFromRight
                   forView:self.view cache:YES];
```

After we set the transition, we make two calls, one on each of the views being used in the transition:

```
[self.blueViewController viewWillAppear:YES];
[self.yellowViewController viewWillDisappear:YES];
```

When we're all done swapping the views, we make two more calls on those views:

```
[self.yellowViewController viewDidDisappear:YES];
[self.blueViewController viewDidAppear:YES];
```

The default implementations of these methods in `UIViewController` do nothing, so our calls to `viewDidDisappear:` and `viewDidAppear:` don't do anything, since our controllers didn't override those methods. It's important to make these calls even if you know you're not using them.

Why is it important to make these calls even though they do nothing? Even though we're not using those methods now, we might choose to in the future. It's also possible that `UIViewController`'s implementation to those methods won't always be empty, so failing to call these methods could cause our application to behave oddly after a future update of the operating system. The performance hit for making these four calls is meaningless, since they trigger no code, and by putting them in, we can be sure that our application will continue to work.

When we're all done specifying the changes to be animated, we call `commitAnima-tions` on `UIView`. Everything between the start of the animation block and the call to `commitAnimations` will be animated together.

Thanks to Cocoa Touch's use of Core Animation under the hood, we're able to do fairly sophisticated animation with only a handful of code.

Switching Off

Whoo-boy! Creating our own multiview controller was a lot of work, wasn't it? You should have a very good grasp on how multiview applications are put together now that you've built one from scratch. Although Xcode contains project templates for the most common types of multiview applications, you need to understand the overall structure of these types of applications so you can build them yourself from the ground up. The delivered templates are incredible timesavers, but at times, they simply won't meet your needs.

In the next three chapters, we're going to continue building multiview applications to reinforce the concepts from this chapter and to give you a feel for how more complex applications are put together. In the next chapter, we'll construct a tab bar application, and in the two chapters after that, we'll learn how to construct a navigation-based application.

Chapter 7

Tab Bars and Pickers

*i*n the previous chapter, you built your first multiview application. In this chapter, you're going to build a full tab bar application with five different tabs and five different content views. Building this application is going to reinforce a lot of what you learned in the previous chapter, but you're too smart to spend a whole chapter doing stuff you already sorta know how to do, so we're going to use those five content views to show you how to use a type of iPhone control that we have not yet covered. The control is called a **picker view**, or just a **picker**.

You may not be familiar with the name, but you've almost certainly used a picker if you've owned an iPhone for more than, say, 10 minutes. Pickers are the controls with dials that spin. You use them to input dates in the Calendar application or to set a timer in the Clock application (see Figure 7-1).

Pickers are rather more complex than the iPhone controls you've seen so far, and as such, they deserve a little more attention. Pickers can be configured to display one dial or many. By default, pickers display lists of text, but they can also be made to display images.

Figure 7-1. *A picker in the Clock application*

The Pickers Application

This chapter's application, Pickers, will feature a tab bar. As you build Pickers, you'll change the default tab bar so it has five tabs, add an icon to each of the tab bar items, and then create a series of content views and connect each to a tab.

The first content view we'll build will have a **date picker**, which is the easiest type of picker to implement (see Figure 7-2). The view will also have a button that, when tapped, will display an alert that displays the date that was picked.

The second tab will feature a picker with a single list of values (see Figure 7-3). This picker is a little bit more work to implement than a date picker. You'll learn how to specify the values to be displayed in the picker by using a delegate and a datasource.

In the third tab, we're going to create a picker with two separate wheels. The technical term for each of these wheels is a **picker component**, so here we are creating a picker with two components. We'll see how to use the datasource and delegate to provide two independent lists of data to the picker (see Figure 7-4). Each of this picker's components can be changed without impacting the other one.

Figure 7-2. *The first tab will show a date picker.*

Figure 7-3. *A picker displaying a single list of values*

Figure 7-4. *A two-component picker*

In the fourth content view, we're going to build another picker with two components. But this time, the values displayed in the component on the right are going to change based on the value selected in the component on the left. In our example, we're going to display a list of states in the left component and a list of that state's ZIP codes in the right component (see Figure 7-5).

And last, but most certainly not least, we're going to have a little fun with the fifth content view. We're going to see how to add image data to a picker, and we're going to do it by writing a little game that uses a picker with five components. In several places in Apple's documentation, the picker's appearance is described as looking a bit like a slot machine. Well, then, what could be more fitting than writing a little slot machine game (see Figure 7-6)? For this picker, the user won't be able to manually change the values of the components but will be able to select the Spin button to make the five wheels spin to a new, randomly selected value. If three copies of the same image appear in a row, the user wins.

Figure 7-5. *In this picker, one component is dependent on the other. As we select a state in the left component, the right component changes to a list of ZIP codes in that state.*

Figure 7-6. *Our five component picker. Note that we do not condone using your iPhone as a tiny casino.*

Delegates and Datasources

Before we dive in and start building our application, let's look at why pickers are so much more complex than the other controls you've used so far. It's not just a matter of there being more configurable attributes to set in Interface Builder. In fact, the picker actually has very few attributes that can be configured from within Interface Builder. With the exception of the date picker, you can't use a picker by just grabbing one in Interface Builder, dropping it on your content view, and configuring it. You have to also provide it with both a **picker delegate** and a **picker datasource**.

By this point, you should be comfortable using delegates. We've already used application delegates and action sheet delegates, and the basic idea is the same here. The picker defers several jobs to its delegate. The most important of these is the task of determining what to actually draw for each of the rows in each of its components. The picker asks the delegate for either a string or a view that will be drawn at a given spot on a given component. The picker gets its data from the delegate.

In addition to the delegate, pickers need to have a datasource. In this instance, the name "datasource" is a bit of a misnomer. The datasource tells the picker how many components it will be working with and how many rows make up each component. The datasource works similarly to the delegate, in that its methods are called at certain, prespecified times. Without a datasource and a delegate specified, pickers cannot do their job and, in fact, won't even be drawn.

It's very common for the datasource and the delegate to be the same object, and just as common for that object to be the view controller for the picker's enclosing view, which is the approach we'll be using in this application. The view controllers for each content pane will be the datasource and the delegate for their picker.

NOTE

> Here's a pop quiz: is the picker datasource part of the model, view, or controller portion of the application? It's a trick question. A datasource sounds like it must be part of the model, but in fact, it's actually part of the controller. The datasource isn't usually an object designed to hold data. Though in simple applications the datasource might hold data, its true job is to retrieve data from the model and pass it along to the picker.

Let's fire up Xcode and get to it.

Setting Up the Tab Bar Framework

Although Xcode does provide a template for tab bar applications, we're going to build ours from scratch. It's not much extra work, and it's good practice. So, create a new project, selecting the *Window-based Application* template again. When prompted for a name, type *Pickers*, and make sure the checkbox that says *Use Core Data for storage* is unchecked. We're going to walk you through the process of building the whole application, but if, at any step of the way, you feel like challenging yourself by moving ahead of us, by all means, go ahead. If you get stumped, you can always come back. If you don't feel like skipping ahead, that's just fine. We'd love the company.

Creating the Files

In the previous chapter, we created a root controller to manage the process of swapping our application's other views. We'll be doing that again this time, but we won't need to create our own root controller class. Apple provides a very good class for managing tab bar views, so we're just going to use an instance of `UITabBarController` as our root controller. We will create that instance in Interface Builder in a few minutes.

First, we need to create five new classes in Xcode: the five view controllers that the root controller will swap in and out.

Expand the *Classes* and *Resources* folders in the *Groups & Files* pane. Next, single-click the *Classes* folder, and press ⌘N or select **New File...** from the **File** menu.

Select *Cocoa Touch Classes* in the left pane of the new file assistant, and then select the icon for *UIViewController subclass*. In the bottom-right pane, just above the description of the selected template, you should see a checkbox labeled *With XIB for user interface* (Figure 7-7). Make sure that's checked before clicking *Next*. Name the first one *DatePickerViewController.m*, making sure to check *Also create "DatePickerViewController.h"*. After you click the *Finish* button, there will be three new files in your *Classes* folder: *DatePickerViewController.h*, *DatePickerViewController.m*, and *DatePickerViewController.xib*. The nib file doesn't belong in the *Classes* folder, so drag *DatePickerViewController.xib* down to the *Resources* folder.

Repeat those steps four more times, using the names *SingleComponentPickerViewController.m*, *DoubleComponentPickerViewController.m*, *DependentComponentPickerViewController.m*, and *CustomPickerViewController.m*.

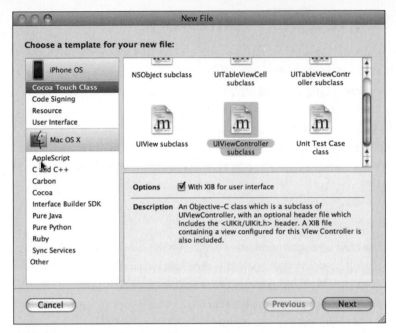

Figure 7-7. *When creating a subclass of UIViewController, Xcode will create the accompanying XIB file for you if you select "With XIB for user interface".*

Adding the Root View Controller

We're going to create our root view controller, which will be an instance of UITabBarController, in Interface Builder. Before we can do that, however, we should declare an outlet for it. Single-click the *PickersAppDelegate.h* class, and add the following code to it:

```
#import <UIKit/UIKit.h>

@interface PickersAppDelegate : NSObject <UIApplicationDelegate> {
    UIWindow *window;
    UITabBarController *rootController;
}

@property (nonatomic, retain) IBOutlet UIWindow *window;
@property (nonatomic, retain) IBOutlet UITabBarController *rootController;
@end
```

Before we move to Interface Builder to create our root view controller, let's add the following code to *PickersAppDelegate.m*:

```
#import "PickersAppDelegate.h"

@implementation PickersAppDelegate
```

```
@synthesize window;
@synthesize rootController;

- (void)applicationDidFinishLaunching:(UIApplication *)application {

    // Override point for customization after app launch
    [window addSubview:rootController.view];
    [window makeKeyAndVisible];
}

- (void)dealloc {
    [rootController release];
    [window release];
    [super dealloc];
}

@end
```

There shouldn't be anything in this code that's a surprise to you. This is pretty much the same thing we did in the previous chapter, except that we're using a controller class provided by Apple this time instead of one we wrote ourselves. Make sure you save both files before continuing.

Tab bars use icons to represent each of the tabs, so we should also add the icons we're going to use before heading over to Interface Builder. You can find some suitable icons in the project archive that accompanies this book in the *07 Pickers/Tab Bar Icons/* folder. The icons should be 24 by 24 pixels and saved in *.png* format. The icon file should have a transparent background. Generally, medium gray icons look the best on a tab bar. Don't worry about trying to match the appearance of the tab bar. Just as it does with the application icon, the iPhone is going to take your image and make it look just right.

You should be comfortable adding resources to your project by this point, so go ahead and add the five icons we've provided by dragging them from the Finder to the *Resources* folder of your Xcode project or selecting **Add to Project...** from the **Project** menu.

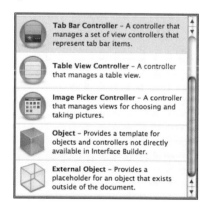

Once you've added the icons, double-click *MainWindow.xib* to open the file in Interface Builder. Drag a *Tab Bar Controller* from the library (see Figure 7-8) over to the nib's main window. Be sure you drag to the window labeled *MainWindow.xib* and not to the window labeled *Window*, which will not accept the drag, so you'll know when you get it right.

Figure 7-8. *Tab Bar Controller in the library*

Once you drop the tab bar controller onto your nib's main window, a new window will appear that looks like Figure 7-9. This tab bar controller will be our root controller. As a reminder, the root controller controls the very first view that the user will see when your program runs.

Single-click the *Tab Bar Controller* icon in your nib's main window, and press ⌘1 to bring up the attributes inspector for it. The attributes inspector for a tab bar controller will look like Figure 7-10.

The part that we're interested in is the top section, which is labeled *View Controllers*. When all is said and done, we'll end up with one view controller for each of our tab controller's tabs. Take a look back at Figure 7-2. As you can see, our program features five tabs, one for each of our five subviews—five subviews, five view controllers.

Turn your attention back to the attributes inspector for the tab bar controller. We need to change our tab bar controller so it has five tabs instead of two. Click the button with the plus sign on it three times to create a total of five controllers. The attributes inspector will show five items, and if you look over at the *Tab Bar Controller* window, you'll see that it now has five buttons instead of two.

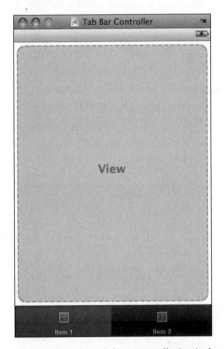

Figure 7-9. *The tab bar controller's window*

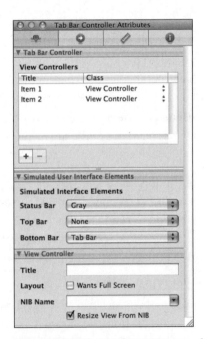

Figure 7-10. *The attributes inspector for the tab bar controller*

Click the tab bar at the bottom of the *Tab Bar Controller* window. Be sure you click the leftmost tab. This should select the controller that corresponds to the leftmost tab, and the inspector should change to look like Figure 7-11. If your inspector doesn't look like Figure 7-11, click the second tab and then back on the first tab.

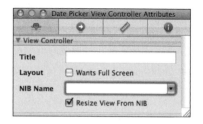

Figure 7-11. *The view controller attributes inspector*

Here's where we associate each tab's view controller with the appropriate nib. This leftmost tab will launch the first of our five subviews. Leave the *Title* field blank. Tab bar controllers don't use this title for anything, though some other kinds of view controllers do. The checkbox labeled *Wants Full Screen* can be used to indicate that the view that comes up when you press that tab will overlap and hide the tabs bar. If you check this checkbox, you must provide an alternative mechanism for navigating off that tab. We will leave this value unchecked for all of our tabs. Finally, specify a *NIB Name* of *DatePickerViewController*. Do not include the *.xib* extension. Leave the *Resize View From NIB* checkbox checked. This won't apply to us, since we'll design our views to not need resizing.

While you are here, press ⌘4. This will bring up the identity inspector for the view controller associated with the leftmost tab. Change the class to *DatePickerViewController*, and press return or tab to set it.

Press ⌘1 to return to the attributes inspector. Click the first tab in the tab bar, and click it again in the same spot. This should cause the inspector to change again, so it looks like Figure 7-12.

Figure 7-12. *The tab bar item attributes inspector*

By clicking the tab bar again in the same spot, we've changed the selection from the view controller associated with the tab bar item to the tab bar item itself. In other words, the first click selected the first of the five subview's view controllers. The second click selects the tab bar item itself so that we can set its title and icon.

The first item on the *Tab Bar Item* inspector is labeled *Badge*. This can be used to put a red icon onto a tab bar item, similar to the red number placed on the *Mail* icon that tells you how many unread e-mails you have. We're not going to use the badge field in this chapter, so you can leave it blank, but we thought you'd want to know what it does.

Under that, there's a pop-up button called *Identifier*. This field allows you to select from a set of commonly used tab bar item names and icons such as *Favorites* and *Search*. If you select one of these, then it will provide the name and icon for the item based on your selection. We're not using standard items, so you can ignore this one for now also.

The next two fields down are where we can specify a title and custom tab icon for a tab bar item. Change the *Title* from *Item 1* to *Date*, click the *Image* combo box, and select the *clockicon.png* image. If you are using your own set of icons, select one of the *.png* files you provided instead. For the rest of this chapter, we'll discuss the resources we provided. Make adjustments for your own media, as necessary.

If you look over at the *Tab Bar Controller* window, you'll see that the leftmost tab bar item now reads *Date* and has a picture of a clock on it. We now need to repeat this process for the other four tab bar items.

Before we do, let's revisit what we just did. First, we single-clicked the first tab and used the attributes inspector to specify the nib name for that first tab's associated view controller. Next, we opened the identity inspector and changed the underlying class of the view controller associated with this tab.

We then clicked the tab again to edit the tab bar item, instead of the view controller. We gave the tab bar item a title and an icon.

Let's repeat this for the next four view controller/tab bar item pairings.

Click the second tab, and bring up the attributes inspector. Change the second view controller's nib name to *SingleComponentPickerViewController*. Switch to the identity inspector, and change the view controller's class to *SingleComponentPickerViewController*. Click the second tab again, and return to the attributes inspector. Give the second tab bar item a title of *Single*, and specify an *Image* of *singleicon.png*.

Click the third tab, and bring up the attributes inspector. Change the third view controller's nib name to *DoubleComponentPickerViewController*. Switch to the identity inspector, and change the view controller's class to *DoubleComponentPickerViewController*. Click the third tab again, and return to the attributes inspector. Give the third tab bar item a title of *Double*, and specify an *Image* of *doubleicon.png*.

Click the fourth tab, and bring up the attributes inspector. Change the fourth view controller's nib name to *DependentComponentPickerViewController*. Switch to the identity inspector, and change the view controller's class to *DependentComponentPickerViewController*. Click the fourth tab again, and return to the attributes inspector. Give the fourth tab bar item a title of *Dependent*, and specify an *Image* of *dependenticon.png*.

Click the fifth tab, and bring up the attributes inspector. Change the fifth view controller's nib name to *SinglePickerViewController*. Switch to the identity inspector, and change the view controller's class to *CustomPickerViewController*. Click the fifth tab again, and return to the attributes inspector. Give the fifth tab bar item a title of *Custom*, and specify an *Image* of *toolicon.png*.

All that we have left to do in this nib file is to control-drag from the *Pickers App Delegate* icon to the *Tab Bar Controller* icon, selecting the *rootController* outlet. Save your nib, and go back to Xcode.

At this point, the tab bar and the content views should all be hooked up and working. Compile and run, and your application should launch with a toolbar that functions; clicking a tab should select it.

There's nothing in the content views now, so the changes won't be very dramatic. But if everything went OK, the basic framework for your multiview application is now set up and working, and we can start designing the individual content views.

If you want to make double sure everything is working, you can add a different label or some other object to each of the content views and then relaunch the application. If everything is working, you'll see the content of the different views change as you select different tabs.

Implementing the Date Picker

To implement the date picker, we'll need a single outlet and a single action. The outlet will be used to grab the value from the date picker. The action will be triggered by a button and will throw up an alert to show the date value pulled from the picker. Single-click *DatePickerViewController.h*, and add the following code:

```
#import <UIKit/UIKit.h>

@interface DatePickerViewController : UIViewController {
    UIDatePicker    *datePicker;
}
@property (nonatomic, retain) IBOutlet UIDatePicker *datePicker;
-(IBAction)buttonPressed;
@end
```

Save this file, and double-click *DatePickerViewController.xib* to open the content view for this first tab in Interface Builder. The first thing we need is to size the view correctly for the space available. The easiest way to do that is to single-click the View icon and press ⌘1 to bring up the attributes inspector. We can use the *Simulated Interface Elements* to have Interface Builder size this view correctly by setting the *Bottom Bar* popup to *Tab Bar*. This will cause Interface Builder to automatically reduce the view's height to 411 pixels and show a simulated tab bar.

Next, we need to add a date picker to this view, so look for *Date Picker* in the library (see Figure 7-13), and drag one over to the *View* window. If the *View* window is not open, open it by double-clicking the *View* icon in the nib's main window.

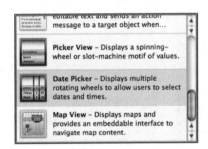

Place the date picker right at the top of the view. It should take up the entire width of your content view and a good portion of the height. Don't use the blue guidelines for the picker; it's designed to fit snugly against the edges of the view (see Figure 7-14).

Figure 7-13. *The Date Picker in the library*

Single-click the date picker if it's not already selected, and press ⌘1 to bring up the attributes inspector. As you can see (in Figure 7-15), a number of attributes can be configured for a date picker. You won't get off this easy with the rest of the pickers, so enjoy it while you can. We're going to leave most of the values at their defaults, though you should feel free to play with the options when we're done to see what they do. The one thing we are going to do is limit the range of the picker to reasonable dates. Look for the heading that says *Constraints*, and check the box that reads *Minimum Date*. Leave the *Minimum* date value at the default of *1/1/1970*. Also check the box that reads *Maximum Date*, and set *Maximum* to *12/31/2200*.

Next, grab a *Round Rect Button* from the library, and place it below the date picker. Double-click it, and give it a title of *Select*, and press ⌘2 to switch to the connections inspector. Drag from the circle next to the *Touch Up Inside* event over to the *File's Owner* icon, and connect to the *buttonPressed* action. Then control-drag from the *File's Owner* icon back to the date picker, and select the *datePicker* outlet. Save, close the nib, and go back to Xcode.

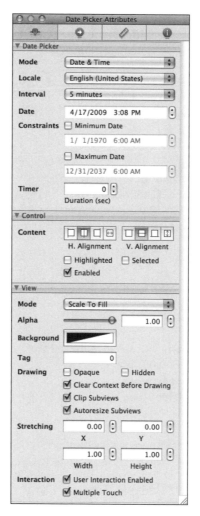

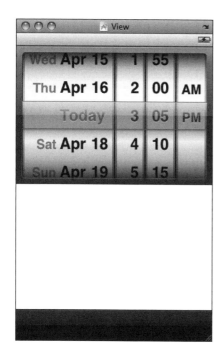

Figure 7-14. *Place all pickers right up against the edges of the view, either at the top or bottom of the view.*

Figure 7-15. *The attributes inspector for a date picker*

Now we just need to implement DatePickerViewController, so click *DatePickerViewController.m*, and first, add the following code at the top of the file:

```
#import "DatePickerViewController.h"

@implementation DatePickerViewController
@synthesize datePicker;

-(IBAction)buttonPressed {
    NSDate *selected = [datePicker date];
    NSString *message = [[NSString alloc] initWithFormat:
        @"The date and time you selected is: %@", selected];
```

```
        UIAlertView *alert = [[UIAlertView alloc]
                initWithTitle:@"Date and Time Selected"
                      message:message
                      delegate:nil
            cancelButtonTitle:@"Yes, I did."
            otherButtonTitles:nil];
        [alert show];
        [alert release];
        [message release];
}
- (void)viewDidLoad {
    NSDate *now = [[NSDate alloc] init];
    [datePicker setDate:now animated:NO];
    [now release];
}
...
```

Next, add two lines to the existing viewDidUnload: method:

```
- (void)viewDidUnload {

    // Release any retained subviews of the main view.
    // e.g. self.myOutlet = nil;
    self.datePicker = nil;
    [super viewDidUnload];
}
```

and one line to the existing dealloc method:

```
- (void)dealloc {
    [datePicker release];
    [super dealloc];
}
```

The first thing we did was to synthesize the accessor and mutator for our datePicker out-let; then we added the implementation of buttonPressed and overrode viewDidLoad. In buttonPressed, we use our datePicker outlet to get the current date value from the date picker, and then we construct a string based on that date and use it to show an alert sheet.

In viewDidLoad, we created a new NSDate object. An NSDate object created this way will hold the current date and time. We then set datePicker to that date, which ensures that every time this view gets loaded from the nib, the picker will reset to the current date and time.

Go ahead and build and run to make sure your date picker checks out. If everything went OK, your application should look like Figure 7-2 when it runs. If you click the *Select* button, an alert sheet will pop up telling you the date and time currently selected in the date picker.

Though the date picker does not allow you to specify seconds or a time zone, the alert that displays the selected date and time displays both seconds and a time zone offset. We could have added some code to simplify the string displayed in the alert, but isn't this chapter long enough already?

Implementing the Single Component Picker

Well, date pickers are easy enough, but let's look at using pickers that let the user select from a list of values. In this example, we're going to create an NSArray to hold the values we want to display in the picker. Pickers don't hold any data themselves. Instead, they call methods on their datasource and delegate to get the data they need to display. The picker doesn't really care where the underlying data is. It asks for the data when it needs it, and the datasource and delegate work together to supply that data. As a result, the data could be coming from a static list, as we'll do in this section, or could be loaded from a file or a URL, or even made up or calculated on the fly.

Declaring Outlets and Actions

As always, we need to make sure our outlets and actions are in place in our controller's header file before we start working in Interface Builder. In Xcode, single-click *SingleCompo-nentPickerViewController.h*. This controller class will act as both the datasource and the delegate for its picker, so we need to make sure it conforms to the protocols for those two roles. In addition, we'll need to declare an outlet and an action. Add the following code:

```
#import <UIKit/UIKit.h>

@interface SingleComponentPickerViewController : UIViewController
    <UIPickerViewDelegate, UIPickerViewDataSource> {
        UIPickerView     *singlePicker;
        NSArray          *pickerData;
}
@property (nonatomic, retain) IBOutlet UIPickerView *singlePicker;
@property (nonatomic, retain) NSArray *pickerData;
- (IBAction)buttonPressed;
@end
```

We start by conforming our controller class to two protocols, UIPickerViewDelegate and UIPickerViewDataSource. After that, we declare an outlet for the picker and a pointer to an NSArray, which will be used to hold the list of items that will be displayed in the picker. Finally, we declare the action method for the button, just as we did for the date picker.

Building the View

Double-click *SingleComponentPickerViewController.xib* to open the content view for the second tab in our tab bar. Single-click the *View* icon and press ⌘1 to bring up the attributes inspector so you can set the *Bottom Bar* to *Tab Bar* in the *Simulated Interface Elements* section. Next, bring over a *Picker View* from the library (see Figure 7-16), and add it to your nib's *View* window, placing it snugly into the top of the view as you did with the date picker view.

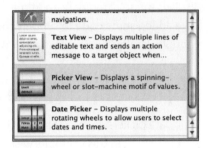

Figure 7-16. *The Picker View in the library*

After placing the picker, control-drag from *File's Owner* to the picker view, and select the *singlePicker* outlet. Next, single-click the picker if it's not already selected, and press ⌘2 to bring up the connections inspector. If you look at the connections available for the picker view, you'll see that the first two items are *Data-Source* and *Delegate*. Drag from the circle next to *DataSource* to the *File's Owner* icon. Then drag again from the circle next to *Delegate* to the *File's Owner* icon. Now this picker knows that the instance of the `SingleComponentPickerViewController` class in the nib is its datasource and delegate and will ask it to supply the data to be displayed. In other words, when the picker needs information about the data it is going to display, it asks the `SingleComponentPickerViewController` instance that controls this view for that information.

Drag a *Round Rect Button* to the view, double-click it, and give it a title of *Select*. Press return to commit the change. In the connections inspector, drag from the circle next to *Touch Up Inside* to the *File's Owner* icon, selecting the *buttonPressed* action. Save the nib file, close it, and go back to Xcode.

Implementing the Controller as Datasource and Delegate

To make our controller work properly as the picker's datasource and delegate, we are going to have to implement a few methods that you've never seen before. Single-click *SingleComp onentPickerViewController.m*, and add the following code at the beginning of the file:

```
#import "SingleComponentPickerViewController.h"

@implementation SingleComponentPickerViewController
@synthesize singlePicker;
@synthesize pickerData;
- (IBAction)buttonPressed {
    NSInteger row = [singlePicker selectedRowInComponent:0];
    NSString *selected = [pickerData objectAtIndex:row];
    NSString *title = [[NSString alloc] initWithFormat:
                    @"You selected %@!", selected];
```

```
        UIAlertView *alert = [[UIAlertView alloc] initWithTitle:title
                                         message:@"Thank you for choosing."
                                         delegate:nil
                              cancelButtonTitle:@"You're Welcome"
                              otherButtonTitles:nil];
        [alert show];
        [alert release];
        [title release];
}
- (void)viewDidLoad {
        NSArray *array = [[NSArray alloc] initWithObjects:@"Luke", @"Leia",
               @"Han", @"Chewbacca", @"Artoo", @"Threepio", @"Lando", nil];
        self.pickerData = array;
        [array release];
}
...
```

These two methods should be familiar to you by now. The buttonPressed method is nearly identical to the one we used with the date picker. Unlike the date picker, a regular picker can't tell us what data it holds, because it doesn't maintain the data. It hands that job off to the delegate and datasource. Instead, we have to ask the picker which row is selected and then grab the corresponding data from our pickerData array.

Here is how we ask it for the selected row:

```
NSInteger row = [singlePicker selectedRowInComponent:0];
```

Notice that we had to specify which component we want to know about. We have only one component in this picker, so we simply pass in 0, which is the index of the first component.

NOTE

Did you notice that there is no asterisk between NSInteger and row? Although on the iPhone the prefix "NS" often indicates an Objective-C class from the Foundation framework, this is one of the exceptions to that general rule. NSInteger is always defined as an integer datatype, either an int or a long. We use NSInteger rather than int or long, because when we use NSInteger, the compiler automatically chooses whichever size is best for the platform for which we are compiling. It will create a 32-bit int when compiling for a 32-bit processor and a longer 64-bit long when compiling for a 64-bit architecture. Currently, there is no 64-bit iPhone, but who knows? Someday in the future, there may be. You might also write classes for your iPhone applications that you'll later want to recycle and use in Cocoa applications for Mac OS X, which already does run on both 32- and 64-bit machines.

In viewDidLoad, we create an array with several objects so that we have data to feed the picker. Usually, your data will come from other sources, like a property list in your project's

Resources folder. By embedding a list of items in our code the way we've done here, we are making it much harder on ourselves if we need to update this list or if we want to have our application translated into other languages. But this approach is the quickest and easiest way to get data into an array for demonstration purposes. Even though you won't usually create your arrays like this, you will almost always cache the data you are using into an array here in the `viewDidLoad` method so that you're not constantly going to disk or to the network every time the picker asks you for data.

TIP

> If you're not supposed to create arrays from lists of objects in your code as we just did in `viewDidLoad`, how should you do it? Embed the lists in property list files, and add those files to the *Resources* folder of your project. Property list files can be changed without recompiling your source code, which means no risk of introducing new bugs when you do so. You can also provide different versions of the list for different languages, as you'll see in Chapter 17. Property lists can be created using the Property List Editor application located at */Developer/Applications/Utilities/Property List Editor.app* or right in Xcode, which supports the editing of property lists in the editor pane. Both `NSArray` and `NSDictionary` offer a method called `initWithContentsOfFile:` to allow you to initialize instances from a property file, something we'll do in this chapter when implementing the *Dependent* tab.

Next, insert the following new lines of code into the existing `viewDidUnload` and `dealloc` methods:

```
...
- (void)viewDidUnload {
    // Release any retained subviews of the main view.
    // e.g. self.myOutlet = nil;
    self.singlePicker = nil;
    self.pickerData = nil;
    [super viewDidUnload];
}
- (void)dealloc {
    [singlePicker release];
    [pickerData release];
    [super dealloc];
}
...
```

One thing to notice here is that we've set both `singlePicker` and `pickerData` to nil. In most cases, you'll set only outlets to `nil` and not other instance variables. However, setting `pickerData` to `nil` is appropriate here because the `pickerData` array will get re-created each time the view gets reloaded, and we want to free up that memory when the view is unloaded. Anything that gets created in the viewDidLoad method can be flushed in viewDidUnload because viewDidLoad will fire again when the view gets reloaded.

Finally, insert the following new code at the end of the file:

```
#pragma mark -
#pragma mark Picker Data Source Methods
- (NSInteger)numberOfComponentsInPickerView:(UIPickerView *)pickerView {
    return 1;
}
- (NSInteger)pickerView:(UIPickerView *)pickerView
        numberOfRowsInComponent:(NSInteger)component {
    return [pickerData count];
}
#pragma mark Picker Delegate Methods
- (NSString *)pickerView:(UIPickerView *)pickerView
        titleForRow:(NSInteger)row
        forComponent:(NSInteger)component {
    return [pickerData objectAtIndex:row];
}
@end
```

At the bottom of the file, we get into the new methods required to implement the picker. The first two methods after dealloc are from the UIPickerViewDataSource protocol, and they are both required for all pickers (except date pickers). Here's the first one:

```
- (NSInteger)numberOfComponentsInPickerView:(UIPickerView *)pickerView {
    return 1;
}
```

Pickers can have more than one spinning wheel, or component, and this is how the picker asks how many components it should display. We want to display only one list this time, so we simply return a value of 1. Notice that a UIPickerView is passed in as a parameter. This parameter points to the picker view that is asking us the question, which makes it possible to have multiple pickers being controlled by the same datasource. In our case, we know that we have only one picker, so we can safely ignore this argument because we already know which picker is calling us.

The second datasource method is used by the picker to ask how many rows of data there are for a given component:

```
- (NSInteger)pickerView:(UIPickerView *)pickerView
        numberOfRowsInComponent:(NSInteger)component {
    return [pickerData count];
}
```

#PRAGMA WHAT?

Did you notice these lines of code from *SingleComponentPickerViewController.m*?

```
#pragma mark -
#pragma mark Picker Data Source Methods
```

Any line of code that begins with #pragma is technically a compiler directive, specifically, a **pragmatic**, or compiler-specific, directive that won't necessarily work with other compilers or in other environments. If the compiler doesn't recognize the directive, it ignores it, though it may generate a warning. In this case, the #pragma directives are actually directives to the IDE, not the compiler, and they tell Xcode's editor to put a break in the pop-up menu of methods and functions at the top of the editor pane, as shown in the following screen shot. The first one puts a divider line in the menu. The second creates a bold entry.

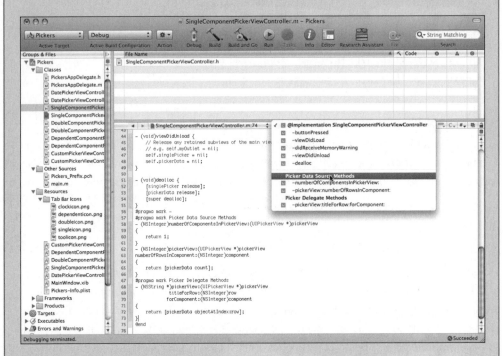

Some of your classes, especially some of your controller classes, are likely to get rather long, and the methods and functions pop-up menu makes navigating around your code much easier. Putting in #pragma directives and logically organizing your code will make that pop-up more efficient to use.

Once again, we are told which picker view is asking and which component that picker is asking about. Since we know that we have only one picker and one component, we don't bother with either of the arguments and simply return the count of objects from our sole data array.

After the two datasource methods, we implement one delegate method. Unlike the datasource methods, all of the delegate methods are optional. The term "optional" is a bit deceiving because you do have to implement at least one delegate method. You will usually implement the method that we are implementing here. As you'll see when we get to the custom picker, if you want to display something other than text in the picker, you have to implement a different method instead.

```
- (NSString *)pickerView:(UIPickerView *)pickerView
        titleForRow:(NSInteger)row
        forComponent:(NSInteger)component {
    return [pickerData objectAtIndex:row];
}
```

In this method, the picker is asking us to provide the data for a specific row in a specific component. We are provided with a pointer to the picker that is asking, along with the component and row that it is asking about. Since our view has one picker with one component, we simply ignore everything except the row argument and use that to return the appropriate item from our data array.

Go ahead and compile and run again. When the simulator comes up, switch to the second tab—the one labeled *Single*—and check out your new custom picker, which should look like Figure 7-3.

When you're done reliving all those *Star Wars* memories, come on back to Xcode and we'll see how to implement a picker with two components. If you feel up to a challenge, this next content view is actually a good one for you to attempt on your own. You've already seen all the methods you'll need for this picker, so go ahead, take a crack at it. We'll wait here. You might want to start off with a good look at Figure 7-4, just to refresh your memory. When you're done, read on, and you'll see how we tackled this problem.

Implementing a Multicomponent Picker

The next content pane will have a picker with two components or wheels, and each wheel will be independent of the other wheel. The left wheel will have a list of sandwich fillings, and the right wheel will have a selection of bread types. As we mentioned a moment ago, we'll write the same datasource and delegate methods that we did for the single component picker; we'll just have to write a little additional code in some of those methods to make sure we're returning the right value and row count for each component.

Declaring Outlets and Actions

Single-click *DoubleComponentPickerViewController.h*, and add the following code:

```
#import <UIKit/UIKit.h>

#define kFillingComponent 0
#define kBreadComponent 1

@interface DoubleComponentPickerViewController : UIViewController
    <UIPickerViewDelegate, UIPickerViewDataSource>
{
    UIPickerView *doublePicker;
    NSArray *fillingTypes;
    NSArray *breadTypes;
}
@property(nonatomic, retain) IBOutlet UIPickerView *doublePicker;
@property(nonatomic, retain) NSArray *fillingTypes;
@property(nonatomic, retain) NSArray *breadTypes;
-(IBAction)buttonPressed;
@end
```

As you can see, we start out by defining two constants that will represent the two components, which is just to make our code easier to read. Components are assigned numbers, with the leftmost component being assigned zero and increasing by one each move to the right.

Next, we conform our controller class to both the delegate and datasource protocols, and we declare an outlet for the picker, as well as for two arrays to hold the data for our two picker components. After declaring properties for each of our instance variables, we declare a single action method for the button, just as we did in the last two context panes. Save this, and double-click *DoubleComponentPickerViewController.xib* to open the nib file in Interface Builder.

Building the View

Select the *View* icon, and use the attributes inspector to set the *Bottom Bar* to *Tab Bar* in the *Simulated Interface* section.

Add a picker and a button to the *View*, and then make the necessary connections. We're not going to walk you through it this time, but you can refer to the previous section if you need a step-by-step guide, since the two applications are identical in terms of the nib file. Here's a summary of what you need to do:

1. Connect the *doublePicker* outlet on *File's Owner* to the picker.

2. Connect the *DataSource* and *Delegate* connections on the picker view to *File's Owner* (use the connections inspector).

3. Connect the *Touch Up Inside* event of the button to the *buttonPressed* action on *File's Owner* (use the connections inspector).

Make sure you save your nib and close it before you head back to Xcode. Oh, and dog-ear this page (or use a bookmark, if you prefer). You'll be referring to it in a bit.

Implementing the Controller

Single-click *DoubleComponentPickerViewController.m*, and add the following code at the top of the file:

```
#import "DoubleComponentPickerViewController.h"

@implementation DoubleComponentPickerViewController
@synthesize doublePicker;
@synthesize fillingTypes;
@synthesize breadTypes;
-(IBAction)buttonPressed
{
    NSInteger breadRow = [doublePicker selectedRowInComponent:
                              kBreadComponent];
    NSInteger fillingRow = [doublePicker selectedRowInComponent:
                              kFillingComponent];

    NSString *bread = [breadTypes objectAtIndex:breadRow];
    NSString *filling = [fillingTypes objectAtIndex:fillingRow];

    NSString *message = [[NSString alloc] initWithFormat:
            @"Your %@ on %@ bread will be right up.", filling, bread];

    UIAlertView *alert = [[UIAlertView alloc] initWithTitle:
                                          @"Thank you for your order"
                                                  message:message
                                                  delegate:nil
                                      cancelButtonTitle:@"Great!"
                                      otherButtonTitles:nil];
    [alert show];
    [alert release];
    [message release];

}
- (void)viewDidLoad {
    NSArray *breadArray = [[NSArray alloc] initWithObjects:@"White",
        @"Whole Wheat", @"Rye", @"Sourdough", @"Seven Grain",nil];
    self.breadTypes = breadArray;
    [breadArray release];

    NSArray *fillingArray = [[NSArray alloc] initWithObjects:@"Ham",
                  @"Turkey", @"Peanut Butter", @"Tuna Salad",
                  @"Chicken Salad", @"Roast Beef", @"Vegemite", nil];
    self.fillingTypes = fillingArray;
```

```
        [fillingArray release];
    }
    ...
```

Also, add the following lines of code to the existing `dealloc` and `viewDidUnload` methods:

```
...
- (void)viewDidUnload {
    // Release any retained subviews of the main view.
    // e.g. self.myOutlet = nil;
    self.doublePicker = nil;
    self.breadTypes = nil;
    self.fillingTypes = nil;
    [super viewDidUnload];


}

- (void)dealloc {
    [doublePicker release];
    [breadTypes release];
    [fillingTypes release];
    [super dealloc];
}
...
```

And add the delegate and datasource methods at the bottom:

```
#pragma mark -
#pragma mark Picker Data Source Methods
- (NSInteger)numberOfComponentsInPickerView:(UIPickerView *)pickerView {
    return 2;
}
- (NSInteger)pickerView:(UIPickerView *)pickerView
    numberOfRowsInComponent:(NSInteger)component {
    if (component == kBreadComponent)
        return [self.breadTypes count];

    return [self.fillingTypes count];
}
#pragma mark Picker Delegate Methods
- (NSString *)pickerView:(UIPickerView *)pickerView
    titleForRow:(NSInteger)row
    forComponent:(NSInteger)component {
    if (component == kBreadComponent)
        return [self.breadTypes objectAtIndex:row];
```

```
        return [self.fillingTypes objectAtIndex:row];
}
@end
```

The `buttonPressed` method is a little more involved this time, but there's very little there that's new to you; we just have to specify which component we are talking about when we request the selected row using those constants we defined earlier, `kBreadComponent` and `kFillingComponent`.

```
NSInteger breadRow = [doublePicker selectedRowInComponent:
        kBreadComponent];
NSInteger fillingRow = [doublePicker selectedRowInComponent:
        kFillingComponent];
```

You can see here that using the two constants instead of 0 and 1 makes our code considerably more readable. From this point on, the `buttonPressed` method is fundamentally the same as the last one we wrote.

`viewDidLoad:` is also very similar to the one we wrote for the previous section. The only difference is that we are loading two arrays with data rather than just one. Again, we're just creating arrays from a hard-coded list of strings, something you generally won't do in your own applications.

When we get down to the datasource methods, that's where things start to change a bit. In the first method, we specify that our picker should have two components rather than just one:

```
- (NSInteger)numberOfComponentsInPickerView:(UIPickerView *)pickerView {
    return 2;
}
```

Easy enough. This time, when we are asked for the number of rows, we have to check which component the picker is asking about and return the correct row count for the corresponding array:

```
- (NSInteger)pickerView:(UIPickerView *)pickerView
    numberOfRowsInComponent:(NSInteger)component {
    if (component == kBreadComponent)
        return [self.breadTypes count];

    return [self.fillingTypes count];
}
```

Then, in our delegate method, we do the same thing. We check the component and use the correct array for the requested component to fetch and return the right value.

```
- (NSString *)pickerView:(UIPickerView *)pickerView
    titleForRow:(NSInteger)row
      forComponent:(NSInteger)component {
    if (component == kBreadComponent)
        return [self.breadTypes objectAtIndex:row];

    return [self.fillingTypes objectAtIndex:row];
}
```

That wasn't so hard, was it? Compile and run your application, and make sure the *Double* content pane looks like Figure 7-4. Notice that each wheel is completely independent of the other one. Turning one has no effect on the other. That's appropriate in this case. But there are going to be times when one component is dependent on another. A good example of this is in the date picker. When you change the month, the dial that shows the number of days in the month may have to change because not all months have the same number of days. Implementing this isn't really hard once you know how, but it's not the easiest thing to figure out on your own, so let's do that next.

Implementing Dependent Components

We're picking up steam now. For this next section, we're not going to hold your hand quite as much when it comes to material we've already covered. Instead, we'll focus on the new stuff. Our new picker will display a list of US states in the left component and a list of ZIP codes in the right component that correspond to the state currently selected in the left.

We'll need a separate list of ZIP code values for each item in the left-hand component. We'll declare two arrays, one for each component, as we did last time. We'll also need an NSDictionary. In the dictionary, we're going to have an NSArray for each state (see Figure 7-16). Later, we'll implement a delegate method that will notify us when the picker's selection changes. If the value on the left changes, we will grab the correct array out of the dictionary and assign it to the array being used for the right-hand component. Don't worry if you didn't catch all that; we'll talk about it more as we get into the code.

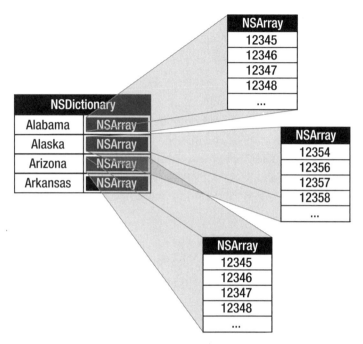

Figure 7-17. *Our application's data: for each state there will be one entry in a dictionary with the name of the state as the key. Stored under that key will be an* NSArray *instance containing all the ZIP codes from that state.*

Add the following code to your *DependentComponentPickerViewController.h* file:

```
#import <UIKit/UIKit.h>
#define kStateComponent    0
#define kZipComponent      1

@interface DependentComponentPickerViewController : UIViewController
    <UIPickerViewDelegate, UIPickerViewDataSource> {
    UIPickerView     *picker;

    NSDictionary     *stateZips;
    NSArray          *states;
    NSArray          *zips;
}
@property (retain, nonatomic) IBOutlet UIPickerView *picker;
@property (retain, nonatomic) NSDictionary *stateZips;
@property (retain, nonatomic) NSArray *states;
@property (retain, nonatomic) NSArray *zips;
- (IBAction) buttonPressed;
@end
```

Now move to Interface Builder, and build the content view. That process will be almost identical to the last two component views we built. If you get lost, flip back a few pages to the last *Building the View* section, and follow those step-by-step instructions. Here's a hint: start off by opening *DependentComponentPickerViewController.xib*. When you're done, make sure you save, close the nib, and then come back to Xcode.

OK, take a deep breath. Let's implement this controller class. This implementation may seem a little gnarly at first. By making one component dependent on the other, we have added a whole new level of complexity to our controller class. Although the picker displays only two lists at a time, our controller class has to know about and manage fifty-one lists. The technique we're going to use here actually simplifies that process. The datasource methods look almost identical to the one we implemented for the *DoublePicker* view. All of the additional complexity is handled elsewhere, between `viewDidLoad` and a new delegate method called `pickerView:didSelectRow:inComponent:`.

Before we write the code, we need some data to display, however. Up to now, we've created arrays in code by specifying a list of strings. But, we've also told you you're not going to do it that way. So, because we didn't want you to have to type in several thousand values and because we figured we ought to show you the correct way to do this, we're going to load the data from a property list. As we've mentioned, both `NSArray` and `NSDictionary` objects can be created from property lists. We've included a property list called *statedictionary.plist* in the projects archive, under the *07 Pickers* folder.

Add that file into the *Resources* area in your Xcode project. If you single-click it in the project window, you can see and even edit the data that it contains (see Figure 7-18).

Key	Type	Value
▼ Root	Dictionary	(50 items)
▶ Alabama	Array	(657 items)
▶ Alaska	Array	(251 items)
▶ Arizona	Array	(376 items)
▶ Arkansas	Array	(618 items)
▶ California	Array	(1757 items)
▶ Colorado	Array	(501 items)
▶ Connecticut	Array	(276 items)
▶ Delaware	Array	(68 items)
▶ Florida	Array	(972 items)
▶ Georgia	Array	(736 items)
▼ Hawaii	Array	(92 items)
Item 1	String	96701
Item 2	String	96703
Item 3	String	96704
Item 4	String	96705
Item 5	String	96706
Item 6	String	96707
Item 7	String	96708
Item 8	String	96710
Item 9	String	96712
Item 10	String	96713
Item 11	String	96714
Item 12	String	96716
Item 13	String	96717
Item 14	String	96718
Item 15	String	96719

Figure 7-18. *The statedictionary.plist file*

Now, let's write some code. Add the following to *DependentComponentPickerViewController.m*, and then we'll break it down into more digestible chunks:

```
#import "DependentComponentPickerViewController.h"

@implementation DependentComponentPickerViewController
@synthesize picker;
@synthesize stateZips;
@synthesize states;
@synthesize zips;

- (IBAction) buttonPressed {
    NSInteger stateRow = [picker selectedRowInComponent:kStateComponent];
    NSInteger zipRow = [picker selectedRowInComponent:kZipComponent];

    NSString *state = [self.states objectAtIndex:stateRow];
    NSString *zip = [self.zips objectAtIndex:zipRow];

    NSString *title = [[NSString alloc] initWithFormat:
                        @"You selected zip code %@.", zip];
    NSString *message = [[NSString alloc] initWithFormat:
                          @"%@ is in %@", zip, state];

    UIAlertView *alert = [[UIAlertView alloc] initWithTitle:title
                                               message:message
                                               delegate:nil
                                 cancelButtonTitle:@"OK"
                                 otherButtonTitles:nil];
    [alert show];
    [alert release];
    [title release];
    [message release];
}

- (void)viewDidLoad {

    NSBundle *bundle = [NSBundle mainBundle];
    NSString *plistPath = [bundle pathForResource:
                            @"statedictionary" ofType:@"plist"];

    NSDictionary *dictionary = [[NSDictionary alloc]
                                 initWithContentsOfFile:plistPath];
    self.stateZips = dictionary;
    [dictionary release];

    NSArray *components = [self.stateZips allKeys];
    NSArray *sorted = [components sortedArrayUsingSelector:
```

```
                    @selector(compare:)];
    self.states = sorted;

    NSString *selectedState = [self.states objectAtIndex:0];
    NSArray *array = [stateZips objectForKey:selectedState];
    self.zips = array;
}
...
```

Next, add the following lines of code to the existing viewDidUnload and dealloc methods:

```
- (void)viewDidUnload {
    // Release any retained subviews of the main view.
    // e.g. self.myOutlet = nil;
    self.picker = nil;
    self.stateZips = nil;
    self.states = nil;
    self.zips = nil;
    [super viewDidUnload];
}


- (void)dealloc {
    [picker release];
    [stateZips release];
    [states release];
    [zips release];
    [super dealloc];
}
```

And, finally, add the delegate and datasource methods at the bottom of the file:

```
...
#pragma mark -
#pragma mark Picker Data Source Methods
- (NSInteger)numberOfComponentsInPickerView:(UIPickerView *)pickerView {
    return 2;
}
- (NSInteger)pickerView:(UIPickerView *)pickerView
        numberOfRowsInComponent:(NSInteger)component {
    if (component == kStateComponent)
        return [self.states count];
    return [self.zips count];
}
#pragma mark Picker Delegate Methods
- (NSString *)pickerView:(UIPickerView *)pickerView
        titleForRow:(NSInteger)row
        forComponent:(NSInteger)component {
    if (component == kStateComponent)
```

```
            return [self.states objectAtIndex:row];
        return [self.zips objectAtIndex:row];
}

- (void)pickerView:(UIPickerView *)pickerView
        didSelectRow:(NSInteger)row
        inComponent:(NSInteger)component {
    if (component == kStateComponent) {
        NSString *selectedState = [self.states objectAtIndex:row];
        NSArray *array = [stateZips objectForKey:selectedState];
        self.zips = array;
        [picker selectRow:0 inComponent:kZipComponent animated:YES];
        [picker reloadComponent:kZipComponent];
    }
}
@end
```

There's no need to talk about the `buttonPressed` method; it's fundamentally the same as the last one. We should talk about the `viewDidLoad` method, though. There's some stuff going on there that you need to understand, so pull up a chair, and let's chat.

The first thing we do in this new `viewDidLoad` method is grab a reference to our application's **main bundle**.

```
NSBundle *bundle = [NSBundle mainBundle];
```

What is a bundle, you ask? Well, a **bundle** is just a special type of folder whose contents follow a specific structure. Applications and frameworks are both bundles, and this call returns a bundle object that represents our application. One of the primary uses of `NSBundle` is to get to resources that you added to the *Resources* folder of your project. Those files will get copied into your application's bundle when you build your application. We've added resources like images to our projects, but up to now, we've only used those in Interface Builder. If we want to get to those resources in our code, we usually have to use `NSBundle`. We use the main bundle to retrieve the path of the resource in which we're interested:

```
NSString *plistPath = [bundle pathForResource:@"statedictionary"
    ofType:@"plist"];
```

This will return a string containing the location of the *statedictionary.plist* file. We can then use that path to create an `NSDictionary` object. Once we do that, the entire contents of that property list will be loaded into the newly created `NSDictionary` object, which we then assign to `stateZips`.

```
NSDictionary *dictionary = [[NSDictionary alloc]
    initWithContentsOfFile:plistPath];
self.stateZips = dictionary;
[dictionary release];
```

The dictionary we just loaded uses the names of the states as the keys and contains an NSArray with all the ZIP codes for that state as the values. To populate the array for the left-hand component, we get the list of all keys from our dictionary and assign those to the states array. Before we assign it, though, we sort it alphabetically.

```
NSArray *components = [self.stateZips allKeys];
NSArray *sorted = [components sortedArrayUsingSelector:
    @selector(compare:)];
self.states = sorted;
```

Unless we specifically set the selection to another value, pickers start with the first row (row 0) selected. In order to get the zips array that corresponds to the first row in the states array, we grab the object from the states array that's at index 0. That will return the name of the state that will be selected at launch time. We then use that state name to grab the array of ZIP codes for that state, which we assign to the zips array that will be used to feed data to the right-hand component.

```
NSString *selectedState = [self.states objectAtIndex:0];
NSArray *array = [stateZips objectForKey:selectedState];
self.zips = array;
```

The two datasource methods are practically identical to the last version; we return the number of rows in the appropriate array. The same is true for the first delegate method we implemented. The second delegate method is the new one, and it's where the magic happens:

```
- (void)pickerView:(UIPickerView *)pickerView
        didSelectRow:(NSInteger)row
        inComponent:(NSInteger)component {
    if (component == kStateComponent) {
        NSString *selectedState = [self.states objectAtIndex:row];
        NSArray *array = [stateZips objectForKey:selectedState];
        self.zips = array;
        [picker selectRow:0 inComponent:kZipComponent animated:YES];
        [picker reloadComponent:kZipComponent];
    }
}
```

In this method, which is called any time the picker's selection changes, we look at the component and see whether the left-hand component changed. If it did, we grab the array that corresponds to the new selection and assign it to the zips array. Then we set the right-hand component back to the first row and tell it to reload itself. By swapping the zips array whenever the state changes, the rest of the code remains pretty much the same as it was in the *DoublePicker* example.

We're not quite done yet. Compile and run your application, and check out the *Dependent* tab, as illustrated in Figure 7-19. Do you see anything there you don't like?

The two components are equal in size. Even though the ZIP code will never be more than five characters long, it's been given equal billing with the state. Since states like Mississippi and Massachusetts won't fit in half of the picker, this seems less than ideal. Fortunately, there's another delegate method we can implement to indicate how wide each component should be. We have about 295 pixels available to the picker components in portrait orientation, but for every additional component we add, we lose a little bit of space to drawing the edges of the new component. You might need to experiment a little with values to get it to look right. Add the following method to the delegate section of *Dependent-ComponentPickerViewController.m*:

Figure 7-19. *Do we really want the two components to be equal size?*

```
- (CGFloat)pickerView:(UIPickerView *)pickerView
    widthForComponent:(NSInteger)component {
    if (component == kZipComponent)
        return 90;
    return 200;
}
```

In this method, we return a number that represents how many pixels wide each component should be, and the picker will do its best to accommodate this. Save, compile, and run, and the picker on the *Dependent* tab will look more like the one shown in Figure 7-5.

Well, by this point, you should be pretty darn comfortable with both pickers and tab bar applications. We have one more thing to show you about pickers, but let's have a little fun while doing it. Let's create a simple slot machine game.

Creating a Simple Game with a Custom Picker

Next up, we're going to create an actual working slot machine. Well, OK, it won't dispense silver dollars, but it does look pretty cool. Take a look back at Figure 7-6 before proceeding so you know what the view we're building is going to look like.

Writing the Controller Header File

Add the following code to *CustomPickerViewController.h* for starters:

```objc
#import <UIKit/UIKit.h>

@interface CustomPickerViewController : UIViewController
        <UIPickerViewDataSource, UIPickerViewDelegate> {
    UIPickerView *picker;
    UILabel *winLabel;

    NSArray *column1;
    NSArray *column2;
    NSArray *column3;
    NSArray *column4;
    NSArray *column5;
}
@property(nonatomic, retain) IBOutlet UIPickerView *picker;
@property(nonatomic, retain) IBOutlet UILabel *winLabel;
@property(nonatomic, retain) NSArray *column1;
@property(nonatomic, retain) NSArray *column2;
@property(nonatomic, retain) NSArray *column3;
@property(nonatomic, retain) NSArray *column4;
@property(nonatomic, retain) NSArray *column5;
-(IBAction)spin;
@end
```

We're declaring two outlets, one for a picker view and one for a label. The label will be used to tell users when they've won, which happens when they get three of the same symbol in a row.

We also create five pointers to NSArray objects. We'll use these to hold the image views containing the images we want the picker to draw. Even though we're using the same images in all five columns, we need separate arrays for each one with its own set of image views, because each view can be drawn in only one place in the picker at a time. We also declare an action method, this time called spin.

Building the View

Even though the picker in Figure 7-6 looks quite a bit fancier than the other ones we've built, there's actually very little difference in the way we'll design our nib. All the extra work is done in the delegate methods of our controller.

Make sure you've saved your new source code, and then double-click *CustomPickerView-Controller.xib* to open the file in Interface Builder. Set the *Simulated Interface Elements* to simulate a tab bar at the bottom of the view, and then add a label, a picker, and a button. Give the button a title of *Spin*. Next, select the label and use the resize handles to increase the size so that it takes up the width from left margin to right margin, and most of the available height left between the button and picker. Next, use the Fonts palette (press ⌘T) to make the label's text nice and big. You can also assign your label a nice festive color using the attributes inspector. While you're there, be sure to set the text alignment to centered. After getting the text the way you want it, delete the word *Label* from it, since we don't want any text displayed until the first time the user wins.

After that, make all the connections to outlets and actions. You need to connect the file's owner's `picker` outlet to the picker view, the file's owner's `winLabel` outlet to the label, and the button's touch up inside event to the `spin` action. After that, just make sure to specify the *Delegate* and the *DataSource* for the picker.

Oh, and there's one additional thing that you need to do. Select the picker, and bring up the attributes inspector. You need to uncheck the checkbox labeled *User Interaction Enabled* so that the user can't manually change the dial and cheat. Once you've done all that, save and return to Xcode.

CAUTION

> Be careful when using the Fonts palette in Interface Builder for designing iPhone interfaces. Interface Builder will let you assign any font that's on your Mac to the label, but the iPhone has a very limited selection of fonts. You should limit your font selections to one of the following font families: American Typewriter, AppleGothic, Arial, Arial Rounded MT Bold, Arial Unicode MS, Courier, Courier New, DB LCD Temp, Georgia, Helvetica, Helvetica Neue, Hiragino Kaku Gothic ProN W3, Hiragino Kaku Gothic ProN W6, Marker Felt, STHeiti J, STHeiti K, STHeiti SC, STHeiti TC, Times New Roman, Trebuchet MS, Verdana, or Zapfino.

Adding Image Resources

Once you're back in Xcode, we need to add the images that we'll be using in our game. We've included a set of six image files (*seven.png*, *bar.png*, *crown.png*, *cherry.png*, *lemon.png*, and *apple.png*) for you in the project archive under the *07 Pickers/Custom Picker Images* folder. Add all of those files to the *Resources* folder of your project. It's probably a good idea to copy them into the project folder when prompted to do so.

Implementing the Controller

We've got a bunch of new stuff to cover in the implementation of this controller. Add the following code at the beginning of *CustomPickerViewController.m* file:

```
#import "CustomPickerViewController.h"

@implementation CustomPickerViewController
@synthesize picker;
@synthesize winLabel;
@synthesize column1;
```

```
@synthesize column2;
@synthesize column3;
@synthesize column4;
@synthesize column5;

-(IBAction)spin {
    BOOL win = NO;
    int numInRow = 1;
    int lastVal = -1;
    for (int i = 0; i < 5; i++) {
        int newValue = random() % [self.column1 count];

        if (newValue == lastVal)
            numInRow++;
        else
            numInRow = 1;

        lastVal = newValue;
        [picker selectRow:newValue inComponent:i animated:YES];
        [picker reloadComponent:i];
        if (numInRow >= 3)
            win = YES;
    }

    if (win)
        winLabel.text = @"WIN!";
    else
        winLabel.text = @"";
}

- (void)viewDidLoad {

    UIImage *seven = [UIImage imageNamed:@"seven.png"];
    UIImage *bar = [UIImage imageNamed:@"bar.png"];
    UIImage *crown = [UIImage imageNamed:@"crown.png"];
    UIImage *cherry = [UIImage imageNamed:@"cherry.png"];
    UIImage *lemon = [UIImage imageNamed:@"lemon.png"];
    UIImage *apple = [UIImage imageNamed:@"apple.png"];

    for (int i = 1; i <= 5; i++) {
        UIImageView *sevenView = [[UIImageView alloc] initWithImage:seven];
        UIImageView *barView = [[UIImageView alloc] initWithImage:bar];
        UIImageView *crownView = [[UIImageView alloc] initWithImage:crown];
        UIImageView *cherryView = [[UIImageView alloc]
                                    initWithImage:cherry];
        UIImageView *lemonView = [[UIImageView alloc] initWithImage:lemon];
        UIImageView *appleView = [[UIImageView alloc] initWithImage:apple];
```

```objc
        NSArray *imageViewArray = [[NSArray alloc] initWithObjects:
                    sevenView, barView, crownView, cherryView, lemonView,
                               appleView, nil]];

        NSString *fieldName =
        [[NSString alloc] initWithFormat:@"column%d", i];
        [self setValue:imageViewArray forKey:fieldName];
        [fieldName release];
        [imageViewArray release];

        [sevenView release];
        [barView release];
        [crownView release];
        [cherryView release];
        [lemonView release];
        [appleView release];
    }

    srandom(time(NULL));
}
...
```

Next, insert the following new lines into the `viewDidUnload` and `dealloc` methods:

```objc
...
- (void)viewDidUnload {
    // Release any retained subviews of the main view.
    // e.g. self.myOutlet = nil;
    self.picker = nil;
    self.winLabel = nil;
    self.column1 = nil;
    self.column2 = nil;
    self.column3 = nil;
    self.column4 = nil;
    self.column5 = nil;
    [super viewDidUnload];
}
- (void)dealloc {
    [picker release];
    [winLabel release];
    [column1 release];
    [column2 release];
    [column3 release];
    [column4 release];
    [column5 release];
    [super dealloc];
}
...
```

Finally, add the following code to the end of the file. When you're done, we'll look at each new thing in turn:

```
...
#pragma mark -
#pragma mark Picker Data Source Methods
- (NSInteger)numberOfComponentsInPickerView:(UIPickerView *)pickerView {
    return 5;
}

- (NSInteger)pickerView:(UIPickerView *)pickerView
    numberOfRowsInComponent:(NSInteger)component {
    return [self.column1 count];
}
#pragma mark Picker Delegate Methods
- (UIView *)pickerView:(UIPickerView *)pickerView
        viewForRow:(NSInteger)row
            forComponent:(NSInteger)component reusingView:(UIView *)view {
    NSString *arrayName = [[NSString alloc] initWithFormat:@"column%d",
        component+1];
    NSArray *array = [self valueForKey:arrayName];
    [arrayName release];
    return [array objectAtIndex:row];
}
@end
```

There's a lot going on there, huh? Let's take the new stuff method by method.

The spin Method

The `spin` method method fires when the user touches the *Spin* button. In it, we first declare a few variables that will help us keep track of whether the user has won. We'll use `win` to keep track of whether we've found three in a row by setting it to YES if we have. We'll use `numInRow` to keep track of how many of the same value we've gotten in a row so far, and we will keep track of the previous component's value in `lastVal` so that we have a way to compare the current value to the previous. We initialize `lastVal` to –1 because we know that value won't match any of the real values:

```
BOOL win = NO;
int numInRow = 1;
int lastVal = -1;
```

Next, we loop through all five components and set each one to a new, randomly generated row selection. We get the count from the `column1` array to do that, which is a shortcut we can use because we know that all five columns have the same number of values:

```
for (int i = 0; i < 5; i++) {
    int newValue = random() % [self.column1 count];
```

We compare the new value to the last value and increment numInRow if it matches. If the value didn't match, we reset numInRow back to 1. We then assign the new value to lastVal so we'll have it to compare the next time through the loop:

```
if (newValue == lastVal)
    numInRow++;
else
    numInRow = 1;
lastVal = newValue;
```

After that, we set the corresponding component to the new value, telling it to animate the change, and we tell the picker to reload that component:

```
[picker selectRow:newValue inComponent:i animated:YES];
[picker reloadComponent:i];
```

The last thing we do each time through the loop is look to see whether we got three in a row and set win to YES if we have:

```
    if (numInRow >= 3)
        win = YES;
}
```

Once we're done with the loop, we set the label to say whether the spin was a win or not:

```
if (win)
    winLabel.text = @"Win!";
else
    winLabel.text = @"";
```

The viewDidLoad Method

The new version of viewDidLoad is somewhat scary looking, isn't it? Don't worry; once we break it down, it won't seem quite so much like the monster in the closet. The first thing we do is load six different images. We do this using a convenience method on the UIImage class called imageNamed:.

```
UIImage *seven = [UIImage imageNamed:@"seven.png"];
UIImage *bar = [UIImage imageNamed:@"bar.png"];
UIImage *crown = [UIImage imageNamed:@"crown.png"];
UIImage *cherry = [UIImage imageNamed:@"cherry.png"];
UIImage *lemon = [UIImage imageNamed:@"lemon.png"];
UIImage *apple = [UIImage imageNamed:@"apple.png"];
```

We've warned you in the past about using convenience class methods to initialize objects because they use the autorelease pool, but we're making an exception here for two reasons. First, this code fires once only when the application launches, and second, it's just so darn convenient. By using this method, we avoid having to determine the location of each image on the iPhone and then use that information to load each image. It's probably saving us a dozen lines of code or more without adding meaningful memory overhead.

Once we have the six images loaded, we then need to create instances of `UIImageView`, one for each image, for each of the five picker components. We do that in a loop:

```
for (int i = 1; i <= 5; i++) {
    UIImageView *sevenView = [[UIImageView alloc] initWithImage:seven];
    UIImageView *barView = [[UIImageView alloc] initWithImage:bar];
    UIImageView *crownView = [[UIImageView alloc] initWithImage:crown];
    UIImageView *cherryView = [[UIImageView alloc]
        initWithImage:cherry];
    UIImageView *lemonView = [[UIImageView alloc] initWithImage:lemon];
    UIImageView *appleView = [[UIImageView alloc] initWithImage:apple];
```

Once we have the image views, we put them into an array. This array is the one that will be used to provide data to the picker for one of its five components.

```
NSArray *imageViewArray = [[NSArray alloc] initWithObjects:
    sevenView, barView, crownView, cherryView, lemonView,
    appleView, nil];
```

Now, we just need to assign this array to one of our five arrays. To do that, we're going to create a string that matches the name of one of the arrays. The first time through the loop, this string will be `column1`, which is the name of the array we'll use to feed the first component in the picker. The second time through, it will equal `column2`, and so on:

```
NSString *fieldName = [[NSString alloc]
            initWithFormat:@"column%d", i];
```

Once we have the name of one of the five arrays, we can assign this array to that property using a very handy method called `setValue:forKey:`. This method lets you set a property based on its name. So, if we call this with a value of "column1", it is exactly the same as calling the mutator method `setColumn1:`.

```
[self setValue:imageViewArray forKey:fieldName];
```

After that, we just do a little memory cleanup:

```
[fieldName release];
[imageViewArray release];
```

```
        [sevenView release];
        [barView release];
        [crownView release];
        [cherryView release];
        [lemonView release];
        [appleView release];
    }
```

The last thing we do in this method is to seed the random number generator. If we don't do that, the game will play the same every time you play it, which gets kind of boring.

```
        srandom(time(NULL));
}
```

That wasn't so bad, was it? But, um, what do we do with those five arrays now that we've filled them up with image views? If you scroll down through the code you just typed, you'll see that two datasource methods look pretty much the same as before, but if you look down further into the delegate methods, you'll see that we're using a completely different delegate method to provide data to the picker. The one that we've used up to now returned an `NSString *`, but this one returns a `UIView *`.

Using this method instead, we can supply the picker with anything that can be drawn into a `UIView`. Of course, there are limitations on what will work here and look good at the same time, given the small size of the picker. But this method gives us a lot more freedom in what we display, though it is a little bit more work.

```
- (UIView *)pickerView:(UIPickerView *)pickerView
        viewForRow:(NSInteger)row
      forComponent:(NSInteger)component
       reusingView:(UIView *)view {
```

This method returns one of the image views from one of the five arrays. To do that, we once again create an `NSString` with the name of one of the arrays. Because component is zero-indexed, we add one to it, which gives us a value between `column1` and `column5` and which will correspond to the component for which the picker is requesting data.

```
        NSString *arrayName = [[NSString alloc] initWithFormat:@"column%d",
            component+1];
```

Once we have the name of the array to use, we retrieve that array using a method called `valueForKey:`. `valueForKey:` is the counterpart to the `setValue:forKey:` method that we used in `viewDidLoad`. Using it is the same as calling the accessor method for the property you specify. So, calling `valueForKey:` and specifying "column1" is the same as using the `column1` accessor method. Once we have the right array for the component, we just return the image view from the array that corresponds to the selected row.

```
    NSArray *array = [self valueForKey:arrayName];
    return [array objectAtIndex:row];
}
```

Wow, take a deep breath. You got through all of it in one piece and now you get to take it for a spin.

Final Details

Our little game is rather fun, especially when you think about how little effort it took to build it. Let's make a couple more tweaks to it, though. There are two things about this game right now that really bug us. The first is that it's so darn quiet. Slot machines aren't quiet! The second thing is that it tells us that we've won before the dials have finished spinning, which is a minor thing, but it does tend to eliminate the anticipation.

First things first: the *07 Pickers/Custom Picker Sounds* folder in the projects archive that accompanies the book contains two sound files: *crunch.wav* and *win.wav*. Add both of these to your project's *Resources* folder. These are the sounds we'll play, respectively, when the users tap the spin button and when they win.

To work with sounds, we'll need access to the iPhone's Audio Toolbox classes. Insert this line at the top of *CustomPickerViewController.m*:

```
#import <AudioToolbox/AudioToolbox.h>
```

Next, we need to add an outlet that will point to the button. While the wheels are spinning, we're going to hide the button. We don't want users tapping the button again until the current spin is all done. Add the following code to *CustomPickerViewController.h*:

```
#import <UIKit/UIKit.h>

@interface CustomPickerViewController : UIViewController
        <UIPickerViewDataSource, UIPickerViewDelegate> {
    UIPickerView *picker;
    UILabel *winLabel;

    NSArray *column1;
    NSArray *column2;
    NSArray *column3;
    NSArray *column4;
    NSArray *column5;

    UIButton *button;
}
@property(nonatomic, retain) IBOutlet UIPickerView *picker;
@property(nonatomic, retain) IBOutlet UILabel *winLabel;
@property(nonatomic, retain) NSArray *column1;
```

```
@property(nonatomic, retain) NSArray *column2;
@property(nonatomic, retain) NSArray *column3;
@property(nonatomic, retain) NSArray *column4;
@property(nonatomic, retain) NSArray *column5;
@property(nonatomic, retain) IBOutlet UIButton *button;
-(IBAction)spin;

@end
```

After you type that and save, double-click *CustomPickerViewController.xib* to open the file in Interface Builder. Once it's open, control-drag from *File's Owner* to the *Spin* button, and connect it to the new `button` outlet we just created. Save, and go back to Xcode.

Now, we need to do a few things in the implementation of our controller class. First, we need to synthesize the accessor and mutator for our new outlet, so open *CustomPickerView Controller.m* and add the following line:

```
@implementation CustomPickerViewController
@synthesize picker;
@synthesize winLabel;
@synthesize column1;
@synthesize column2;
@synthesize column3;
@synthesize column4;
@synthesize column5;
@synthesize button;
...
```

We also need a couple of methods added to our controller class. Add the following two methods to *CustomPickerViewController.m* as the first two methods in the class:

```
-(void)showButton {
    button.hidden = NO;
}

-(void)playWinSound {
    NSString *path = [[NSBundle mainBundle] pathForResource:@"win"
        ofType:@"wav"];
    SystemSoundID soundID;
    AudioServicesCreateSystemSoundID((CFURLRef)[NSURL fileURLWithPath:path]
        , &soundID);
    AudioServicesPlaySystemSound (soundID);
    winLabel.text = @"WIN!";
    [self performSelector:@selector(showButton) withObject:nil
        afterDelay:1.5];
}
```

The first method is used to show the button. We're going to hide the button when the user taps it, because if the wheels are already spinning, there's no point in letting them spin again until they've stopped.

The second method will be called when the user wins. The first line of this method asks the main bundle for the path to the sound called *win.wav*, just as we did when we loaded the property list for the *Dependent* picker view. Once we have the path to that resource, the next three lines of code load the sound file in and play it. Then we set the label to *WIN!* and call the showButton method, but we call the show button method in a special way using a method called performSelector:withObject:afterDelay:. This is a very handy method available to all objects; it lets you call the method sometime in the future, in this case, one and a half seconds in the future, which will give the dials time to spin to their final locations before telling the user the result.

We also have to make some changes to the spin: method. We have to write code to play a sound and to call the playerWon method if the player, in fact, won. Make the following changes to it now:

```
-(IBAction)spin {
    BOOL win = NO;
    int numInRow = 1;
    int lastVal = -1;
    for (int i = 0; i < 5; i++) {
        int newValue = random() % [self.column1 count];

        if (newValue == lastVal)
            numInRow++;
        else
            numInRow = 1;

        lastVal = newValue;
        [picker selectRow:newValue inComponent:i animated:YES];
        [picker reloadComponent:i];
        if (numInRow >= 3)
            win = YES;

    }

    button.hidden = YES;
    NSString *path = [[NSBundle mainBundle] pathForResource:@"crunch"
        ofType:@"wav"];
    SystemSoundID soundID;
    AudioServicesCreateSystemSoundID((CFURLRef)[NSURL fileURLWithPath:path]
        , &soundID);
    AudioServicesPlaySystemSound (soundID);
```

```
    if (win)
        [self performSelector:@selector(playWinSound)
            withObject:nil
            afterDelay:.5];
    else
        [self performSelector:@selector(showButton)
            withObject:nil
            afterDelay:.5];

    winLabel.text = @"";

    if (win)
        winLabel.text = @"WIN!";
    else
        winLabel.text = @"";
}
```

The first line of code we added hides the *Spin!* button. The next four lines play a sound to let the player know they've spun the wheels. Then, instead of setting the label to *WIN!* as soon as we know the user has won, we do something tricky. We call one of the two methods we just created, but we do it after a delay using `performSelector:afterDelay:`. If the user won, we call our `playerWon` method half a second into the future, which will give time for the dials to spin into place; otherwise, we just wait a half a second and reenable the *Spin!* button.

The only thing left is to make sure we release our button outlet, so make the following changes to your `dealloc` and `viewDidUnload` methods:

```
...
- (void)viewDidUnload {
    // Release any retained subviews of the main view.
    // e.g. self.myOutlet = nil;
    self.picker = nil;
    self.winLabel = nil;
    self.column1 = nil;
    self.column2 = nil;
    self.column3 = nil;
    self.column4 = nil;
    self.column5 = nil;
    self.button = nil;
    [super viewDidUnload];
}
- (void)dealloc {
    [picker release];
    [winLabel release];
    [column1 release];
    [column2 release];
```

```
        [column3 release];
        [column4 release];
        [column5 release];
        [button release];
        [super dealloc];
}
...
```

Linking in the Audio Toolbox Framework

If you try to compile now, you'll get another linking error. Turns out, it's those functions we called to load and play sounds. Yeah, they're not in any of the frameworks that are linked in by default. A quick command–double-click on the AudioServicesCreateSystemSoundID function takes us to the header file where it's declared. If we scroll up to the top of that header file, we see this:

```
/*===================================================================
        File:       AudioToolbox/AudioServices.h

        Contains:   API for general high level audio services.

        Copyright:  (c) 2006 - 2008 by Apple Inc., all rights reserved.
...
```

This tells us that the function we're trying to call is part of the Audio Toolbox, so we have to manually link our project to that framework.

Right-click (control-click if you have an older single-button mouse) on the *Frameworks* folder in the *Groups & Files* pane in Xcode and select **Existing Frameworks. . .** from the **Add** sub-menu. Navigate to the frameworks folder for the iPhone simulator at:

/Developer/Platforms/iPhoneSimulator.platform/Developer/SDKs/iPhoneSimulator3.0.sdk/ System/Library/Frameworks

Once you're there, select *AudioToolbox.framework*, and add it to your project. When prompted, select a *Reference Type* of *Relative to Current SDK*. By selecting that option, when you switch between the simulator and iPhone, or between different versions of the iPhone SDK, it will automatically link to the correct version of the AudioToolbox framework. Now, your application should compile just fine, and you can play the game with sound and all.

Final Spin

By now, you certainly should be comfortable with tab bar applications and pickers. In this chapter, you got to build a full-fledged tab bar application from scratch containing five different content views. You learned how to use pickers in a number of different configurations.

You learned how to create pickers with multiple components and even how to make the values in one component dependent on the value selected in another component. You also learned how to make the picker display images rather than just text.

Along the way, you also learned about picker delegates and datasources and saw how to load images, play sounds, create dictionaries from property lists, and link your project to additional frameworks. It was a long chapter, so congratulations on making it through! When you're ready to tackle table views, turn the page, and we'll keep going.

Chapter 8

Introduction to Table Views

*i*n our next chapter, we're going to build a hierarchical navigation-based application similar to the Mail application that ships on the iPhone. Our application will allow the user to drill down into nested lists of data and edit that data. But, before we can do that, you need to master the concept of table views. And that's the goal of this chapter.

Table views are the most common mechanism used to display lists of data to the user. They are highly configurable objects that can be made to look practically any way you want them to. Mail uses table views to show lists of accounts, folders, and messages, but table views are not just limited to the display of textual data. Table views are also used in the YouTube, Settings, and iPod applications, even though these applications all have very different appearances (see Figure 8-1).

Figure 8-1. *Though they all look different, the Settings, iPod, and YouTube applications all use table views to display their data.*

Table View Basics

Tables display lists of data. Each item in a table's list is a row. iPhone tables can have an unlimited number of rows, constrained only by the amount of available memory. iPhone tables can be only one column wide.

A table view is the view object that displays a table's data and is an instance of the class UITableView. Each visible row of the table is implemented by the class UITableViewCell. So a table view is the object that displays the visible part of a table, and a table view cell is responsible for displaying a single row of the table (see Figure 8-2).

Figure 8-2. *Each table view is an instance of UITableView, and each visible row is an instance of UITableViewCell.*

Table views are not responsible for storing your table's data. They store only enough data to draw the rows that are currently visible. Table views get their configuration data from an object that conforms to the UITableViewDelegate protocol and their row data from an object that conforms to the UITableViewDataSource protocol. You'll see how all this works when we get into our sample programs later in the chapter.

As mentioned, all tables are implemented as a single column. But the YouTube application, shown on the right side of Figure 8-1, does have the appearance of having at least two columns, perhaps even three if you count the icons. But no, each row in the table is represented by a single UITableViewCell. Each UITableViewCell object can be configured with an image, some text, and an optional accessory icon, which is a small icon on the right side that we'll cover in detail in the next chapter.

You can put even more data in a cell if you need to. There are two basic ways to do this. One is to add subviews to UITableViewCell; the other is by creating a subclass of UITableViewCell. You can lay the table view cell out in any way you like and include any subviews that you want. So the single column limitation is far less limiting than it probably sounds at first. If this is confusing, don't worry; we'll show you both of these techniques later in this chapter.

Grouped and Plain Tables

Table views come in two basic styles. One style is called **grouped**. Each group in a grouped table is a set of rows embedded in a rounded rectangle, as shown in the leftmost picture in Figure 8-3. Note that a grouped table can consist of a single group.

The other style is called **plain** (in a few places, it's also referred to as **indexed** when an index is used). Plain is the default style. Any table that doesn't feature rounded rectangles is a plain table view.

If your datasource provides the necessary information, the table view will let the user navigate your list using an index that is displayed down the right-hand side. Figure 8-3 shows a grouped table, a plain table without an index, and a plain table with an index (an indexed table).

Figure 8-3. *The same table view displayed as a grouped table (left); a plain table without an index, (middle); and an plain table with an index, also called an indexed table (right)*

Each division of your table is known to your datasource as a **section**. In a grouped table, each group is a section (see Figure 8-4). In an indexed table, each indexed grouping of data is a section. For example, in the indexed tables shown in Figure 8-3, all the names beginning with "A" would be one section, those beginning with "B" another, and so on.

Figure 8-4. *Sections and rows in a grouped table are obvious, but all tables support them.*

Sections have two primary purposes. In a grouped table, each section represents one group. In an indexed table, each section corresponds to one index entry. So, if you wanted to display a list indexed alphabetically with an index entry for every letter, for example, you would have 26 sections, each containing all the values that begin with a particular letter.

CAUTION

It is technically possible to create a grouped table with an index. Even though it's possible, you should not provide an index for a grouped table view. The *iPhone Human Interface Guidelines* specifically state that grouped tables should not provide indexes.

We'll create both types of tables in this chapter.

Implementing a Simple Table

Let's look at the simplest possible example of a table view to get a feel for how it works. In this example, we're just going to display a list of text values.

Create a new project in Xcode. For this chapter, we're going back to the view-based application template, so select that one, and call your project Simple Table.

Designing the View

Expand the *Resources* folder and the *Classes* folder. This is such a simple application that we're not even going to need any outlets or actions, so double-click *Simple_TableView Controller.xib* to open the file in Interface Builder. The *View* window should already be open, so just look in the library for a *Table View* (see Figure 8-5) and drag that over to the *View* window.

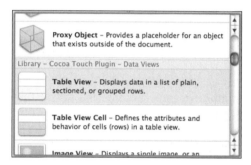

Figure 8-5. *The Table View in the library*

The table view should automatically size itself to the height and width of the view (see Figure 8-6). This is exactly what we want. Table views are designed to take up the entire width of the screen and as much of the height as isn't taken up by your application's navigation bars, tool bars, or tab bars.

After dropping the table view onto the *View* window, it should still be selected. If it's not, single-click it to select it, and press ⌘2 to bring up the connections inspector. You'll notice that the first two available connections for the table view are the same as the first two for the picker view: *dataSource* and *delegate*. Drag from the circle next to each of those connections over to the *File's Owner* icon. By doing this, we are making our controller class both the datasource and delegate for this table. After doing that, save, close, and go back to Xcode.

Figure 8-6. *The View window after the table view is placed*

Writing the Controller

Next stop is our controller class's header file. Single-click *Simple_TableViewController.h*, and add the following code:

```
#import <UIKit/UIKit.h>

@interface Simple_TableViewController : UIViewController
        <UITableViewDelegate, UITableViewDataSource>
{
    NSArray *listData;
}
@property (nonatomic, retain) NSArray *listData;
@end
```

All we're doing here is conforming our class to the two protocols that are needed for it to act as the delegate and datasource for the table view and then declaring an array that will hold the data to be displayed.

Switch over to *Simple_TableViewController.m*, and add the following code at the beginning of the file:

```
#import "Simple_TableViewController.h"

@implementation Simple_TableViewController
@synthesize listData;
- (void)viewDidLoad {
    NSArray *array = [[NSArray alloc] initWithObjects:@"Sleepy", @"Sneezy",
        @"Bashful", @"Happy", @"Doc", @"Grumpy", @"Dopey", @"Thorin",
        @"Dorin", @"Nori", @"Ori", @"Balin", @"Dwalin", @"Fili", @"Kili",
        @"Oin", @"Gloin", @"Bifur", @"Bofur", @"Bombur", nil];
    self.listData = array;
    [array release];
    [super viewDidLoad];
}
...
```

Next, add the following lines of code to the existing `viewDidUnload` and `dealloc` methods:

```
...
- (void)viewDidUnload {
    // Release any retained subviews of the main view.
    // e.g. self.myOutlet = nil;
    self.listData = nil;
    [super viewDidUnload];
}
```

```
- (void)dealloc {
    [listData release];
    [super dealloc];
}
...
```

Finally, add the following code at the end of the file:

```
...
#pragma mark -
#pragma mark Table View Data Source Methods
- (NSInteger)tableView:(UITableView *)tableView
    numberOfRowsInSection:(NSInteger)section {
    return [self.listData count];
}
- (UITableViewCell *)tableView:(UITableView *)tableView
        cellForRowAtIndexPath:(NSIndexPath *)indexPath {

    static NSString *SimpleTableIdentifier = @"SimpleTableIdentifier";

    UITableViewCell *cell = [tableView dequeueReusableCellWithIdentifier:
        SimpleTableIdentifier];
    if (cell == nil) {
        cell = [[[UITableViewCell alloc]
            initWithStyle:UITableViewCellStyleDefault
            reuseIdentifier:SimpleTableIdentifier] autorelease];
    }

    NSUInteger row = [indexPath row];
    cell.textLabel.text = [listData objectAtIndex:row];
    return cell;
}
@end
```

We added three methods to the controller. You should be very comfortable with the first one, viewDidLoad, since we've done similar things in the past. We're simply creating an array of data to pass to the table. In a real application, this array would likely come from another source, such as a text file, property list, or URL.

If you scroll down to the end, you can see we added two datasource methods. The first one, tableView:numberOfRowsInSection:, is used by the table to ask how many rows are in a particular section. As you might expect, the default number of sections is one, and this method will be called to get the number of rows in the one section that makes up the list. We just return the number of items in our array.

The next method probably requires a little explanation, so let's look at it more closely:

```
- (UITableViewCell *)tableView:(UITableView *)tableView
        cellForRowAtIndexPath:(NSIndexPath *)indexPath {
```

This method is called by the table view when it needs to draw one of its rows. You'll notice that the second argument to this method is an NSIndexPath instance. This is the mechanism that table views use to wrap the section and row into a single object. To get the row or the section out of an NSIndexPath, you just call either its row method or its section method, both of which return an int.

The first parameter, tableView, is a reference to the table doing the asking. This allows us to create classes that act as a datasource for multiple tables.

Next, we declare a static string instance.

```
static NSString *SimpleTableIdentifier = @"SimpleTableIdentifier";
```

This string will be used as a key to represent a single kind of table cell. We'll be using only one kind of cell in this table, so we define a single identifier. A table view can display only a few rows at a time on iPhone's small screen, but the table itself can conceivably hold considerably more. Remember that each row in the table is represented by an instance of UITableViewCell, which is a subclass of UIView, which means each row can contain sub-views. With a large table, this could represent a huge amount of overhead if the table were to try and keep one table view cell instance for every row in the table regardless of whether that row was currently being displayed. Fortunately, tables don't work that way.

Instead, as table view cells scroll off the screen, they are placed into a queue of cells available to be reused. If the system runs low on memory, the table view will get rid of the cells in the queue, but as long as it's got some available memory for them, it will hold on to them in case you want to use them again.

Every time a table view cell rolls off the screen, there's a pretty good chance that another one just rolled onto the screen on the other side. If that new row can just reuse one of the cells that has already rolled off the screen, the system can avoid the overhead associated with constantly creating and releasing those views. To take advantage of this mechanism, we'll ask the table view to give us one of its **dequeued** cells of the type we want. Note that we're making use of the NSString identifier we declared earlier. In effect, we're asking for a reusable cell of type SimpleTableIdentifier:

```
UITableViewCell *cell = [tableView dequeueReusableCellWithIdentifier:
    SimpleTableIdentifier];
```

Now, it's completely possible that the table view won't have any spare cells, so we check cell after the call to see whether it's nil. If it is, we manually create a new table view cell using that identifier string. At some point, we'll inevitably reuse one of the cells we create here, so we need to make sure it has the correct type.

```
if (cell == nil) {
    cell = [[[UITableViewCell alloc]
            initWithStyle:UITableViewCellStyleDefault
            reuseIdentifier: SimpleTableIdentifier] autorelease];
}
```

We now have a table view cell that we can return for the table view to use. All we need to do now is place whatever information we want displayed in this cell. Displaying text in a row of a table is a very common task, so the table view cell provides a UILabel property called textLabel that we can set in order to display strings. To do that, all we have to do is get the right string out of our listData array and use it to set the cell's textLabel.

NOTE

Are you curious about what UITableViewCellStyleDefault does? Hold onto that thought for just a few minutes, and we'll show you!

To get the correct value, however, we need to know which row the table view is asking for. We get that information out of the indexPath variable, like so:

```
NSUInteger row = [indexPath row];
```

We use the row number of the table to get the corresponding string from the array, assign it to the cell's textLabel.text property, and then return the cell.

```
    cell.textLabel.text = [listData objectAtIndex:row];
    return cell;
}
```

That wasn't so bad, was it? Compile and run your application and you should see the array values displayed in a table view (see Figure 8-7).

NOTE

Using cell.textLabel.text will work only when working in the iPhone SDK 3.0 and later. In prior versions, you would use cell.text instead.

Figure 8-7. *The Simple Table application, in all its dwarven glory*

Adding an Image

It'd be nice if we could add an image to each row. Guess we'd have to create a subclass of UITableViewCell or add subviews in order to do that, huh? Actually, no, not if you can live with the image being on the left-hand side of each row. The default table view cell can handle that situation just fine. Let's check it out.

In the *08 Simple Table* folder, in the project archive, grab the file called *star.png*, and add it to your project's *Resources* folder. *star.png* is a small icon we prepared just for this project.

Next, let's get to the code. In the file *Simple_TableViewController.m*, add the following code to the tableView:cellForRowAtIndexPath: method:

```
- (UITableViewCell *)tableView:(UITableView *)tableView
        cellForRowAtIndexPath:(NSIndexPath *)indexPath {

    static NSString *SimpleTableIdentifier = @" SimpleTableIdentifier ";
```

```
    UITableViewCell *cell = [tableView dequeueReusableCellWithIdentifier:
        SimpleTableIdentifier];
    if (cell == nil) {
        cell = [[[UITableViewCell alloc] initWithFrame:CGRectZero
            reuseIdentifier: SimpleTableIdentifier] autorelease];
    }

    UIImage *image = [UIImage imageNamed:@"star.png"];
    cell.imageView.image = image;

    NSUInteger row = [indexPath row];
    cell.textLabel.text = [listData objectAtIndex:row];

    return cell;
}
@end
```

Yep, that's it. Each cell has an `imageView` property. Each `imageView` has an `image` property, as well as a `highlightedImage` property. The image appears to the left of the cell's text and is replaced by the `highlightedImage`, if one is provided, when the cell is selected.

We just set the cell's `imageView.image` property to whatever image we want to display. If you compile and run your application now, you should get a list with a bunch of nice little star icons to the left of each row (see Figure 8-8). Of course, if we wanted to, we could have included a different image for each row in the table. Or, with very little effort, we could have used one icon for all of Mr. Disney's dwarves and a different one for Mr. Tolkein's.

If you like, make a copy of *star.png*, colorize it a bit, add it to the project, load it with `imageNamed:`, and use it to set `imageView.highlightedImage`. Now, if you click a cell, your new image will be drawn. If you don't feel like coloring, use the *star2.png* icon we provided in the project archive.

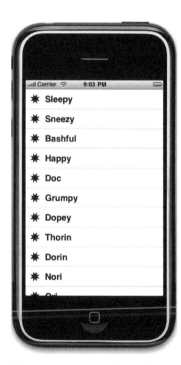

Figure 8-8. *We used the cell's image property to add an image to each of the table view's cells.*

NOTE

It's okay to use imageNamed: in this way. UIImage uses a caching mechanism based on the filename, so it won't load a new image property each time, but instead will use the already cached version.

Table View Cell Styles

Versions of the iPhone SDK prior to SDK 3.0 were limited to a single cell style, the one shown in Figure 8-8. With the release of SDK 3.0, Apple added a bit more variety to the standard table cell design.

For starters, Apple introduced the concept of a cell style. Cell styles make use of three different cell elements:

- **Image**: If an image is part of the specified style, the image is displayed to the left of the cell's text.

- **Text Label**: This is the cell's primary text. In the style we used earlier, `UITableViewCellStyleDefault`, the text label is the only text shown in the cell.

- **Detail Text Label**: This is the cell's secondary text, usually used as an explanatory note or label. We'll show an example of a style that uses detail text in a moment.

To see what these new style additions look like, add the following code to `tableView:cellF orRowAtIndexPath:` in *Simple_TableViewController.m*:

```
- (UITableViewCell *)tableView:(UITableView *)tableView
        cellForRowAtIndexPath:(NSIndexPath *)indexPath {

    static NSString *SimpleTableIdentifier = @"SimpleTableIdentifier";

    UITableViewCell *cell = [tableView dequeueReusableCellWithIdentifier:
                            SimpleTableIdentifier];
    if (cell == nil) {
        cell = [[[UITableViewCell alloc]
            initWithStyle:UITableViewCellStyleDefault
            reuseIdentifier: SimpleTableIdentifier] autorelease];
    }

    UIImage *image = [UIImage imageNamed:@"star.png"];
    cell.image = image;

    NSUInteger row = [indexPath row];
    cell.textLabel.text = [listData objectAtIndex:row];

    if (row < 7)
        cell.detailTextLabel.text = @"Mr. Disney";
    else
        cell.detailTextLabel.text = @"Mr. Tolkein";

    return cell;
}
```

All we've done here is set the cell's detail text. We use the string @"Mr. Disney" for the first seven rows and @"Mr. Tolkein" for the rest. When you run this code, each cell will look like just the same as it did before (see Figure 8-9). That's because we are using the style UITableViewCell-StyleDefault, which does not make use of the detail text.

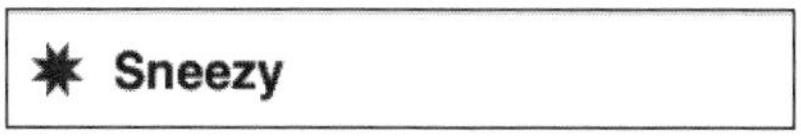

Figure 8-9. *The default cell style shows the image and text label in a straight row.*

Figure 8-10. *The subtitle style shows the detail text in smaller, gray letters below the text label.*

Now, change UITableViewCellStyleDefault to UITableViewCellStyleSubtitle and run again. With the subtitle style, both text elements are shown, one below the other (Figure 8-10).

Change UITableViewCellStyleSubtitle to UITableViewCellStyleValue1 and then build and run. This style doesn't use the cell's image, but places the text label and detail text label on the same line on opposite sides of the cell (Figure 8-11).

Figure 8-11. *The Style Value 1 will place the text label on the left side in black letters, the detail text right-justified on the right side in blue letters, but doesn't show the cell's image.*

One last time, let's change UITableViewCellStyleValue1 to UITableViewCellStyleValue2. This format is often used to display information along with a descriptive label. It also doesn't show the

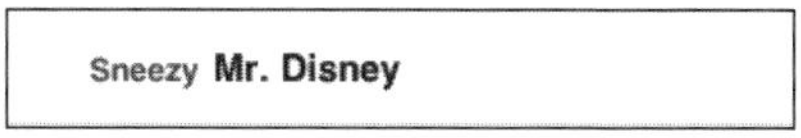

Figure 8-12. *The Style Value 2 places the detail text label in blue letters to the left of the text label.*

cell's icon, but places the detail text label to the left of the text label. In this layout, the detail text label acts as a label describing the type of data held in the text label.

Now that you've seen the cell styles that are available, go ahead and change back to using UITableViewCellStyleDefault before continuing on. Later, you'll see how to customize the appearance of your table. But before decide to do that, make sure you consider the available styles to see whether one of them will suit your needs.

Additional Configurations

You may have noticed that we made our controller both the datasource and delegate for this table view, but up to now, we haven't actually implemented any of the methods from UITableViewDelegate. Unlike picker views, simpler table views don't require a delegate to do their thing. The datasource provides all the data needed to draw the table. The purpose of the delegate is to configure the appearance of the table view and to handle certain user interactions. Let's take a look at a few of the configuration options now. We'll look at more in the next chapter.

Setting the Indent Level

The delegate can be used to specify that some rows should be indented. In the file *Simple_TableViewController.m*, add the following method to your code, just above the @end declaration:

```
#pragma mark -
#pragma mark Table Delegate Methods

- (NSInteger)tableView:(UITableView *)tableView
    indentationLevelForRowAtIndexPath:(NSIndexPath *)indexPath {
        NSUInteger row = [indexPath row];
    return row;
}
```

This method sets the **indent level** for each row to its row number, so row 0 will have an indent level of 0, row 1 will have an indent level of 1, and so on. An indent level is simply an integer that tells the table view to move that row a little to the right. The higher the number, the further to the right the row will be indented. You might use this technique, for example, to indicate that one row is subordinate to another row, as Mail does when representing subfolders.

When we run the application again, you can see that each row is now drawn a little further to the right than the last one (see Figure 8-13).

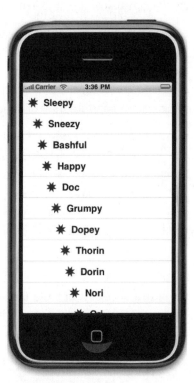

Figure 8-13. *Each row of the table is drawn with an indent level higher than the row before it.*

Handling Row Selection

The table's delegate can use two methods to determine if the user has selected a particular row. One method gets called before the row gets selected and can be used to prevent the row from being selected or can even change which row gets selected. Let's implement that method and specify that the first row is not selectable. Add the following method to the end of *Simple_TableViewController.m*, just before the @end declaration:

```
-(NSIndexPath *)tableView:(UITableView *)tableView
    willSelectRowAtIndexPath:(NSIndexPath *)indexPath {
    NSUInteger row = [indexPath row];
```

```
    if (row == 0)
        return nil;

    return indexPath;
}
```

This method gets passed `indexPath`, which represents the item that's about to get selected. Our code looks at which row is about to be selected. If the row is the first row, which is always index zero, then it returns `nil`, which indicates that no row should actually be selected. Otherwise, it returns `indexPath`, which is how we indicate that it's OK for the selection to proceed.

Before you compile and run, let's also implement the delegate method that gets called after a row has been selected, which is typically where you'll actually handle the selection. This is where you take whatever action is appropriate when the user selects a row. In the next chapter, we'll use this method to handle the drill-downs, but in this chapter, we'll just throw up an alert to show that the row was selected. Add the following method to the bottom of *Simple_TableViewController.m*, just before the @end declaration again.

```
- (void)tableView:(UITableView *)tableView
        didSelectRowAtIndexPath:(NSIndexPath *)indexPath {
    NSUInteger row = [indexPath row];
    NSString *rowValue = [listData objectAtIndex:row];

    NSString *message = [[NSString alloc] initWithFormat:
        @"You selected %@", rowValue];
    UIAlertView *alert = [[UIAlertView alloc]
        initWithTitle:@"Row Selected!"
              message:message
             delegate:nil
    cancelButtonTitle:@"Yes I Did"
    otherButtonTitles:nil];
    [alert show];

    [message release];
    [alert release];
    [tableView deselectRowAtIndexPath:indexPath animated:YES];
}
```

Once you've added this method, compile and run and take it for a spin. See whether you can select the first row (you shouldn't be able to), and then select one of the other rows. The selected row should highlight, and then your alert should pop up telling you which row you selected while the selected row fades in the background (see Figure 8-14).

Note that you can also modify the index path before you pass it back, which would cause a different row and/or section to be selected. You won't do that very often, as you should have a very good reason for changing the user's selection on them. In the vast majority of cases, when you use this method, you will either return indexPath unmodified to allow the selection, or else nil to or disallow it.

Figure 8-14. *In this example, the first row is not selectable, and an alert is displayed when any other row is selected. This was done using the delegate methods.*

Changing Font Size and Row Height

Let's say that we want to change the size of the font being used in the table view. In most situations, you shouldn't override the default font; it's what users expect to see. But there are valid reasons to do this at times. Add the following line of code to your tableView:cellForRowAtIndexPath: method and then compile and run:

```
- (UITableViewCell *)tableView:(UITableView *)tableView
        cellForRowAtIndexPath:(NSIndexPath *)indexPath
{
```

```
    static NSString *SimpleTableIdentifier = @"SimpleTableIdentifier";

    UITableViewCell *cell = [tableView dequeueReusableCellWithIdentifier:
                            SimpleTableIdentifier];
    if (cell == nil) {
        cell = [[[UITableViewCell alloc]
            initWithStyle:UITableViewCellStyleDefault
            reuseIdentifier: SimpleTableIdentifier] autorelease];

    }

    UIImage *image = [UIImage imageNamed:@"star.png"];
    cell.image = image;

    NSUInteger row = [indexPath row];
    cell.textLabel.text = [listData objectAtIndex:row];
    cell.textLabel.font = [UIFont boldSystemFontOfSize:50];

    if (row < 7)
        cell.detailTextLabel.text = @"Mr. Disney";
    else
        cell.detailTextLabel.text = @"Mr. Tolkein";

    return cell;
}
```

When you run the application now, the values in your list get drawn really large, but they don't exactly fit in the row (see Figure 8-15).

Well, here comes the table view delegate to the rescue! The table view delegate can specify the height of the table rows. In fact, it can specify unique values for each row if you need to. Go ahead and add this method to your controller class, just before @end:

```
- (CGFloat)tableView:(UITableView *)tableView
    heightForRowAtIndexPath:(NSIndexPath *)indexPath {
    return 70;
}
```

We've just told the table view to set the row height for all rows to 70 pixels tall. Compile and run, and your table's rows should be much taller now (see Figure 8-16).

Figure 8-15. *Look how nice and big! But, um, it would be nice if we could see everything.*

Figure 8-16. *Changing the row size using the delegate*

What Else Can the Delegate Do?

There are more tasks that the delegate handles, but most of the remaining ones come into play when we start working with hierarchical data in the next chapter. To learn more, use the documentation browser to explore the UITableViewDelegate protocol and see what other methods are available.

Customizing Table View Cells

You can do a lot with table views right out of the box, but often, you will want to format the data for each row in ways that simply aren't supported by UITableViewCell directly. In those cases, there are two basic approaches, one that involves adding subviews to UITableViewCell and a second that involves creating a subclass of UITableViewCell. Let's look at both techniques.

The Cells Application

To show how to use custom cells, we're going to create a new application with another table view. In each row, we'll display two lines of information along with two labels (see Figure 8-17). Our application will display the name and color of a series of potentially familiar computer models, and we'll display both of those pieces of information in the same table cell by adding subviews to the table view cell.

Adding Subviews to the Table View Cell

Although the four provided table view cell styles offer a fair amount of flexibility, there will still be situations where you need more flexibility than those built-in styles allow. We're going to create a project that adds subviews to the table view cell in order to work around that limitation, enabling us to display two lines of data in each cell.

Create a new Xcode project using the view-based application template. Name the project *Cells*. Double-click *CellsViewController.xib* to open the nib file in Interface Builder. Add a *Table View* to the main view, and set its delegate and datasource to *File's Owner* as we did in the previous section. Save the nib, and come back to Xcode. You can refer to the "Building the View" section earlier in the chapter for the exact steps if you need to.

Figure 8-17. *Adding subviews to the table view cell can give you multiline rows.*

Modifying the Controller Header File

Single-click *CellsViewController.h*, and add the following code:

```
#import <UIKit/UIKit.h>
#define kNameValueTag     1
#define kColorValueTag    2


@interface CellsViewController : UIViewController
    <UITableViewDataSource, UITableViewDelegate>
{
    NSArray     *computers;
}
@property (nonatomic, retain) NSArray *computers;
@end
```

The first thing that you'll notice here is that we have defined two constants. We're going to use these in a few moments to assign **tags** to some of the subviews that we'll be adding to the table view cell. We're going to add four subviews to the cell, and two of those need to be changed for every row. In order to do that, we need some mechanism that will allow us to retrieve the two fields from the cell when we go to update that cell with a particular row's data. If we set unique tag values for each label that we'll need to use again, we'll be able to retrieve them from the table view cell and set their value.

Implementing the Controller's Code

In our controller, we need to set up some data to use, and then implement the table data-source methods to feed that data to the table. Single-click *CellsViewController.m*, and add the following code at the beginning of the file:

```
#import "CellsViewController.h"

@implementation CellsViewController
@synthesize computers;
- (void)viewDidLoad {

    NSDictionary *row1 = [[NSDictionary alloc] initWithObjectsAndKeys:
                    @"MacBook", @"Name", @"White", @"Color", nil];
    NSDictionary *row2 = [[NSDictionary alloc] initWithObjectsAndKeys:
                    @"MacBook Pro", @"Name", @"Silver", @"Color", nil];
    NSDictionary *row3 = [[NSDictionary alloc] initWithObjectsAndKeys:
                    @"iMac", @"Name", @"White", @"Color", nil];
    NSDictionary *row4 = [[NSDictionary alloc] initWithObjectsAndKeys:
                    @"Mac Mini", @"Name", @"White", @"Color", nil];
    NSDictionary *row5 = [[NSDictionary alloc] initWithObjectsAndKeys:
                    @"Mac Pro", @"Name", @"Silver", @"Color", nil];

    NSArray *array = [[NSArray alloc] initWithObjects:row1, row2,
                    row3, row4, row5, nil];
    self.computers = array;

    [row1 release];
    [row2 release];
    [row3 release];
    [row4 release];
    [row5 release];
    [array release];
}
...
```

Of course, we need to be good memory citizens, so make the following changes to the existing `dealloc` and `viewDidUnload` methods:

```
...
- (void)viewDidUnload {
    // Release any retained subviews of the main view.
    // e.g. self.myOutlet = nil;
    self.computers = nil;
}
- (void)dealloc {
    [computers release];
    [super dealloc];
}
...
```

and add this code at the end of the file, above the @end declaration:

```
...
#pragma mark -
#pragma mark Table Data Source Methods
- (NSInteger)tableView:(UITableView *)tableView
    numberOfRowsInSection:(NSInteger)section {
    return [self.computers count];
}
-(UITableViewCell *)tableView:(UITableView *)tableView
    cellForRowAtIndexPath:(NSIndexPath *)indexPath {
    static NSString *CellTableIdentifier = @"CellTableIdentifier ";

    UITableViewCell *cell = [tableView dequeueReusableCellWithIdentifier:
        CellTableIdentifier];
    if (cell == nil) {
        cell = [[[UITableViewCell alloc]
            initWithStyle:UITableViewCellStyleDefault
            reuseIdentifier:CellTableIdentifier] autorelease];

        CGRect nameLabelRect = CGRectMake(0, 5, 70, 15);
        UILabel *nameLabel = [[UILabel alloc] initWithFrame:nameLabelRect];
        nameLabel.textAlignment = UITextAlignmentRight;
        nameLabel.text = @"Name:";
        nameLabel.font = [UIFont boldSystemFontOfSize:12];
        [cell.contentView addSubview: nameLabel];
        [nameLabel release];

        CGRect colorLabelRect = CGRectMake(0, 26, 70, 15);
        UILabel *colorLabel = [[UILabel alloc] initWithFrame:
            colorLabelRect];
        colorLabel.textAlignment = UITextAlignmentRight;
        colorLabel.text = @"Color:";
        colorLabel.font = [UIFont boldSystemFontOfSize:12];
        [cell.contentView addSubview: colorLabel];
        [colorLabel release];
```

```
            CGRect nameValueRect = CGRectMake(80, 5, 200, 15);
            UILabel *nameValue = [[UILabel alloc] initWithFrame:
                nameValueRect];
            nameValue.tag = kNameValueTag;
            [cell.contentView addSubview:nameValue];
            [nameValue release];

            CGRect colorValueRect = CGRectMake(80, 25, 200, 15);
            UILabel *colorValue = [[UILabel alloc] initWithFrame:
                colorValueRect];
            colorValue.tag = kColorValueTag;
            [cell.contentView addSubview:colorValue];
            [colorValue release];

        }

        NSUInteger row = [indexPath row];
        NSDictionary *rowData = [self.computers objectAtIndex:row];
        UILabel *name = (UILabel *)[cell.contentView viewWithTag:
            kNameValueTag];
        name.text = [rowData objectForKey:@"Name"];

        UILabel *color = (UILabel *)[cell.contentView viewWithTag:
            kColorValueTag];
        color.text = [rowData objectForKey:@"Color"];
        return cell;
    }
@end
```

The viewDidLoad method this time creates a bunch of dictionaries. Each dictionary contains the name and color information for one row in the table. The name for that row is held in the dictionary under the key Name, and the color is held under the key Color. We stick all the dictionaries into a single array, which is our data for this table.

Let's focus on tableView:cellForRowWithIndexPath:, since that's where we're really getting into some new stuff. The first two lines of code are just like our earlier versions. We create an identifier and ask the table to dequeue a table view cell if it has one.

If the table doesn't have any cells available for reuse, we have to create a new cell. When we do this, we also need to create and add the subviews that we'll be using to implement our two-line-per-row table. Let's look at that code a little more closely. First, we create a cell. This is, essentially, the same technique as before. We specify the default style, although the style actually won't matter, because we'll be adding our own subviews to display our data rather than using the provided ones.

```
cell = [[[UITableViewCell alloc]
    initWithStyle:UITableViewCellStyleDefault
    reuseIdentifier:CellTableIdentifier] autorelease];
```

After that, we create four UILabels and add them to the table view cell. The table view cell already has a UIView subview called contentView, which it uses to group all of its subviews, much the way we grouped those two switches inside of a UIView back in Chapter 4. As a result, we don't add the labels as subviews directly to the table view cell, but rather to its contentView.

```
[cell.contentView addSubview:colorValue];
```

Two of these labels contain static text. The label nameLabel contains the text *Name:* and the label colorLabel contains the text *Color:*. Those are just static labels that we won't change. The other two labels, however, will be used to display our row-specific data. Remember, we need some way of retrieving these fields later on, so we assign values to both of them. For example, we assign the constant kNameValueTag into nameValue's tag field:

```
nameValue.tag = kNameValueTag;
```

In a moment, we'll use that tag to retrieve the correct label from the cell.

Once we're done creating our new cell, we use the indexPath argument that was passed in to determine which row the table is requesting a cell for and then use that row value to grab the correct dictionary for the requested row. Remember that that dictionary has two key/value pairs, one with name and another with color.

```
NSUInteger row = [indexPath row];
NSDictionary *rowData = [self.computers objectAtIndex:row];
```

Remember those tags we set before? Well, here, we use them to retrieve the label whose value we need to set.

```
UILabel *name = (UILabel *)[cell.contentView viewWithTag:kNameValueTag];
```

Once we have that label, we just set its text to one of the values we pull from the dictionary that represents this row.

```
name.text = [rowData objectForKey:@"Name"];
```

Compile and run your application, and you should get rows with two lines of data in it, just as in Figure 8-17. Being able to add views to the table view provides a lot more flexibility than using the standard table view cell alone, but it can get a little tedious creating, positioning, and adding all the subviews programmatically. Gosh, it sure would be nice if we could design the table view cell in Interface Builder, wouldn't it?

Using a Custom Subclass of UITableViewCell

Well, we're in luck. It just so happens that you can use Interface Builder to design your table cell views. We're going to re-create that same two-line interface we just built in code using Interface Builder. To do this, we'll create a subclass of `UITableViewCell` and a new nib file that will contain the table view cell. Then, when we need a table view cell to represent a row, instead of adding subviews to a standard table view cell, we'll just load in our subclass from the nib file and use two outlets we'll add to set the name and color. Make sense? Let's do it.

Right-click (or control-click) on the *Classes* folder in Xcode and select **New File. . .** from the **Add** submenu that comes up, or just press ⌘N. When the new file assistant comes up, select *Cocoa Touch Class* from the left pane, select Objective-C class in the upper-right pane, and then select *UITableViewCell subclass* from the pop-up in the lower-right pane. Click the *Next* button; give the new file a name of *CustomCell.m*; and make sure that *Also create "CustomCell.h"* is checked.

Once that file is created, right-click the *Resources* folder in Xcode, and select **Add▶New File. . .** again. This time, in the left pane of the new file assistant, click *User Interface*, and from the upper right pane, select *Empty XIB*. When prompted for a name, type *CustomCell.xib*.

Creating the UITableViewCell Subclass

Now that we have all the new files we need, let's go ahead and create our new subclass of `UITableViewCell`.

We're going to use outlets in our subclass to make it easier to set the value that needs to change for each row. We could use tags again and avoid creating a subclass altogether, but by doing it this way, our code will be much more concise and easy to read, because we'll be able to set the labels on each row's cell just by setting properties, like so:

```
cell.nameLabel = @"Foo";
```

Single-click *CustomCell.h*, and add the following code:

```
#import <UIKit/UIKit.h>

@interface CustomCell : UITableViewCell {
    UILabel *nameLabel;
    UILabel *colorLabel;
}
@property (nonatomic, retain) IBOutlet UILabel *nameLabel;
@property (nonatomic, retain) IBOutlet UILabel *colorLabel;
@end
```

That's all we need to do here, so let's switch over to *CustomCell.m* and add two more lines:

```
#import "CustomCell.h"

@implementation CustomCell
@synthesize nameLabel;
@synthesize colorLabel;
- (id)initWithFrame:(CGRect)frame
    reuseIdentifier:(NSString *)reuseIdentifier {
    if (self = [super initWithFrame:frame
        reuseIdentifier:reuseIdentifier]) {
        // Initialization code
    }
    return self;
}

- (void)setSelected:(BOOL)selected animated:(BOOL)animated {

    [super setSelected:selected animated:animated];

    // Configure the view for the selected state
}

- (void)dealloc {
    [nameLabel release];
    [colorLabel release];
    [super dealloc];
}

@end
```

Make sure you save both of those, and we're done with our custom subclass.

Designing the Table View Cell in Interface Builder

Next, double-click *CustomCell.xib* to open the file in Interface Builder. There are only two icons in this nib's main window: *File's Owner* and *First Responder*. Look in the library for a *Table View Cell* (see Figure 8-18), and drag one of those over to your nib's main window.

Make sure the table view cell is selected, and press ⌘4 to bring up the identity inspector. Change the class from *UITableViewCell* to *CustomCell*.

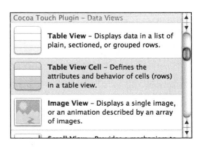

Figure 8-18. *Table View Cell in the library*

After that, press ⌘3 to bring up the size inspector, and change the table view cell's height from *44* to *65*. That will give us a little bit more room to play with.

Finally, press ⌘1 to go to the attributes inspector (Figure 8-19). The first field you'll see there is *Identifier*, and that's the reuse identifier that we've been using in our code. If this does not ring a bell, scan back through the chapter and look for SimpleTableIdentifier. Set the *Identifier* to *CustomCellIdentifier*.

Remember, even though UITableViewCell is a subclass of UIView, it uses a content view to hold and group its subviews. Double-click the *Custom Cell* icon, which will open a new window. You'll notice a gray dashed rounded rectangle labeled *Content View* (see Figure 8-20). That's Interface Builder's way of telling you that you should add something, so look in the library for a *View*, and drag that onto the *Custom Cell* window.

When you release the view, it will be the wrong size for our window. Let's fix this. With the new view selected, go to the size inspector. Change *View*'s size and position to match the *Custom Cell* by setting *x* to *0*, *y* to *0*, *w* to *320*, and *h* to *65*.

Now we're all set. We have a canvas we can use to design our table view cell in Interface Builder. Let's do this.

Drag four labels over from the library to the *Custom Cell* window, and place and rename them as shown in Figure 8-21. To make the *Name:* and *Color:* fields bold, select them, and press ⌘B. Next, select the upper right label, and make it wider. Drag its right edge all the way to the right blue line. Do the same for the lower right label. We want to make sure we have plenty of room for the name and color data.

Now, control-drag from the *Custom Cell* icon to the top-right label on the view, assigning it to the outlet *nameLabel*. Then, control-drag again from the *Custom Cell* icon to the lower right label, assigning it to the *colorLabel* outlet.

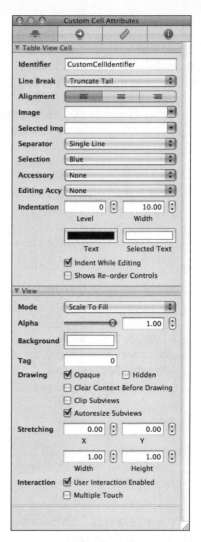

Figure 8-19. *The attribute inspector for a table view cell*

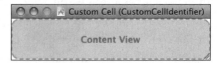

Figure 8-20. *The table view cell's window*

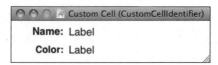

Figure 8-21. *The table view cell's design*

<u>NOTE</u>

Although the blue margins are useful in this context for positioning labels against the left and the right, because the cells will be drawn with a separator against it, the top and bottom guides cannot be relied on here. We ended up putting the top labels a little higher than the guides suggested, and the bottom labels a little lower to get everything to look right when the program is run.

You might be wondering why we're not doing anything with the *File's Owner* icon. The reason is that we just don't need to. We're using this table cell to display data, but all the interaction with the user is going to go through the table view, so it doesn't need its own controller class. We're really just using the nib as a sort of template so we can design our table cells visually.

Save the nib; close it; and let's go back to Xcode.

Using the New Table View Cell

To use the cell we designed, we have to make some pretty drastic changes to the tableView:cellForRowAtIndexPath: method in *CellsViewController.m*. Delete the one you currently have, and replace it with this new version:

```
- (UITableViewCell *)tableView:(UITableView *)tableView
        cellForRowAtIndexPath:(NSIndexPath *)indexPath {
    static NSString *CustomCellIdentifier = @"CustomCellIdentifier ";

    CustomCell *cell = (CustomCell *)[tableView
        dequeueReusableCellWithIdentifier: CustomCellIdentifier];
    if (cell == nil) {
        NSArray *nib = [[NSBundle mainBundle] loadNibNamed:@"CustomCell"
                                            owner:self options:nil];
        for (id oneObject in nib)
            if ([oneObject isKindOfClass:[CustomCell class]])
                cell = (CustomCell *)oneObject;
    }
    NSUInteger row = [indexPath row];
    NSDictionary *rowData = [self.computers objectAtIndex:row];
    cell.colorLabel.text = [rowData objectForKey:@"Color"];
    cell.nameLabel.text = [rowData objectForKey:@"Name"];
    return cell;
}
```

While you're mucking around in *CellsViewController.m*, go ahead and add this line near the top:

```
#import "CustomCell.h"
```

Because we've designed the table view cell in a nib file, if there are no reusable cells, we simply load one from the nib. When we load the nib, we get an array that contains all the objects in the nib. The objects and order of those objects is undocumented and has changed in the past, so rather than rely on the table view cell being at a specific index in the nib, we'll loop through all the objects in the nib and look for an instance of our `CustomCell` class.

There's one other addition we have to make. Because we change the height of our table view cell from the default value, we have to inform the table view of that fact; otherwise, it won't leave enough space for the cell to display properly. We do that by adding this delegate method to *CellsViewController.m*, just before the @end:

```
- (CGFloat)tableView:(UITableView *)tableView
    heightForRowAtIndexPath:(NSIndexPath *)indexPath {
    return kTableViewRowHeight;
}
```

Unfortunately, we can't get this value from the cell because this delegate method may be called before the cell exists, so we have to hard-code the value. Add this constant definition to the top of *CellsViewController.h*, and delete the tag constants, which are no longer needed.

```
#define kTableViewRowHeight    66
#define kNameValueTag          1
#define kColorValueTag         2
```

That's it. Build and run. Now your two line table cells are based on your mad Interface Builder design skillz.

Grouped and Indexed Sections

Our next project will explore another fundamental aspect of tables. We're still going to use a single table view—no hierarchies yet—but we're going to divide data into sections. Create a new Xcode project using the view-based application template again, this time calling it *Sections*.

Building the View

Open the *Classes* and *Resources* folders, and double-click *SectionsViewController.xib* to open the file in Interface Builder. Drop a table view onto the *View* window, as we did before. Then press ⌘2, and connect the *dataSource* and *delegate* connections to the *File's Owner* icon.

Next, make sure the table view is selected, and press ⌘1 to bring up the attributes inspector. Change the table view's *Style* from *Plain* to *Grouped* (see Figure 8-22). If you need a reminder, we discussed the difference between indexed and grouped styles at the beginning of the chapter. Save and return to Xcode.

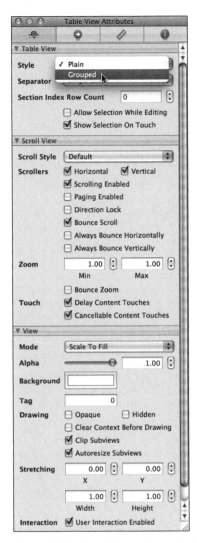

Figure 8-22. *The attributes inspector for the table view*

Importing the Data

This project needs a fair amount of data to do its thing. To save you a few hours worth of typing, we've provided another property list for your tabling pleasure. Grab the file named *sortednames.plist* from the *08 Sections* folder in the projects archive that came with this book, and add it to your project's *Resources* folder.

Once it's added to your project, single-click *sortednames.plist* just to get a sense of what it looks like (see Figure 8-23). It's a property list that contains a dictionary, with one entry for each letter of the alphabet. Underneath each letter is a list of names that start with that letter.

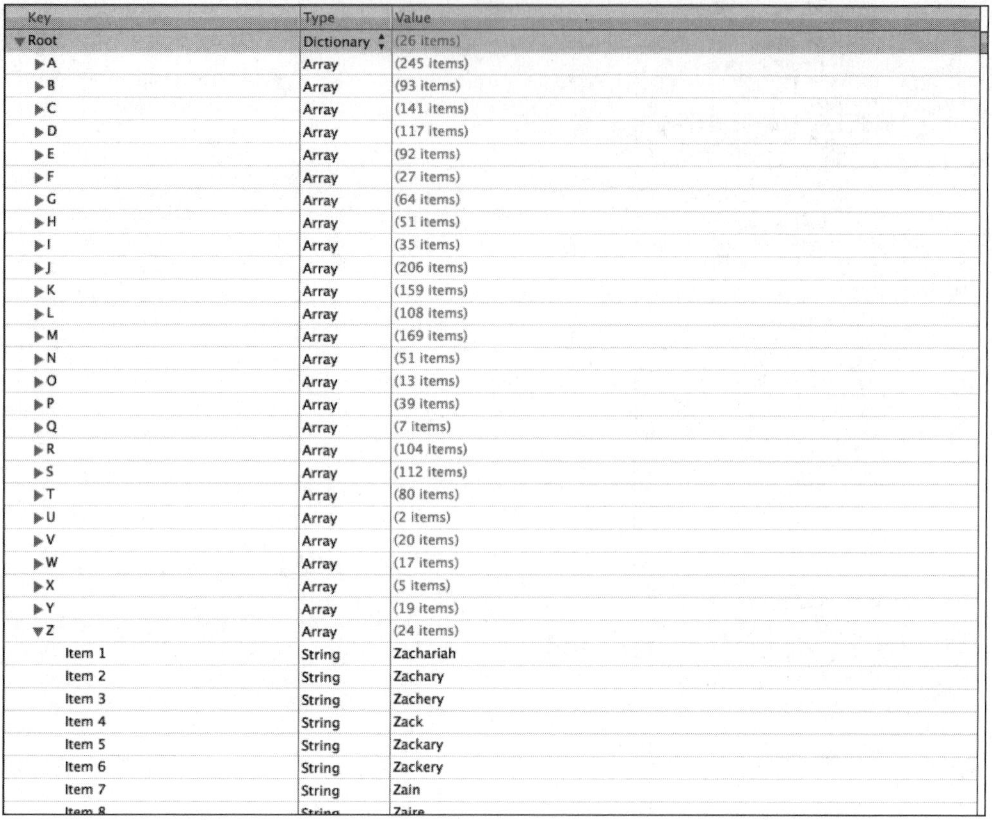

Key	Type	Value
▼ Root	Dictionary ⬍	(26 items)
▶ A	Array	(245 items)
▶ B	Array	(93 items)
▶ C	Array	(141 items)
▶ D	Array	(117 items)
▶ E	Array	(92 items)
▶ F	Array	(27 items)
▶ G	Array	(64 items)
▶ H	Array	(51 items)
▶ I	Array	(35 items)
▶ J	Array	(206 items)
▶ K	Array	(159 items)
▶ L	Array	(108 items)
▶ M	Array	(169 items)
▶ N	Array	(51 items)
▶ O	Array	(13 items)
▶ P	Array	(39 items)
▶ Q	Array	(7 items)
▶ R	Array	(104 items)
▶ S	Array	(112 items)
▶ T	Array	(80 items)
▶ U	Array	(2 items)
▶ V	Array	(20 items)
▶ W	Array	(17 items)
▶ X	Array	(5 items)
▶ Y	Array	(19 items)
▼ Z	Array	(24 items)
Item 1	String	Zachariah
Item 2	String	Zachary
Item 3	String	Zachery
Item 4	String	Zack
Item 5	String	Zackary
Item 6	String	Zackery
Item 7	String	Zain
Item 8	String	Zaire

Figure 8-23. *The sortednames.plist property list file*

We'll use the data from this property list to feed the table view, creating a section for each letter.

Implementing the Controller

Single-click the *SectionsViewController.h* file, and add both an NSDictionary and an NSArray instance variable and corresponding property declarations. The dictionary will hold all of our data. The array will hold the sections sorted in alphabetical order. We also need to conform the class to the UITableViewDataSource and UITableViewDelegate protocols:

```
#import <UIKit/UIKit.h>

@interface SectionsViewController : UIViewController
    <UITableViewDataSource, UITableViewDelegate>
{
    NSDictionary *names;
    NSArray      *keys;
}
```

```
@property (nonatomic, retain) NSDictionary *names;
@property (nonatomic, retain) NSArray *keys;
@end
```

Now, switch over to *SectionsViewController.m*, and add the following code to the beginning of that file:

```
#import "SectionsViewController.h"

@implementation SectionsViewController
@synthesize names;
@synthesize keys;
- (void)viewDidLoad {
    NSString *path = [[NSBundle mainBundle] pathForResource:@"sortednames"
                                                ofType:@"plist"];
    NSDictionary *dict = [[NSDictionary alloc]
                        initWithContentsOfFile:path];
    self.names = dict;
    [dict release];

    NSArray *array = [[names allKeys] sortedArrayUsingSelector:
                    @selector(compare:)];
    self.keys = array;
}
...
```

Insert the following lines of code in the existing `dealloc` and `viewDidUnload` methods:

```
...
- (void)viewDidUnload {
    // Release any retained subviews of the main view.
    // e.g. self.myOutlet = nil;
    self.names = nil;
    self.keys = nil;
}
- (void)dealloc {
    [names release];
    [keys release];
    [super dealloc];
}
...
```

And add the following code at the end of the file, just above the @end declaration:

```
...
#pragma mark -
#pragma mark Table View Data Source Methods
- (NSInteger)numberOfSectionsInTableView:(UITableView *)tableView {
```

```
        return [keys count];
}
- (NSInteger)tableView:(UITableView *)tableView
    numberOfRowsInSection:(NSInteger)section {
    NSString *key = [keys objectAtIndex:section];
    NSArray *nameSection = [names objectForKey:key];
    return [nameSection count];
}
- (UITableViewCell *)tableView:(UITableView *)tableView
    cellForRowAtIndexPath:(NSIndexPath *)indexPath {
    NSUInteger section = [indexPath section];
    NSUInteger row = [indexPath row];

    NSString *key = [keys objectAtIndex:section];
    NSArray *nameSection = [names objectForKey:key];

    static NSString *SectionsTableIdentifier = @"SectionsTableIdentifier";

    UITableViewCell *cell = [tableView dequeueReusableCellWithIdentifier:
        SectionsTableIdentifier;
    if (cell == nil) {
        cell = [[[UITableViewCell alloc]
            initWithStyle:UITableViewCellStyleDefault
            reuseIdentifier:SectionsTableIdentifier] autorelease];
    }

    cell.textLabel.text = [nameSection objectAtIndex:row];
    return cell;

}
- (NSString *)tableView:(UITableView *)tableView
    titleForHeaderInSection:(NSInteger)section {
    NSString *key = [keys objectAtIndex:section];
    return key;
}
@end
```

Most of this isn't too different from what you've seen before. In the viewDidLoad method, we created an NSDictionary instance from the property list we added to our project and assigned it to names. After that, we grabbed all the keys from that dictionary and sorted them to give us an ordered NSArray with all the key values in the dictionary in alphabetical order. Remember, the NSDictionary uses the letters of the alphabet as its keys, so this array will have 26 letters, in order from "A" to "Z," and we'll use that array to help us keep track of the sections.

Scroll down to the datasource methods. The first one we added to our class specifies the number of sections. We didn't implement this method last time because we were happy with the default setting of 1. This time, we're telling the table view that we have one section for each key in our dictionary.

```
- (NSInteger)numberOfSectionsInTableView:(UITableView *)tableView {
    return [keys count];
}
```

The next method calculates the number of rows in a specific section. Last time, we had only one section, so we just returned the number of rows we had in our array. This time, we have to break it down per section. We can do that by retrieving the array that corresponds to the section in question and returning the count from that array.

```
- (NSInteger)tableView:(UITableView *)tableView
    numberOfRowsInSection:(NSInteger)section {
    NSString *key = [keys objectAtIndex:section];
    NSArray *nameSection = [names objectForKey:key];
    return [nameSection count];
}
```

In our `tableView:cellForRowAtIndexPath:` method, we have to extract both the section and row from the index path and use that to determine which value to use. The section will tell us which array to pull out of the names dictionary, and then we can use the row to figure out which value from that array to use. Everything else in that method is basically the same as the version in the Simple Table application.

The method `tableView:titleForHeaderInSection` allows you to specify an optional header value for each section, and we simply return the letter for this group.

```
- (NSString *)tableView:(UITableView *)tableView
    titleForHeaderInSection:(NSInteger)section {
    NSString *key = [keys objectAtIndex:section];
    return key;
}
```

Why don't you compile and run the project and revel in its grooviness? Remember that we changed the table's *Style* to *Grouped*, so we ended up with a grouped table with 26 sections, which should look like Figure 8-24.

As a contrast, let's change our table view back to the indexed style and see what an indexed table view with multiple sections looks like. Double-click *SectionViewController.xib* to open the file in Interface Builder. Select the table view, and use the attributes inspector to change the view back to *Plain*. Save, and go back to Xcode to build and run it—same data, different grooviness (see Figure 8-25).

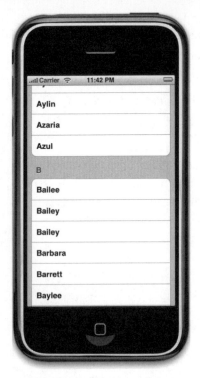

Figure 8-24. *A grouped table with multiple sections*

Figure 8-25. *An indexed table view with sections*

Adding an Index

One problem with our current table is the sheer number of rows. There are two thousand names in this list. Your finger will get awfully tired looking for Zachariah or Zebediah, not to mention Zojirishu.

One solution to this problem is to add an index down the right side of the table view. Now that we've set our table view style back to indexed, that's actually relatively easy to do. Add the following method to the bottom of *SectionsViewController.m*, just above the @end:

```
- (NSArray *)sectionIndexTitlesForTableView:(UITableView *)tableView {
    return keys;
}
```

Yep, that's it. In this method, the delegate is asking for an array of the values to display in the index. You must have more than one section in your table view to use the index, and the entries in this array must correspond to those sections. The returned array must have the same number of entries as you have sections, and the values must correspond to the appropriate section. In other words, the first item in this array will take the user to the first section, which is section 0.

Compile and run again, and you'll have yourself a nice index (see Figure 8-26).

Implementing a Search Bar

The index is helpful, but even so, we still have an awful lot of names here. If we want to see whether the name Arabella is in the list, for example, we're still going to have to scroll for a while even after using the index. It'd be nice if we could let the user pare down the list by specifying a search term, wouldn't it? That'd be darn user friendly. Well, it's a little bit of extra work, but it's not too bad. We're going to implement a standard iPhone search bar, like the one shown in Figure 8-27.

Rethinking the Design

Before we set about doing this, we need to put some thought into how it's going to work. Currently, we have a dictionary that holds a bunch of arrays, one for each letter of the alphabet. The dictionary is immutable, which means we can't add or delete values from it, and so are the arrays that it holds. We also have to retain the ability to get back to the original dataset when the user hits cancel or erases their search term.

What we can do is to create two dictionaries: an immutable dictionary to hold the full dataset and a mutable copy that we can remove rows from. The delegate and datasources will read from the mutable dictionary, and when the search criteria change or the search is cancelled, we can refresh the mutable dictionary from the immutable one. Sounds like a plan. Let's do it.

CAUTION

This next project is a bit advanced and may cause a distinct burning sensation if taken too quickly. If some of these concepts give you a headache, retrieve your copy of *Learn Objective-C* (Mark Dalrymple and Scott Knaster, Apress 2009) and review the bits about categories and mutability.

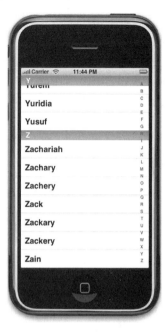

Figure 8-26. *The indexed table view with an index*

Figure 8-27. *The application with a search bar added to it*

A Deep Mutable Copy

There's one problem. NSDictionary conforms to the NSMutableCopying protocol, which returns an NSMutableDictionary, but that method creates what's called a "shallow" copy. This means that when you call the mutableCopy method, it will create a new NSMutableDictionary object that has all the objects that the original dictionary had. They won't be copies; they will be the same actual objects. This would be fine if, say, we were dealing with a dictionary storing strings, because removing a value from the copy wouldn't do anything to the original. Since we have a dictionary full of arrays, however, if we were to remove objects from the arrays in the copy, we'd also be removing them from the arrays in the original, because both the copies and the original point to the same objects.

In order to deal with this properly, we need to be able to make a deep mutable copy of a dictionary full of arrays. That's not too hard to do, but where should we put this functionality?

If you said, "in a category," then great, now you're thinking with portals! If you didn't, don't worry, it takes a while to get used to this language. Categories, in case you've forgotten, allow you to add additional methods to existing objects without subclassing them. Categories are frequently overlooked by folks new to Objective-C, because they're a feature most other languages don't have.

With categories, we can add a method to NSDictionary to do a deep copy, returning an NSMutableDictionary with the same data but not containing the same actual objects.

In your project window, select the *Classes* folder, and press ⌘N to create a new file. When the assistant comes up, select *Other* from the very bottom of the left side. Unfortunately, there's no file template for categories, so we'll just create a couple of empty files to hold it. Select the *Empty File* icon, and give this first one a name of *NSDictionary-MutableDeepCopy.h*. Repeat the process, the second time using a name of *NSDictionary-MutableDeepCopy.m*.

TIP

A faster way to create the two files needed for the category is to select the *NSObject subclass* template and then delete the file contents. This option will give you both the header and implementation file, saving you one step.

Put the following code in *NSDictionary-MutableDeepCopy.h*:

```
#import <Foundation/Foundation.h>

@interface NSDictionary(MutableDeepCopy)
- (NSMutableDictionary *)mutableDeepCopy;
@end
```

Flip over to *NSDictionary-MutableDeepCopy.m*, and add the implementation:

```
#import "NSDictionary-MutableDeepCopy.h"

@implementation NSDictionary (MutableDeepCopy)
- (NSMutableDictionary *) mutableDeepCopy {
    NSMutableDictionary *ret = [[NSMutableDictionary alloc]
        initWithCapacity:[self count]];
    NSArray *keys = [self allKeys];
    for (id key in keys) {
        id oneValue = [self valueForKey:key];
        id oneCopy = nil;

        if ([oneValue respondsToSelector:@selector(mutableDeepCopy)])
            oneCopy = [oneValue mutableDeepCopy];
        else if ([oneValue respondsToSelector:@selector(mutableCopy)])
            oneCopy = [oneValue mutableCopy];
        if (oneCopy == nil)
            oneCopy = [oneValue copy];
        [ret setValue:oneCopy forKey:key];
    }
    return ret;
}
@end
```

This method creates a new mutable dictionary and then loops through all the keys of the original dictionary, making mutable copies of each array it encounters. Since this method will behave just as if it were part of `NSDictionary`, any reference to `self` is a reference to the dictionary that this method is being called on. The method first attempts to make a deep mutable copy, and if the object doesn't respond to the `mutableDeepCopy` message, it tries to make a mutable copy. If the object doesn't respond to the `mutableCopy` message, it falls back on making a regular copy to ensure that all the objects contained in the dictionary do get copied. By doing it this way, if we were to have a dictionary containing dictionaries (or other objects that supported deep mutable copies), the contained ones would also get deep copied.

For a few of you, this might be the first time you've seen this syntax in Objective-C:

```
for (id key in keys)
```

There's a new feature of Objective-C 2.0, called fast enumeration. **Fast enumeration** is a language-level replacement for `NSEnumerator`, which you'll find covered in *Learn Objective C*. It allows you to quickly iterate through a collection, such as an `NSArray`, without the hassle of creating additional objects or loop variables.

All of the delivered Cocoa collection classes, including NSDictionary, NSArray, and NSSet support fast enumeration, and you should use this syntax any time you need to iterate over a collection. It will ensure you get the most efficient loop possible.

You may have noticed that it looks like we have a memory leak here. We allocate and initialize ret, but we never release it. That's OK. Because our method has "copy" in its name, it follows the same memory rules as the copyWithZone: method, which are supposed to return an object with a retain count of 1.

If we include the *NSDictionary-MutableDeepCopy.h* header file in one of our other classes, we'll be able to call mutableDeepCopy on any NSDictionary object we like. Let's take advantage of that now.

Updating the Controller Header File

Next, we need to add some outlets to our controller class header file. We'll need an outlet for the table view. Up until now, we haven't needed a pointer to the table view outside of the datasource methods, but we're going to need one now, since we'll need to tell the table to reload itself based on the result of the search.

We're also going to need an outlet to a search bar, which is a control used for, well, searching. In addition to those two outlets, we're also going to need an additional dictionary. The existing dictionary and array are both immutable objects, and we need to change both of them to the corresponding mutable version, so the NSArray becomes an NSMutableArray and the NSDictionary becomes an NSMutableDictionary.

We won't need any new action methods in our controller, but we will need a couple of new methods. For now, just declare them, and we'll talk about them in detail once we enter the code.

We'll also need to conform our class to the UISearchBarDelegate protocol. We'll need to become the search bar's delegate in addition to being the table view's delegate.

Make the following changes to *SectionsViewController.h*:

```
#import <UIKit/UIKit.h>

@interface SectionsViewController : UIViewController
<UITableViewDataSource, UITableViewDelegate, UISearchBarDelegate>
{
    UITableView *table;
    UISearchBar *search;
    NSDictionary *allNames;
    NSMutableDictionary *names;
    NSMutableArray  *keys;
    NSDictionary *names;
```

```
    NSArray *keys;
}
@property (nonatomic, retain) NSDictionary *names;
@property (nonatomic, retain) NSArray *keys;
@property (nonatomic, retain) IBOutlet UITableView *table;
@property (nonatomic, retain) IBOutlet UISearchBar *search;
@property (nonatomic, retain) NSDictionary *allNames;
@property (nonatomic, retain) NSMutableDictionary *names;
@property (nonatomic, retain) NSMutableArray *keys;
- (void)resetSearch;
- (void)handleSearchForTerm:(NSString *)searchTerm;
@end
```

Here's what we just did. The outlet `table` will point to our table view; the outlet `search` will point to the search bar; the dictionary `allNames` will hold the full data set; the dictionary `names` will hold the data set that matches the current search criteria; and `keys` will hold the index values and section names. If you're clear on everything, let's now modify our view in Interface Builder.

Modifying the View

Double-click *SectionsViewController.xib* to open the file in Interface Builder. Next, grab a *Search Bar* from the library (see Figure 8-28), and add it to the top of the table view.

Figure 8-28. *The Search Bar in the library*

You're trying to drop it into the table view's header section, a special part of the table view that lies before the first section. In Interface Builder, the way to do this is to drop the search bar at the top of the view. Before you let go of the mouse button, you should see a rounded blue rectangle at the top of the view (Figure 8-29). That's your indication that if you drop the search bar now, it will go into the table header. Let go of the mouse button to drop the search bar once you see that blue rectangle.

Now control-drag from the *File's Owner* icon to the table view, and select the *table* outlet. Repeat with the search bar, and select the *search* outlet. Single-click the search bar, and go to the attributes inspector by pressing ⌘1. It should look like Figure 8-30.

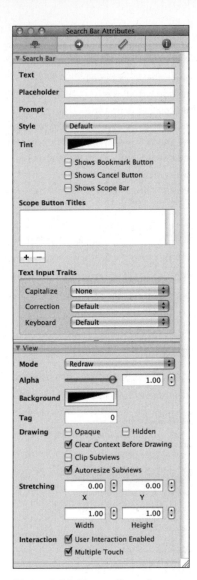

Figure 8-29. *The new version of our view with both a table view and a search bar*

Figure 8-30. *The attributes inspector for the search bar*

Type *search* in the *Placeholder* field. The word "*search*" will appear, very lightly, in the search field. Check the box that says *Shows Cancel Button*. A *Cancel* button will appear to the right of the search field. The user can tap this button to cancel the search. Under the *Text Input Traits*, set the popup button labeled *Correction* to *No* to indicate that the search bar should not try and correct the user's spelling.

Switch to the connections inspector by pressing ⌘2, and drag from the *delegate* connection to the *File's Owner* icon to tell this search bar that our view controller is also the search bar's delegate.

That should be everything we need here, so make sure to save, and let's head back to Xcode.

Modifying the Controller Implementation

The changes to accommodate the search bar are fairly drastic. Make the following changes to *SectionsViewController.m*, and then come on back so we can walk through the changes.

```
#import "SectionsViewController.h"
#import "NSDictionary-MutableDeepCopy.h"

@implementation SectionsViewController
@synthesize names;
@synthesize keys;
@synthesize table;
@synthesize search;
@synthesize allNames;
#pragma mark -
#pragma mark Custom Methods
- (void)resetSearch {
    NSMutableDictionary *allNamesCopy = [self.allNames mutableDeepCopy];
    self.names = allNamesCopy;
    [allNamesCopy release];
    NSMutableArray *keyArray = [[NSMutableArray alloc] init];
    [keyArray addObjectsFromArray:[[self.allNames allKeys]
            sortedArrayUsingSelector:@selector(compare:)]];
    self.keys = keyArray;
    [keyArray release];
}
- (void)handleSearchForTerm:(NSString *)searchTerm {
    NSMutableArray *sectionsToRemove = [[NSMutableArray alloc] init];
    [self resetSearch];

    for (NSString *key in self.keys) {
        NSMutableArray *array = [names valueForKey:key];
        NSMutableArray *toRemove = [[NSMutableArray alloc] init];
        for (NSString *name in array) {
            if ([name rangeOfString:searchTerm
                options:NSCaseInsensitiveSearch].location == NSNotFound)
                [toRemove addObject:name];
        }

        if ([array count] == [toRemove count])
            [sectionsToRemove addObject:key];

        [array removeObjectsInArray:toRemove];
        [toRemove release];
    }
    [self.keys removeObjectsInArray:sectionsToRemove];
```

```objc
        [sectionsToRemove release];
        [table reloadData];
    }
    - (void)viewDidLoad {
        NSString *path = [[NSBundle mainBundle] pathForResource:@"sortednames"
            ofType:@"plist"];
        NSDictionary *dict = [[NSDictionary alloc]
            initWithContentsOfFile:path];
        self.names = dict;
        self.allNames = dict;

        [dict release];

        NSArray *array = [[names allKeys] sortedArrayUsingSelector:
            @selector(compare:)];
        self.keys = array;

        [self resetSearch];
        [table reloadData];
        [table setContentOffset:CGPointMake(0.0, 44.0) animated:NO];
    }

    - (void)didReceiveMemoryWarning {;
        [super didReceiveMemoryWarning];
        // Releases the view if it doesn't have a superview
        // Release anything that's not essential, such as cached data
    }

    - (void)viewDidUnload {
        // Release any retained subviews of the main view.
        // e.g. self.myOutlet = nil;
        self.table = nil;
        self.search = nil;
        self.allNames = nil;
        self.names = nil;
        self.keys = nil;
    }

    - (void)dealloc {
        [table release];
        [search release];
        [allNames release];
        [keys release];
        [names release];
        [super dealloc];
    }
```

```
#pragma mark -
#pragma mark Table View Data Source Methods
- (NSInteger)numberOfSectionsInTableView:(UITableView *)tableView {
    return [keys count];
    return ([keys count] > 0) ? [keys count] : 1;
}


- (NSInteger)tableView:(UITableView *)aTableView
        numberOfRowsInSection:(NSInteger)section {
    if ([keys count] == 0)
        return 0;
    NSString *key = [keys objectAtIndex:section];
    NSArray *nameSection = [names objectForKey:key];
    return [nameSection count];
}


- (UITableViewCell *)tableView:(UITableView *)aTableView
        cellForRowAtIndexPath:(NSIndexPath *)indexPath {
    NSUInteger section = [indexPath section];
    NSUInteger row = [indexPath row];

    NSString *key = [keys objectAtIndex:section];
    NSArray *nameSection = [names objectForKey:key];

    static NSString *sectionsTableIdentifier = @"sectionsTableIdentifier";

    UITableViewCell *cell = [aTableView dequeueReusableCellWithIdentifier:
        sectionsTableIdentifier];
    if (cell == nil) {
        cell = [[[UITableViewCell alloc] initWithFrame:CGRectZero
            reuseIdentifier: sectionsTableIdentifier] autorelease];
    }

    cell.text = [nameSection objectAtIndex:row];
    return cell;
}

- (NSString *)tableView:(UITableView *)tableView
    titleForHeaderInSection:(NSInteger)section {
    if ([keys count] == 0)
        return nil;

    NSString *key = [keys objectAtIndex:section];
    return key;
}
- (NSArray *)sectionIndexTitlesForTableView:(UITableView *)tableView {
    return keys;
```

```
}
#pragma mark -
#pragma mark Table View Delegate Methods
- (NSIndexPath *)tableView:(UITableView *)tableView
    willSelectRowAtIndexPath:(NSIndexPath *)indexPath {
    [search resignFirstResponder];
    return indexPath;
}
#pragma mark -
#pragma mark Search Bar Delegate Methods
- (void)searchBarSearchButtonClicked:(UISearchBar *)searchBar {
    NSString *searchTerm = [searchBar text];
    [self handleSearchForTerm:searchTerm];
}

- (void)searchBar:(UISearchBar *)searchBar
    textDidChange:(NSString *)searchTerm {
    if ([searchTerm length] == 0) {
        [self resetSearch];
        [table reloadData];
        return;
    }
    [self handleSearchForTerm:searchTerm];
}

- (void)searchBarCancelButtonClicked:(UISearchBar *)searchBar {
    search.text = @"";
    [self resetSearch];
    [table reloadData];
    [searchBar resignFirstResponder];
}
@end
```

Copying Data from allNames

Wow, are you still with us after all that typing? Let's break it down and see what we just did.
We'll start with the two new methods we added. Here's the first one:

```
- (void)resetSearch {
    self.names = [self.allNames mutableDeepCopy];
    NSMutableArray *keyArray = [[NSMutableArray alloc] init];
    [keyArray addObjectsFromArray:[[self.allNames allKeys]
            sortedArrayUsingSelector:@selector(compare:)]];
    self.keys = keyArray;
    [keyArray release];
}
```

This method will get called any time the search is cancelled or the search term changes. All it does is create a mutable copy of allNames, assign it to names, and then refresh the keys array so it includes all the letters of the alphabet. We have to refresh the keys array because, if a search eliminates all values from a section, we need to get rid of that section too. Otherwise, the screen gets filled up with headers and empty sections, and it doesn't look good. We also don't want to provide an index to something that doesn't exist, so as we cull the names based on the search terms, we also cull the empty sections.

Implementing the Search

The other new method is the actual search:

```
- (void)handleSearchForTerm:(NSString *)searchTerm {
    NSMutableArray *sectionsToRemove = [[NSMutableArray alloc] init];
    [self resetSearch];

    for (NSString *key in self.keys) {
        NSMutableArray *array = [names valueForKey:key];
        NSMutableArray *toRemove = [[NSMutableArray alloc] init];
        for (NSString *name in array) {
            if ([name rangeOfString:searchTerm
                options:NSCaseInsensitiveSearch].location == NSNotFound)
                    [toRemove addObject:name];
        }

        if ([array count] == [toRemove count])
            [sectionsToRemove addObject:key];

        [array removeObjectsInArray:toRemove];
        [toRemove release];
    }
    [self.keys removeObjectsInArray:sectionsToRemove];
    [sectionsToRemove release];
    [table reloadData];
}
```

Although we'll kick off the search in the search bar delegate methods, we pulled handleSearchForTerm: into its own method, since we're going to need to use the exact same functionality in two different delegate methods. By embedding the search in the handleSearchForTerm: method, we consolidate the functionality into a single place so it's easier to maintain and then just call this new method as required.

Since this is the real meat (or tofu, if you prefer) of this section, let's break this method down into smaller chunks. First, we create an array that's going to hold the empty sections as we find them. We use this array to remove those empty sections later, because it is not safe to remove objects from a collection while iterating that collection. Since we are using fast enumeration, attempting to do that will raise an exception. So, since we won't be able to remove keys while we're iterating through them, we store the sections to be removed in an array, and after we're all done enumerating, we remove all the objects at once. After allocating the array, we reset the search.

```
NSMutableArray *sectionsToRemove = [[NSMutableArray alloc] init];
[self resetSearch];
```

Next, we enumerate through all the keys in the newly restored keys array.

```
for (NSString *key in self.keys) {
```

Each time through the loop, we grab the array of names that corresponds to the current key and create another array to hold the values we need to remove from the names array. Remember, we're removing names and sections, so we have to keep track of which keys are empty as well as which names don't match the search criteria.

```
NSMutableArray *array = [names valueForKey:key];
NSMutableArray *toRemove = [[NSMutableArray alloc] init];
```

Next, we iterate through all the names in the current array. So, if we're currently working through the key of "A," this loop will enumerate through all the names that begin with "A."

```
for (NSString *name in array) {
```

Inside this loop, we use one of NSString's methods that returns the location of a substring within a string. We specify an option of NSCaseInsensitiveSearch to tell it we don't care about the search term's case. In other words, "A" is the same as "a." The value returned by this method is an NSRange struct with two members, location and length. If the search term was not found, the location will be set to NSNotFound, so we just check for that. If the NSRange that is returned contains NSNotFound, we add the name to the array of objects to be removed later.

```
if ([name rangeOfString:searchTerm
    options:NSCaseInsensitiveSearch].location == NSNotFound)
        [toRemove addObject:name];
}
```

After we've looped through all the names for a given letter, we check to see whether the array of names to be removed is the same length as the array of names. If it is, we know this section is now empty, and we add it to the array of keys to be removed later.

```
if ([array count] == [toRemove count])
    [sectionsToRemove addObject:key];
```

Next, we actually remove the nonmatching names from this section's arrays and then release the array we used to keep track of the names. It's very important to avoid using convenience methods inside of loops like this as much as possible, because they will put something into the autorelease pool every time through the loop. However, the autorelease pool can't get flushed until we're all done with our loop.

```
    [array removeObjectsInArray:toRemove];
    [toRemove release];
}
```

Finally, we remove the empty sections, release the array used to keep track of the empty sections, and tell the table to reload its data.

```
    [self.keys removeObjectsInArray:sectionsToRemove];
    [sectionsToRemove release];
    [table reloadData];
}
```

Changes to viewDidLoad

Down in viewDidLoad, we made a few changes. First of all, we now load the property list into the allNames dictionary instead of the names dictionary and delete the code that load the keys array because that is now done in the resetSearch method. We then call the resetSearch method, which populates the names mutable dictionary and the keys array for us. After that, we call reloadData on our tableView. In the normal flow of the program, reloadData will get called before the user ever sees the table, so most of the time it's not necessary to call it in viewDidLoad:. However, in order for the line after it, setContentOffset:animated: to work, we need to make sure that the table is all set up before we do that, and the way we do that is to call reloadData on the table.

```
    [table reloadData];
    [table setContentOffset:CGPointMake(0.0, 44.0) animated:NO];
```

So, what does setContentOffset:animated: do? Well, it does exactly what it sounds like. It offsets the contents of the table, in our case, by 44 pixels, the height of the search bar. This causes the search bar to be scrolled off the top when the table first comes up.

Changes to Datasource Methods

If you skip down to the datasource methods, you'll see we made a few minor changes there. Because the names dictionary and keys array are still being used to feed the datasource, these methods are basically the same as they were before. We did have to account for the facts that table views always have a minimum of one section and yet the search could potentially exclude all names from all sections. So, we added a little code to check for the situation where all sections were removed, and in those cases, we feed the table view a single section with no rows and a blank name. This avoids any problems and doesn't give any incorrect feedback to the user.

Adding a Table View Delegate Method

Below the datasource methods, we've added a single delegate method. If the user clicks a row while using the search bar, we want the keyboard to go away. We accomplish this by implementing `tableView:willSelectRowAtIndexPath:` and telling the search bar to resign first responder status, which will cause the keyboard to retract. Next, we return `indexPath` unchanged. We could also have done this in `tableView:didSelectRowAtIndex Path:`, but because we're doing it here, the keyboard retracts a tiny bit sooner.

```
- (NSIndexPath *)tableView:(UITableView *)tableView
    willSelectRowAtIndexPath:(NSIndexPath *)indexPath {
    [search resignFirstResponder];
    return indexPath;
}
```

Adding Search Bar Delegate Methods

The search bar has a number of methods that it calls on its delegate. When the user taps return or the search key on the keyboard, `searchBarSearchButtonClicked:` will be called. Our version of this method grabs the search term from the search bar and calls our search method, which will remove the nonmatching names from `names` and the empty sections from `keys`.

```
- (void)searchBarSearchButtonClicked:(UISearchBar *)searchBar {
    NSString *searchTerm = [searchBar text];
    [self handleSearchForTerm:searchTerm];
}
```

The `searchBarSearchButtonClicked:` method should be implemented any time you use a search bar. We also implement another search bar delegate method in addition to that one, but the next requires a bit of caution. This next method implements a live search. Every time the search term changes, regardless of whether the user has selected the search button or tapped return, we redo the search. This behavior is very user friendly, as the users can see the results change while typing. If users pare the list down far enough on the third character, they can stop typing and select the row they want.

You can easily hamstring the performance of your application implementing live search, especially if you're displaying images or have a complex data model. In this case, with 2,000 strings and no images or accessory icons, things actually work pretty well, even on a first-generation iPhone or iPod touch.

Do not assume that snappy performance in the simulator translates to snappy performance on your device. If you're going to implement a live search like this, you need to test extensively on actual hardware to make sure your application stays responsive. When in doubt, don't use it. Your users will likely be perfectly happy tapping the search button.

Now that you've been adequately warned, here's how you handle a live search. You implement the search bar delegate method `searchBar:textDidChange:` like so:

```
- (void)searchBar:(UISearchBar *)searchBar
    textDidChange:(NSString *)searchTerm {
    if ([searchTerm length] == 0) {
        [self resetSearch];
        [table reloadData];
        return;
    }
    [self handleSearchForTerm:searchTerm];
}
```

Notice that we check for an empty string. If the string is empty, we know all names are going to match it, so we simply reset the search and reload the data, without bothering to enumerate over all the names.

Last, we implement a method that allows us to get notified when the user clicks the *Cancel* button on the search bar:

```
- (void)searchBarCancelButtonClicked:(UISearchBar *)searchBar {
    search.text = @"";
    [self resetSearch];
    [table reloadData];
    [searchBar resignFirstResponder];
}
```

When the user clicks *Cancel*, we set the search term to an empty string, reset the search, and reload the data so that all names are showing. We also tell the search bar to yield first responder status so that the keyboard drops away and the user can resume working with the table view.

If you haven't done so already, fire it up and try out the search functionality. Remember, the search bar is scrolled just off the top of the screen, so drag down to bring it into view. Click in the search field and start typing. The name list should trim to match the text you type. It works, right?

But, there's one thing that's not quite right. The index is overlapping the *Cancel* button (Figure 8-31).

Figure 8-31. *The way things are working now, the search bar cancel button is overlapped by the index.*

It's a subtle thing, but iPhone users often notice subtle things. How does Apple deal with this problem in the Contacts application? They make the index disappear when you tap the search bar. We can do that. First, let's add an instance variable to keep track of whether the user is currently using the search bar. Add the following to *SectionsViewController.h*:

```
@interface SectionsViewController : UIViewController
<UITableViewDataSource, UITableViewDelegate, UISearchBarDelegate>
{
    UITableView *table;
    UISearchBar *search;
    NSDictionary *allNames;
    NSMutableDictionary *names;
    NSMutableArray  *keys;

    BOOL    isSearching;
}
@property (nonatomic, retain) IBOutlet UITableView *table;
@property (nonatomic, retain) IBOutlet UISearchBar *search;
@property (nonatomic, retain) NSDictionary *allNames;
@property (nonatomic, retain) NSMutableDictionary *names;
@property (nonatomic, retain) NSMutableArray *keys;
- (void)resetSearch;
- (void)handleSearchForTerm:(NSString *)searchTerm;
@end
```

Then we need to modify `sectionIndexTitlesForTableView:` method to return `nil` if the user is searching:

```
- (NSArray *)sectionIndexTitlesForTableView:(UITableView *)tableView {
    if (isSearching)
        return nil;

    return keys;
}
```

We need to implement a new delegate method to set isSearching to YES when searching begins. Add the following method to *SectionsViewController.m*:

```
- (void)searchBarTextDidBeginEditing:(UISearchBar *)searchBar {
    isSearching = YES;
    [table reloadData];
}
```

This method gets called when the search bar is tapped. In it, we set isSearching to YES, then we tell the table to reload itself, which causes the index to disappear. We also have to remember to set isSearching to NO when the user is done searching. There are two ways that can happen: the user can press the Cancel button, or they can tap a row in the table. Therefore, we have to add code to the searchBarCancelButtonClicked: method:

```
- (void)searchBarCancelButtonClicked:(UISearchBar *)searchBar {
    isSearching = NO;
    search.text = @"";
    [self resetSearch];
    [table reloadData];
    [searchBar resignFirstResponder];
}
```

and also to the tableView:willSelectRowAtIndexPath: method:

```
- (NSIndexPath *)tableView:(UITableView *)tableView
  willSelectRowAtIndexPath:(NSIndexPath *)indexPath {
    [search resignFirstResponder];
    isSearching = NO;
    search.text = @"";
    [tableView reloadData];
    return indexPath;
}
```

Now, try it again, and when you tap the search bar, the index will disappear until you're done searching.

Adding a Magnifying Glass to the Index

Because we offset the tableview's content, the search bar is not visible when the application first launches, but a quick flick down brings the search bar into view so it can be used. It is also acceptable to put a search bar above rather than in the table view so that it's always visible, but this eats up valuable screen real estate. Having the search bar scroll with the table uses the iPhone's small screen more efficiently, and the user can always get to the search bar quickly by tapping in the status bar at the top of the screen. But, not everybody knows that tapping in the status bar takes you to the top of the current table. What would be ideal, would be if we could put a magnifying glass at the top of the index the way that the Contacts application does (Figure 8-32).

Figure 8-32. *The Contacts application has a magnifying glass icon in the index that takes you to the search bar. Prior to SDK 3, this was not available to other applications, but now it is.*

Well, guess what? We can. One of the new features in iPhone SDK 3 is the ability to put a magnifying glass in a table index. Let's do that now for our application. There are only three steps involved in this. First, we have to add a special value to our keys array to indicate we want the magnifying glass, we have to prevent the iPhone from printing a section header in the table for that special value, and we need to tell the table to scroll to the top when that item is selected. Let's tackle them in order.

ADDING THE SPECIAL VALUE TO THE KEYS ARRAY

To add the special value to our keys array, all we have to do is add one line of code to the resetSearch method:

```
- (void)resetSearch {
    self.names = [self.allNames mutableDeepCopy];
    NSMutableArray *keyArray = [[NSMutableArray alloc] init];
    [keyArray addObject:UITableViewIndexSearch];
```

```
    [keyArray addObjectsFromArray:[[self.allNames allKeys]
            sortedArrayUsingSelector:@selector(compare:)]];
    self.keys = keyArray;
    [keyArray release];
}
```

SUPPRESSING THE SECTION HEADER

Now, we need to suppress that value from coming up as a section title. We do that, by adding a check in the existing `tableView:titleForHeaderInSection:` method, and return
`nil` when it asks for the title for the special search section:

```
- (NSString *)tableView:(UITableView *)tableView
titleForHeaderInSection:(NSInteger)section {
    if ([keys count] == 0)
        return nil;

    NSString *key = [keys objectAtIndex:section];
    if (key == UITableViewIndexSearch)
        return nil;
    return key;
}
```

TELLING THE TABLE VIEW WHAT TO DO

Finally, we have to tell the tableview what to do when the user taps on the magnifying glass
in the index. When the user taps the magnifying class, the delegate method `tableView:`
`sectionForSectionIndexTitle:atIndex:` gets called, if it is implemented.

Add this method to the bottom of *SectionsViewController.m*, just above the @end:

```
- (NSInteger)tableView:(UITableView *)tableView
sectionForSectionIndexTitle:(NSString *)title
              atIndex:(NSInteger)index {
    NSString *key = [keys objectAtIndex:index];
    if (key == UITableViewIndexSearch) {
        [tableView setContentOffset:CGPointZero animated:NO];
        return NSNotFound;
    }
    else return index;
}
```

To tell it to go to the search box, we have to do two things. First, we have to get rid of
the content offset we added earlier, and then we have to return NSNotFound. When the
tableview gets this response, it knows to scroll up to the top, so now that we've removed
the offset, it will scroll to the search bar rather than to the top section.

And there you have it—live searching in an iPhone table, with a magnifying glass in the index!

SDK 3 added even more cool search stuff. Interested? Go to the documentation browser and do a search for `UISearchDisplay` to read up on `UISearchDisplayController` and `UISearchDisplayDelegate`. You'll likely find this much easier to understand once you've made your way through Chapter 9.

Putting It All on the Table

Well, how are you doing? This was a pretty hefty chapter, and you've learned a ton! You should have a very solid understanding of the way flat tables work. You should understand how to customize tables and table view cells as well as how to configure table views. You also know how to implement a search bar, which is a vital tool in any iPhone application that presents large volumes of data. Make sure you understand everything we did in this chapter, because we're going to build on it.

We're going to continue working with table views in the next chapter, and you're going to learn how to use them to present hierarchical data. You'll see how to create content views that allow the user to edit data selected in a table view, as well as how to present checklists in tables, embed controls in table rows, and delete rows.

Chapter 9

Navigation Controllers and Table Views

*i*n the previous chapter, you mastered the basics of working with table views. In this chapter, you're going to get a whole lot more practice, because we're going to explore **navigation controllers**. Table views and navigation controllers work hand in hand. Strictly speaking, a navigation controller doesn't need a table view in order to do its thing. As a practical matter, however, when you implement a navigation controller, you almost always implement at least one table, and usually several, because the strength of the navigation controller is in the ease with which it handles complex hierarchical data. On the iPhone's small screen, hierarchical data is best presented using a succession of table views.

In this chapter, we're going to build an application progressively, just as we did with the Pickers application back in Chapter 7. We're going to get the navigation controller and the first view controller working, and then we'll start adding more controllers and more layers to the hierarchy. Each view controller we create will reinforce some aspect of table use or configuration. You're going to see how to drill down from table views into child tables and also from table views down into content views where detailed data can be viewed and even edited. You're also going to see how to use a table list to allow the user to select from multiple values and learn how to use edit mode to allow rows to be deleted from a table view.

That is a lot, isn't it? Well, nothing for it but to get started. Let's go!

Navigation Controllers

The main tool you'll use to build hierarchical applications is `UINavigationController`. `UINavigationController` is similar to `UITabBarController` in that it manages, and swaps in and out, multiple content views. The main difference between the two is that `UINavigationController` is implemented as a **stack**, which makes it well suited to working with hierarchies.

Already know everything there is to know about stacks? Scan through this section and we'll meet you at the beginning of the next section, "A Stack of Controllers." New to stacks? Fortunately, it's a pretty easy concept.

Stacky Goodness

A stack is a commonly used data structure that works on the principle of last in, first out. Believe it or not, a Pez dispenser is a great example of a stack. Ever try to load one? According to the little instruction sheet that comes with each and every Pez dispenser, there are a few easy steps. First, unwrap the pack of Pez candy. Second, open the dispenser by tipping its head straight back. Third, grab the stack (notice the clever way we inserted the word "stack" in there!) of candy, holding it firmly between your pointer finger and thumb, and insert the column into the open dispenser. Fourth, pick up all the little pieces of candy that flew all over the place because these instructions just never work.

OK, that example was not particularly useful. But what happens next is: as you pick up the pieces and jam them, one at a time, into the dispenser, you are working with a stack. Remember, we said a stack was last in, first out. That also means first in, last out. The first piece of Pez you push into the dispenser will be the last piece that pops out. The last piece of Pez you push in there will be the first piece you pop out.

A computer stack follows the same rules. When you add an object to a stack, it's called a **push**: you push an object onto the stack. When you remove an object from the stack, it's called a **pop**. When you pop an object off the stack, it's always the last one you pushed onto the stack. The first object you push onto the stack will always be the last one you pop off the stack.

A Stack of Controllers

A navigation controller maintains a stack of view controllers. Any kind of view controller is fair game for the stack. When you design your navigation controller, you'll need to specify the very first view the user sees. That view is the bottommost view in the view hierarchy and its controller is called the **root view controller**. The root view controller is the very first view controller the navigation controller pushes onto its stack. As the user selects the next view to look at, a new view controller is pushed onto the stack, and the view it controls is shown to the user. We refer to these new view controllers as **subcontrollers**. As you'll see, this chapter's application, Nav, is made up of a navigation controller and six subcontrollers.

Take a look at Figure 9-1. Notice the **navigation button** in the upper-left corner of the current view. The navigation button is similar to a web browser's back button. When the user taps that button, the current view controller is popped off the stack, and the previous view becomes the current view.

We love this design pattern. It allows you to build complex hierarchical applications iteratively. You don't have to know the entire hierarchy to get things up and running. Each controller only needs to know about its child controllers so it can push the appropriate new controller object onto the stack when the user makes a selection. You can build up a large application from many small pieces this way, which is exactly what we're going to do in this chapter.

Figure 9-1. *The Settings application uses a navigation controller. In the upper left (1) is the navigation button used to pop the current view controller off the stack, returning you to the previous level of the hierarchy. The title (2) of the current content view controller is also displayed.*

Nav, a Hierarchical Application in Six Parts

The application we're about to build will show you how to do most of the common tasks associated with displaying a hierarchy of data. When the application launches, you'll be presented with a list of options (see Figure 9-2). Each of the rows in this top-level view represents a different view controller that will get pushed onto the navigation controller's stack when that row is selected.

The icons on the right side of each row are called **accessory icons**. This particular accessory icon (the gray arrow) is called a **disclosure indicator** and is used to tell the user that touching that row will drill down to another table view.

Using a disclosure indicator to drill down to a view with detailed information about the selected row is not appropriate. Instead, use a **detail disclosure button**, as shown in Figure 9-3, which shows the first of our application's six subcontrollers. This view appears when you select *Disclosure Buttons* from the top view shown in Figure 9-2. A detail disclosure button tells you that selecting that row will reveal, and perhaps allow you to edit, more detailed information about the current row.

Figure 9-2. *This chapter's application's top-level view. Note the accessory icons on the right side of the view. This particular type of accessory icon is called a disclosure indicator and tells the user that touching that row will drill down to another table view.*

Figure 9-3. *The first of the Nav application's six subcontrollers implements a table whose rows each contain a detail disclosure button.*

Unlike the disclosure indicator, the detail disclosure button is not just an icon but a control that the user can tap, so you can have two different options available for a given row. One action is triggered when the user selects the row. The other action is triggered when the user taps the disclosure button.

A good example of the proper use of the detail disclosure button is found in the Phone application. Selecting a person's row from the *Favorites* tab places a call to the person whose row you touched, but selecting the disclosure button next to a name takes you to detailed contact information. The YouTube application is another great example. Selecting a row plays a video, but tapping the detail disclosure button takes you to more detailed information about the video.

In the Contacts application, the list of contacts does not feature detail disclosure buttons even though selecting a row does take you to a detail view. Since there is only one option available for each row in the Contacts application, no accessory icon is displayed.

To restate, if tapping a row takes you to a more detailed view of that row, you'll either use no accessory icon or use a detail disclosure button, if you want to support two different options for the row. If tapping a row takes you to another view entirely, one that is not a more detailed view of that row, use a disclosure indicator (gray arrow) to mark the row.

The second of our application's six subcontrollers is shown in Figure 9-4. This is the view that appears when you select *Check One* in Figure 9-2.

This view comes in handy when you want to present a list from which only one item can be selected. This approach is to iPhone as radio buttons are to Mac OS X. These lists use a check-mark to mark the currently selected row.

The third of our application's six subcontrollers is shown in Figure 9-5. This view features a tappable button in each row's **accessory view**. The accessory view is the far right part of the table view cell that usually holds the accessory icon but can be used for more. When we get to this part of our application, you'll see how to create controls in the accessory view.

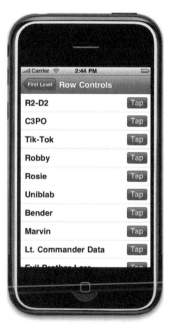

Figure 9-4. *The second of the Nav application's six subcontrollers allows you to select one row from many.*

Figure 9-5. *The third of the Nav application's six subcontrollers adds a button to the accessory view of each table view cell.*

The fourth of our application's six subcontrollers is shown in Figure 9-6. In this view, we'll let the user rearrange the order of the rows in a list by having the table enter **edit mode** (more on this when we get to it in code later in this chapter).

The fifth of our application's six subcontrollers is shown in Figure 9-7. In this view, we're going to show another use of edit mode by allowing the user to delete rows from our table.

The sixth and last of our application's six subcontrollers is shown in Figure 9-8, and it shows an editable detail view using a grouped table. This technique for detail view is used widely by the applications that ship on the iPhone.

So very much to do. Let's get started!

Figure 9-6. *The fourth of the Nav application's six subcontrollers lets the user rearrange rows in a list by touching and dragging the move icon.*

Figure 9-7. *The fifth of the Nav application's six subcontrollers implements edit mode to allow the user to delete items from the table.*

Figure 9-8. *The sixth and last of the Nav application's six subcontrollers implements an editable detail view using a grouped table.*

Constructing the Nav Application's Skeleton

Xcode offers a perfectly good template for creating navigation-based applications, and you will likely use it much of the time when you need to create hierarchical applications. However, we're not going to use that one today. Nope. We're going to construct our navigation-based application from the ground up so you get a feel for how everything fits together. It's not really very different from the way we built the tab bar controller in Chapter 7, so you shouldn't have any problems keeping up. Using the provided template is no different from what we'll be doing today except that you'll be able to skip the first several steps in the future.

In Xcode, press ⌘⇧N to create a new project, and select *Window-Based Application* from the iPhone template list, making sure that *Use Core Data for storage* is not checked. Give your new project a name of *Nav*. As you'll see, if you click the *Classes* and *Resources* folders, this template gives you an application delegate, a *MainWindow.xib*, and not much else. We need to add a navigation controller to *MainWindow.xib,* which will be our application's root controller. And, since all navigation controllers have to have their own root view controller, we'll need to create that as well. Since we're already in Xcode, let's create the files needed to implement the root view controller.

Creating the First Level View Controller

In this chapter, we're going to be subclassing `UITableViewController` instead of `UIViewController` for our table views. When we subclass `UITableViewController`, we inherit some nice functionality from that class that will create a table view with no need for a nib file. We can provide a table view in a nib, as we did last chapter, but if we don't, `UITableViewController` will create a table view automatically, that takes up the entire space available and will connect the appropriate outlets in our controller class and make our controller class the delegate and datasource for that table. When all you need for a specific controller is a table, subclassing `UITableViewController` is the way to go.

In your project window, select the *Classes* folder in the *Groups & Files* pane, expanding as necessary, and then press ⌘N or select **New File...** from the **File** menu. When the new file assistant comes up, select *Cocoa Touch Class*, select *Objective-C class*, and then select *NSObject* from the *Subclass of* pop-up menu. Click *Next*. Give this file a name of *FirstLevelViewController.m*, and make sure that you check *Also create "FirstLevelViewController.h"*.

You may have noticed an entry named *UITableViewController* in the *Subclass of* pop-up menu. When creating your own applications, please feel free to use that template. We didn't use that template, purely to keep things simple. We didn't want you to have to spend time sorting through all the unneeded template methods trying to figure out where to insert or delete code. By creating an *NSObject* subclass and, in its declaration, changing the superclass to `UITableViewController`, we get a smaller, more manageable file. Once the files have been created, single-click *FirstLevelViewController.h*, and make the following change so `FirstLevelViewController` is a subclass of `UITableViewController`:

```
#import <UIKit/UIKit.h>

@interface FirstLevelViewController : NSObject {
@interface FirstLevelViewController : UITableViewController {

}
@end
```

The two files we just created contain the controller class for the first table the user sees. This is not, however, going to be our application's root controller. As with the Pickers application in Chapter 7, the root controller for our application will be a class provided by Apple called a navigation controller, which we don't even need to subclass.

Setting Up the Navigation Controller

Before we get into our code, let's talk about the names we use to refer to the various controllers that make up our application. At the root of our application is the controller whose view gets added to the window, known as the root controller. In our case, the root controller is the navigation controller that will swap in and out all the other views that make up our hierarchy of views.

Here's where things get a bit confusing. As it turns out, the UINavigationController class refers to a root view controller. For example, the UINavigationController class features methods called initWithRootViewController: and popToRootViewControllerAnimated:. This reference to a root view controller is really talking about the view controller on the bottom of the navigation stack, which is the first view presented to the user when launching the application for the first time. This is different from the "root controller," which is the navigation controller itself. Confusing, right?

In our case, the navigation controller's root view controller is the six-row view shown in Figure 9-2. This can be a point of confusion, however, since our application's root view controller (the UINavigationController) will itself have a root view controller. In order to avoid confusion between the two root controllers, we won't be using the term "root view controller" for either. Instead, we'll refer to the application's root controller as navController, and as you just saw in the previous section, we'll refer to navController's root view controller as FirstLevelController, because it's the first level in the visual hierarchy presented to the user.

Take a moment to make sense of all this and file it away in permanent storage. And now, back to our regularly scheduled program.

Let's start by adding an outlet for our application's root view controller, navController, in *NavAppDelegate.h*:

```
#import <UIKit/UIKit.h>

@interface NavAppDelegate : NSObject <UIApplicationDelegate> {
    UIWindow *window;
    UINavigationController *navController;
}

@property (nonatomic, retain) IBOutlet UIWindow *window;
@property (nonatomic, retain) IBOutlet UINavigationController
```

```
    *navController;
@end
```

Next, we need to hop over to the implementation file and add the `@synthesize` statement for navController. We'll also add navController's view as a subview of our application's window so that it gets shown to the user. Single-click *NavAppDelegate.m*, and make the following changes:

```
#import "NavAppDelegate.h"

@implementation NavAppDelegate

@synthesize window;
@synthesize navController;

- (void)applicationDidFinishLaunching:(UIApplication *)application {

    // Override point for customization after application launch
    [window addSubview: navController.view];
    [window makeKeyAndVisible];
}
- (void)dealloc {
    [window release];
    [navController release];
    [super dealloc];
}
@end
```

Save both of these files. Next, we have to create a navigation controller, connect it to the navController outlet we just declared, and then tell the navigation controller what to use as its root view controller.

Expand the *Resources* folder in the *Groups & Files* pane if necessary; then double-click *MainWindow.xib* to open that file in Interface Builder. Look in the library for a *Navigation Controller* (see Figure 9-9), and drag one over to the nib's main window, which is the window labeled *MainWindow.xib*, not the one labeled *Window*.

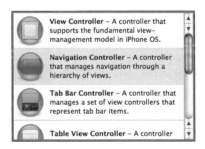

Figure 9-9. *The Navigation Controller in the library*

Control-drag from the *Nav App Delegate* icon to the new *Navigation Controller* icon, and select the *navController* outlet. We're almost done, but the next task is a little tricky. We need to tell the navigation controller where to find its root view controller. The easiest way to do that is to change the nib's main window into list mode using the middle *View Mode* button in the toolbar of that window (see Figure 9-10).

Click the little disclosure triangle to the left of *Navigation Controller* to expand it. Underneath it, you'll find two items, *Navigation Bar* and *View Controller (Root View Controller)*.

Single-click the *View Controller (Root View Controller)* icon, and press ⌘4 to bring up the identity inspector. Change the underlying class to *FirstLevelViewController*, and press return to commit the change. Switch to the attributes inspector using ⌘1. Here, if we wanted to, we could also specify a nib file from which it should load the root-level view. Instead, we're going to leave the *NIB Name* field blank, which is how we indicate that the table view controller should create a table view instance for us. That's all the changes we need here, so save, close the window, and go back to Xcode.

Figure 9-10. *Switching MainWindow. xib's main window into list mode*

Now, of course, we need a list for our root view to display. In the last chapter, we used simple arrays of strings. In this application, the first level view controller is going to manage a list of its subcontrollers, which we will be building throughout the chapter. Tapping any row will cause an instance of the selected view controller to get pushed onto the navigation controller's stack. We also want to be able to display an icon next to each row, so instead of adding a `UIImage` property to every subcontroller that we create, we're going to create a subclass of `UITableViewController` that has a `UIImage` property to hold the row icon. We will then subclass this new class instead of subclassing `UITableViewController` directly, and as a result, all of our subclasses will get that `UIImage` property for free, which will make our code much cleaner.

We will never actually create an instance of this new class. It exists solely to let us add a common item to the rest of the controllers we're going to write. In many languages, we would declare this as an **abstract class**, but Objective-C doesn't support abstract classes. We can make classes that aren't intended to be instantiated, but the compiler won't prevent us from actually creating them the way it does in many other languages. Objective-C is a much more permissive language than most other popular languages, and this can be a little hard to get used to.

Single-click the *Classes* folder in Xcode, and press ⌘N to bring up the new file assistant. Select *Cocoa Touch Class* from the left pane, select *Objective-C class*, and select *NSObject for Subclass of*. Give the new file the name *SecondLevelViewController.m*. Be sure to create the *.h* file as well. Once the new files are created, select *SecondLevelViewController.h*, and make the following changes:

```
#import <UIKit/UIKit.h>

@interface SecondLevelViewController : NSObject {
@interface SecondLevelViewController : UITableViewController {
    UIImage    *rowImage;
}
@property (nonatomic, retain) UIImage *rowImage;
@end
```

Over in *SecondLevelViewController.m*, add the following line of code:

```
#import "SecondLevelViewController.h"

@implementation SecondLevelViewController
@synthesize rowImage;
@end
```

Any controller class that we want to implement as a second-level controller—in other words, any controller that the user can navigate directly to from the first table shown in our application—should subclass SecondLevelViewController instead of UITableViewController. Because we're subclassing SecondLevelViewController, all of those classes will have a property they can use to store a row image, and we can write our code in FirstLevelViewController before we've actually written any concrete second-level controller classes by using SecondLevelViewController as a placeholder.

Let's do that now. First, declare an array in *FirstLevelViewController.h*:

```
#import <UIKit/UIKit.h>

@interface FirstLevelViewController : UITableViewController {
        NSArray *controllers;
}
@property (nonatomic, retain) NSArray *controllers;
@end
```

The array we just added will hold the instances of the second-level view controllers. We'll use it to feed data to our table.

Add the following code to *FirstLevelViewController.m*, and then come on back and gossip with us, 'K?

```
#import "FirstLevelViewController.h"
#import "SecondLevelViewController.h"

@implementation FirstLevelViewController
@synthesize controllers;
- (void)viewDidLoad {
    self.title = @"First Level";
```

```objc
    NSMutableArray *array = [[NSMutableArray alloc] init];
    self.controllers = array;
    [array release];
    [super viewDidLoad];
}
- (void)viewDidUnload {
    self.controllers = nil;
    [super viewDidUnload];
}
- (void)dealloc {
    [controllers release];
    [super dealloc];
}
#pragma mark -
#pragma mark Table Data Source Methods
- (NSInteger)tableView:(UITableView *)tableView
 numberOfRowsInSection:(NSInteger)section {
    return [self.controllers count];
}
- (UITableViewCell *)tableView:(UITableView *)tableView
        cellForRowAtIndexPath:(NSIndexPath *)indexPath {

    static NSString *FirstLevelCell= @"FirstLevelCell";

    UITableViewCell *cell = [tableView dequeueReusableCellWithIdentifier:
                            FirstLevelCell];
    if (cell == nil) {
        cell = [[[UITableViewCell alloc]
                initWithStyle:UITableViewCellStyleDefault
                reuseIdentifier: FirstLevelCell] autorelease];
    }
    // Configure the cell
    NSUInteger row = [indexPath row];
    SecondLevelViewController *controller =
    [controllers objectAtIndex:row];
    cell.textLabel.text = controller.title;
    cell.imageView.image = controller.rowImage;
    cell.accessoryType = UITableViewCellAccessoryDisclosureIndicator;
    return cell;
}
#pragma mark -
#pragma mark Table View Delegate Methods
- (void)tableView:(UITableView *)tableView
didSelectRowAtIndexPath:(NSIndexPath *)indexPath {
    NSUInteger row = [indexPath row];
    SecondLevelViewController *nextController = [self.controllers
                                        objectAtIndex:row];
```

```
[self.navigationController pushViewController:nextController
                                    animated:YES];
}
@end
```

The first thing we want you to notice is that we've imported that new *SecondLevelView-Controller.h* header file. Doing that lets us use the SecondLevelViewController class in our code so that the compiler will know about the rowImage property.

Next comes the viewDidLoad method. The first thing we do is set self.title. A navigation controller knows what to display in the title of its navigation bar by asking the currently active controller for its title. Therefore, it's important to set the title for all controller instances in a navigation-based application, so the user knows where they are at all times.

We then create a mutable array and assign it to the controllers property we declared earlier. Later, when we're ready to add rows to our table, we will add view controllers to this array, and they will show up in the table automatically. Selecting any row will automatically cause the corresponding controller's view to get presented to the user.

TIP

Did you notice that our property is declared as an NSArray, but that we're creating an NSMutable Array? It's perfectly acceptable to assign a subclass to a property like this. In this case, we use the mutable array in viewDidLoad to make it easier to add new controllers in an iterative fashion, but we leave the property declared as an immutable array as a message to other code that they shouldn't be modifying this array.

The final piece of the viewDidLoad method is the call to [super viewDidLoad]. We do this because we are subclassing UITableViewController. You should always call [super viewDidLoad] when you override the viewDidLoad method, because there's no way to know if our parent class does something important in its own viewDidLoad method.

The tableView:numberOfRowsInSection: method here is identical to ones you've seen in the past; it simply returns the count from our array of controllers. The tableView:cellForRowAtIndexPath: method is also very similar to ones we've written in the past. It gets a dequeued cell, or creates a new one if there aren't any, and then grabs the controller object from the array corresponding to the row being asked about. It then sets the cell's textLabel and image properties using the title and rowImage from that controller.

Notice that we are assuming the object retrieved from the array is an instance of Second LevelViewController and are assigning the controller's rowImage property to a UIImage. This step will make more sense when we declare and add the first concrete second-level controller to the array in a few minutes.

The last method we added is the most important one here, and it's the only functionality that's truly new. You've seen the `tableView:didSelectRowAtIndexPath:` method before, of course. It's the one that gets called after a user taps a row. If tapping a row needs to trigger a drill down, this is how we do it. First, we get the row from `indexPath`:

```
NSUInteger row = [indexPath row];
```

Next, we grab the correct controller from our array that corresponds to that row:

```
SecondLevelViewController *nextController =
    [self.controllers objectAtIndex:row];
```

Next, we use our `navigationController` property, which points to our application's navigation controller, to push the next controller, the one we pulled from our array, onto the navigation controller's stack:

```
[self.navigationController pushViewController:nextController
                                    animated:YES];
```

That's really all there is to it. Each controller in the hierarchy need only know about its children. When a row is selected, the active controller is responsible for getting or creating a new subcontroller, setting its properties if necessary (it's not necessary here), and then pushing that new subcontroller onto the navigation controller's stack. Once you've done that, everything else is handled automatically by the navigation controller.

At this point, the application skeleton is done. Save all your files, and build and run to make sure all your typing took hold. If all is well, the application should launch, and a navigation bar with the title *First Level* should appear. Since our array is currently empty, no rows will display at this point (see Figure 9-11).

Now, we're ready to start developing the second-level views. Before we do that, go grab the image icons from the *09 Nav* directory. A subdirectory called *Images* should have eight *.png* images, six that will act as row images and an additional two that we'll use to make a button look nice later in the chapter. Add all eight of them to the *Resources* folder of your Xcode project before proceeding.

Figure 9-11. *The application skeleton in action*

Our First Subcontroller: The Disclosure Button View

Let's implement the first of our second-level view controllers. To do that, we'll first need to create a subclass of `SecondLevelViewController`.

Select the *Classes* folder in Xcode, and press ⌘N to bring up the new file assistant again. Select *Cocoa Touch Class* in the left pane, and then select *Objective-C class* and *NSObject* for *Subclass of*. Name the file *DisclosureButtonController.m*, and make sure the checkbox for creating the header file is checked. This class will manage the table of movies that will be displayed when the user clicks the *Disclosure Buttons* item from the top-level view (see Figure 9-3).

When the user clicks any movie title, the application will drill down into another view that will report which row was selected. As a result, we're also going to need a **detail view** for the user to drill down into, so repeat the steps to create another file, and call it *DisclosureDetailController.m*. Be sure to check the checkbox so the header file is created as well.

The detail view will be a very simple view with just a single label that we can set. It won't be editable, and we'll just use this to show how to pass values into a child controller. Because this controller will not be responsible for a table view, we also need a nib to go along with the controller class. Before we create the nib, let's quickly add the outlet for the label. Make the following changes to *DisclosureDetailController.h*:

```
#import <Foundation/Foundation.h>

@interface DisclosureDetailController : NSObject {
@interface DisclosureDetailController : UIViewController {
    UILabel     *label;
    NSString    *message;
}
@property (nonatomic, retain) IBOutlet UILabel *label;
@property (nonatomic, retain) NSString *message;
@end
```

Why, pray tell, are we adding both a label and a string? Remember the concept of lazy loading? Well, view controllers use lazy loading behind the scenes as well. When we create our controller, it won't load its nib file until it actually gets displayed. When the controller is pushed onto the navigation controller's stack, we can't count on there being a `label` to set. If the nib file has not been loaded, `label` will just be a pointer set to `nil`. Yeesh. But it's OK. Instead, we'll set `message` to the value we want, and in the `viewWillAppear:` method, we'll set the label based on the value in `message`.

Why are we using `viewWillAppear:` to do our updating instead of using `viewDidLoad`, as we've done in the past? The problem is that `viewDidLoad` gets called only the first time the controller's view is loaded. But in our case, we are reusing the `DisclosureDetail Controller`'s view. No matter which fine Pixar flick you pick, when you click the disclosure button, the detail message appears in the same `DisclosureDetailController` view. If we used `viewDidLoad` to manage our updates, that view would get updated only the very first time the `DisclosureDetailController` view appeared. When we picked our second fine Pixar flick, we'd still see the detail message from the first fine Pixar flick (try saying that ten times fast). Not good. Since `viewWillAppear:` gets called every time a view is about to be drawn, we'll be fine using it for our updating.

Add the following code to *DisclosureDetailController.m*:

```
#import "DisclosureDetailController.h"

@implementation DisclosureDetailController
@synthesize label;
@synthesize message;
- (void)viewWillAppear:(BOOL)animated {
    label.text = message;
    [super viewWillAppear:animated];
}
- (void)viewDidUnload {
    self.label = nil;
    self.message = nil;
    [super viewDidUnload];
}
- (void)dealloc {
    [label release];
    [message release];
    [super dealloc];
}
@end
```

That's all pretty straightforward, right? OK, let's go create the nib to go along with this file. Be sure you've saved your source changes.

Select the *Resources* folder in Xcode, and press ⌘N to create another new file. This time, select *User Interface* on the left pane and *View XIB* from the upper-right. Give this nib file the name *DisclosureDetail.xib*.

Let's set up the nib first. Double-click *DisclosureDetail.xib* in Xcode to open the file in Interface Builder. Once it's open, single-click *File's Owner*, and press ⌘4 to bring up the identity inspector. Change the underlying class to *DisclosureDetailController*. Now control-drag from the *File's Owner* icon to the *View* icon, and select the *view* outlet to reestablish the link from the controller to its view that was broken when we changed its class.

Drag a *Label* from the library, and place it on the *View* window. Resize it so that it takes up most of the width of the view, using the blue guide lines to place it correctly, and then use the attributes inspector to change the text alignment to centered. Control-drag from *File's Owner* to the label, and select the *label* outlet. Save, close the nib, and head back to Xcode.

For this example, our list is just going to show a number of rows from an array, so we will declare an NSArray named list. We also need to declare an instance variable to hold one instance of our child controller, which will point to an instance of the DisclosureDetailController class we just built. We could allocate a new instance of that controller class every time the user taps a detail disclosure button, but it's more efficient to create one and then keep reusing it. Make the following changes to *DisclosureButtonController.h*:

```
#import <Foundation/Foundation.h>
#import <UIKit/UIKit.h>
#import "SecondLevelViewController.h"
@class DisclosureDetailController;

@interface DisclosureButtonController : NSObject {
@interface DisclosureButtonController : SecondLevelViewController {
    NSArray     *list;
    DisclosureDetailController *childController;
}
@property (nonatomic, retain) NSArray *list;
@end
```

Notice that we didn't declare a property for the childController. We are using this instance variable internally in our class and don't want to expose it to others, so we don't advertise its existence by declaring a property.

Now, we get to the juicy part. Type the following changes into *DisclosureButtonController.m*. We'll talk about what's going on afterward.

```
#import "DisclosureButtonController.h"
#import "NavAppDelegate.h"
#import "DisclosureDetailController.h"
@implementation DisclosureButtonController
@synthesize list;
- (void)viewDidLoad {
    NSArray *array = [[NSArray alloc] initWithObjects:@"Toy Story",
                     @"A Bug's Life", @"Toy Story 2", @"Monsters, Inc.",
                     @"Finding Nemo", @"The Incredibles", @"Cars",
                     @"Ratatouille", @"WALL-E", @"Up", @"Toy Story 3",
                     @"Cars 2", @"The Bear and the Bow", @"Newt", nil];
    self.list = array;
    [array release];
    [super viewDidLoad];
```

```
}
- (void)viewDidUnload {
    self.list = nil;
    [childController release];
    childController = nil;
}
- (void)dealloc {
    [list release];
    [childController release];
    [super dealloc];
}
#pragma mark -
#pragma mark Table Data Source Methods
- (NSInteger)tableView:(UITableView *)tableView
 numberOfRowsInSection:(NSInteger)section {
    return [list count];
}
- (UITableViewCell *)tableView:(UITableView *)tableView
        cellForRowAtIndexPath:(NSIndexPath *)indexPath {

    static NSString * DisclosureButtonCellIdentifier =
    @"DisclosureButtonCellIdentifier";

    UITableViewCell *cell = [tableView dequeueReusableCellWithIdentifier:
                            DisclosureButtonCellIdentifier];
    if (cell == nil) {
        cell = [[[UITableViewCell alloc]
            initWithStyle:UITableViewCellStyleDefault
            reuseIdentifier: DisclosureButtonCellIdentifier] autorelease];
    }
    NSUInteger row = [indexPath row];
    NSString *rowString = [list objectAtIndex:row];
    cell.textLabel.text = rowString;
    cell.accessoryType = UITableViewCellAccessoryDetailDisclosureButton;
    [rowString release];
    return cell;
}
#pragma mark -
#pragma mark Table Delegate Methods
- (void)tableView:(UITableView *)tableView
didSelectRowAtIndexPath:(NSIndexPath *)indexPath {

    UIAlertView *alert = [[UIAlertView alloc] initWithTitle:
        @"Hey, do you see the disclosure button?"
        message:@"If you're trying to drill down, touch that instead"
        delegate:nil
        cancelButtonTitle:@"Won't happen again"
```

```
                otherButtonTitles:nil];
        [alert show];
        [alert release];
    }
    - (void)tableView:(UITableView *)tableView
    accessoryButtonTappedForRowWithIndexPath:(NSIndexPath *)indexPath {
        if (childController == nil)
            childController = [[DisclosureDetailController alloc]
                              initWithNibName:@"DisclosureDetail" bundle:nil];

        childController.title = @"Disclosure Button Pressed";
        NSUInteger row = [indexPath row];

        NSString *selectedMovie = [list objectAtIndex:row];
        NSString *detailMessage  = [[NSString alloc]
                initWithFormat:@"You pressed the disclosure button for %@.",
                selectedMovie];
        childController.message = detailMessage;
        childController.title = selectedMovie;
        [detailMessage release];
        [self.navigationController pushViewController:childController
                                        animated:YES];
    }
    @end
```

By now, you should be fairly comfortable with everything up to and including the three datasource methods we just added. Let's look at our two new delegate methods.

The first method, `tableView:didSelectRowAtIndexPath:`, which gets called when the row is selected, puts up a polite little alert telling the user to tap the disclosure button instead of selecting the row. If the user actually taps the detail disclosure button, the last of our new delegate methods, `tableView:accessoryButtonTappedForRowWithIndexPath:`, is called. Let's look at this one a little more closely.

The first thing we do here is check the `childController` instance variable to see if it's `nil`. If it is, we have not yet allocated and initialized a new instance of `DetailDisclosure Controller`, so we do that next.

```
    if (childController == nil)
        childController = [[DisclosureDetailController alloc]
                          initWithNibName:@"DisclosureDetail" bundle:nil];
```

This gives us a new controller that we can push onto the navigation stack, just as we did earlier in `FirstLevelViewController`. Before we push it onto the stack, though, we need to give it some text to display.

```
    childController.title = @"Disclosure Button Pressed";
```

In this case, we set message to reflect the row whose disclosure button was tapped. We also set the new view's title based on the selected row.

```
NSUInteger row = [indexPath row];

NSString *selectedMovie = [list objectAtIndex:row];
NSString *detailMessage  = [[NSString alloc]
        initWithFormat:@"You pressed the disclosure button for %@.",
        selectedMovie];
childController.message = detailMessage;
childController.title = selectedMovie;
[detailMessage release];
```

Then, finally, we push the detail view controller onto the navigation stack.

```
[self.navigationController pushViewController:childController
                                    animated:YES];
```

And, with that, our first second-level controller is done, as is our detail controller. The only remaining task is to create an instance of our second level controller and add it to FirstLevelViewController's controllers.

Single-click *FirstLevelViewController.m*, and insert the following code into the viewDidLoad method:

```
- (void)viewDidLoad {
    self.title = @"First Level";
    NSMutableArray *array = [[NSMutableArray alloc] init];

    // Disclosure Button
    DisclosureButtonController *disclosureButtonController =
        [[DisclosureButtonController alloc]
        initWithStyle:UITableViewStylePlain];
    disclosureButtonController.title = @"Disclosure Buttons";
    disclosureButtonController.rowImage = [UIImage
        imageNamed:@"disclosureButtonControllerIcon.png"];
    [array addObject:disclosureButtonController];
    [disclosureButtonController release];

    self.controllers = array;
    [array release];
    [super viewDidLoad];
}
```

All that we're doing is creating a new instance of DisclosureButtonController. We specify UITableViewStylePlain to indicate that we want an indexed table, not a grouped table. Next, we set the title and the image to one of the *.png* files we had you add to your project, add the controller to the array, and release the controller. Up at the top of the file, you'll need to add one line of code to import the header class for our new file. Insert this line right above the @implementation declaration:

```
#import "DisclosureButtonController.h"
```

Save everything, and try building. If everything went as planned, your project should compile and then launch in the simulator. When it comes up, there should be just a single row (see Figure 9-12).

If you touch the one row, it will take you down to the table view we just implemented (see Figure 9-13).

Notice that the title that we set for our controller is now displayed in the navigation bar, and the title of the view controller we were previously at (*First Level*) is contained in a navigation button. Tapping that button will take the user back up to the first level. Select any row in this table, and you will get a gentle reminder that the detail disclosure button is there for drilling down (see Figure 9-14).

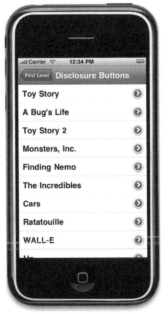

Figure 9-12. *Our application after adding the first of six second-level controllers*

Figure 9-13. *The Disclosure Buttons view*

Figure 9-14. *Selecting the row does not drill down when there is a detail disclosure button visible.*

If you touch the detail disclosure button itself, you drill
down into another view. The new view (see Figure 9-15)
shows information that we passed into it. Even though this
is a simple example, the same basic technique is used anytime you show a detail view.

Notice that when we drill down to the detail view, the title
again changes, as does the back button, which now takes us
to the previous view instead of the root view. That finishes
up the first view controller. Do you see now how the design
Apple used here with the navigation controller makes it
possible to build your application in small chunks? That's
pretty cool, isn't it?

Our Second Subcontroller: The Checklist

Figure 9-15. *The detail view*

The next second-level view we're going to implement is
another table view, but this time, we're going to use the
accessory icon to let the user select one and only one item from the list. We'll use the accessory icon to place a checkmark next to the currently selected row, and we'll change the
selection when the user touches another row.

Since this view is a table view and it has no detail view, we don't need a new nib, but we do
need to create another subclass of SecondLevelViewController. Select the *Classes* folder
in the *Groups & Files* pane in Xcode, and then press ⌘N or select **New File. . .** from the **File**
menu. Select *Cocoa Touch Class*, and then select *Objective-C class* and *NSObject* for *Subclass
of*. Click the *Next* button, and when prompted for a name, type *CheckListController.m*, and
make sure that the header file is created as well.

To present a checklist, we're going to need a way to keep track of which row is currently
selected. We'll declare an NSIndexPath property to track the last row selected. Single-click
CheckListController.h, and add the following code:

```
#import <Foundation/Foundation.h>
#import <UIKit/UIKit.h>
#import "SecondLevelViewController.h"

@interface CheckListController : NSObject {
@interface CheckListController : SecondLevelViewController {
    NSArray        *list;
    NSIndexPath    *lastIndexPath;
}
```

```
@property (nonatomic, retain) NSArray *list;
@property (nonatomic, retain) NSIndexPath * lastIndexPath;
@end
```

Then switch over *CheckListController.m* and add the following code:

```
#import "CheckListController.h"

@implementation CheckListController
@synthesize list;
@synthesize lastIndexPath;
- (void)viewDidLoad {

    NSArray *array = [[NSArray alloc] initWithObjects:@"Who Hash",
        @"Bubba Gump Shrimp Étouffée", @"Who Pudding", @"Scooby Snacks",
        @"Everlasting Gobstopper", @"Green Eggs and Ham", @"Soylent Green",
        @"Hard Tack", @"Lembas Bread",  @"Roast Beast", @"Blancmange", nil];
    self.list = array;
    [array release];

    [super viewDidLoad];
}
- (void)viewDidUnload {
    self.list = nil;
    self.lastIndexPath = nil;
    [super viewDidUnload];
}
- (void)dealloc {
    [list release];
    [lastIndexPath release];
    [super dealloc];
}
#pragma mark -
#pragma mark Table Data Source Methods
- (NSInteger)tableView:(UITableView *)tableView
 numberOfRowsInSection:(NSInteger)section {
    return [list count];
}
- (UITableViewCell *)tableView:(UITableView *)tableView
        cellForRowAtIndexPath:(NSIndexPath *)indexPath {

    static NSString *CheckMarkCellIdentifier = @"CheckMarkCellIdentifier";

    UITableViewCell *cell = [tableView dequeueReusableCellWithIdentifier:
                            CheckMarkCellIdentifier];
    if (cell == nil) {
        cell = [[[UITableViewCell alloc]
            initWithStyle:UITableViewCellStyleDefault
```

```
                reuseIdentifier:CheckMarkCellIdentifier] autorelease];
    }
    NSUInteger row = [indexPath row];
    NSUInteger oldRow = [lastIndexPath row];
    cell.textLabel.text = [list objectAtIndex:row];
    cell.accessoryType = (row == oldRow && lastIndexPath != nil) ?
    UITableViewCellAccessoryCheckmark : UITableViewCellAccessoryNone;

    return cell;
}
#pragma mark -
#pragma mark Table Delegate Methods
- (void)tableView:(UITableView *)tableView
didSelectRowAtIndexPath:(NSIndexPath *)indexPath {

    int newRow = [indexPath row];
    int oldRow = (lastIndexPath != nil) ? [lastIndexPath row] : -1;

    if (newRow != oldRow) {
        UITableViewCell *newCell = [tableView cellForRowAtIndexPath:
                                    indexPath];
        newCell.accessoryType = UITableViewCellAccessoryCheckmark;

        UITableViewCell *oldCell = [tableView cellForRowAtIndexPath:
                                    lastIndexPath];
        oldCell.accessoryType = UITableViewCellAccessoryNone;
        lastIndexPath = indexPath;
    }

    [tableView deselectRowAtIndexPath:indexPath animated:YES];
}
@end
```

Look first at the `tableView:cellForRowAtIndexPath:` method, because there are a few new things in there worth noticing. The first several lines should be familiar to you:

```
    static NSString *CheckMarkCellIdentifier = @"CheckMarkCellIdentifier";

    UITableViewCell *cell = [tableView dequeueReusableCellWithIdentifier:
        CheckMarkCellIdentifier];
    if (cell == nil) {
        cell = [[[UITableViewCell alloc]
                initWithStyle:UITableViewCellStyleDefault
                reuseIdentifier:CheckMarkCellIdentifier] autorelease];
    }
```

Here's where things get interesting, though. First, we extract the row from this cell and from the current selection:

```
NSUInteger row = [indexPath row];
NSUInteger oldRow = [lastIndexPath row];
```

We grab the value for this row from our array and assign it to the cell's title:

```
cell.textLabel.text = [list objectAtIndex:row];
```

Then, we set the accessory to show either a checkmark or nothing, depending on whether the two rows are the same. In other words, if the row the table is requesting a cell for is the currently selected row, we set the accessory icon to be a checkmark; otherwise, we set it to be nothing. Notice that we also check `lastIndexPath` to make sure it's not `nil`. We do this because a `nil` `lastIndexPath` indicates no selection. However, calling the `row` method on a `nil` object will return a 0, which is a valid row, but we don't want to put a checkmark on row 0 when, in reality, there is no selection.

```
cell.accessoryType = (row == oldRow && lastIndexPath != nil) ?
    UITableViewCellAccessoryCheckmark : UITableViewCellAccessoryNone;
```

After that, we just release the string we declared and return the cell.

```
[rowTitle release];
return cell;
```

Now skip down to the last method. You've seen the `tableView:didSelectRowAtIndexPath:` method before, but we're doing something new here. We grab not only the row that was just selected but also the row that was previously selected.

```
int newRow = [indexPath row];
int oldRow = [lastIndexPath row];
```

We do this so if the new row and the old row are the same, we don't bother making any changes:

```
if (newRow != oldRow) {
```

Next, we grab the cell that was just selected and assign a checkmark as its accessory icon:

```
        UITableViewCell *newCell = [tableView
            cellForRowAtIndexPath:indexPath];
        newCell.accessoryType = UITableViewCellAccessoryCheckmark;
```

We then grab the previously selected cell, and we set its accessory icon to none:

```
UITableViewCell *oldCell = [tableView cellForRowAtIndexPath:
    lastIndexPath];
oldCell.accessoryType = UITableViewCellAccessoryNone;
```

After that, we store the index path that was just selected in lastIndexPath, so we'll have it next time a row is selected:

```
lastIndexPath = indexPath;
}
```

When we're all done, we tell the table view to deselect the row that was just selected, because we don't want the row to stay highlighted. We've already marked the row with a checkmark; leaving it blue would just be a distraction.

```
[tableView deselectRowAtIndexPath:indexPath animated:YES];
}
```

Next, we just need to add an instance of this controller to FirstLevelViewController's controllers array. We do that by adding the following code to the viewDidLoad method in *FirstLevelViewController.m*:

```
- (void)viewDidLoad {
    self.title = @"First Level";
    NSMutableArray *array = [[NSMutableArray alloc] init];

    // Disclosure Button
    DisclosureButtonController *disclosureButtonController =
        [[DisclosureButtonController alloc]
        initWithStyle:UITableViewStylePlain];
    disclosureButtonController.title = @"Disclosure Buttons";
    disclosureButtonController.rowImage = [UIImage imageNamed:
        @"disclosureButtonControllerIcon.png"];
    [array addObject:disclosureButtonController];
    [disclosureButtonController release];

    // Check List
    CheckListController *checkListController = [[CheckListController alloc]
            initWithStyle:UITableViewStylePlain];
    checkListController.title = @"Check One";
    checkListController.rowImage = [UIImage imageNamed:
        @"checkmarkControllerIcon.png"];
    [array addObject:checkListController];
    [checkListController release];
```

```
        self.controllers = array;
        [array release];
        [super viewDidLoad];
}
```

Finally, you'll need to import the new header file, so add this line just after all the other #import statements, toward the top of the file:

```
#import "CheckListController.h"
```

Well, what are you waiting for? Save everything, compile, and run. If everything went smoothly, the application launched again in the simulator, and there was much rejoicing. This time there will be two rows (see Figure 9-16).

If you touch the *Check One* row, it will take you down to the view controller we just implemented (see Figure 9-17). When it first comes up, no rows will be selected and no checkmarks will be visible. If you tap a row, a checkmark will appear. If you then tap a different row, the checkmark will switch to the new row. Huzzah!

Figure 9-16. *Two second-level controllers, two rows. What a coincidence!*

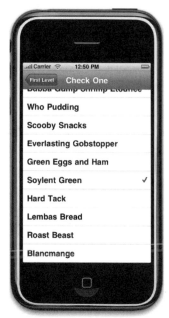

Figure 9-17. *The checklist view. Note that only a single item can be checked at a time. Soylent Green, anyone?*

Our Third Subcontroller: Controls on Table Rows

In the previous chapter, we showed you how to add subviews to a table view cell to customize its appearance, but we didn't put any active controls into the content view, only labels. It's time to try adding controls to a table view cell. In our example, we'll add a button to each row, but the same technique will work with most controls. We'll add the control to the accessory pane this time, which means that when tapping the accessory pane, the user will tap the button, similar to the way they would tap a disclosure button.

To add another row to our root view's table, we need another controller. You know the drill: select the *Classes* folder in the *Groups & Files* pane in Xcode, and then press ⌘N or select **New File. . .** from the **File** menu. Select *Cocoa Touch Class*, select Objective-C class, and select *Objective-C class* and *NSObject* for *Subclass of*. When prompted for a name, type *RowControlsController.m*, and make sure the checkbox for creating the header file is checked. Just as with the last section, this controller can be completely implemented with a single table view; no nib file is necessary.

Single-click *RowControlsController.h*, and add the following code:

```
#import <Foundation/Foundation.h>
#import <UIKit/UIKit.h>
#import "SecondLevelViewController.h"

@interface RowControlsController : NSObject {
@interface RowControlsController : SecondLevelViewController {
    NSArray *list;
}
@property (nonatomic, retain) NSArray *list;
- (IBAction)buttonTapped:(id)sender;
@end
```

Not much there, huh? We change the parent class, create an array to hold our table data, then we define a property for that array, and declare an action method that will get called when the row buttons are pressed.

NOTE

> Strictly speaking, we don't need to make this method an action method, since we won't be triggering it from controls in a nib file. Since it is an action method and will be called by a control, however, it's still a good idea to use the `IBAction` keyword.

Switch over to *RowControlsController.m*, and make the following changes:

```objc
#import "RowControlsController.h"

@implementation RowControlsController
@synthesize list;
- (IBAction)buttonTapped:(id)sender
{
    UIButton *senderButton = (UIButton *)sender;
    UITableViewCell *buttonCell =
        (UITableViewCell *)[senderButton superview];
    NSUInteger buttonRow = [[self.tableView
        indexPathForCell:buttonCell] row];
    NSString *buttonTitle = [list objectAtIndex:buttonRow];
    UIAlertView *alert = [[UIAlertView alloc]
                    initWithTitle:@"You tapped the button"
                    message:[NSString stringWithFormat:
                        @"You tapped the button for %@", buttonTitle]
                    delegate:nil
                    cancelButtonTitle:@"OK"
                    otherButtonTitles:nil];
    [alert show];
    [alert release];
}
- (void)viewDidLoad {
    NSArray *array = [[NSArray alloc] initWithObjects:@"R2-D2",
            @"C3PO", @"Tik-Tok", @"Robby", @"Rosie", @"Uniblab",
            @"Bender", @"Marvin", @"Lt. Commander Data",
            @"Evil Brother Lore", @"Optimus Prime", @"Tobor", @"HAL",
            @"Orgasmatron", nil];
    self.list = array;
    [array release];
    [super viewDidLoad];
}
- (void)viewDidUnload {
    self.list = nil;
    [super viewDidUnload];
}
- (void)dealloc {
    [list release];
    [super dealloc];
}
#pragma mark -
#pragma mark Table Data Source Methods
- (NSInteger)tableView:(UITableView *)tableView
 numberOfRowsInSection:(NSInteger)section {
    return [list count];
}
```

```objectivec
- (UITableViewCell *)tableView:(UITableView *)tableView
        cellForRowAtIndexPath:(NSIndexPath *)indexPath {

    static NSString *ControlRowIdentifier = @"ControlRowIdentifier";

    UITableViewCell *cell = [tableView
        dequeueReusableCellWithIdentifier:ControlRowIdentifier];
    if (cell == nil) {
        cell = [[[UITableViewCell alloc]
                    initWithStyle:UITableViewCellStyleDefault
                    reuseIdentifier:ControlRowIdentifier] autorelease];
        UIImage *buttonUpImage = [UIImage imageNamed:@"button_up.png"];
        UIImage *buttonDownImage = [UIImage imageNamed:@"button_down.png"];
        UIButton *button = [UIButton buttonWithType:UIButtonTypeCustom];
        button.frame = CGRectMake(0.0, 0.0, buttonUpImage.size.width,
            buttonUpImage.size.height);
        [button setBackgroundImage:buttonUpImage
            forState:UIControlStateNormal];
        [button setBackgroundImage:buttonDownImage
            forState:UIControlStateHighlighted];
        [button setTitle:@"Tap" forState:UIControlStateNormal];
        [button addTarget:self action:@selector(buttonTapped:)
            forControlEvents:UIControlEventTouchUpInside];
        cell.accessoryView = button;
    }
    NSUInteger row = [indexPath row];
    NSString *rowTitle = [list objectAtIndex:row];
    cell.textLabel.text = rowTitle;

    return cell;
}
#pragma mark -
#pragma mark Table Delegate Methods
- (void)tableView:(UITableView *)tableView
didSelectRowAtIndexPath:(NSIndexPath *)indexPath {
    NSUInteger row = [indexPath row];
    NSString *rowTitle = [list objectAtIndex:row];
    UIAlertView *alert = [[UIAlertView alloc]
                            initWithTitle:@"You tapped the row."
                            message:[NSString
                            stringWithFormat:@"You tapped %@.", rowTitle]
                            delegate:nil
                            cancelButtonTitle:@"OK"
                            otherButtonTitles:nil];
    [alert show];
    [alert release];
```

```
    [tableView deselectRowAtIndexPath:indexPath animated:YES];
}
@end
```

Let's look first at our new action method. The first thing we do is declare a new `UIButton` instance and set it to sender. This is just so we don't have to cast sender multiple times throughout our method:

```
UIButton *senderButton = (UIButton *)sender;
```

Next, we get the button's superview, which is the table view cell for the row it's in, and we use that to determine the row that was pressed and to retrieve the title for that row:

```
UITableViewCell *buttonCell =
    (UITableViewCell *)[senderButton superview];
NSUInteger buttonRow = [[self.tableView
    indexPathForCell:buttonCell] row];
NSString *buttonTitle = [list objectAtIndex:buttonRow];
```

Then we show an alert, telling the user that they pressed the button:

```
UIAlertView *alert = [[UIAlertView alloc]
                initWithTitle:@"You tapped the button"
                message:[NSString stringWithFormat:
                    @"You tapped the button for %@", buttonTitle]
                delegate:nil
                cancelButtonTitle:@"OK"
                otherButtonTitles:nil];
[alert show];
[alert release];
```

Everything from there to `tableView:cellForRowAtIndexPath:` should be familiar to you, so skip down to that method, which is where we set up the table view cell with the button. The method starts as usual. We declare an identifier and then use it to request a reusable cell:

```
static NSString *ControlRowIdentifier = @"ControlRowIdentifier";

UITableViewCell *cell = [tableView
    dequeueReusableCellWithIdentifier:ControlRowIdentifier];
```

If there are no reusable cells, we create one:

```
if (cell == nil) {
    cell = [[[UITableViewCell alloc]
                initWithStyle:UITableViewCellStyleDefault
                reuseIdentifier:ControlRowIdentifier] autorelease];
```

To create the button, we're going to load in two of the images that were in the images folder you imported earlier. One will represent the button in the normal state, the other will represent the button in its highlighted state or, in other words, when the button is being tapped:

```
UIImage *buttonUpImage = [UIImage imageNamed:@"button_up.png"];
UIImage *buttonDownImage = [UIImage imageNamed:@"button_down.png"];
```

Next, we create a button. Because the `buttonType` property of `UIButton` is declared read-only, we have to create the button using the factory method `buttonWithType:`. We can't create it using `alloc` and `init`, because we wouldn't be able to change the button's type to `UIButtonTypeCustom`, which we need to do in order to use the custom button images:

```
UIButton *button = [UIButton buttonWithType:UIButtonTypeCustom];
```

Next, we set the button's size to match the images, assign the images for the two states, and give the button a title:

```
button.frame = CGRectMake(0.0, 0.0, buttonUpImage.size.width,
    buttonUpImage.size.height);
[button setBackgroundImage:buttonUpImage
    forState:UIControlStateNormal];
[button setBackgroundImage:buttonDownImage
    forState:UIControlStateHighlighted];
[button setTitle:@"Tap" forState:UIControlStateNormal];
```

Finally, we tell the button to call our action method on the Touch Up Inside event and assign it to the cell's accessory view:

```
[button addTarget:self action:@selector(buttonTapped:)
    forControlEvents:UIControlEventTouchUpInside];
cell.accessoryView = button;
```

Everything else in the method is just like we've done it in the past.

The last method we implemented is `tableView:didSelectRowAtIndexPath:`, which, as you know by now, is the delegate method that gets called after the user selects a row. All we do here is find out which row was selected and grab the appropriate title from our array:

```
NSUInteger row = [indexPath row];
NSString *rowTitle = [list objectAtIndex:row];
```

Then we create an another alert to inform the user that they tapped the row, but not the button:

```
UIAlertView *alert = [[UIAlertView alloc]
                    initWithTitle:@"You tapped the row."
                    message:[NSString
                    stringWithFormat:@"You tapped %@.", rowTitle]
```

```
                            delegate:nil
                            cancelButtonTitle:@"OK"
                            otherButtonTitles:nil];
    [alert show];
    [alert release];
    [tableView deselectRowAtIndexPath:indexPath animated:YES];
```

Now, all we have to do is add this controller to the array in FirstLevelViewController.
Single-click *FirstLevelViewController.m*, and add the following code to viewDidLoad:

```
- (void)viewDidLoad {
    self.title = @"Root Level";
    NSMutableArray *array = [[NSMutableArray alloc] init];

    // Disclosure Button
    DisclosureButtonController *disclosureButtonController =
        [[DisclosureButtonController alloc]
        initWithStyle:UITableViewStylePlain];
    disclosureButtonController.title = @"Disclosure Buttons";
    disclosureButtonController.rowImage = [UIImage
        imageNamed:@"disclosureButtonControllerIcon.png"];
    [array addObject:disclosureButtonController];
    [disclosureButtonController release];

    // Check List
    CheckListController *checkListController = [[CheckListController alloc]
            initWithStyle:UITableViewStylePlain];
    checkListController.title = @"Check One";
    checkListController.rowImage = [UIImage
        imageNamed:@"checkmarkControllerIcon.png"];
    [array addObject:checkListController];
    [checkListController release];

    // Table Row Controls
    RowControlsController *rowControlsController =
        [[RowControlsController alloc]
        initWithStyle:UITableViewStylePlain];
    rowControlsController.title = @"Row Controls";
    rowControlsController.rowImage = [UIImage imageNamed:
        @"rowControlsIcon.png"];
    [array addObject:rowControlsController];
    [rowControlsController release];

    self.controllers = array;
    [array release];
    [super viewDidLoad];
}
```

In order for this code to compile, we have to also import the header file for the RowControls Controller class, so add the following line of code just before the @implementation line in the same file:

```
#import "RowControlsController.h"
```

Save everything, and compile it. This time, assuming everything went OK, you'll get yet another row when your application launches (see Figure 9-18).

If you tap this new row, it will take you down to a new list where every row has a button control on the right side of the row. Tapping either the button or the row will show an alert telling you which one you tapped (Figure 9-19).

Tapping a row anywhere but on its switch will display an alert telling you whether the switch for that row is turned on or off. At this point, you should be getting pretty comfortable with how this all works, so let's try a slightly more difficult case, shall we? Let's look at how to allow the user to reorder the rows in a table.

Figure 9-18. *The row controls controller added to the root level controller*

Figure 9-19. *The table with buttons in the accessory view*

Our Fourth Subcontroller: Moveable Rows

How you doing? Hanging in there? This chapter is very long, and you've already accomplished a lot. Why not take a break, and grab a Fresca and a Pastel de Belém? We'll do the same. When you're refreshed and ready to move on, we'll build another second-level view controller and add it to our application.

Editing Mode

Moving and deleting rows, as well as inserting rows at a specific spot in the table are all tasks that can be implemented fairly easily. All three are done by turning on something called **editing mode**, which is done using the `setEditing:animated:` method on the table view. This method takes two `Boolean`s. The first indicates whether you are turning on or off editing mode, and the second indicates whether the table should animate the transition. If you set editing to the mode it's already in (in other words, turning it on when it's already on or off when it's already off), the transition will not be animated regardless of what you specify in the second parameter.

In the follow-on controller, we'll again use editing mode, this time to allow the user to delete rows from the table. Allowing row reordering is the easiest of the editing mode tasks, so we'll tackle it first.

Once editing mode is turned on, a number of new delegate methods come into play. The table view uses them to ask if a certain row can be moved or edited and again to notify you if the user actually does move or edit a specific row. It sounds more complex than it is. Let's see it in action.

Creating a New Second-Level Controller

Because we don't have to display a detail view, the Move Me view controller can be implemented without a nib and with just a single controller class. So, select the *Classes* folder in the *Groups & Files* pane in Xcode, and then press ⌘N or select **New File...** from the **File** menu. Select *Cocoa Touch Class*, select *Objective-C class* and *NSObject* for *Subclass of*. When prompted for a name, type *MoveMeController.m*, and create the header file as well.

In our header file, we need two things. First, we need a mutable array to hold our data and keep track of the order of the rows. It has to be mutable because we need to be able to move items around as we get notified of moves. We also need an action method to toggle edit mode on and off. The action method will be called by a navigation bar button that we will create. Single-click *MoveMeController.h*, and make the following changes:

```
#import <Foundation/Foundation.h>
#import <UIKit/UIKit.h>
#import "SecondLevelViewController.h"

@interface MoveMeController : NSObject {
@interface MoveMeController : SecondLevelViewController {
    NSMutableArray *list;
}
@property (nonatomic, retain) NSMutableArray *list;
-(IBAction)toggleMove;
@end
```

Now, switch over to *MoveMeController.m* and add the following code:

```
#import "MoveMeController.h"

@implementation MoveMeController
@synthesize list;
-(IBAction)toggleMove{
    [self.tableView setEditing:!self.tableView.editing animated:YES];

    if (self.tableView.editing)
        [self.navigationItem.rightBarButtonItem setTitle:@"Done"];
    else
        [self.navigationItem.rightBarButtonItem setTitle:@"Move"];
}
- (void)dealloc {
    [list release];
    [super dealloc];
}
- (void)viewDidLoad {
    if (list == nil)
    {
        NSMutableArray *array = [[NSMutableArray alloc] initWithObjects:
                    @"Eeny", @"Meeny", @"Miney", @"Moe", @"Catch", @"A",
                    @"Tiger", @"By", @"The", @"Toe", nil];
        self.list = array;
        [array release];
    }

    UIBarButtonItem *moveButton = [[UIBarButtonItem alloc]
                                    initWithTitle:@"Move"
                                    style:UIBarButtonItemStyleBordered
                                    target:self
                                    action:@selector(toggleMove)];
    self.navigationItem.rightBarButtonItem = moveButton;
    [moveButton release];
    [super viewDidLoad];
```

```objc
}
#pragma mark -
#pragma mark Table Data Source Methods
- (NSInteger)tableView:(UITableView *)tableView
 numberOfRowsInSection:(NSInteger)section {
    return [list count];
}
- (UITableViewCell *)tableView:(UITableView *)tableView
        cellForRowAtIndexPath:(NSIndexPath *)indexPath {

    static NSString *MoveMeCellIdentifier = @"MoveMeCellIdentifier";

    UITableViewCell *cell = [tableView
        dequeueReusableCellWithIdentifier:MoveMeCellIdentifier];
    if (cell == nil) {
        cell = [[[UITableViewCell alloc]
                  initWithStyle:UITableViewCellStyleDefault
                  reuseIdentifier:MoveMeCellIdentifier] autorelease];
        cell.showsReorderControl = YES;

    }
    NSUInteger row = [indexPath row];
    cell.textLabel.text = [list objectAtIndex:row];

    return cell;
}
- (UITableViewCellEditingStyle)tableView:(UITableView *)tableView
        editingStyleForRowAtIndexPath:(NSIndexPath *)indexPath {
    return UITableViewCellEditingStyleNone;
}
- (BOOL)tableView:(UITableView *)tableView
canMoveRowAtIndexPath:(NSIndexPath *)indexPath {
    return YES;
}
- (void)tableView:(UITableView *)tableView
moveRowAtIndexPath:(NSIndexPath *)fromIndexPath
      toIndexPath:(NSIndexPath *)toIndexPath {
    NSUInteger fromRow = [fromIndexPath row];
    NSUInteger toRow = [toIndexPath row];

    id object = [[list objectAtIndex:fromRow] retain];
    [list removeObjectAtIndex:fromRow];
    [list insertObject:object atIndex:toRow];
    [object release];
}
@end
```

Let's take this one step at a time. The first code we added was the implementation of our action method:

```
-(IBAction)toggleMove{
    [self.tableView setEditing:!self.tableView.editing animated:YES];

    if (self.tableView.editing)
        [self.navigationItem.rightBarButtonItem setTitle:@"Done"];
    else
        [self.navigationItem.rightBarButtonItem setTitle:@"Move"];
}
```

All that we're doing here is toggling edit mode and then setting the button's title to an appropriate value. Easy enough, right?

Then we have a standard dealloc method, but no viewDidUnload method. That's intentional. We have no outlets, and if we were to flush our list array, we would lose any reordering that the user had done when the view gets flushed, which we don't want. Therefore, since we have nothing to do in the viewDidUnload method, we don't bother to override it.

The next method we touched is viewDidLoad. The first part of that method doesn't do anything you haven't seen before. It checks to see if list is nil, and if it is (meaning this is the first time this method has been called), it creates a mutable array, filled with values, so our table has some data to show. After that, though, there is something new.

```
UIBarButtonItem *moveButton = [[UIBarButtonItem alloc]
            initWithTitle:@"Move"
            style:UIBarButtonItemStyleBordered
            target:self
            action:@selector(toggleMove)];
    self.navigationItem.rightBarButtonItem = moveButton;
    [moveButton release];
```

Here, we're creating a button bar item, which is a button that will sit on the navigation bar. We give it a title of *Move* and specify a constant, UIBarButtonItemStyleBordered, to indicate that we want a standard bordered bar button. The last two arguments, target and action, tell the button what to do when it is tapped. By passing self as the target and giving it a selector to the toggleMove method as the action, we are telling the button to call our toggleMove method whenever the button is tapped. As a result, anytime the user taps this button, editing mode will be toggled. After we create the button, we add it to the right side of the navigation bar, and then release it.

Now, skip down to the tableView:cellForRowAtIndexPath: method we just added. Did you notice this new line of code?

```
cell.showsReorderControl = YES;
```

Standard accessory icons can be specified by setting the `accessoryType` property of the cell. But, the reorder control is not a standard accessory icon: it's a special case that's shown only when the table is in edit mode. To enable the reorder control, we have to set a property on the cell itself. Note, though, that setting this property to YES doesn't actually display the reorder control until the table gets put into edit mode. Everything else in this method is stuff we've done before.

The next new method is short but important. In our table view, we want to be able to reorder the rows, but we don't want the user to be able to delete or insert rows. As a result, we implement the method `tableView:editingStyleForRowAtIndexPath:`. This method allows the table view to ask if a specific row can be deleted or if a new row can be inserted at a specific spot. By returning `UITableViewCellEditingStyleNone` for each row, we are indicating that we don't support inserts or deletes for any row.

Next comes the method `tableView:canMoveRowAtIndexPath:`. This method gets called for each row, and it gives you the chance to disallow the movement of specific rows. If you return NO from this method for any row, the reorder control will not be shown for that row, and the user will be unable to move it from its current position. We want to allow full reordering, so we just return YES for every row.

The last method, `tableView:moveRowAtIndexPath:fromIndexPath:`, is the method that will actually get called when the user moves a row. The two parameters besides `tableView` are both `NSIndexPath` instances that identify the row that was moved and the row's new position. The table view has already moved the rows in the table so the user is seeing the right thing, but we need to update our data model to keep the two in sync and avoid causing display problems.

First, we retrieve the row that needs to be moved. Then, we retrieve the row's new position.

```
NSUInteger fromRow = [fromIndexPath row];
NSUInteger toRow = [toIndexPath row];
```

We now need to remove the specified object from the array and reinsert it at its new location. But before we do that, we retrieve a pointer to the about-to-be-moved object and retain it so that the object doesn't get released when we remove it from the array. If the array is the only object that has retained the object we're removing (and in our case, it is), removing the selected object from the array will cause its retain count to drop to 0, meaning it will probably disappear on us. By retaining it first, we prevent that from happening.

```
id object = [[list objectAtIndex:fromRow] retain];
[list removeObjectAtIndex:fromRow];
```

After we've removed it, we need to reinsert it into the specified new location:

```
[list insertObject:object atIndex:toRow];
```

And, finally, because we've retained it, we need to release it to avoid leaking memory:

```
[object release];
```

Well, there you have it. We've implemented a table that allows reordering of rows. Now, we just need to add an instance of this new class to FirstLevelViewController's array of controllers. You're probably comfortable doing this by now, but we'll walk you through it just to keep you company.

In *FirstLevelViewController.m*, import the new view's header file by adding the following line of code just before the @implementation declaration:

```
#import "MoveMeController.h"
```

Now, add the following code to the viewDidLoad method in the same file:

```
- (void)viewDidLoad {
    self.title = @"First Level";
    NSMutableArray *array = [[NSMutableArray alloc] init];

    // Disclosure Button
    DisclosureButtonController *disclosureButtonController =
        [[DisclosureButtonController alloc]
        initWithStyle:UITableViewStylePlain];
    disclosureButtonController.title = @"Disclosure Buttons";
    disclosureButtonController.rowImage = [UIImage
        imageNamed:@"disclosureButtonControllerIcon.png"];
    [array addObject:disclosureButtonController];
    [disclosureButtonController release];

    // Check List
    CheckListController *checkListController = [[CheckListController alloc]
        initWithStyle:UITableViewStylePlain];
    checkListController.title = @"Check One";
    checkListController.rowImage = [UIImage
        imageNamed:@"checkmarkControllerIcon.png"];
    [array addObject:checkListController];
    [checkListController release];

    // Table Row Controls
    RowControlsController *rowControlsController =
        [[RowControlsController alloc]
        initWithStyle:UITableViewStylePlain];
```

```
rowControlsController.title = @"Row Controls";
rowControlsController.rowImage = [UIImage imageNamed:
    @"rowControlsIcon.png"];
[array addObject:rowControlsController];
[rowControlsController release];

// Move Me
MoveMeController *moveMeController = [[MoveMeController alloc]
    initWithStyle:UITableViewStylePlain];
moveMeController.title = @"Move Me";
moveMeController.rowImage = [UIImage imageNamed:@"moveMeIcon.png"];
[array addObject:moveMeController];
[moveMeController release];

self.controllers = array;
[array release];
[super viewDidLoad];
}
```

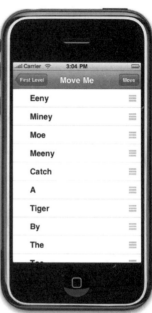

OK, let's go ahead and compile this bad boy and see what shakes out. If everything went smoothly, our application will launch in the simulator with (count 'em) four rows in the root-level table. If you click the new one, called *Move Me*, it'll take you down to a list of rows. If you want to try moving the rows, click the *Move* button, and the reorder controls should appear (see Figure 9-20).

If you tap in the reorder control and then drag, the row should move as you drag, as in Figure 9-6. Move the row as you like. The row should settle into its new position nicely. You can even navigate back up to the top level and come back down, and your rows will be right where you left them. If you quit and come back in, they will get restored, but don't worry; in a few chapters, we'll teach you how to save and restore data.

Figure 9-20. *The Move Me view controller when you first drill down*

NOTE

If you find you have a bit of trouble making contact with the move control, don't panic. If you are very careful to actually click the pixels of the move control, you should be able to experience moving goodness. The difficulty here is that you are interfacing with the simulator using a single-pixel hot-spot cursor. If you downloaded the application onto your iPhone or iPod touch (which you can't do until you are accepted into one of Apple's for-pay iPhone Developer Programs), you'd be using your big, fat fingers, which, presumably, are several pixels wide and will have no trouble making contact with the move control.

In case you hadn't noticed, this chapter is a bit of a marathon. If you're feeling a little over-whelmed, this is probably a good time to take a break. There's a lot of stuff in this chapter to absorb, but it's important. The vast majority of iPhone applications will use table views in some respect. When you're ready to move on, we'll look at another use of edit mode. This time, we'll let the user delete our precious rows. Gasp!

Our Fifth Subcontroller: Deletable Rows

Letting users delete rows isn't really significantly harder than letting them move rows. Let's take a look at that process. Instead of creating an array from a hard-coded list of objects, we're going to load a property list file this time, just to save some typing. You can grab the file called *computers.plist* out of the *09 Nav* folder in the projects archive that accompanies this book and add it to the *Resources* folder of your Xcode project.

Select the *Classes* folder in the *Groups & Files* pane in Xcode, and then press ⌘N or select **New File...** from the **File** menu. Select *Cocoa Touch Class*, select *Objective-C class* and *NSObject* for *Subclass of*. When prompted for a name, this time type *DeleteMeController.m*.

Once you've got your new files, let's start by editing *DeleteMeController.h*. The changes we're going to make there should look familiar, as they're nearly identical to the ones we made in the last view controller we built. Go ahead and make these changes now:

```
#import <Foundation/Foundation.h>
#import <UIKit/UIKit.h>
#import "SecondLevelViewController.h"

@interface DeleteMeController : NSObject {
@interface DeleteMeController : SecondLevelViewController {
    NSMutableArray *list;
}
@property (nonatomic, retain) NSMutableArray *list;
-(IBAction)toggleEdit:(id)sender;
@end
```

No surprises here, right? We're changing the superclass from NSObject to Second LevelViewController. After that, we declare a mutable array to hold our data and an action method to toggle edit mode. In the last controller we built, we used edit mode to let the users reorder rows. In this version, edit mode will be used to let them delete rows. You can actually combine both in the same table if you like. We separated them so the con-cepts would be a bit easier to follow, but the delete and reorder operations do play nicely together. A row that can be reordered will display the reorder icon anytime that the table is in edit mode. When you tap the red circular icon on the left side of the row (see Figure 9-7), the *Delete* button will pop up, obscuring the reorder icon but only temporarily.

Switch over to *DeleteMeController.m*, and add the following code:

```
#import "DeleteMeController.h"

@implementation DeleteMeController
@synthesize list;
-(IBAction)toggleEdit:(id)sender {
    [self.tableView setEditing:!self.tableView.editing animated:YES];

    if (self.tableView.editing)
        [self.navigationItem.rightBarButtonItem setTitle:@"Done"];
    else
        [self.navigationItem.rightBarButtonItem setTitle:@"Delete"];
}
- (void)viewDidLoad {
    if (list == nil)
    {
        NSString *path = [[NSBundle mainBundle]
            pathForResource:@"computers" ofType:@"plist"];
        NSMutableArray *array = [[NSMutableArray alloc]
                                 initWithContentsOfFile:path];
        self.list = array;
        [array release];
    }
    UIBarButtonItem *editButton = [[UIBarButtonItem alloc]
                                   initWithTitle:@"Delete"
                                   style:UIBarButtonItemStyleBordered
                                   target:self
                                   action:@selector(toggleEdit:)];
    self.navigationItem.rightBarButtonItem = editButton;
    [editButton release];

    [super viewDidLoad];
}
- (void)dealloc {
    [list release];
    [super dealloc];
}
#pragma mark -
#pragma mark Table Data Source Methods
- (NSInteger)tableView:(UITableView *)tableView
 numberOfRowsInSection:(NSInteger)section {
    return [list count];
}
- (UITableViewCell *)tableView:(UITableView *)tableView
        cellForRowAtIndexPath:(NSIndexPath *)indexPath {
```

```
static NSString *DeleteMeCellIdentifier = @"DeleteMeCellIdentifier";

UITableViewCell *cell = [tableView dequeueReusableCellWithIdentifier:
                            DeleteMeCellIdentifier];
if (cell == nil) {
    cell = [[[UITableViewCell alloc]
        initWithStyle:UITableViewCellStyleDefault
        reuseIdentifier:DeleteMeCellIdentifier] autorelease];
}
NSInteger row = [indexPath row];
cell.textLabel.text = [self.list objectAtIndex:row];
return cell;
}


#pragma mark -
#pragma mark Table View Data Source Methods
- (void)tableView:(UITableView *)tableView
commitEditingStyle:(UITableViewCellEditingStyle)editingStyle
forRowAtIndexPath:(NSIndexPath *)indexPath {

    NSUInteger row = [indexPath row];
    [self.list removeObjectAtIndex:row];
    [tableView deleteRowsAtIndexPaths:[NSArray arrayWithObject:indexPath]
                withRowAnimation:UITableViewRowAnimationFade];
}
@end
```

Let's look at what we did. The new action method, toggleEdit:, is pretty much the same
as our last version. It sets edit mode to on if it's currently off and vice versa, and then sets
the button's title as appropriate. The viewDidLoad method is also similar to the one from
the previous view controller and, again, we have no viewDidUnload method because we
have no outlets and we want to preserve changes made to our mutable array in edit mode.
The only difference is that we're loading our array from a property list rather than feeding it
a hard-coded list of strings. The property list we're using is a flat array of strings containing
a variety of computer model names that might be a bit familiar. We also assign a different
name to the edit button this time, naming it *Delete* to make the button's effect obvious to
the user.

The two data source methods contain nothing new, but the last method in the class is something you've never seen before, so let's take a closer look at it:

```
- (void)tableView:(UITableView *)tableView
      commitEditingStyle:(UITableViewCellEditingStyle)editingStyle
      forRowAtIndexPath:(NSIndexPath *)indexPath {
```

This method is called by the table view when the user has made an edit, which means a delete or an insert. The first argument is the table view on which a row was edited. The second parameter, editingStyle, is a constant that tells us what kind of edit just happened. Currently, there are three editing styles defined. One of them is UITable ViewCellEditingStyleNone, which we used in the last section to indicate that a row can't be edited. The other two styles are UITableViewCellEditingStyleDelete, which is the default option, and UITableViewCellEditingStyleInsert. The option UITableView CellEditingStyleNone will never be passed into this method, because it is used to indicate that editing is not allowed for this row.

We ignore this parameter, because the default editing style for rows is the delete style, so we know that every time this method is called, it will be requesting a delete. You can use this parameter to allow both inserts and deletes within a single table. The other editing style, UITableViewCellEditingStyleInsert, is generally used when you need to let the user insert rows at a specific spot in a list. In a list whose order is maintained by the system, such as an alphabetical list of names, the user will usually tap a toolbar or navigation bar button to ask the system to create a new object in a detail view. Once the user is done specifying the new object, the system will place in the appropriate row. We won't be covering the use of inserts, but the insert functionality works in fundamentally the same way as the delete we are about to implement. The only difference is that, instead of deleting the specified row from your data model, you have to create a new object and insert it at the specified spot.

The last parameter, indexPath, tells us which row is being edited. For a delete, this index path represents the row to be deleted. For an insert, it represents the index where the new row should be inserted.

In our method, we first retrieve the row that is being edited from indexPath:

```
NSUInteger row = [indexPath row];
```

Then, we remove the object from the mutable array we created earlier:

```
[self.list removeObjectAtIndex:row];
```

Finally, we tell the table to delete the row, specifying the constant UITableViewRow AnimationFade, which represents one type of animation the iPhone will use when removing rows. There are several other options in addition to this one, which causes the row to fade away. You can look up the UITableViewRowAnimation in Xcode's document browser to see what other animations are available.

```
[tableView deleteRowsAtIndexPaths:[NSArray arrayWithObject:indexPath]
    withRowAnimation:UITableViewRowAnimationFade];
}
```

And that's all she wrote, folks. That's the whole enchilada for this class, so let's add an instance of it to our root view controller and try it out. In *FirstLevelViewController.m*, we first need to import our new controller class's header file, so add the following line of code right before the @implementation declaration:

```
#import "DeleteMeController.h"
```

Now, add the following code to the viewDidLoad method:

```
- (void)viewDidLoad {
    self.title = @"First Level";
    NSMutableArray *array = [[NSMutableArray alloc] init];

    // Disclosure Button
    DisclosureButtonController *disclosureButtonController =
        [[DisclosureButtonController alloc]
        initWithStyle:UITableViewStylePlain];
    disclosureButtonController.title = @"Disclosure Buttons";
    disclosureButtonController.rowImage = [UIImage imageNamed:
        @"disclosureButtonControllerIcon.png"];
    [array addObject:disclosureButtonController];
    [disclosureButtonController release];

    // Check List
    CheckListController *checkListController = [[CheckListController alloc]
        initWithStyle:UITableViewStylePlain];
    checkListController.title = @"Check One";
    checkListController.rowImage = [UIImage imageNamed:
        @"checkmarkControllerIcon.png"];
    [array addObject:checkListController];
    [checkListController release];

    // Table Row Controls
    RowControlsController *rowControlsController =
        [[RowControlsController alloc]
        initWithStyle:UITableViewStylePlain];
    rowControlsController.title = @"Row Controls";
    rowControlsController.rowImage = [UIImage imageNamed:
        @"rowControlsIcon.png"];
    [array addObject:rowControlsController];
    [rowControlsController release];

    // Move Me
    MoveMeController *moveMeController = [[MoveMeController alloc]
        initWithStyle:UITableViewStylePlain];
    moveMeController.title = @"Move Me";
    moveMeController.rowImage = [UIImage imageNamed:@"moveMeIcon.png"];
```

```
[array addObject:moveMeController];
[moveMeController release];

// Delete Me
DeleteMeController *deleteMeController = [[DeleteMeController alloc]
    initWithStyle:UITableViewStylePlain];
deleteMeController.title = @"Delete Me";
deleteMeController.rowImage = [UIImage imageNamed:@"deleteMeIcon.png"];
[array addObject:deleteMeController];
[deleteMeController release];

self.controllers = array;
[array release];
[super viewDidLoad];
}
```

Save everything, compile, and let her rip. When the simulator comes up, the root level will now have—can you guess?—five rows. If you select the new *Delete Me* row, you'll be presented with a list of computer models (see Figure 9-21). How many of these have you owned?

Notice that we again have a button on the right side of the navigation bar, this time labeled *Delete*. If we tap that, the table enters edit mode, which looks like Figure 9-22.

Figure 9-21. *The delete me view when it first launches*

Figure 9-22. *The delete me view in edit mode*

Next to each editable row is now a little icon that looks a little like a "Do Not Enter" street sign. If you tap the icon, it rotates sideways, and a button labeled *Delete* appears (see Figure 9-7). Tapping that button will cause its row to be deleted, both from the underlying model as well as from the table, using the animation style we specified.

And when you implement edit mode to allow deletes, you get additional functionality for free. Swipe your finger horizontally across a row. Look at that! The delete button comes up for just that row, just like in the Mail application.

Our Sixth Subcontroller: An Editable Detail Pane

We're coming around the bend, now, and the finish line is in sight, albeit still a little ways in the distance. If you're still with us, give yourself a pat on the back, or have someone do it for you. This is a long, tough chapter.

The next concept we're going to explore is how to implement a reusable editable detail view. You may notice as you look through the various applications that come on your iPhone, that many of those applications, including the Contacts application, implement their detail views as a grouped table (see Figure 9-23).

Figure 9-23. *An example of a grouped table view being used to present an editable table view*

Let's look at how to do this now. Before we begin, we need some data to show, and we need more than just a list of strings. In the last two chapters, when we needed more complex data, such as with the multiline table in Chapter 7 or the ZIP codes picker in Chapter 6, we used an NSArray to hold a bunch of NSDictionary instances filled with our data. That works fine and is very flexible, but it's a little hard to work with. For this table's data, let's create a custom Objective-C data object to hold the individual instances that will be displayed in the list.

Creating the Data Model Object

The property list we'll be using in this section of the application contains data about the US presidents: each president's name, his party, the year he took office, and the year he left office. Let's create the class to hold that data.

Once again, single-click the *Classes* folder in Xcode to select it, and then press ⌘N to bring up the new file assistant. Select *Cocoa Touch Class* from the left pane, and then select

Objective-C class and *NSObject* for *Subclass of*. Name this class *President.m*, and make sure the checkbox for creating the header file is checked.

Click *President.h*, and make the following changes:

```
#define kPresidentNumberKey          @"President"
#define kPresidentNameKey            @"Name"
#define kPresidentFromKey            @"FromYear"
#define kPresidentToKey              @"ToYear"
#define kPresidentPartyKey           @"Party"

#import <Foundation/Foundation.h>

@interface President : NSObject {
@interface President : NSObject <NSCoding> {
    int         number;
    NSString    *name;
    NSString    *fromYear;
    NSString    *toYear;
    NSString    *party;
}
@property int number;
@property (nonatomic, retain) NSString *name;
@property (nonatomic, retain) NSString *fromYear;
@property (nonatomic, retain) NSString *toYear;
@property (nonatomic, retain) NSString *party;
@end
```

The five constants will be used to identify the fields when they are read from the file system. Conforming this class to the `NSCoding` protocol is what allows this object to be written to and created from files. The rest of the new stuff we've added to this header file is there to implement the properties needed to hold our data. Switch over to *President.m*, and make these changes:

```
#import "President.h"

@implementation President
@synthesize number;
@synthesize name;
@synthesize fromYear;
@synthesize toYear;
@synthesize party;

-(void)dealloc{
    [name release];
    [fromYear release];
    [toYear release];
```

```
        [party release];
        [super dealloc];
}
#pragma mark -
#pragma mark NSCoding
- (void)encodeWithCoder:(NSCoder *)coder {
        [coder encodeInt:self.number forKey:kPresidentNumberKey];
        [coder encodeObject:self.name forKey:kPresidentNameKey];
        [coder encodeObject:self.fromYear forKey:kPresidentFromKey];
        [coder encodeObject:self.toYear   forKey:kPresidentToKey];
        [coder encodeObject:self.party forKey:kPresidentPartyKey];
}
- (id)initWithCoder:(NSCoder *)coder {
    if (self = [super init]) {
        self.number = [coder decodeIntForKey:kPresidentNumberKey];
        self.name = [coder decodeObjectForKey:kPresidentNameKey];
        self.fromYear = [coder decodeObjectForKey:kPresidentFromKey];
        self.toYear = [coder decodeObjectForKey:kPresidentToKey];
        self.party = [coder decodeObjectForKey:kPresidentPartyKey];
    }
    return self;
}
@end
```

Don't worry too much about the encodeWithCoder: and initWithCoder: methods. We'll be covering those in more detail in Chapter 11. All you need to know for now is that these two methods are part of the NSCoding protocol which can be used to save objects to disk and load them back in. encodeWithCoder: encodes our object to be saved; initWithCoder: is used to create new objects from the saved file. These methods will allow us to create President objects from a property list archive file. Everything else in this class should be fairly self-explanatory.

We've provided you with a property list file that contains data for all the US presidents and can be used to create new instances of the President object we just wrote. We will be using this in the next section, so you won't have to type in a whole bunch of data. Grab the *Presidents.plist* file from the *09 Nav* folder in the projects archive, and add it to the *Resources* folder of your project.

Now, we're ready to write our two controller classes.

Creating the Controllers

For this part of the application, we're going to need two new controllers, one that will show the list to be edited and another one to view and edit the details of the item selected in that list. Since both of these view controllers will be based on tables, we won't need to create any nib files, but we will need two separate controller classes. Let's create the files for both classes now and then implement them.

Select the *Classes* folder in the *Groups & Files* pane in Xcode, and then press ⌘N or select **New File…** from the **File** menu. Select *Cocoa Touch Class*, select *Objective-C class* and *NSObject* for *Subclass of*. For a name, type *PresidentsViewController.m*, and make sure to have it create the header file also. Repeat the same process a second time using the name *PresidentDetailController.m*.

NOTE

In case you were wondering, `PresidentDetailController` is singular (as opposed to `Presidents DetailController`) because it deals with detail on a single president. Yes, we actually had a fistfight about that little detail, but one intense paintball session later, we are friends again.

Let's create the view controller that shows the list of presidents first. Single-click *Presidents ViewController.h*, and make the following changes:

```
#import <Foundation/Foundation.h>
#import "SecondLevelViewController.h"

@interface PresidentsViewController : NSObject {
@interface PresidentsViewController : SecondLevelViewController {
        NSMutableArray *list;
}
@property (nonatomic, retain) NSMutableArray *list;
@end
```

Then switch over to *PresidentsViewController.m* and make the following changes:

```
#import "PresidentsViewController.h"
#import "PresidentDetailController.h"
#import "President.h"

@implementation PresidentsViewController
@synthesize list;
- (void)viewDidLoad {
    NSString *path = [[NSBundle mainBundle] pathForResource:@"Presidents"
                                                     ofType:@"plist"];

    NSData *data;
    NSKeyedUnarchiver *unarchiver;

    data = [[NSData alloc] initWithContentsOfFile:path];
    unarchiver = [[NSKeyedUnarchiver alloc] initForReadingWithData:data];
```

```objc
        NSMutableArray *array = [unarchiver decodeObjectForKey:@"Presidents"];
        self.list = array;
        [unarchiver finishDecoding];
        [unarchiver release];
        [data release];

        [super viewDidLoad];
}
- (void)viewWillAppear:(BOOL)animated {
    [self.tableView reloadData];
    [super viewWillAppear:animated];
}
- (void)dealloc {
    [list release];
    [super dealloc];
}
#pragma mark -
#pragma mark Table Data Source Methods
- (NSInteger)tableView:(UITableView *)tableView
 numberOfRowsInSection:(NSInteger)section {
    return [list count];
}
- (UITableViewCell *)tableView:(UITableView *)tableView
         cellForRowAtIndexPath:(NSIndexPath *)indexPath {

    static NSString *PresidentListCellIdentifier =
        @"PresidentListCellIdentifier";

    UITableViewCell *cell = [tableView
        dequeueReusableCellWithIdentifier:PresidentListCellIdentifier];
    if (cell == nil) {
        cell = [[[UITableViewCell alloc]
            initWithStyle:UITableViewCellStyleSubtitle
            reuseIdentifier:PresidentListCellIdentifier] autorelease];
    }
    NSUInteger row = [indexPath row];
    President *thePres = [self.list objectAtIndex:row];
    cell.textLabel.text = thePres.name;
    cell.detailTextLabel.text = [NSString stringWithFormat:@"%@ - %@",
        thePres.fromYear, thePres.toYear];
    return cell;
}
#pragma mark -
#pragma mark Table Delegate Methods
- (void)tableView:(UITableView *)tableView
didSelectRowAtIndexPath:(NSIndexPath *)indexPath {
```

```
    NSUInteger row = [indexPath row];
    President *prez = [self.list objectAtIndex:row];

    PresidentDetailController *childController =
    [[PresidentDetailController alloc]
     initWithStyle:UITableViewStyleGrouped];

    childController.title = prez.name;
    childController.president = prez;

    [self.navigationController pushViewController:childController
        animated:YES];
    [childController release];
}
@end
```

Most of the code you just entered is stuff you've seen before. One new thing is in the viewDidLoad method, where we used an NSKeyedUnarchiver method to create an array full of instances of the President class from our property list file. It's not important that you understand exactly what's going on there as long as you understand that we're loading an array full of Presidents.

First, we get the path for the property file:

```
    NSString *path = [[NSBundle mainBundle] pathForResource:@"Presidents"
        ofType:@"plist"];
```

Next, we declare a data object that will temporarily hold the encoded archive and an NSKeyedUnarchiver, which we'll use to actually restore the objects from the archive:

```
    NSData *data;
    NSKeyedUnarchiver *unarchiver;
```

We load the property list into data, and then use data to initialize unarchiver:

```
    data = [[NSData alloc] initWithContentsOfFile:path];
    unarchiver = [[NSKeyedUnarchiver alloc] initForReadingWithData:data];
```

Now, we decode an array from the archive. The key @"Presidents" is the same value that was used to create this archive:

```
    NSMutableArray *array = [unarchiver decodeObjectForKey:@"Presidents"];
```

We then assign this decoded array to our list property, finalize the decoding process, clean up our memory, and make our call to super:

```
    self.list = array;
    [unarchiver finishDecoding];
    [unarchiver release];
    [data release];

    [super viewDidLoad];
```

We also need to tell our tableView to reload its data in the viewWillAppear: method. If the user changes something in the detail view, we need to make sure that the parent view shows that new data. Rather than testing for a change, we force the parent view to reload its data and redraw each time it appears.

```
- (void)viewWillAppear:(BOOL)animated {
    [self.tableView reloadData];
    [super viewWillAppear:animated];
}
```

There's one other change from the last time we created a detail view. It's in the last method, tableView:didSelectRowAtIndexPath:. When we created the *Disclosure Button* view, we reused the same child controller every time and just changed its values. That's relatively easy to do when you've got a nib with outlets. When you're using a table view to implement your detail view, the methods that fire the first time and the ones that fire subsequent times are different. Also, the table cells that are used to display and change the data get reused. The combination of these two details means your code can get very, very complex if you're trying to make it behave exactly the same way every time and to make sure that you are able to keep track of all the changes. As a result, it's well worth the little bit of additional overhead from allocating and releasing new controller objects to keep down the complexity of our controller class.

Let's look at the detail controller, because that's where the bulk of the new stuff is this time. This new controller gets pushed onto the navigation stack when the user taps one of the rows in the PresidentsViewController table to allow data entry for that president. Let's implement the detail view now.

Creating the Detail View Controller

Please fasten your seatbelts, ladies and gentlemen; we're expecting a little turbulence ahead. Air sickness bags are located in the seat pocket in front of you.

This next controller is just a little on the gnarly side, but we'll get through it safely. Please remain seated. Single-click *PresidentDetailController.h*, and make the following changes:

```
#import <Foundation/Foundation.h>

@class President;
```

```
#define kNumberOfEditableRows          4
#define kNameRowIndex                  0
#define kFromYearRowIndex              1
#define kToYearRowIndex                2
#define kPartyIndex                    3

#define kLabelTag                      4096

@interface PresidentDetailController : NSObject {
@interface PresidentDetailController : UITableViewController
        <UITextFieldDelegate> {
    President *president;
    NSArray *fieldLabels;
    NSMutableDictionary *tempValues;
    UITextField *textFieldBeingEdited;
}
@property (nonatomic, retain) President *president;
@property (nonatomic, retain) NSArray *fieldLabels;
@property (nonatomic, retain) NSMutableDictionary *tempValues;
@property (nonatomic, retain) UITextField *textFieldBeingEdited;

- (IBAction)cancel:(id)sender;
- (IBAction)save:(id)sender;
- (IBAction)textFieldDone:(id)sender;
@end
```

Well, now, what the heck is going on here? This is new. In all our previous table view examples, each table row corresponded to a single row in an array. The array provided all the data the table needed. So, for example, our table of Pixar movies was driven by an array of strings, each string containing the title of a single Pixar movie.

Our presidents example features two different tables. One is a list of presidents, by name, and is driven by an array with one president per row. The second table implements a detail view of a selected president. Since this table has a fixed number of fields, instead of using an array to supply data to this table, we define a series of constants we will use in our table data source methods. These constants define the number of editable fields, along with the index value for the row that will hold each of those properties.

There's also a constant called kLabelTag that we'll use to retrieve the UILabel from the cell so that we can set the label correctly for the row. Shouldn't there be another tag for the UITextField? Normally, yes, but we will need to use the tag property of the text field for another purpose. We'll have to use another slightly less convenient mechanism to retrieve the text field when we need to set its value. Don't worry if that seems confusing; everything should become clear when we actually write the code.

You should notice that this class conforms to three protocols this time: the table data-source and delegate protocols and a new one, `UITextFieldDelegate`. By conforming to `UITextFieldDelegate`, we'll be notified when a user makes a change to a text field so that we can save the field's value. This application doesn't have enough rows for the table to ever have to scroll, but in many applications, a text field could scroll off the screen and, perhaps, be deallocated or reused. If the text field is lost, the value stored in it is lost, so saving the value when the user makes a change is the way to go.

Down a little further, we declare a pointer to a `President` object. This is the object that we will actually be editing using this view, and it's set in the `tableView:didSelectRowAt IndexPath:` of our parent controller based on the row selected there. When the user taps the row for Thomas Jefferson, the `PresidentsViewController` will create an instance of the `PresidentDetailController`. The `PresidentsViewController` will then set the `president` property of that instance to the object that represents Thomas Jefferson, and push the newly created instance of `PresidentDetailController` onto the navigation stack.

The second instance variable, `fieldLabels`, is an array that holds a list of labels that correspond to the constants kNameRowIndex, kFromYearRowIndex, kToYearRowIndex, and kPartyIndex. For example, kNameRowIndex is defined as 0. So, the label for the row that shows the president's name is stored at index 0 in the `fieldLabels` array. You'll see this in action when we get to it in code in a minute.

Next, we define a mutable dictionary, `tempValues`, that will hold values from fields the user changes. We don't want to make the changes directly to the `president` object because if the user selects the *Cancel* button, we need the original data so we can go back to it. Instead, what we will do is store any value that gets changed in our new mutable dictionary, `tempValues`. So if, for example, the user edited the *Name:* field and then tapped the *Party:* field to start editing that one, the `PresidentDetailController` would get notified at that time that the *Name:* field had been edited, because it is the text field's delegate.

When the `PresidentDetailController` gets notified of the change, it stores the new value in the dictionary using the name of the property it represents as the key. In our example, we'd store a change to the *Name:* field using the key @"name". That way, regardless of whether users save or cancel, we have the data we need to handle it. If the users cancel, we just discard this dictionary, and if they save, we copy the changed values over to `president`.

Next up is a pointer to a `UITextField`, named `textFieldBeingEdited`. The moment the users click in one of the `PresidentDetailController` text fields, `textFieldBeingEdited` is set to point to that text field. Why do we need this text field pointer? We have an interesting timing problem, and `textFieldBeingEdited` is the solution.

Users can take one of two basic paths to finish editing a text field. First, they can touch another control or text field that becomes first responder. In this case, the text field that was being edited loses first responder status, and the delegate method `textFieldDidEndEditing:` is called. You'll see `textFieldDidEndEditing:` in a few pages when we enter the code for *PresidentDetailController.m*. In this case, `textFieldDidEndEditing:` takes the new value of the text field and stores it in `tempValues`.

The second way the users can finish editing a text field is by tapping the *Save* or *Cancel* button. When they do this, the `save:` or `cancel:` action method gets called. In both methods, the `PresidentDetailController` view must be popped off the stack, since both the save and cancel actions end the editing session. This presents a problem. The `save:` and `cancel:` action methods do not have a simple way of finding the just-edited text field to save the data.

`textFieldDidEndEditing:`, the delegate method we discussed in the previous paragraph, does have access to the text field, since the text field is passed in as a parameter. That's where `textFieldBeingEdited` comes in. The `cancel:` action method ignores `textFieldBeingEdited`, since the user did not want to save changes, so the changes can be lost with no problem. But the `save:` method does care about those changes and needs a way to save them.

Since `textFieldBeingEdited` is maintained as a pointer to the current text field being edited, `save:` uses that pointer to copy the value in the text field to `tempValues`. Now, `save:` can do its job and pop the `PresidentDetailController` view off the stack, which will bring our list of presidents back to the top of the stack. When the view is popped off the stack, the text field and its value are lost. That's OK; we've saved that sucker already, so all is cool.

Single-click *PresidentDetailController.m*, and make the following changes:

```
#import "PresidentDetailController.h"
#import "President.h"

@implementation PresidentDetailController
@synthesize president;
@synthesize fieldLabels;
@synthesize tempValues;
@synthesize textFieldBeingEdited;

-(IBAction)cancel:(id)sender {
    [self.navigationController popViewControllerAnimated:YES];
}
- (IBAction)save:(id)sender {

    if (textFieldBeingEdited != nil) {
        NSNumber *tagAsNum= [[NSNumber alloc]
                            initWithInt:textFieldBeingEdited.tag];
```

```objc
        [tempValues setObject:textFieldBeingEdited.text forKey: tagAsNum];
        [tagAsNum release];

    }
    for (NSNumber *key in [tempValues allKeys]) {
        switch ([key intValue]) {
            case kNameRowIndex:
                president.name = [tempValues objectForKey:key];
                break;
            case kFromYearRowIndex:
                president.fromYear = [tempValues objectForKey:key];
                break;
            case kToYearRowIndex:
                president.toYear = [tempValues objectForKey:key];
                break;
            case kPartyIndex:
                president.party = [tempValues objectForKey:key];
            default:
                break;
        }
    }
    [self.navigationController popViewControllerAnimated:YES];

    NSArray *allControllers = self.navigationController.viewControllers;
    UITableViewController *parent = [allControllers lastObject];
    [parent.tableView reloadData];
}
-(IBAction)textFieldDone:(id)sender {
    [sender resignFirstResponder];
}
#pragma mark -
- (void)viewDidLoad {
    NSArray *array = [[NSArray alloc] initWithObjects:@"Name:", @"From:",
                      @"To:", @"Party:", nil];
    self.fieldLabels = array;
    [array release];

    UIBarButtonItem *cancelButton = [[UIBarButtonItem alloc]
                                      initWithTitle:@"Cancel"
                                      style:UIBarButtonItemStylePlain
                                      target:self
                                      action:@selector(cancel:)];
    self.navigationItem.leftBarButtonItem = cancelButton;
    [cancelButton release];

    UIBarButtonItem *saveButton = [[UIBarButtonItem alloc]
                                    initWithTitle:@"Save"
```

```
                                style:UIBarButtonItemStyleDone
                                target:self
                                action:@selector(save:)];
    self.navigationItem.rightBarButtonItem = saveButton;
    [saveButton release];

    NSMutableDictionary *dict = [[NSMutableDictionary alloc] init];
    self.tempValues = dict;
    [dict release];
    [super viewDidLoad];
}
- (void)dealloc {
    [textFieldBeingEdited release];
    [tempValues release];
    [president release];
    [fieldLabels release];

    [super dealloc];
}


#pragma mark -
#pragma mark Table Data Source Methods
- (NSInteger)tableView:(UITableView *)tableView
 numberOfRowsInSection:(NSInteger)section {
    return kNumberOfEditableRows;
}
- (UITableViewCell *)tableView:(UITableView *)tableView
        cellForRowAtIndexPath:(NSIndexPath *)indexPath {
    static NSString *PresidentCellIdentifier = @"PresidentCellIdentifier";

    UITableViewCell *cell = [tableView dequeueReusableCellWithIdentifier:
                            PresidentCellIdentifier];
    if (cell == nil) {

        cell = [[[UITableViewCell alloc]
            initWithStyle:UITableViewCellStyleDefault
            reuseIdentifier:PresidentCellIdentifier] autorelease];
        UILabel *label = [[UILabel alloc] initWithFrame:
                        CGRectMake(10, 10, 75, 25)];
        label.textAlignment = UITextAlignmentRight;
        label.tag = kLabelTag;
        label.font = [UIFont boldSystemFontOfSize:14];
        [cell.contentView addSubview:label];
        [label release];

        UITextField *textField = [[UITextField alloc] initWithFrame:
                        CGRectMake(90, 12, 200, 25)];
```

```objc
        textField.clearsOnBeginEditing = NO;
        [textField setDelegate:self];
        textField.returnKeyType = UIReturnKeyDone;
        [textField addTarget:self
                    action:@selector(textFieldDone:)
            forControlEvents:UIControlEventEditingDidEndOnExit];
        [cell.contentView addSubview:textField];
    }
    NSUInteger row = [indexPath row];

    UILabel *label = (UILabel *)[cell viewWithTag:kLabelTag];
    UITextField *textField = nil;
    for (UIView *oneView in cell.contentView.subviews) {
        if ([oneView isMemberOfClass:[UITextField class]])
            textField = (UITextField *)oneView;
    }
    label.text = [fieldLabels objectAtIndex:row];
    NSNumber *rowAsNum = [[NSNumber alloc] initWithInt:row];
    switch (row) {
        case kNameRowIndex:
            if ([[tempValues allKeys] containsObject:rowAsNum])
                textField.text = [tempValues objectForKey:rowAsNum];
            else
                textField.text = president.name;
            break;
        case kFromYearRowIndex:
            if ([[tempValues allKeys] containsObject:rowAsNum])
                textField.text = [tempValues objectForKey:rowAsNum];
            else
                textField.text = president.fromYear;
            break;
        case kToYearRowIndex:
            if ([[tempValues allKeys] containsObject:rowAsNum])
                textField.text = [tempValues objectForKey:rowAsNum];
            else
                textField.text = president.toYear;
            break;
        case kPartyIndex:
            if ([[tempValues allKeys] containsObject:rowAsNum])
                textField.text = [tempValues objectForKey:rowAsNum];
            else
                textField.text = president.party;
        default:
            break;
    }
    if (textFieldBeingEdited == textField)
        textFieldBeingEdited = nil;
```

```
        textField.tag = row;
        [rowAsNum release];
        return cell;
}
#pragma mark -
#pragma mark Table Delegate Methods
- (NSIndexPath *)tableView:(UITableView *)tableView
  willSelectRowAtIndexPath:(NSIndexPath *)indexPath {
        return nil;
}
#pragma mark Text Field Delegate Methods
- (void)textFieldDidBeginEditing:(UITextField *)textField {
        self.textFieldBeingEdited = textField;
}
- (void)textFieldDidEndEditing:(UITextField *)textField {
        NSNumber *tagAsNum = [[NSNumber alloc] initWithInt:textField.tag];
        [tempValues setObject:textField.text forKey:tagAsNum];
        [tagAsNum release];
}
@end
```

The first new method is our cancel: action method. This gets called, appropriately enough, when the user taps the *Cancel* button. When the *Cancel* button is tapped, the current view will be popped off the stack, and the previous view will rise to the top of the stack. Ordinarily, that job would be handled by the navigation controller, but a little later in the code, we're going to manually set the left bar button item. This means we're replacing the button that the navigation controller uses for that purpose. We can pop the current view off the stack by getting a reference to the navigation controller and telling it to do just that.

```
-(IBAction)cancel:(id)sender {
    NavAppDelegate *delegate =
        [[UIApplication sharedApplication] delegate];
    [delegate.navController popViewControllerAnimated:YES];

}
```

The next method is save:, which gets called when the user taps the *Save* button. When the *Save* button is tapped, the values that the user has entered have already been stored in the tempValues dictionary, unless the keyboard is still visible and the cursor is still in one of the text fields. In that case, there may well be changes to that text field that have not yet been put into our tempValues dictionary. To account for this, the first thing the save: method does is check to see if there is a text field that is currently being edited. Whenever the user starts editing a text field, we store a pointer to that text field in textFieldBeingEdited. If textFieldBeingEdited is not nil, we grab its value and stick it in tempValues:

```
    if (textFieldBeingEdited != nil) {
        NSNumber *tfKey= [[NSNumber alloc] initWithInt:
            textFieldBeingEdited.tag];
        [tempValues setObject:textFieldBeingEdited.text forKey:tfKey];
        [tagAsNum release];
    }
```

We then use fast enumeration to step through all the key values in the dictionary, using the row numbers as keys. We can't store raw datatypes like `int` in an `NSDictionary`, so we create `NSNumber` objects based on the row number and use those instead. We use `intValue` to turn the number represented by `key` back into an `int`, and then use a `switch` on that value using the constants we defined earlier and assign the appropriate value from the `tempValues` array back to the designated field on our `president` object.

```
    for (NSNumber *key in [tempValues allKeys]) {
        switch ([key intValue]) {
            case kNameRowIndex:
                president.name = [tempValues objectForKey:key];
                break;
            case kFromYearRowIndex:
                president.fromYear = [tempValues objectForKey:key];
                break;
            case kToYearRowIndex:
                president.toYear = [tempValues objectForKey:key];
                break;
            case kPartyIndex:
                president.party = [tempValues objectForKey:key];
            default:
                break;
        }
    }
```

Now, our `president` object has been updated, and we need to move up a level in the view hierarchy. Tapping a *Save* or *Done* button on a detail view should generally bring the user back up to the previous level, so we grab our application delegate and use its navController outlet to pop ourselves off of the navigation stack, sending the user back up to the list of presidents:

```
    NavAppDelegate *delegate =
        [[UIApplication sharedApplication] delegate];
    [delegate.navController popViewControllerAnimated:YES];
```

There's one other thing we have to do here, which is to tell our parent view's table to reload its data. Because one of the fields that the user can edit is the name field, which is displayed in the `PresidentsViewController` table, if we don't have that table reload its data, it will continue to show the old value.

```
UINavigationController *navController = [delegate navController];
NSArray *allControllers = navController.viewControllers;
UITableViewController *parent = [allControllers lastObject];
[parent.tableView reloadData];
```

The third action method will be called when the user taps the *Done* button on the keyboard. Without this method, the keyboard won't retract when the user taps *Done*. This approach isn't strictly necessary in our application, since the four rows that can be edited here fit in the area above the keyboard. That said, you'll need this method if you add a row or in a future application that requires more screen real estate. It's a good idea to keep the behavior consistent from application to application even if doing so is not critical to your application's functionality.

```
-(IBAction)textFieldDone:(id)sender {
    [sender resignFirstResponder];
}
```

The `viewDidLoad` method doesn't contain anything too surprising. We create the array of field names and assign it the `fieldLabels` property.

```
NSArray *array = [[NSArray alloc] initWithObjects:@"Name:",
        @"From:", @"To:", @"Party:", nil];
self.fieldLabels = array;
[array release];
```

Next, we create two buttons and add them to the navigation bar. We put the *Cancel* button in the left bar button item spot, which supplants the navigation button put there automatically. We put the *Save* button in the right spot and assign it the style `UIBarButtonItemStyleDone`. This style was specifically designed for this occasion, for a button users tap when they are happy with their changes and ready to leave the view. A button with this style will be blue instead of gray and usually will carry a label of *Save* or *Done*.

```
UIBarButtonItem *cancelButton = [[UIBarButtonItem alloc]
        initWithTitle:@"Cancel"
        style:UIBarButtonItemStylePlain
        target:self
        action:@selector(cancel:)];
self.navigationItem.leftBarButtonItem = cancelButton;
[cancelButton release];

UIBarButtonItem *saveButton = [[UIBarButtonItem alloc]
        initWithTitle:@"Save"
        style:UIBarButtonItemStyleDone
        target:self
        action:@selector(save:)];
self.navigationItem.rightBarButtonItem = saveButton;
[saveButton release];
```

Finally, we create a new mutable dictionary and assign it to `tempValues` so that we have a place to stick the changed values. If we made the changes directly to the `president` object, we'd have no easy way to roll back to the original data when the user tapped *Cancel*.

```
NSMutableDictionary *dict = [[NSMutableDictionary alloc] init];
self.tempValues = dict;
[dict release];
[super viewDidLoad];
```

We can skip over the `dealloc` method and the first data source method, as there are is nothing new under the sun there. We do need to stop and chat about `tableView:cellForRowAtIndexPath:`, however, because there are a few gotchas there. The first part of the method is exactly like every other `tableView:cellForRowAtIndexPath:` method we've written.

```
- (UITableViewCell *)tableView:(UITableView *)tableView
    cellForRowAtIndexPath:(NSIndexPath *)indexPath {
    static NSString *PresidentCellIdentifier = @"PresidentCellIdentifier";

    UITableViewCell *cell = [tableView dequeueReusableCellWithIdentifier:
        PresidentCellIdentifier];
    if (cell == nil) {

        cell = [[[UITableViewCell alloc] initWithFrame:CGRectZero
                    reuseIdentifier:PresidentCellIdentifier] autorelease];
```

When we create a new cell, we create a label, make it right-aligned and bold, and assign it a tag so that we can retrieve it again later. Next, we add it to the cell's `contentView` and release it. It's pretty straightforward:

```
UILabel *label = [[UILabel alloc] initWithFrame:
    CGRectMake(10, 10, 75, 25)];
label.textAlignment = UITextAlignmentRight;
label.tag = kLabelTag;
label.font = [UIFont boldSystemFontOfSize:14];
[cell.contentView addSubview:label];
[label release];
```

After that, we create a new text field. The user actually types in this field. We set it so it does not clear the current value when editing so we don't lose the existing data, and we set `self` as the text field's delegate. By setting the text field's delegate to `self`, we can get notified by the text field when certain events occur by implementing appropriate methods from the `UITextFieldDelegate` protocol. As you'll see in a moment, we've implemented two text field delegate methods in this class. Those methods will get called by the text fields on all rows when the user begins and ends editing the text they contain. We also set the keyboard's **return key type**, which is how we specify the text for the key in the bottom-right of

the keyboard. The default value is *Return*, but since we have only single-line fields, we want
the key to say *Done* instead, so we pass `UIReturnKeyDone`.

```
UITextField *textField = [[UITextField alloc] initWithFrame:
    CGRectMake(90, 12, 200, 25)];
textField.clearsOnBeginEditing = NO;
    [textField setDelegate:self];
textField.returnKeyType = UIReturnKeyDone;
```

After that, we tell the text field to call our `textFieldDone:` method on the *Did End on Exit*
event. This is exactly the same thing as dragging from the *Did End on Exit* event in the connections inspector in Interface Builder to *File's Owner* and selecting an action method. Since
we don't have a nib file, we have to do it programmatically, but the result is the same.

When we're all done configuring the text field, we add it to the cell's content view. Notice,
however, that we did not set a `tag` before we added it to that view.

```
[textField addTarget:self
            action:@selector(textFieldDone:)
            forControlEvents:UIControlEventEditingDidEndOnExit];
[cell.contentView addSubview:textField];
}
```

At this point, we know that we've either got a brand new cell or a reused cell, but we don't
know which. The first thing we do is figure out which row this darn cell is going to represent:

```
NSUInteger row = [indexPath row];
```

Next, we need to get a reference to the label and the text field from inside this cell. The label
is easy; we just use the tag we assigned to it to retrieve it from `cell`:

```
UILabel *label = (UILabel *)[cell viewWithTag:kLabelTag];
```

The text field, however, isn't going to be quite as easy, because we need the tag in order
to tell our text field delegates which text field is calling them. So we're going to rely on the
fact that there's only one text field that is a subview of our cell's `contentView`. We'll use fast
enumeration to work through all of its subviews, and when we find a text field, we assign it
to the pointer we declared a moment earlier. When the loop is done, the `textField` pointer
should be pointing to the one and only text field contained in this cell.

```
UITextField *textField = nil;

for (UIView *oneView in cell.contentView.subviews) {
    if ([oneView isMemberOfClass:[UITextField class]])
        textField = (UITextField *)oneView;
}
```

Now that we have pointers to both the label and the text field, we can assign them the correct values based on which field from the `president` object this row represents. Once again, the label gets its value from the `fieldLabels` array:

```
label.text = [fieldLabels objectAtIndex:row];
```

Assigning the value to the text field is not quite as easy. We have to first check to see if there is a value in the `tempValues` dictionary corresponding to this row. If there is, we assign it to the text field. If there isn't any corresponding value in `tempValues`, we know there have been no changes entered for this field, so we assign this field the corresponding value from `president`.

```
NSNumber *rowAsNum = [[NSNumber alloc] initWithInt:row];
switch (row) {
        case kNameRowIndex:
            if ([[tempValues allKeys] containsObject:rowAsNum])
                textField.text = [tempValues objectForKey:rowAsNum];
            else
                textField.text = president.name;
            break;
        case kFromYearRowIndex:
            if ([[tempValues allKeys] containsObject:rowAsNum])
                textField.text = [tempValues objectForKey:rowAsNum];
            else
                textField.text = president.fromYear;
            break;
        case kToYearRowIndex:
            if ([[tempValues allKeys] containsObject:rowAsNum])
                textField.text = [tempValues objectForKey:rowAsNum];
            else
                textField.text = president.toYear;
            break;
        case kPartyIndex:
            if ([[tempValues allKeys] containsObject:rowAsNum])
                textField.text = [tempValues objectForKey:rowAsNum];
            else
                textField.text = president.party;
        default:
            break;
    }
```

If the field we're using is the one that is currently being edited, that's an indication that that the value we're holding in `textFieldBeingEdited` is no longer valid, so we set `textFieldBeingEdited` to `nil`. If the text field did get released or reused, our text field delegate would have been called, and the correct value would already be in the `tempValues` dictionary.

```
    if (textFieldBeingEdited == textField)
        textFieldBeingEdited = nil;
```

Next, we set the text field's `tag` to the row it represents, which will allow us to know which field is calling our text field delegate methods:

```
    textField.tag = row;
```

Finally, we release `rowAsNum` to be a good memory citizen and return the `cell`:

```
    [rowAsNum release];
    return cell;
}
```

We do implement one table delegate method this time, which is `tableView:willSelectRowAtIndexPath:`. Remember, this method gets called before a row gets selected and gives us a chance to disallow the row selection. In this view, we never want a row to appear selected. We need to know that the user selected a row so we can place a checkmark next to it, but we don't want the row to actually be highlighted. Don't worry. A row doesn't need to be selected for a text field on that row to be editable, so this method just keeps the row from staying highlighted after it is touched.

```
- (NSIndexPath *)tableView:(UITableView *)tableView
        willSelectRowAtIndexPath:(NSIndexPath *)indexPath {
    return nil;
}
```

All that's left now are the two text field delegate methods. The first one we implement, `textFieldDidBeginEditing:`, gets called whenever a text field for which we are the delegate becomes first responder. So, if the user taps a field and the keyboard pops up, we get notified. In this method, we store a pointer to the field currently being edited so that we have a way to get to the last changes made before the *Save* button was tapped.

```
(void)textFieldDidBeginEditing:(UITextField *)textField {
    self.textFieldBeingEdited = textField;
}
```

The last method we wrote gets called when the user stops editing a text field by tapping a different text field or pressing the *Done* button or when another field became the first responder, which will happen, for example, when the user navigates back up to the list of presidents. Here, we save the value from that field in the `tempValues` dictionary so that we will have them if the user taps the *Save* button to confirm the changes.

```
- (void)textFieldDidEndEditing:(UITextField *)textField {
    NSNumber *tagAsNum = [[NSNumber alloc] initWithInt:textField.tag];
    [tempValues setObject:textField.text forKey:tagAsNum];
```

```
    [tagAsNum release];
}
```

And that's it. We're done with these two view controllers, so all we have to do is add an instance of this class to the top-level view controller. You know how to do this by now. Single-click *FirstLevelViewController.m*.

First, import the header from the new second-level view by adding the following line of code right before the @implementation declaration:

```
#import "PresidentsViewController.h"
```

And then add the following code to the viewDidLoad method:

```
- (void)viewDidLoad {
    self.title = @"Top Level";
    NSMutableArray *array = [[NSMutableArray alloc] init];

    // Disclosure Button
    DisclosureButtonController *disclosureButtonController =
        [[DisclosureButtonController alloc]
            initWithStyle:UITableViewStylePlain];
    disclosureButtonController.title = @"Disclosure Buttons";
    disclosureButtonController.rowImage = [UIImage
        imageNamed:@"disclosureButtonControllerIcon.png"];
    [array addObject:disclosureButtonController];
    [disclosureButtonController release];

    // Check List
    CheckListController *checkListController = [[CheckListController alloc]
            initWithStyle:UITableViewStylePlain];
    checkListController.title = @"Check One";
    checkListController.rowImage = [UIImage
        imageNamed:@"checkmarkControllerIcon.png"];
    [array addObject:checkListController];
    [checkListController release];

    // Table Row Controls
    RowControlsController *rowControlsController =
        [[RowControlsController alloc]
        initWithStyle:UITableViewStylePlain];
    rowControlsController.title = @"Row Controls";
    rowControlsController.rowImage =
        [UIImage imageNamed:@"rowControlsIcon.png"];
    [array addObject:rowControlsController];
    [rowControlsController release];
```

```
    // Move Me
    MoveMeController *moveMeController = [[MoveMeController alloc]
        initWithStyle:UITableViewStylePlain];
    moveMeController.title = @"Move Me";
    moveMeController.rowImage = [UIImage imageNamed:@"moveMeIcon.png"];
    [array addObject:moveMeController];
    [moveMeController release];

    // Delete Me
    DeleteMeController *deleteMeController = [[DeleteMeController alloc]
            initWithStyle:UITableViewStylePlain];
    deleteMeController.title = @"Delete Me";
    deleteMeController.rowImage = [UIImage imageNamed:@"deleteMeIcon.png"];
    [array addObject:deleteMeController];
    [deleteMeController release];

    // President View/Edit
    PresidentsViewController *presidentsViewController =
        [[PresidentsViewController alloc]
        initWithStyle:UITableViewStylePlain];
    presidentsViewController.title = @"Detail Edit";
    presidentsViewController.rowImage = [UIImage imageNamed:
        @"detailEditIcon.png"];
    [array addObject:presidentsViewController];
    [presidentsViewController release];

    self.controllers = array;
    [array release];
    [super viewDidLoad];
}
```

Save everything, sigh deeply, hold your breath, and then build that sucker. If everything is in order, the simulator will launch, and a sixth and final row will appear, just like the one in Figure 9-2. If you click the new row, you'll be taken to a list of US presidents (see Figure 9-24).

Tapping any of the rows will take you down to the detail view that we just built (see Figure 9-8), and you'll be able to edit the values. If you select the *Done* button in the keyboard, the keyboard should retract. Tap one of the editable values, and the keyboard will reappear. Make some changes, and tap *Cancel*, and the application will pop back to the list of presidents. If you revisit the president you just cancelled out of, your changes will be gone. On the other hand, if you make some changes and tap *Save*, your changes will be reflected in the parent table, and when you come back into the detail view, the new values will still be there.

Figure 9-24. *Our sixth and final subcontroller presents a list of US presidents. Tap one of the presidents, and you'll be taken to a detail view (or a secret service agent will wrestle you to the ground).*

But There's One More Thing...

There's one more little bit of polish we need to add to make our application behave the way it should. In the version we just built, the keyboard incorporates a *Done* button that, when tapped, makes the keyboard retract. That behavior is proper if there are other controls on the view that the user might need to get to. Since every row on this table view is a text field, however, we need a slightly different solution. The keyboard should feature a *Return* button instead of a *Done* button. When tapped, that button should take the user to the next row's text field.

In order to accomplish this, the first thing we need to do is replace the *Done* button with a *Return* button. We can accomplish this by deleting a single line of code from *PresidentDetailController.m*. In the `tableView:cellForRowAtIndexPath:` method, delete the following line of code:

```
- (UITableViewCell *)tableView:(UITableView *)tableView
      cellForRowAtIndexPath:(NSIndexPath *)indexPath {
    static NSString *PresidentCellIdentifier = @"PresidentCellIdentifier";
```

```
UITableViewCell *cell = [tableView dequeueReusableCellWithIdentifier:
    PresidentCellIdentifier];
if (cell == nil) {

    cell = [[[UITableViewCell alloc] initWithFrame:CGRectZero
                reuseIdentifier:PresidentCellIdentifier] autorelease];
    UILabel *label = [[UILabel alloc] initWithFrame:
        CGRectMake(10, 10, 75, 25)];
    label.textAlignment = UITextAlignmentRight;
    label.tag = kLabelTag;
    label.font = [UIFont boldSystemFontOfSize:14];
    [cell.contentView addSubview:label];
    [label release];

    UITextField *textField = [[UITextField alloc] initWithFrame:
        CGRectMake(90, 12, 200, 25)];
    textField.clearsOnBeginEditing = NO;
    [textField setDelegate:self];
    textField.returnKeyType = UIReturnKeyDone;
    [textField addTarget:self
                action:@selector(textFieldDone:)
                forControlEvents:UIControlEventEditingDidEndOnExit];
    [cell.contentView addSubview:textField];



}
NSUInteger row = [indexPath row];
...
```

The next step isn't quite as straightforward. In our `textFieldDone:` method, instead of simply telling `sender` to resign first responder status, we need to somehow figure out what the next field should be and tell that field to become the first responder. Replace your current version of `textFieldDone:` with this new version, and then we'll chat about how it works:

```
-(IBAction)textFieldDone:(id)sender {
    UITableViewCell *cell =
        (UITableViewCell *)[[sender superview] superview];
    UITableView *table = (UITableView *)[cell superview];
    NSIndexPath *textFieldIndexPath = [table indexPathForCell:cell];
    NSUInteger row = [textFieldIndexPath row];
    row++;
    if (row >= kNumberOfEditableRows)
        row = 0;
    NSUInteger newIndex[] = {0, row};
    NSIndexPath *newPath = [[NSIndexPath alloc] initWithIndexes:newIndex
        length:2];
    UITableViewCell *nextCell = [self.tableView
```

```
        cellForRowAtIndexPath:newPath];
    [newPath release];
    UITextField *nextField = nil;
    for (UIView *oneView in nextCell.contentView.subviews) {
        if ([oneView isMemberOfClass:[UITextField class]])
            nextField = (UITextField *)oneView;
    }
    [nextField becomeFirstResponder];
}
```

Unfortunately, cells don't know what row they represent. The table view, however, does know which row a given cell is currently representing. So, we get a reference to the table view cell. We know that the text field that is triggering this action method is a subview of the table cell view's content view, so we just need to get sender's superview's superview (now say *that* ten times fast).

If that sounded confusing, think of it this way. Sender, in this case, is the text field being edited. Sender's superview is the content view that groups the text field and its label. Sender's superview's superview is the cell that encompasses that content view.

```
UITableViewCell *cell = (UITableViewCell *)[[(UIView *)sender
        superview]superview];
```

We also need access to the cell's enclosing table view, which is easy enough, since it's the superview of the cell:

```
UITableView *table = (UITableView *)[cell superview];
```

We then ask the table which row the cell represents. The response is an NSIndexPath, and we get the row from that:

```
NSIndexPath *textFieldIndexPath = [table indexPathForCell:cell];
NSUInteger row = [textFieldIndexPath row];
```

Next, we increment row by one, which represents the next row in the table. If incrementing the row number puts us beyond the last one, we reset row to 0:

```
row++;
if (row >= kNumberOfEditableRows)
    row = 0;
```

Then we build a new NSIndexPath to represent the next row, and use that index path to get a reference to the cell currently representing the next row:

```
NSUInteger newIndex[] = {0, row};
NSIndexPath *newPath = [[NSIndexPath alloc] initWithIndexes:newIndex
        length:2];
```

```
UITableViewCell *nextCell = [self.tableView
    cellForRowAtIndexPath:newPath];
[newPath release];
```

For the text field, we're already using `tag` for another purpose, so we have to loop through the subviews of the cell's content view to find the text field rather than using `tag` to retrieve it:

```
UITextField *nextField = nil;
for (UIView *oneView in nextCell.contentView.subviews) {
    if ([oneView isMemberOfClass:[UITextField class]])
    nextField = (UITextField *)oneView;
}
```

And finally, we can tell that new text field to become the first responder:

```
[nextField becomeFirstResponder];
```

Now, compile and run, and when you drill down to the detail view, tapping the *Return* button will take you to the next field in the table, which will make entering data much easier for your users.

Breaking the Tape

This chapter was a marathon, and if you're still standing, you should feel pretty darn good about yourself. Dwelling on these mystical table view and navigation controller objects is important, because they are the backbone of a great many iPhone applications, and their complexity can definitely get you into trouble if you don't truly understand them.

As you start building your own tables, check back to this chapter and the previous one, and don't be afraid of Apple's documentation, either. Table views are extraordinarily complex, and we could never cover every conceivable permutation, but you should now have a very good set of table view building blocks you can use as you design and build your own applications. As always, please do feel free to reuse this code in your own applications. It's a gift from us to you. Enjoy!

In the next chapter, we're going to look at application settings, the mechanism the iPhone uses to gather and store user preferences. Once you've completed your cooldown, drink plenty of fluids, and proceed to the next chapter. Oh, and don't forget to stretch.

Chapter 10

Application Settings and User Defaults

*a*ll but the simplest computer programs today have a preferences window where the user can set application-specific options. On Mac OS X, the **Preferences…** menu item is usually found in the application menu. Selecting it brings up a window where the user can enter and change various options. The iPhone has a dedicated application called Settings, which you no doubt have played with any number of times. In this chapter, we'll show you how to add settings for your application to the Settings application, and we'll show you how to access those settings from within your application.

Getting to Know Your Settings Bundle

The Settings application (see Figure 10-1) lets the user enter and change preferences for any application that has a settings bundle. A settings bundle is a group of files built into an application that tells the Settings application what preferences the application wishes to collect from the user.

Pick up your iPhone or iPod touch, and locate your Settings icon. You'll find it on the home screen. When you touch the icon, the Settings application will launch. Ours is shown in Figure 10-2.

Figure 10-1. *The Settings application icon is the third one down in the last column. It may be in a different spot on your iPhone or iPod touch, but it's always available.*

Figure 10-2. *The Settings application*

The Settings application acts as a common user interface for the iPhone's User Defaults mechanism. User Defaults is the part of Application Preferences that stores and retrieves preferences. User Defaults is implemented by the NSUserDefaults class. If you've done Cocoa programming on the Mac, you're probably already familiar with NSUserDefaults, because it is the same class that is used to store and read preferences on the Mac. Your applications will use NSUserDefaults to read and store preference data using a key value, just as you would access keyed data from an NSDictionary. The difference is that NSUserDefaults data is persisted to the file system rather than stored in an object instance in memory.

In this chapter, we're going to create an application, add and configure a settings bundle, and then access and edit those preferences from within our application.

One nice thing about the Settings application is that you don't have to design a user interface for your preferences. You create a property list defining your application's available settings, and the Settings application creates the interface for you. There are limits to what you can do with the Settings application, however. Any preference that the user might need to change while your application is running should not be limited to the Settings application because your user would be forced to quit your application to change those values.

Immersive applications, such as games, generally should provide their own preferences view so that the user doesn't have to quit in order to make a change. Even utility and productivity applications might, at times, have preferences that a user should be able to change without leaving the application. We'll also show you to how to collect preferences from the user right in your application and store those in iPhone's User Defaults.

The AppSettings Application

We're going to build a simple application in this chapter. First, we'll implement a settings bundle so that when the user launches the Settings application, there will be an entry for our application (see Figure 10-3).

If the user selects our application, it will drill down into a view that shows the preferences relevant to our application. As you can see from Figure 10-4, the Settings application is using text fields, secure text fields, switches, and sliders to coax values out of our intrepid user.

You should also notice that there are two items on the view that have disclosure indicators. The first one, *Protocol*, takes the user to another table view that displays the available options for that item. From that table view, the user can select a single value (see Figure 10-5).

Figure 10-3. *The settings application showing an entry for our application in the simulator*

Figure 10-4. *Our application's primary settings view*

Figure 10-5. *Selecting a single preference item from a list*

The other disclosure indicator on our application's main view in the Settings application allows the user to drill down to another set of preferences (see Figure 10-6). This child view can have the same kinds of controls as the main settings view and can even have its own child views. You may have noticed that the Settings application uses a navigation controller, which it needs because it supports the building of hierarchical preference views.

When users actually launch our application, they will be presented with a list of the preferences gathered in the Settings application (see Figure 10-7).

In order to show how to update preferences from within our application, we also provide a little information button in the lower-right corner that will take the user to another view to set two of the preference values right in our application (see Figure 10-8).

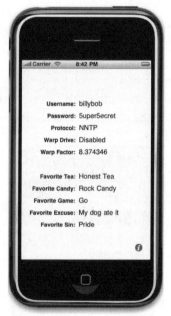

Figure 10-6. *A child settings view in our application*

Figure 10-7. *Our application's main view*

Figure 10-8. *Setting some preferences right in our application*

Let's get started, shall we?

Creating the Project

In Xcode, press ⌘⇧N or select **New Project...** from the **File** menu. When the new project assistant comes up, select *Application* from under the *iPhone* heading in the left pane, and then click the *Utility Application* icon before clicking the *Choose...* button. Name your new project *AppSettings*.

This is a new project template that we haven't used before, so let's take a second to look at the project before we proceed. This template creates an application very similar to the one we built in Chapter 6. The application has a main view and a secondary view called the **flip-side view**. Tapping the information button on the main view takes you to the flipside view, and tapping the *Done* button on the flipside view takes you back to the main view.

You'll notice that, for the first time, there is no *Classes* folder in our Xcode project (see Figure 10-9). Because it takes several files to implement this type of application, the template very kindly organizes the files in groups for us to make our lives easier. Expand the folders *Main View*, *Flipside View*, and *Application Delegate*. Heck, while you're in the folder-expanding groove, flip open *Resources* too.

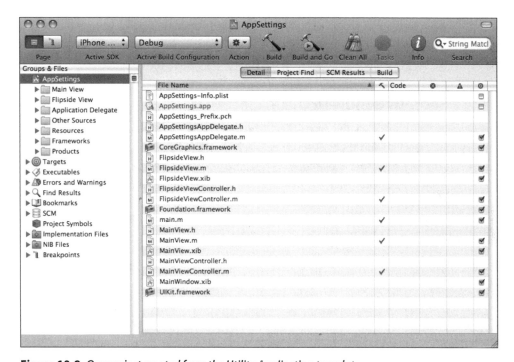

Figure 10-9. *Our project created from the Utility Application template*

All the classes that make up the main view, including the view controller and a subclass of UIView, are included in the folder called *Main View*. Likewise, all source code files needed to implement the flipside view are contained in the folder called *Flipside View*. Finally, the application delegate is contained in a folder called (wait for it...) *Application Delegate*.

This template has provided us with a custom subclass of UIView for both the main and flipside views. We won't actually need to subclass UIView in this application for either of our views, but we'll leave both FlipsideView and MainView in our project. It won't hurt anything to leave them as is, but if we remove them, we will have to go rewire the nibs to point to UIView.

Working with the Settings Bundle

The Settings application bases the display of preferences for a given application on the contents of the settings bundle inside that application. Each settings bundle must have a property list, called *Root.plist*, which defines the root level preferences view. This property list must follow a very precise format, which we'll talk about in a few minutes. If it finds a settings bundle with an appropriate *Root.plist* file, the Settings application will build a settings view for our application based on the contents of the property list. If we want our preferences to include any subviews, we have to add additional property lists to the bundle and add an entry to *Root.plist* for each child view. You'll see exactly how to do that in this chapter.

 One small wrinkle with this process is that you can't add or delete items from a settings bundle from within Xcode. You can change the contents of files that are already in the settings bundle from Xcode, but if you need to actually add or remove items, you'll have to do it in the Finder. No worries, we'll show you how to do this a bit further down.

Adding a Settings Bundle to Our Project

In the *Groups & Files* pane, click the root object (the one called *AppSettings*, which should be at the very top of the list) and then select **New File...** from the **File** menu or press ⌘N. In the left pane, select *Resource* under the *iPhone OS* heading, and then select the *Settings Bundle* icon (see Figure 10-10). Click the *Next* button, and choose the default name of *Settings. bundle* by pressing return.

Figure 10-10. *Creating a settings bundle*

You should now see a new item in Xcode's *Groups & File* pane called *Settings.bundle*. Expand *Settings.bundle*, and you should see two items, an icon named *Root.plist* and a folder named *en.lproj*. We'll discuss *en.lproj* in Chapter 17 when we talk about localizing your application into other languages. For the moment, let's just concentrate on *Root.plist*.

Setting Up the Property List

Single-click *Root.plist*, and take a look at the editor pane. You're looking at Xcode's property list editor. This editor functions in the same way as the Property List Editor application in */Developer/Applications/Utilities*.

Property lists all have a root node, which has a node type of *Dictionary*, which means it stores items using a key value, just as an NSDictionary does. All of the children of a *Dictionary* node need to have both a key and a value. There can be only one root node in any given property list, and all nodes must come under it.

There are several different types of nodes that can be put into a property list. In addition to *Dictionary* nodes, which allow you to store other nodes under a key, there are also *Array* nodes, which store an ordered list of other nodes similar to an NSArray. The *Dictionary* and *Array* types are the only property list node types that can contain other nodes. There are also a number of other node types designed to hold data. The data node types are *Boolean*, *Data*, *Date*, *Number*, and *String*.

TIP

Although you can use most kinds of objects as a key in an NSDictionary, keys in property list dictionary nodes have to be strings, though you are free to use any node type for the values.

When creating a settings property list, you have to follow a defined format. Fortunately, when you added the settings bundle to your project, a properly formatted property list, called *Root.plist*, was created for you. This is the *Root.plist* that you just clicked in the settings bundle.

In the *Root.plist* editor pane, expand the node named *PreferenceSpecifiers* (see Figure 10-11).

Key	Type	Value
▼ Root	Dictionary	(2 items)
StringsTable	String	Root
▼ PreferenceSpecifiers	Array	(4 items)
▶ Item 1	Dictionary	(2 items)
▶ Item 2	Dictionary	(8 items)
▶ Item 3	Dictionary	(4 items)
▶ Item 4	Dictionary	(7 items)

Figure 10-11. *Root.plist in the editor pane*

Before we add our preference specifiers, let's look at the property list so you can see the required format. We'll talk about the first item, *StringsTable*, in Chapter 17 as well; a strings table is also used in translating your application into another language. Since it is optional, you can delete that entry now by clicking it and pressing the delete key. You can leave it there if you like, since it won't do any harm.

The next item under the root node is *PreferenceSpecifiers*, and it's an array. Click its disclosure triangle to reveal its subitems. This array node is designed to hold a set of dictionary nodes, each of which represents a single preference that the user can enter or a single child view that the user can drill down into. You'll notice that Xcode's template kindly gave us four nodes. Those nodes aren't likely to reflect our actual preferences, so delete *Item 2*, *Item 3*, and *Item 4* by single-clicking each of those rows and pressing the delete key.

Single-click *Item 1* but don't expand it. Look at the right edge of the row, and notice the button with the plus icon. That button is used to add a sibling node after this row. In other words, it will add another node at the same level as this one. If we click that icon now (don't click it, just follow along), we will get a new row called *Item 2* right after *Item 1*.

Now expand *Item 1*, and notice that the button changes to a different icon, one with three horizontal lines. That new icon indicates that clicking that button now will add a child node, so if we click it now (again, don't click it, just follow along), we will get a new row underneath *Item 1*.

The first row under *Item 1* has a key of *Type*, and every property list node in the Preference Specifiers array must have an entry with this key. It's typically the first one, but order doesn't matter in a dictionary, so the *Type* key doesn't have to be first. The *Type* key tells the Settings application what type of data is associated with this item.

Take a look at the *Type* field under *Item 1*. The value of this *Type* field, *PSGroupSpecifier*, is used to indicate that this item represents the start of a new group. Each item that follows will be part of this group, until the next item with a *Type* of *PSGroupSpecifier*. If you look back at Figure 10-4, you'll see that the Settings application presents the settings in a grouped table. *Item 1* in the *PreferenceSpecifiers* array in a settings bundle property list should always be a *PSGroupSpecifier* so the settings start in a new group, because you need at least one group in every Settings table.

The only other entry in *Item 1* has a key of *Title*, and this is used to set an optional header just above the group that's being started. If you look again back at Figure 10-4, you'll see that our first group is called *General Info*. Double-click the value next to *Title*, and change it from *Group* to *General Info*.

Adding a Text Field Setting

We now need to add a second item in this array, which will represent the first actual preference field. We're going to start with a simple text field. If we single-click the *Preference-Specifiers* row in the editor pane, and click the button to add a child, the new row will be inserted at the beginning of the list, which is not what we want. We want to add a row at the end of the array. To do this, click the disclosure triangle to the left of *Item 1* to close it, and then select *Item 1* and click the plus button at the end of the row, which will give us a new sibling row after the current row (see Figure 10-12).

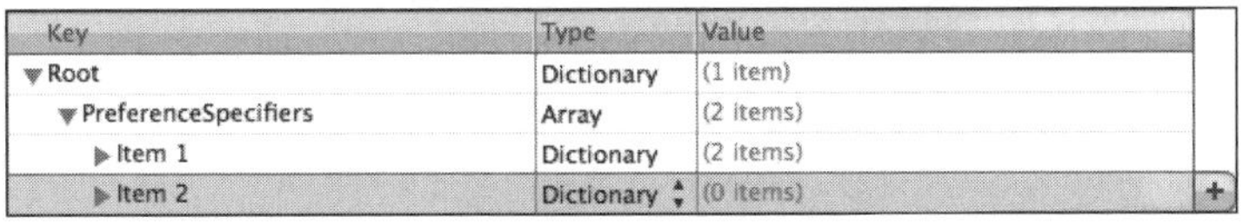

Key	Type	Value	
▼ Root	Dictionary	(1 item)	
▼ PreferenceSpecifiers	Array	(2 items)	
▶ Item 1	Dictionary	(2 items)	
▶ Item 2	Dictionary ⬍	(0 items)	+

Figure 10-12. *Adding a new sibling row to Item 1*

The new row will default to a *String* node type, which is not what we want. Remember, each item in the *PreferenceSpecifiers* array has to be a dictionary, so click the word *String*, and change the node type to *Dictionary*. Now, click the disclosure triangle next to *Item 2* to expand it. It doesn't actually contain anything yet, so the only differences you'll see are that the disclosure triangle will point down and the button to add sibling nodes will change to let you add child nodes. Click the *add child node* button (the button to the right with three lines) now to add our first entry to this dictionary.

A new row will come up and default to a *String* type, which *is* what we want. The new row's key value will default to *New item*. Change it to *Type*, and then double-click the *Value* column, and enter *PSTextFieldSpecifier*, which is the type value used to tell the Settings application that we want the user to edit this setting in a text field.

In this example, *PSTextFieldSpecifier* is a type. More specifically, it is the type of a specific preference field. When you see *Type* in the *Key* column, we're defining the type of field that will be used to edit the preference.

Click the button with the plus icon to the right of the *Type* row to add another item to our dictionary. This next row will specify the label that will be displayed next to the text field. Change the key from *New item* to *Title*. Now press the tab key. Notice that you are now all set to edit the value in the *Value* column. Set it to *Username*. Now press the plus button at the end of the *Title* row to add yet another item to our dictionary.

Change the key for this new entry to *Key* (no, that's not a misprint, you're really setting the key to "Key"). For a value, type in *username*. Recall that we said that user defaults work like a dictionary? Well, this entry tells the Settings application what key to use when it stores the value entered in this text field. Recall what we said about NSUserDefaults? It lets you store values using a key, similar to an NSDictionary. Well, the Settings application will do the same thing for each of the preferences it saves on your behalf. If you give it a key value of *foo*, then later in your application, you can request the value for *foo,* and it will give you the value the user entered for that preference. We will use this same key value later to retrieve this setting from the user defaults in our application.

<u>NOTE</u>

Notice that our *Title* had a value of *Username* and our *Key* a value of *username*. This uppercase/lowercase difference will happen frequently. The *Title* is what appears on the screen, so the capital "U" makes sense. The *Key* is a text string we'll use to retrieve preferences from the user defaults, so all lowercase makes sense there. Could we use all lowercase for a *Title*? You bet. Could we use all capitals for *Key*? Sure! As long as you capitalize it the same way when you save and when you retrieve, it doesn't matter what convention you use for your preference keys.

Add another item to our dictionary, giving this one a key of *AutocapitalizationType*, and a value of *None*. This specifies that the text field shouldn't attempt to autocapitalize what the user types in.

Create one last new row and give it a key of *AutocorrectionType* and a value of *No*. This will tell the Settings application not to try to autocorrect values entered into this text field. If you did want the text field to use autocorrection, then you would change the value in this row to *Yes*. When you're all done, your property list should look like the one shown in Figure 10-13.

Key	Type	Value
▼ Root	Dictionary	(1 item)
▼ PreferenceSpecifiers	Array	(2 items)
▶ Item 1	Dictionary	(2 items)
▼ Item 2	Dictionary	(5 items)
Type	String	PSTextFieldSpecifier
Title	String	Username
Key	String	username
AutocapitalizationType	String	None
AutocorrectionType	String	No

Figure 10-13. *The finished text field specified in Root.plist*

Save the property file, and let's see if everything is set up and working. We should be able to compile and run the application now. Even though our application doesn't do anything yet, we should be able to click the home button on the iPhone simulator, and then select the Settings application to see an entry for our application (see Figure 10-3).

Try it now by selecting **Build and Run** from the **Build** menu. If you click the home button and then the icon for the Settings application, you should find an entry for our application, which uses the application icon we added earlier. If you click the *AppSettings* row, you should be presented with a simple settings view with a single text field, as shown in Figure 10-14.

Adding a Secure Text Field Setting

Quit the simulator, and go back to Xcode. We're not done yet, but you should now have a sense of how easy adding preferences to your application is. Let's add the rest of the fields for our root settings view. The first one we'll add is a secure text field for the user's password.

Figure 10-14. *Our root view in the Settings application after adding a group and a text field*

Here's an easy way to add another node. Collapse *Item 2* in the *PreferenceSpecifiers* array. Now select *Item 2*. Press ⌘C to copy it to the clipboard, and then press ⌘V to paste it back. This will create a new *Item 3* that is identical to *Item 2*. Expand the new item, and change the *Title* to *Password* and the *Key* to *password*.

Next, add one more child to the new item. Remember, the order of items does not matter, so feel free to place it right below the *Key* item. Give the new item a *Key* of *IsSecure*, and change the *Type* to *Boolean*. Once you do that, the space where you normally type in a value will change to a checkbox. Click it to check the box, which tells the Settings application that this field needs to be a password field rather than just an ordinary text field.

Adding a Multivalue Field

The next item we're going to add is a multivalue field. This type of field will automatically generate a row with a disclosure indicator, and clicking it will take you down to another table where you can select one of several rows. Collapse *Item 3*; select the row; and click the plus icon at the end of the row to add *Item 4*. Change *Item 4's Type* to *Dictionary*, and expand *Item 4* by clicking the disclosure triangle.

Give it a child row with a key of *Type* and a value of *PSMultiValueSpecifier*. Add a second row with a key of *Title* and value of *Protocol*. Now create a third row with a key of *Key* and a value of *protocol*. The next part is a little tricky, so let's talk about it before we do it.

We're going to add two more children to *Item 4*, but they are going to be *Array* type nodes, not *String* type nodes. One, called *Titles*, is going to hold a list of the values that the user can select from. The other, called *Values*, is going to hold a list of the values that actually get stored in the User Defaults. So, if the user selects the first item in the list, which corresponds to the first item in the *Titles* array, the Settings application will actually store the first value from the *Values* array. This pairing of *Titles* and *Values* lets you present user-friendly text to the user but actually store something else, like a number, a date, or a different string. Both of these arrays are required. If you want them both to be the same, you can create one array, copy it, paste it back in, and change the key so that you have two arrays with the same content but stored under different keys. We'll actually do just that.

Add a new child to *Item 4*. Change its key to *Values* and set its type to *Array*. Expand the array, and add five child nodes. All five nodes should be *String* type nodes and should contain the following values: *HTTP*, *SMTP*, *NNTP*, *IMAP*, and *POP3*.

TIP

Note that if you enter the first value and press return, you'll be editing the value just beneath it. Shortcut!

Once you've entered all five, collapse *Values*, and select it. Then, press ⌘C to copy it, and press ⌘V to paste it back. This will create a new item with a key of *Values - 2*. Double-click *Values - 2*, and change it to *Titles*.

We're almost done with our multivalue field. There's just one more required value in the dictionary, which is the default value. Multivalue fields must have one and only one row selected, so we have to specify the default value to be used if none has yet been selected, and it needs to correspond to one of the items in the *Values* array (not the *Titles* array if they are different). Add another child to *Item 4*. Give it a key of *DefaultValue* and a value of *SMTP*.

Let's check our work. Save the property list, build, and run again. When your application starts up, press the home button and launch the Settings application. When you select *AppSettings*, you should now have three fields on your root level view (see Figure 10-15). Go ahead and play with your creation, and then let's move on.

Figure 10-15. *Three fields down*

Adding a Toggle Switch Setting

The next item we need to get from the user is a Boolean value that indicates whether the warp engines are turned on. To capture a Boolean value in our preferences, we are going to tell the Settings application to use a `UISwitch` by adding another item to our *Preference-Specifiers* array with a type of *PSToggleSwitchSpecifier*.

Collapse *Item 4* if it's currently expanded, and then single-click it to select it. Click the plus icon at the right side of the row to create *Item 5*. Change its type to *Dictionary*, and then expand *Item 5*, and add a child row. Give the child row a key of *Type* and a value of

PSToggleSwitchSpecifier. Add another child row with a key of *Title* and a value of *Warp Drive*. Next, add a third child row with a key of *Key* and a value of *warp*.

By default, a toggle switch will cause a Boolean YES or NO to get saved into the user defaults. If you would prefer to assign a different value to the on and off positions, you can do that by specifying the optional keys *TrueValue* and *FalseValue*. You can assign strings, dates or numbers to either the on position (*TrueValue*) or the off position (*FalseValue*) so that the Settings application will store the string you specify instead of just storing YES or NO. Let's set the on position to save the string *Engaged* and the off position to store *Disabled*.

Do this by adding two more children to *Item 5*, one with a key of *TrueValue* and a value of *Engaged*, and a second one with a key of *FalseValue* and a value of *Disabled*.

We have one more required item in this dictionary, which is the default value. If we had not supplied the option *FalseValue* and *TrueValue* items, we would create a new row with a key of *DefaultValue* and change the type from *String* to *Boolean*. However, because we did add those two items, the value we put in *DefaultValue* has to match either the value passed in *TrueValue* or the one passed in *FalseValue*.

Let's make our warp engines on by default, so create one last child to *Item 5*, give it a key of *DefaultValue* and a value of *Engaged*. Note that the string "Engaged" is what will be stored in the user defaults, not what will appear on the screen. We just wanted to be clear on that.

Adding the Slider Setting

The next item we need to implement is a slider. In the Settings application, a slider can have a small image at each end, but it can't have a label. Let's put the slider in its own group with a header so that the user will know what the slider does.

Single-click *Item 1* under *PreferenceSpecifiers*, and press ⌘C to copy it to the clipboard. Now, select *Item 5*, making sure it's collapsed, and then press ⌘V to paste. Since *Item 1* was a group specifier, the item we just pasted in as the new *Item 6* is also a group specifier and will tell the Settings application to start a new group at this location.

Expand *Item 6*, double-click the value in the row labeled *Title* and change the value to *Warp Factor*.

Collapse *Item 6* and select it. Then, click the button at the end of its row to add a new sibling row. Change the *Type* of the new row, *Item 7*, from *String* to *Dictionary* and then expand the new row. Add a child row, and give it a key of *Type* and a value of *PSSliderSpecifier*, which indicates to the Settings application that it should use a UISlider to get this information from the user. Add another child with a key of *Key* and a value of *warpFactor* so that the Settings application knows what key to use when storing this value.

We're going to allow the user to enter a value from one to ten, and we'll set the default to *warp 5*. Sliders need to have a minimum value, a maximum value, and a starting (or default) value, and all of these need to be stored as numbers, not strings, in your property list. To do this, add three more child rows to *Item 7*, setting the *Type* of all three rows from *String* to *Number*. Give the first one a key of *DefaultValue* and a value of *5*. Give the second one a key of *MinimumValue* and a value of *1*, and give the final one a key of *MaximumValue* and a value of *10*.

If you want to test the slider, go ahead, but hurry back. We're going to do just a bit more customization. Sliders allow placement of a small 21-pixel × 21-pixel image at each end of the slider. Let's provide little icons to indicate that moving the slider to the left slows us down, and moving it to the right speeds us up.

In the *10 AppSettings* folder in the project archive that accompanies this book, you'll find two icons called *rabbit.png* and *turtle.png*. We need to add both of these to our settings bundle. Because these images need to be used by the Settings application, we can't just put them in our *Resources* folder, we need to put them in the settings bundle so the Settings application can get them. To do that, go to the Finder and navigate to wherever you saved your Xcode project. In that same folder, you'll find an icon named *Settings.bundle*.

Remember, bundles look like files in the Finder, but they are really folders, and you can get to their contents by right-clicking (or control-clicking) the bundle's icon and selecting Show Package Contents. This will open a new window, and you should see the same two items that you see in *Settings. bundle* in Xcode. Copy the two icon files, *rabbit.png* and *turtle.png*, from the *10 AppSettings* folder to this folder.

You can leave this window open in the Finder, as we'll need to copy another file here in a few minutes. For now, go back to Xcode, and let's tell the slider to use these two images.

Go back to *Root.plist* and add two more child rows under *Item 7*. Give one a key of *MinimumValueImage* and a value of *turtle.png*. Give the other a key of *MaximumValueImage* and a value of *rabbit.png*. Save your property list, and let's build and run to make sure everything is still hunky-dory. If everything is, you should be able to navigate to the Settings application and find the slider waiting for you with the sleepy turtle and the happy rabbit at each end of the slider (see Figure 10-16).

Figure 10-16. *We have text fields, multivalue fields, a toggle switch, and a slider. We're almost done.*

Adding a Child Settings View

We're going to add another preference specifier to tell the Settings application that we want it to display a child settings view. This specifier will present a row with a disclosure indicator that, when tapped, will take the user down to a whole new view full of preferences. Before we add that node, however, since we don't want this new preference to be grouped with the slider, we're going to copy the group specifier in *Item 1* and paste it at the end of the *PreferenceSpecifiers* array to create a new group for our child settings view. In *Root.plist*, collapse *Item 1* if it's expanded, and then single-click it to select it and press ⌘**C** to copy it to the clipboard. Next, collapse *Item 7* if it's expanded; single-click it to select it, and then press ⌘**V** to paste in a new *Item 8*. Expand Item 8, and double-click the value column next to the key *Title*, changing it from *General Info* to *Additional Info*.

Now, collapse *Item 8* again. Select it, and press the *add sibling* button at the right end of the row to add *Item 9*, which will be our actual child view. Change the new row's type from *String* to *Dictionary* and expand it by clicking the disclosure triangle. Add a child row, and give it a key of *Type* and a value of *PSChildPaneSpecifier*. Add another child row with a key of *Title* and a value of *More Settings*.

We need to add one final row, which will tell the Settings application which property list to load for the *More Settings* view.

Add another child row and give it a key of *File* and a value of *More*. The file extension *.plist* is assumed and must not be included, or the Settings application won't find the property list file.

We are adding a child view to our main preference view. That settings in that child view are specified in the *More.plist* file. We need to copy *More.plist* into the settings bundle. We can't add new files to the bundle in Xcode, and the Property List Editor's *Save* dialog will not let us save into a bundle. So, we have to create a new property list, save it somewhere else, and then drag it into the *Settings.bundle* window using the Finder.

You've now seen all the different types of preference fields that you can use in a settings bundle property list file, so to save yourself some typing, why don't you grab *More.plist* out of the *10 AppSettings* folder in the projects archive that accompanies this book, and drag it into that *Settings.bundle* window we left open earlier.

TIP

> When you create your own child settings views, the easiest way to do it is to make a copy of *Root.plist* and give it a new name. Then delete all of the existing preference specifiers except the first one, and add whatever preference specifiers you need to that new file.

We're done with our settings bundle. Feel free to compile, run, and test out the Settings application. You should be able to reach the child view and set values for all the other fields. Go ahead and play with it, and make changes to the property list if you want. We've covered almost every configuration option available (at least at the time of this writing), but you can find the full documentation of the settings property list format in the document called *Settings Application Schema Reference* in the iPhone Dev Center. You'll find it on this page, along with a ton of other useful reference documents:

```
http://developer.apple.com/iphone/library/navigation/Reference.html
```

Before we continue on, we've included an application icon with this chapter's code to make sure your program looks like ours. First, open the *10 AppSettings* folder in the project archive, grab the three image files there (*icon.png*, *rabbit.png*, and *turtle.png*) and add them to the *Resources* folder of your project. Then, make *icon.png* your application icon by single-clicking *AppSettings-Info.plist* in the *Resources* folder, and setting the value of the *Icon* file row to *icon. png*. Be sure to save *AppSettings-Info.plist* when you are done.

NOTE

> You might have noticed that two of the icons you just added are exactly the same ones you added to your settings bundle earlier, and you might be wondering why. Remember: Applications on the iPhone can't read files out of other applications' sandboxes. The settings bundle doesn't become part of our application's sandbox, it becomes part of the Settings application's sandbox. Since we also want to use those icons in our application, we need to add them separately to our *Resources* folder so they get copied into our application's sandbox as well.

Reading Settings in Our Application

We've now solved half of our problem. The user can get to our preferences, but how do we get to them? As it turns out, that's the easy part.

We'll take advantage of a class called NSUserDefaults to read in the user's settings. NSUserDefaults is implemented as a singleton, which means there is only one instance of NSUserDefaults running in your application. To get access to that one instance, we call the class method standardUserDefaults, like so:

```
NSUserDefaults *defaults = [NSUserDefaults standardUserDefaults];
```

Once we have a pointer to the standard user defaults, we use it just like an NSDictionary. To get a value out of it, we can call objectForKey: which will return an Objective-C object like an NSString, NSDate, or NSNumber. If we want to retrieve the value as a scalar like an int, float, or BOOL, we can use other methods, such as intForKey:, floatForKey:, or boolForKey:.

When you were creating the property list for this application, you created an array of *PreferenceSpecifiers*. Some of those specifiers were used to create groups. Others created interface objects that the user used to set their settings. Those are the specifiers we are really interested in, because that's where the real data is. Every specifier that was tied to a user setting had a *Key* named *Key*. Take a minute to go back and check. For example, the *Key* for our slider had a value of *warpfactor*. The *Key* for our *Password* field was *password*. We'll use those keys to retrieve the user settings.

So that we have a place to display the settings, let's quickly set up our main view with a bunch of labels. Before going over to Interface Builder, let's create outlets for all the labels we'll need. Single-click *MainViewController.h*, and make the following changes:

```
#import "FlipsideViewController.h"
#define kUsernameKey         @"username"
#define kPasswordKey         @"password"
#define kProtocolKey         @"protocol"
#define kWarpDriveKey        @"warp"
#define kWarpFactorKey       @"warpFactor"
#define kFavoriteTeaKey      @"favoriteTea"
#define kFavoriteCandyKey    @"favoriteCandy"
#define kFavoriteGameKey     @"favoriteGame"
#define kFavoriteExcuseKey   @"favoriteExcuse"
#define kFavoriteSinKey      @"favoriteSin"

@interface MainViewController : UIViewController
        <FlipsideViewControllerDelegate> {
    UILabel *usernameLabel;
    UILabel *passwordLabel;
    UILabel *protocolLabel;
    UILabel *warpDriveLabel;
    UILabel *warpFactorLabel;

    UILabel *favoriteTeaLabel;
    UILabel *favoriteCandyLabel;
    UILabel *favoriteGameLabel;
    UILabel *favoriteExcuseLabel;
    UILabel *favoriteSinLabel;
}
@property (nonatomic, retain) IBOutlet UILabel *usernameLabel;
@property (nonatomic, retain) IBOutlet UILabel *passwordLabel;
@property (nonatomic, retain) IBOutlet UILabel *protocolLabel;
@property (nonatomic, retain) IBOutlet UILabel *warpDriveLabel;
@property (nonatomic, retain) IBOutlet UILabel *warpFactorLabel;
```

```
@property (nonatomic, retain) IBOutlet UILabel *favoriteTeaLabel;
@property (nonatomic, retain) IBOutlet UILabel *favoriteCandyLabel;
@property (nonatomic, retain) IBOutlet UILabel *favoriteGameLabel;
@property (nonatomic, retain) IBOutlet UILabel *favoriteExcuseLabel;
@property (nonatomic, retain) IBOutlet UILabel *favoriteSinLabel;

- (void)refreshFields;
- (IBAction)showInfo;
@end
```

There's nothing new here. We declare a bunch of constants. These are the key values that we used in our property list file for the different preference fields. Then we declare ten outlets, all of them labels, and create properties for each of them. Finally, we declare a method that will read settings out of the user defaults and push those values into the various labels. We put this functionality in its own method, because we have to do this same task in more than one place. Now that we've got our outlets declared, let's head over to Interface Builder.

Double-click *MainView.xib* to open it in Interface Builder. When it comes up, you'll notice that the background of the view is dark gray. Let's change it to white. Single-click the *Main View* icon in the nib's main window, and press ⌘1 to bring up the attributes inspector. Use the color well labeled *Background* to change the background to white. Now double-click the *Main View* icon if the window labeled *Main View* is not already open.

Put the main window (the one titled *MainView.xib*) in list mode (the center *View Mode* button). Next, click the disclosure triangle to the left of the *Main View* icon. This reveals an icon called *Light Info Button* (see Figure 10-17).

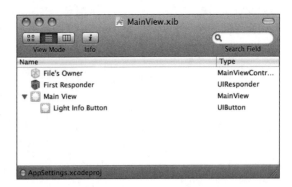

Figure 10-17. *Using the list view mode*

TIP

Got a complex Interface Builder list mode hierarchy that you want to open, all at once? Instead of expanding each of the items individually, you can expand the entire hierarchy by holding down the option key and clicking any of the list's disclosure triangles.

We're going to change this icon so it will look good on a white background. Single-click the *Light Info Button* icon to select it, and then press ⌘1 to bring up the attributes inspector. Change the button's *Type* from *Info Light* to *Info Dark*.

Now we're going to add a bunch of labels to the *Main View* so it looks like the one shown in Figure 10-18. We'll need a grand total of twenty labels. Half of them will be static labels that are right-aligned and **bold**; the other half will be used to display the actual values retrieved from the user defaults and will have outlets pointing to them. Use Figure 10-18 as your guide to build this view. You don't have to match the appearance exactly, but you do need to have one label on the view for each of the outlets we declared. Go ahead and design the view. You don't need our help for this. When you're done and have it looking the way you like, come back, and we'll continue on.

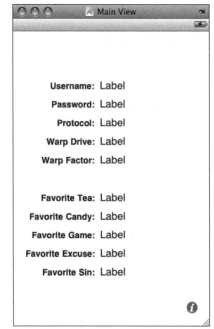

Figure 10-18. *The Main View window in Interface Builder*

The next thing we need to do is control-drag from *File's Owner* to each of the labels intended to display a settings value. You will control-drag a total of ten times, setting each label to a different outlet. Once you have all ten outlets connected to labels, save, close the *MainView.xib* window, and go back to Xcode.

Single-click *MainViewController.m*, and add the following code at the beginning of the file.

```
#import "MainViewController.h"
#import "MainView.h"

@implementation MainViewController
@synthesize usernameLabel;
@synthesize passwordLabel;
@synthesize protocolLabel;
@synthesize warpDriveLabel;
@synthesize warpFactorLabel;
@synthesize favoriteTeaLabel;
@synthesize favoriteCandyLabel;
@synthesize favoriteGameLabel;
@synthesize favoriteExcuseLabel;
@synthesize favoriteSinLabel;
```

```
- (void)refreshFields {
    NSUserDefaults *defaults = [NSUserDefaults standardUserDefaults];
    usernameLabel.text = [defaults objectForKey:kUsernameKey];
    passwordLabel.text = [defaults objectForKey:kPasswordKey];
    protocolLabel.text = [defaults objectForKey:kProtocolKey];
    warpDriveLabel.text = [defaults objectForKey:kWarpDriveKey];
    warpFactorLabel.text = [[defaults objectForKey:kWarpFactorKey]
                            stringValue];
    favoriteTeaLabel.text = [defaults objectForKey:kFavoriteTeaKey];
    favoriteCandyLabel.text = [defaults objectForKey:kFavoriteCandyKey];
    favoriteGameLabel.text = [defaults objectForKey:kFavoriteGameKey];
    favoriteExcuseLabel.text = [defaults objectForKey:kFavoriteExcuseKey];
    favoriteSinLabel.text = [defaults objectForKey:kFavoriteSinKey];
}
- (void)viewDidAppear:(BOOL)animated {
    [self refreshFields];
    [super viewDidAppear:animated];
}
...
```

Also, let's be a good memory citizen by inserting the following code into the existing dealloc and viewDidUnload methods:

```
- (void)viewDidUnload {
    // Release any retained subviews of the main view.
    // e.g. self.myOutlet = nil;
    self.usernameLabel = nil;
    self.passwordLabel = nil;
    self.protocolLabel = nil;
    self.warpDriveLabel = nil;
    self.warpFactorLabel = nil;
    self.favoriteTeaLabel = nil;
    self.favoriteCandyLabel = nil;
    self.favoriteGameLabel = nil;
    self.favoriteExcuseLabel = nil;
    self.favoriteSinLabel = nil;
    [super viewDidUnload];
}
- (void)dealloc {
    [usernameLabel release];
    [passwordLabel release];
    [protocolLabel release];
    [warpDriveLabel release];
    [warpFactorLabel release];
    [favoriteTeaLabel release];
    [favoriteCandyLabel release];
    [favoriteGameLabel release];
    [favoriteExcuseLabel release];
```

```
    [favoriteSinLabel release];
    [super dealloc];
}
...
```

When the user is done using the flipside view where some preferences can be changed, our controller will get notified of the fact. When that happens, we need to make sure our labels are updated to show any changes, so add the following line of code to the existing `flipsideViewControllerDidFinish:` method:

```
- (void)flipsideViewControllerDidFinish:
        (FlipsideViewController *)controller {
    [self refreshFields];
    [self dismissModalViewControllerAnimated:YES];
}
```

There's not really much here that should throw you. The new method, `refreshFields`, does nothing more than grab the standard user defaults, and sets the text property of all the labels to the appropriate object from the user defaults, using the key values that we put in our properties file. Notice that for `warpFactorLabel`, we're calling `stringValue` on the object returned. All of our other preferences are strings, which come back from the user defaults as `NSString` objects. The preference stored by the slider, however, comes back as an `NSNumber`, so we call `stringValue` on it to get a string representation of the value it holds.

After that, we added a `viewDidAppear:` method, where we call our `refreshFields` method. We call `refreshFields` again when we get notified that the flipside controller is being dismissed. This will cause our displayed fields to get set to the appropriate preference values when the view loads, and then to get refreshed when the flipside view gets swapped out. Because the flipside view is handled modally with the main view as its modal parent, `MainViewController`'s `viewDidAppear:` method will not get called when the flipside view is dismissed. Fortunately, the `Utility Application` template we chose has very kindly provided us with a delegate method we can use for exactly that purpose.

This class is done. You should be able to compile and run your application and have it look something like Figure 10-7, except yours will be showing whatever values you entered in your Settings application, of course. Couldn't be much easier, could it?

Changing Defaults from Our Application

Now that we've got the main view up and running, let's build the flipside view. As you can see in Figure 10-19, the flipside view features our warp drive switch, as well as the warp factor slider. We'll use the same controls that the Settings application uses for these two items: a switch and a slider. First, we need to declare our outlets, so single-click *FlipsideViewController.h*, and make the following changes:

```
@protocol FlipsideViewControllerDelegate;

@interface FlipsideViewController : UIViewController {
    id <FlipsideViewControllerDelegate> delegate;
    UISwitch *engineSwitch;
    UISlider *warpFactorSlider;
}

@property (nonatomic, assign) id <FlipsideViewControllerDelegate> delegate;
@property (nonatomic, retain) IBOutlet UISwitch *engineSwitch;
@property (nonatomic, retain) IBOutlet UISlider *warpFactorSlider;

- (IBAction)done;
@end

@protocol FlipsideViewControllerDelegate
- (void)flipsideViewControllerDidFinish:
    (FlipsideViewController *)controller;
@end
```

NOTE

Don't worry too much about the extra code here. As we saw before, the *Utility Application* template makes `MainViewController` a delegate of the `FlipsideViewController`, the extra code here that hasn't been in the other file templates we've used implements that delegate relationship.

Figure 10-19. *Desiging the flipside view in Interface Builder*

Now, double-click *FlipsideView.xib* to open it in Interface Builder. If the *Flipside View* window is not open, double-click the *Flipside View* icon in the nib's main window to open it. First, change the background color using the attribute inspector to a lighter shade of gray, about a 25% gray should work well. The default flipside view background color is too dark for black text to look good, but light enough that white text is hard to read. Next, drag two *Labels* from the library and place them on Flipside View window. Double-click one of them and change it to read *Warp Engines:*. Double-click the other, and call it *Warp Factor:*. You can use Figure 10-19 as a placement guide.

When you're done placing the controls, double-click the word *Title* at the top of the view and change it to read *Warp Settings*.

Next, drag over a *Switch* from the library, and place it against the right side of the view across from the label that reads *Warp Engines*. Control-drag from the *File's Owner* icon to the new switch, and connect it to the *engineSwitch* outlet.

Now drag over a *Slider* from the library, and place it below the label that reads *Warp Factor*. Resize the slider so that it stretches from the blue guide line on the left margin to the one on the right, and then control-drag from the *File's Owner* icon to the slider, and connect it to the *warpFactorSlider* outlet.

Single-click the slider if it's not still selected, and press ⌘1 to bring up the attributes inspector. Set *Minimum* to *1.00*, *Maximum* to *10.00*, and *Initial* to *5.00*. Next, select *turtle.png* for *Min Image* and *rabbit.png* for *Max Image*. Once you're done, the inspector should look like Figure 10-20.

Save and close the nib, and head back to Xcode so we can finish the flipside view controller. Single-click *FlipsideViewController.m*, and make the following changes:

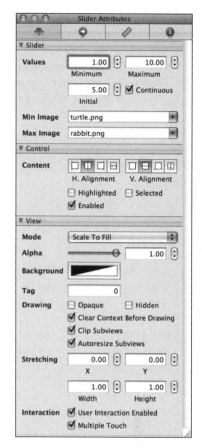

Figure 10-20. *The attributes inspector for our Warp Factor slider*

```
#import "FlipsideViewController.h"
#import "MainViewController.h"

@implementation FlipsideViewController
@synthesize delegate;
@synthesize engineSwitch;
@synthesize warpFactorSlider;

- (void)viewDidLoad {
    self.view.backgroundColor = [UIColor viewFlipsideBackgroundColor];

    NSUserDefaults *defaults = [NSUserDefaults standardUserDefaults];
    engineSwitch.on  = ([[defaults objectForKey:kWarpDriveKey]
        isEqualToString:@"Engaged"]) ? YES : NO;
    warpFactorSlider.value = [defaults floatForKey:kWarpFactorKey];
    [super viewDidLoad];
}
```

```
- (void)viewWillDisappear:(BOOL)animated {
    NSUserDefaults *defaults = [NSUserDefaults standardUserDefaults];
    NSString *prefValue = (engineSwitch.on) ? @"Engaged" : @"Disabled";
    [defaults setObject:prefValue forKey:kWarpDriveKey];
    [defaults setFloat:warpFactorSlider.value forKey:kWarpFactorKey];
    [super viewWillDisappear:animated];
}
...
```

Add the following lines of code to the existing `dealloc` and `viewDidUnload` methods:

```
...
- (void)viewDidUnload {
    // Release any retained subviews of the main view.
    // e.g. self.myOutlet = nil;
    self.engineSwitch = nil;
    self.warpFactorSlider = nil;
    [super viewDidUnload];
}
- (void)dealloc {
    [engineSwitch release];
    [warpFactorSlider release];
    [super dealloc];
}
...
```

In the `viewDidLoad` method, we deleted one line of code and added three (well, four, because one line was too long to fit the page width of this book). The one line of code we deleted wasn't really important. Code in the template set the background color of the view using a class method, and that line of code caused the flipside view to have a textured, dark gray appearance rather than using the background that was set in Interface Builder. The textured background made it difficult to read the text and to see the slider pictures that we used; we deleted it to let the background color from Interface Builder shine through so our text and icons could be seen more easily.

The four lines of code we added get a reference to the standard user defaults and use the outlets for the switch and slider to set them to the values stored in the user defaults. Because we opted to store strings rather than Booleans for the warp drive setting, we have to handle the conversion in our code because a `UISwitch` instance is set using a BOOL property.

```
NSUserDefaults *defaults = [NSUserDefaults standardUserDefaults];
engineSwitch.on = ([[defaults objectForKey:kWarpDriveKey]
        isEqualToString:@"Engaged"]) ? YES : NO;
warpFactorSlider.value = [defaults floatForKey:kWarpFactorKey];
```

We also overrode our parent's `viewWillDisappear:` method so that we could stuff the values from our controls back into the user defaults before the main view is shown again. Because our controller's `viewDidDisappear:` method will fire before the main view's `viewWillAppear:` method, the changed values will already be stored in the user defaults for the view to retrieve, so the main view will get updated with the correct new values.

Beam Me Up, Scotty

At this point, you should have a very solid grasp on both the Settings application and user defaults. You know how to add a settings bundle to your application and how to build a hierarchy of views for your application's preferences. You also saw how to read and write preferences using `NSUserDefaults` and how to let the user change preferences from within your application, and you even got a chance to use a new project template in Xcode. There really shouldn't be much in the way of application preferences that you aren't equipped to handle now.

In the next chapter, we're going to tackle the different approaches to file management on the iPhone. We'll cover different techniques for persisting your objects to the file system and also take a look at using your iPhone's embedded database, SQLite. You'll also get your first look at a very cool technology called Core Data. Ready? Let's go!

Chapter 11

Basic Data Persistence

S o far, we've focused on the controller and view aspects of the Model-View-Controller paradigm. Although several of our applications have read data out of the application bundle, none of our applications has saved their data to any form of persistent storage, persistent storage being any form of nonvolatile storage that survives a restart of the computer or device. With the exception of Application Settings, so far, every sample application either did not store data or used volatile or nonpersistent storage. Every time one of our sample applications launched, it appeared with exactly the same data it had the first time you launched it.

This approach has worked for us up to this point. But in the real world, your applications will need to persist data so that when users make changes, those changes are stored and are there when they launch the program again. A number of different mechanisms are available for persisting data on the iPhone. If you've programmed in Cocoa for Mac OS X, you've likely used some or all of these techniques.

In this chapter, we're going to look at four different mechanisms for persisting data to the iPhone's file system: using property lists, object archives (or archiving), the iPhone's embedded relational database called SQLite3, and Apple's provided persistence tool called Core Data. We will write example applications that use all four approaches.

NOTE

> Property lists, object archives, SQLite3, and Core Data are not the only ways you can persist data on an
> iPhone. They are just the most common and easiest. You always have the option of using traditional C I/O
> calls like `fopen()` to read and write data. You can also use Cocoa's low-level file management tools. In
> almost every case, doing so will result in a lot more coding effort and is rarely necessary, but those tools
> are there if you need them.

Your Application's Sandbox

All four of this chapter's data-persistence mechanisms share an important common element,
your application's */Documents* folder. Every application gets its own */Documents* folder, and
applications are only allowed to read and write from their own */Documents* directory.

To give you some context, let's take a look at what an application looks like on the iPhone.
Open a Finder window, and navigate to your home directory. Within that, drill down into
Library/Application Support/iPhoneSimulator/User/. At this point, you should see five subfold-
ers, one of which is named *Applications* (see Figure 11-1).

NOTE

> If you've installed multiple versions of the SDK, you may see a few additional folders with names like
> *Library.previousInstall*. That's perfectly normal.

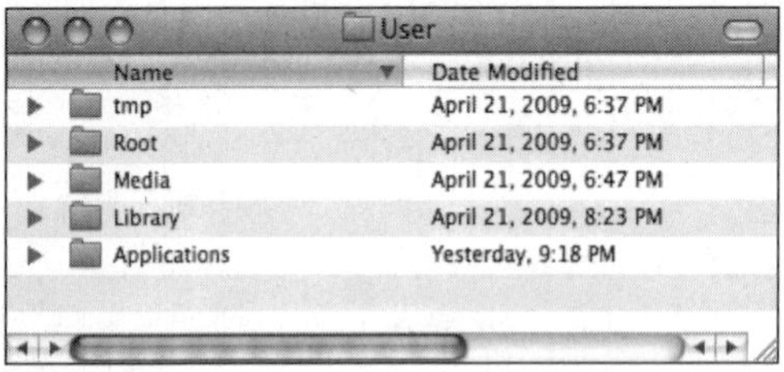

Name	Date Modified
▶ ▣ tmp	April 21, 2009, 6:37 PM
▶ ▣ Root	April 21, 2009, 6:37 PM
▶ ▣ Media	April 21, 2009, 6:47 PM
▶ ▣ Library	April 21, 2009, 8:23 PM
▶ ▣ Applications	Yesterday, 9:18 PM

Figure 11-1. *The layout of the User directory
showing the Applications folder*

Although this listing represents the simulator, the file structure is similar to what's on the
actual device. As is probably obvious, the *Applications* folder is where the iPhone stores its
applications. If you open the *Applications* folder, you'll see a bunch of folders and files with
names that are long strings of characters. These names are generated automatically by
Xcode. Each of these folders contains one application and its supporting folders.

Scattered among those application directories, you may spy the occasional *.sb* file. The *.sb* files contain settings that the simulator uses to launch the program that shares the same name. You should never need to touch those. If you open one of the application subdirectories, however, you should see something that looks a little more familiar. In there, you'll find one of the iPhone applications you've built, along with three support folders: *Documents*, *Library*, and *tmp*. Your application stores its data in *Documents*, with the exception of NSUserDefaults-based preference settings, which get stored in the *Library/Preferences* folder. The *tmp* directory offers a place where your application can store temporary files. Files written into */tmp* will not be backed up by iTunes when your iPhone syncs, but your application does need to take responsibility for deleting the files in */tmp* once they are no longer needed to avoid filling up the file system.

Getting the Documents Directory

Since our application is in a folder with a seemingly random name, how do we retrieve the full path to the *Documents* directory so that we can read and write our files? It's actually quite easy. The C function NSSearchPathForDirectoriesInDomain() will locate various directories for you. This is a Foundation function, so it is shared with Cocoa for Mac OS X. Many of its available options are designed for OS X and won't return any values on the iPhone, either because those locations don't exist on the iPhone (e.g., the *Downloads* folder) or because your application doesn't have rights to access the location due to the iPhone's sandboxing mechanism.

Here's some code to retrieve the path to the *Documents* directory:

```
NSArray *paths = NSSearchPathForDirectoriesInDomains(NSDocumentDirectory,
    NSUserDomainMask, YES);
NSString *documentsDirectory = [paths objectAtIndex:0];
```

The constant NSDocumentDirectory says we are looking for the path to the *Documents* directory. The second constant, NSUserDomainMask, indicates that we want to restrict our search to our application's sandbox. In Mac OS X, this same constant is used to indicate that we want the function to look in the user's home directory, which explains its somewhat odd name.

Though an array of matching paths is returned, we can count on our *Documents* directory residing at index 0 in the array. Why? We know that only one directory meets the criteria we've specified since each application has only one *Documents* directory. We can create a filename, for reading or writing purposes, by appending another string onto the end of the path we just retrieved. We'll use an NSString method designed for just that purpose called stringByAppendingPathComponent:, like so:

```
NSString *filename = [documentsDirectory
    stringByAppendingPathComponent:@"theFile.txt"];
```

After this call, `filename` would contain the full path to a file called *theFile.txt* in our application's *Documents* directory, and we can use `filename` to create, read, and write from that file.

Getting the tmp Directory

Getting a reference to your application's temporary directory is even easier than getting a reference to the *Documents* directory. The Foundation function called `NSTemporaryDirectory()` will return a string containing the full path to your application's temporary directory. To create a filename for a file that will get stored in the temporary directory, we first find the temporary directory:

```
NSString *tempPath = NSTemporaryDirectory();
```

Then, we create a path to a file in that directory by appending a filename to that path, like this:

```
NSString *tempFile = [tempPath
    stringByAppendingPathComponent:@"tempFile.txt"];
```

File Saving Strategies

As a reminder, in this chapter, we're going to look at four different approaches to data persistence. All four approaches make use of your iPhone's file system.

In the case of SQLite3, you'll create a single SQLite3 database file and let SQLite3 worry about storing and retrieving your data. In its simplest form, Core Data takes care of all the file system management for you. With the other two persistence mechanisms, property lists and archiving, you need to put some thought into whether you are going to store your data in a single file or in multiple files.

Single-File Persistence

Using a single file is the easiest approach, and with many applications, it is a perfectly acceptable one. You start off by creating a root object, usually an `NSArray` or `NSDictionary`, though your root object can also be based on a custom class when using archiving. Next, you populate your root object with all the program data that needs to be persisted. Whenever you need to save, your code rewrites the entire contents of that root object to a single file. When your application launches, it reads the entire contents of that file into memory, and when it quits, it writes out the entire contents. This is the approach we'll use in this chapter.

The downside of using a single file is that you have to load all of your application's data into memory, and you have to write all of it to the file system for even the smallest changes. If your application isn't likely to manage more than a few megabytes of data, this approach is probably fine, and its simplicity will certainly make your life easier.

Multiple-File Persistence

The multiple file approach is definitely more complicated. As an example, you might write an e-mail application that stored each e-mail message in its own file. There are obvious advantages to this method. It allows the application to load only data that the user has requested (another form of lazy loading), and when the user makes a change, only the files that changed have to be saved. This method also gives you the opportunity to free up memory when you receive a low-memory notification, since any memory that is being used to store data that the user is not currently looking at can be flushed and simply reloaded from the file system the next time it's needed. The downside of multiple-file persistence is that it adds a fair amount of complexity to your application. For now, we'll stick with single-file persistence.

Persisting Application Data

Let's get into the specifics of each of our persistence methods: property lists, object archives, SQLite3, and Core Data. We'll explore each of these in turn and build an application that uses each mechanism to save some data to the iPhone's file system. We'll start with property lists.

Property List Serialization

Several of our applications have made use of property lists, most recently when we used a property list to specify our application preferences. Property lists are convenient, because they can be edited manually using Xcode or the Property List Editor application, and both `NSDictionary` and `NSArray` instances can be written to and created from property lists as long as the dictionary or array contains only specific serializable objects. A **serialized object** has been converted into a stream of bytes so it can be stored in a file or transferred over a network. Although any object can be made serializable, only certain objects can be placed into a collection class, such as an `NSDictionary` or `NSArray`, and then stored to a property list using the collection classes' `writeToFile:atomically:` method. The Objective-C classes that can be serialized this way are

- `NSArray`

- `NSMutableArray`

- `NSDictionary`

- `NSMutableDictionary`

- `NSData`

- `NSMutableData`

- `NSString`

- `NSMutableString`

- `NSNumber`

- `NSDate`

If you can build your data model from just these objects, you can use property lists to easily save and load your data. In fact, we've used this mechanism in many of the sample applications to provide you with data.

If you're going to use property lists to persist your application data, you'll use either an `NSArray` or an `NSDictionary` to hold the data that needs to be persisted. Assuming that all of the objects that you put into the `NSArray` or `NSDictionary` are serializable objects from the preceding list, you can write a property list by calling the `writeToFile:atomically:` method on the dictionary or array instance, like so:

```
[myArray writeToFile:@"/some/file/location/output.plist" atomically:YES];
```

NOTE

In case you were wondering, the `atomically` parameter tells the method to write the data to an auxiliary file, not to the specified location. Once it has successfully written the file, it will then copy that auxiliary file to the location specified by the first parameter. This is a safer way to write a file, because if the application crashes during the save, the existing file, if there was one, will not be corrupted. It adds a tiny bit of overhead, but in most situations, it's worth the cost.

One problem with the property list approach is that custom objects cannot be serialized into property lists. You also can't use other delivered classes from Cocoa Touch that aren't specified in the previous list of serializable objects, which means that classes like `NSURL`, `UIImage` and `UIColor` cannot be used directly.

Not being able to serialize these objects also means that you can't easily create derived or calculated properties (e.g., a property that is the sum of two other properties), and some of your code that really should be contained in model classes has to be moved to your controller classes. Again, these restrictions are OK for simple data models and simple applications. Most of the time, however, your application will be much easier to maintain if you create dedicated model classes.

However, simple property lists can still be useful in complex applications. They are a great way to include static data in your application. For example, when your application includes a picker, often the best way to include the list of items to go in your picker is to create a property list file and include it in your project's *Resources* folder, which will cause it to get compiled into your application.

Let's a build a simple application that uses property lists to store its data.

The Persistence Application

We're going to build a program that lets you enter data into four text fields, saves those fields to a property list file when the application quits, and then reloads the data back from that property list file the next time the application launches (see Figure 11-2).

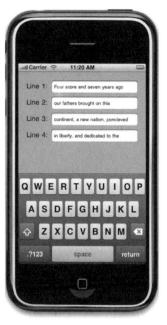

NOTE

In this chapter's applications, we won't be taking the time to set up all the user interface niceties that we have in the past. Tapping the return key, for example, will neither dismiss the keyboard nor take you to the next field. If you want to add that polish to the application, doing so would be good practice, but it's not really material to this chapter's topic, so we won't be walking you through it.

Figure 11-2. *The property list application*

Creating the Persistence Project

In Xcode, create a new project using the view-based application template, and save the project with the name *Persistence*. This project contains all the files that we'll need to build our application, so we can dive right into things. In a minute, we're going to build a view with four text fields. Let's create the outlets we need before we go to Interface Builder. Expand the *Classes* folder. Then, single-click the *PersistenceViewController.h* file, and make the following changes:

```
#import <UIKit/UIKit.h>

#define kFilename        @"data.plist"

@interface PersistenceViewController : UIViewController {
    UITextField *field1;
    UITextField *field2;
    UITextField *field3;
    UITextField *field4;
}
@property (nonatomic, retain) IBOutlet UITextField *field1;
@property (nonatomic, retain) IBOutlet UITextField *field2;
@property (nonatomic, retain) IBOutlet UITextField *field3;
```

```
@property (nonatomic, retain) IBOutlet UITextField *field4;
- (NSString *)dataFilePath;
- (void)applicationWillTerminate:(NSNotification *)notification;
@end
```

In addition to defining four text field outlets, we've also defined a constant for the filename we're going to use, as well as two additional methods. One method, `dataFilePath`, will create and return the full pathname to our data file by concatenating `kFilename` onto the path for the *Documents* directory. The other method, `applicationWillTerminate:`, which we'll discuss in a minute, will get called when our application quits and will save data to the property list file.

Next, expand the *Resources* folder, and double-click *PersistenceViewController.xib* to open the file in Interface Builder.

Designing the Persistence Application View

Once Interface Builder comes up, the *View* window should open as well. If it doesn't, double-click the *View* icon to open it. Drag a *Text Field* from the library, and place it against the top-right blue guide line. Expand it to the left so that it reaches about two-thirds of the way across the window, and then press ⌘1 to bring up the attributes inspector. Uncheck the box labeled *Clear When Editing Begins*.

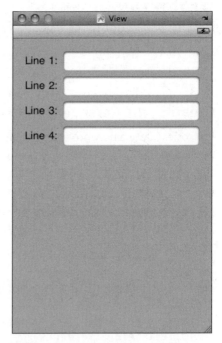

Figure 11-3. *Designing the Persistence application's view*

Next, hold down the option key, and drag the text box downward, which will create a copy of it. Repeat this step two more times so that you have four text fields. Now, drag four labels to the window, and use Figure 11-3 as a placement and design guide. Notice that we've placed the text fields at the top of our view so that there is room for the keyboard.

Once you have all four text fields and labels placed, control-drag from the *File's Owner* icon to each of the four text fields. Connect the topmost text field to the outlet called *field1*, the next one to *field2*, the third to *field3*, and the bottom one to *field4*. When you have all four text fields connected to outlets, save, close *PersistenceViewController.xib*, and go back to Xcode.

Editing the Persistence Classes

Single-click *PersistenceViewController.m*, and add the following code at the beginning of the file:

```
#import "PersistenceViewController.h"

@implementation PersistenceViewController
@synthesize field1;
@synthesize field2;
@synthesize field3;
@synthesize field4;

- (NSString *)dataFilePath {
    NSArray *paths = NSSearchPathForDirectoriesInDomains(
        NSDocumentDirectory, NSUserDomainMask, YES);
    NSString *documentsDirectory = [paths objectAtIndex:0];
    return [documentsDirectory stringByAppendingPathComponent:kFilename];
}
- (void)applicationWillTerminate:(NSNotification *)notification {
    NSMutableArray *array = [[NSMutableArray alloc] init];
    [array addObject:field1.text];
    [array addObject:field2.text];
    [array addObject:field3.text];
    [array addObject:field4.text];
    [array writeToFile:[self dataFilePath] atomically:YES];
    [array release];
}
#pragma mark -
- (void)viewDidLoad {
    NSString *filePath = [self dataFilePath];
    if ([[NSFileManager defaultManager] fileExistsAtPath:filePath]) {
        NSArray *array = [[NSArray alloc] initWithContentsOfFile:filePath];
        field1.text = [array objectAtIndex:0];
        field2.text = [array objectAtIndex:1];
        field3.text = [array objectAtIndex:2];
        field4.text = [array objectAtIndex:3];
        [array release];
    }

    UIApplication *app = [UIApplication sharedApplication];
    [[NSNotificationCenter defaultCenter] addObserver:self
            selector:@selector(applicationWillTerminate:)
            name:UIApplicationWillTerminateNotification
        object:app];
    [super viewDidLoad];
}
...
```

Also, insert the following code into the existing deal1oc and viewDidUnload methods:

```
...
- (void)viewDidUnload {
        // Release any retained subviews of the main view.
    // e.g. self.myOutlet = nil;
    self.field1 = nil;
    self.field2 = nil;
    self.field3 = nil;
    self.field4 = nil;
    [super viewDidUnload];
}
- (void)dealloc {
    [field1 release];
    [field2 release];
    [field3 release];
    [field4 release];
    [super dealloc];
}
...
```

The first method we added, dataFilePath, returns the full pathname of our data file by finding the *Documents* directory and appending kFilename to it. This method will be called from any code that needs to load or save data.

```
- (NSString *)dataFilePath {
    NSArray *paths = NSSearchPathForDirectoriesInDomains(
        NSDocumentDirectory, NSUserDomainMask, YES);
    NSString *documentsDirectory = [paths objectAtIndex:0];
    return [documentsDirectory stringByAppendingPathComponent:kFilename];
}
```

The second new method is called applicationWillTerminate:. Notice that it takes a pointer to an NSNotification as an argument. applicationWillTerminate: is a notification method, and all notifications take a single NSNotification instance as their argument.

A notification is a lightweight mechanism that objects can use to communicate with each other. Any object can define one or more notifications that it will publish to the application's notification center, which is a singleton object that exists only to pass these notifications between objects. Notifications are usually indications that some event occurred, and objects that publish notifications include a list of notifications in their documentation. For example, if you look at Figure 11-4, you can see that the UIApplication class publishes a number of notifications.

Figure 11-4. *UIApplication documentation lists all the notifications that it publishes.*

The purpose of most notifications is usually pretty obvious from their names, but the documentation contains further information if you find one whose purpose is unclear. Our application needs to save its data before the application quits, so we are interested in the notification called UIApplicationWillTerminateNotification. In a minute, when we write our viewDidLoad method, we will subscribe to that notification and tell the notification center to call this method when that notification happens:

```
- (void)applicationWillTerminate:(NSNotification *)notification {
    NSMutableArray *array = [[NSMutableArray alloc] init];
    [array addObject:field1.text];
    [array addObject:field2.text];
    [array addObject:field3.text];
    [array addObject:field4.text];
    [array writeToFile:[self dataFilePath] atomically:YES];
    [array release];
}
```

The method itself is fairly simple. We create a mutable array, add the text from each of the four fields to the array, and then write the contents of that array out to a property list file. That's all there is to saving our data using property lists.

In the viewDidLoad method, we do a few more things. The first thing we do is check to see if a data file already exists. If there isn't one, we don't want to bother trying to load it. If the file does exist, we instantiate an array with the contents of that file and then copy the objects from that array to our four text fields. Because arrays are ordered lists, by copying them in the same order as we saved them, we are always sure to get the right values in the right fields.

```
- (void)viewDidLoad {
    NSString *filePath = [self dataFilePath];
    if ([[NSFileManager defaultManager] fileExistsAtPath:filePath]) {
        NSArray *array = [[NSArray alloc] initWithContentsOfFile:filePath];
        field1.text = [array objectAtIndex:0];
        field2.text = [array objectAtIndex:1];
        field3.text = [array objectAtIndex:2];
        field4.text = [array objectAtIndex:3];
        [array release];
    }
```

After we load the data from the property list, we get a reference to our application instance and use that to subscribe to the UIApplicationWillTerminateNotification, using the default NSNotificationCenter instance and a method called addObserver :selector:name:object:. We pass an observer of self, which means that our PersistenceViewController is the object that needs to get notified. For selector, we pass a selector to the applicationWillTerminate: method we wrote a minute ago, telling the notification center to call that method when the notification is published. The third parameter, name:, is the name of the notification that we're interested in receiving, and the final parameter, object:, is the object we're interested in getting the notification from. If we pass nil for the final parameter, we would then get notified any time any method posted the UIApplicationWillTerminateNotification.

```
    UIApplication *app = [UIApplication sharedApplication];
    [[NSNotificationCenter defaultCenter] addObserver:self
            selector:@selector(applicationWillTerminate:)
            name:UIApplicationWillTerminateNotification
        object:app];
```

After subscribing to the notification, we just give our superclass a chance to respond to viewDidLoad, and we're done.

```
    [super viewDidLoad];
}
```

That wasn't too bad, was it? When our main view is finished loading, we look for a property list file. If it exists, we copy data from it into our text fields. Next, we register to be notified when the application terminates. When the application does terminate, we gather up the values from our four text fields, stick them in a mutable array, and write that mutable array out to a property list.

Why don't you compile and run the application? It should build and then launch in the simulator. Once it comes up, you should be able to type into any of the four text fields. When you've typed something in them, press the home button (the circular button with the rounded square in it at the bottom of the simulator window). It's very important that you press the home button. If you just quit the simulator, that's the equivalent of force quitting your application, and you will never receive the notification that the application is terminating, and your data will never get saved.

Property list serialization is pretty cool and very easy to use, but it's a little limiting, since only a small selection of objects can be stored in property lists. Let's look at a little more robust approach.

Archiving Model Objects

In the last part of Chapter 9, when we built the Presidents data model object, you saw an example of the process of loading archived data using NSCoder. In the Cocoa world, the term "archiving" refers to another form of serialization, but it's a more generic type that any object can implement. Any object specifically written to hold data (model objects) should support archiving. The technique of archiving model objects lets you easily write complex objects to a file and then read them back in. As long as every property you implement in your class is either a scalar like int or float or else is an instance of a class that conforms to the NSCoding protocol, you can archive your objects completely. Since most Foundation and Cocoa Touch classes capable of storing data do conform to NSCoding (though there are a few noteworthy exceptions like UIImage) archiving is actually relatively easy to implement for most classes.

Although not strictly required to make archiving work, another protocol should be implemented along with NSCoding—the NSCopying protocol, which is a protocol that allows your object to be copied. Being able to copy an object gives you a lot more flexibility when using data model objects. For example, in the Presidents application in Chapter 9, instead of that complex code we had to write to store changes the user made so we could handle both the *Cancel* and *Save* buttons, we could have made a copy of the president object and stored the changes in that copy. If the user tapped *Save*, we'd just copy the changed version over to replace the original version.

Conforming to NSCoding

The NSCoding protocol declares two methods, both required. One encodes your object into an archive; the other one creates a new object by decoding an archive. Both methods are passed an instance of NSCoder, which you work with very much like NSUserDefaults from the previous chapter. You can encode and decode both objects and native datatypes like ints and floats using key-value coding.

A method to encode an object might look like this:

```
- (void)encodeWithCoder:(NSCoder *)encoder {
    [encoder encodeObject:foo forKey:kFooKey];
    [encoder encodeObject:bar forKey:kBarKey];
    [encoder encodeInt:someInt forKey:kSomeIntKey];
    [encoder encodeFloat:someFloat forKey:kSomeFloatKey]
}
```

To support archiving in our object, we have to encode each of our instance variables into encoder using the appropriate encoding method, so we need to implement a method that initializes an object from an NSCoder, allowing us to restore an object that was previously archived. If you are subclassing a class that also conforms to NSCoding, you also need to make sure you call encodeWithCoder: on your superclass, meaning your method would look like this instead:

```
- (void)encodeWithCoder:(NSCoder *)encoder {
    [encoder encodeObject:foo forKey:kFooKey];
    [encoder encodeObject:bar forKey:kBarKey];
    [encoder encodeInt:someInt forKey:kSomeIntKey];
    [encoder encodeFloat:someFloat forKey:kSomeFloatKey]
    [super encodeWithCoder:encoder];
}
```

Implementing the initWithCoder: method is slightly more complex than encodeWithcoder:. If you are subclassing NSObject directly, or subclassing some other class that doesn't conform to NSCoding, your method would look something like the following:

```
- (id)initWithCoder:(NSCoder *)decoder {
    if (self = [super init]) {
        self.foo = [decoder decodeObjectForKey:kFooKey];
        self.bar = [decoder decodeObjectForKey:kBarKey];
        self.someInt = [decoder decodeIntForKey:kSomeIntKey];
        self.someFloat = [decoder decodeFloatForKey:kAgeKey];
    }
    return self;
}
```

The method initializes an object instance using [super init], and if that's successful, it sets its properties by decoding values from the passed-in instance of NSCoder. When implementing NSCoding for a class with a superclass that also conforms to NSCoding, the initWithCoder: method needs to look slightly different. Instead of calling init on super, it has to call initWithCoder:, like so:

```
- (id)initWithCoder:(NSCoder *)decoder {
    if (self = [super initWithCoder:decoder]) {
        self.foo = [decoder decodeObjectForKey:kFooKey];
        self.bar = [decoder decodeObjectForKey:kBarKey];
        self.someInt = [decoder decodeIntForKey:kSomeIntKey];
        self.someFloat = [decoder decodeFloatForKey:kAgeKey];
    }
    return self;
}
```

And that's basically it. As long as you implement these two methods to encode and decode all of your object's properties, your object is archivable and can be written to and read from archives.

Implementing NSCopying

As we mentioned a few minutes ago, conforming to NSCopying is a very good idea for any data model objects as well. NSCopying has one method, called copyWithZone:, and it allows objects to be copied. Implementing NSCopying is very similar to implementing initWithCoder:. You just need to create a new instance of the same class and then set all of that new instance's properties to the same values as this objects properties. Here's what a copyWithZone: method might look like:

```
- (id)copyWithZone:(NSZone *)zone {
    MyClass *copy = [[[self class] allocWithZone:zone] init];
    copy.foo = [self.foo copyWithZone:zone];
    copy.bar = [self.bar copyWithZone:zone];
    copy.someInt = self.someInt;
    copy.someFloat = self.someFloat;
    return copy;
}
```

Notice that we do not release or autorelease the new object we created. Copied objects are implicitly retained and should therefore be released or autoreleased in the code that called copy or copyWithZone:.

NOTE

Don't worry too much about the NSZone parameter. This pointer is to a `struct` that is used by the system to manage memory. Only in rare circumstances did developers ever need to worry about zones or create their own, and nowadays, it's almost unheard of to have multiple zones. Calling copy on an object is exactly the same as calling copyWithZone: using the default zone, which is almost always what you want.

Archiving a Data Object

Creating an archive from an object or objects that conforms to NSCoding is relatively easy. First, we create an instance of NSMutableData to hold the encoded data and then create an NSKeyedArchiver instance to archive objects into that NSMutableData instance:

```
NSMutableData *data = [[NSMutableData alloc] init];
NSKeyedArchiver *archiver = [[NSKeyedArchiver alloc]
    initForWritingWithMutableData:data];
```

After creating both of those, we then use key-value coding to archive any objects we wish to include in the archive, like this:

```
[archiver encodeObject:myObject forKey:@"keyValueString"];
```

Once we've encoded all the objects we want to include, we just tell the archiver we're done, write the NSMutableData instance to the file system, and do memory cleanup on our objects.

```
[archiver finishEncoding];
BOOL success = [data writeToFile:@"/path/to/archive" atomically:YES];
[archiver release];
[data release];
```

If anything went wrong while writing the file, success will be set to NO. If success is YES, the data was successfully written to the specified file. Any objects created from this archive will be exact copies of the objects that were last written into the file.

Unarchiving a Data Object

To reconstitute objects from the archive, we go through a similar process. We create an NSData instance from the archive file and create an NSKeyedUnarchiver to decode the data:

```
NSData *data = [[NSData alloc] initWithContentsOfFile:path];
NSKeyedUnarchiver *unarchiver = [[NSKeyedUnarchiver alloc]
    initForReadingWithData:data];
```

After that, we read our objects from the unarchiver using the same key that we used to archive the object:

```
self.object = [unarchiver decodeObjectForKey:@"keyValueString"];
```

Finally, we tell the archiver we are done and do our memory cleanup:

```
[unarchiver finishDecoding];
[unarchiver release];
[data release];
```

If you're feeling a little overwhelmed by archiving, don't worry; it's actually fairly straight-forward. We're going to retrofit our Persistence application to use archiving, so you'll get to see it in action. Once you've done it a few times, archiving will become second nature, as all you're really doing is storing and retrieving your object's properties using key-value coding.

The Archiving Application

Let's retrofit the Persistence application so it uses archiving instead of property lists. We're going to be making some fairly significant changes to the Persistence source code, so you might want to make a copy of your project before continuing.

Implementing the FourLines Class

Once you're ready to proceed and have the Persistence project open in Xcode, single-click the *Classes* folder and press ⌘N or select **New File...** from the **File** menu. When the new file assistant comes up, select *Cocoa Touch Class*, then *Objective-C class* with a *Subclass of NSObject*, and name the file *FourLines.m*, making sure the box to create the header file is checked. This file is going to be our data model, and it's going to hold the data that we're currently storing in a dictionary in the property list application. Single-click *FourLines.h*, and make the following changes:

```
#import <UIKit/UIKit.h>
#define    kField1Key    @"Field1"
#define    kField2Key    @"Field2"
#define    kField3Key    @"Field3"
#define    kField4Key    @"Field4"
```

```
@interface FourLines : NSObject  <NSCoding, NSCopying> {
    NSString *field1;
    NSString *field2;
    NSString *field3;
    NSString *field4;
}
@property (nonatomic, retain) NSString *field1;
@property (nonatomic, retain) NSString *field2;
@property (nonatomic, retain) NSString *field3;
@property (nonatomic, retain) NSString *field4;
@end
```

This is a very straightforward data model class with four string properties. Notice that we've conformed the class to the NSCoding and NSCopying protocols. Now, switch over to *FourLines.m*, and add the following code.

```
#import "FourLines.h"

@implementation FourLines
@synthesize field1;
@synthesize field2;
@synthesize field3;
@synthesize field4;
#pragma mark NSCoding
- (void)encodeWithCoder:(NSCoder *)encoder {
    [encoder encodeObject:field1 forKey:kField1Key];
    [encoder encodeObject:field2 forKey:kField2Key];
    [encoder encodeObject:field3 forKey:kField3Key];
    [encoder encodeObject:field4 forKey:kField4Key];
}
- (id)initWithCoder:(NSCoder *)decoder {
    if (self = [super init]) {
        self.field1 = [decoder decodeObjectForKey:kField1Key];
        self.field2 = [decoder decodeObjectForKey:kField2Key];
        self.field3 = [decoder decodeObjectForKey:kField3Key];
        self.field4 = [decoder decodeObjectForKey:kField4Key];
    }
    return self;
}
#pragma mark -
#pragma mark NSCopying
- (id)copyWithZone:(NSZone *)zone {
    FourLines *copy = [[[self class] allocWithZone: zone] init];
    copy.field1 = [[self.field1 copyWithZone:zone] autorelease];
    copy.field2 = [[self.field2 copyWithZone:zone] autorelease];
    copy.field3 = [[self.field3 copyWithZone:zone] autorelease];
    copy.field4 = [[self.field4 copyWithZone:zone] autorelease];
```

```
        return copy;
}
@end
```

We just implemented all the methods necessary to conform to NSCoding and NSCopying. We encode all four of our properties in encodeWithCoder: and decode all four of them using the same four key values in initWithCoder:. In copyWithZone:, we create a new FourLines object and copy all four strings to it. See? It's not hard at all.

Implementing the PersistenceViewController Class

Now that we have an archivable data object, let's use it to persist our application data. Single click *PersistenceViewController.h*, and make the following changes:

```
#import <UIKit/UIKit.h>

#define kFilename          @"data.plist"
#define kFilename          @"archive"
#define kDataKey           @"Data"


@interface PersistenceViewController : UIViewController {
    UITextField *field1;
    UITextField *field2;
    UITextField *field3;
    UITextField *field4;
}
@property (nonatomic, retain) IBOutlet UITextField *field1;
@property (nonatomic, retain) IBOutlet UITextField *field2;
@property (nonatomic, retain) IBOutlet UITextField *field3;
@property (nonatomic, retain) IBOutlet UITextField *field4;
- (NSString *)dataFilePath;
- (void)applicationWillTerminate:(NSNotification *)notification;
@end
```

All we're doing here is specifying a new filename so that our program doesn't try to load the old property list in as an archive. We've also defined a new constant that will be the key value we use to encode and decode our object.

Let's switch over the *PersistenceViewController.m*, and make the following changes:

```
#import "PersistenceViewController.h"
#import "FourLines.h"

@implementation PersistenceViewController
@synthesize field1;
@synthesize field2;
```

```
@synthesize field3;
@synthesize field4;
- (NSString *)dataFilePath {
    NSArray *paths = NSSearchPathForDirectoriesInDomains(
        NSDocumentDirectory, NSUserDomainMask, YES);
    NSString *documentsDirectory = [paths objectAtIndex:0];
    return [documentsDirectory stringByAppendingPathComponent:kFilename];
}
- (void)applicationWillTerminate:(NSNotification *)notification {
    NSMutableArray *array = [[NSMutableArray alloc] init];
    [array addObject:field1.text];
    [array addObject:field2.text];
    [array addObject:field3.text];
    [array addObject:field4.text];
    [array writeToFile:[self dataFilePath] atomically:YES];
    [array release];


    FourLines *fourLines = [[FourLines alloc] init];
    fourLines.field1 = field1.text;
    fourLines.field2 = field2.text;
    fourLines.field3 = field3.text;
    fourLines.field4 = field4.text;


    NSMutableData *data = [[NSMutableData alloc] init];
    NSKeyedArchiver *archiver = [[NSKeyedArchiver alloc]
        initForWritingWithMutableData:data];
    [archiver encodeObject:fourLines forKey:kDataKey];
    [archiver finishEncoding];
    [data writeToFile:[self dataFilePath] atomically:YES];
    [fourLines release];
    [archiver release];
    [data release];


}
#pragma mark -
- (void)viewDidLoad {

    NSString *filePath = [self dataFilePath];
    if ([[NSFileManager defaultManager] fileExistsAtPath:filePath]) {
        NSMutableArray *array =[[NSMutableArray alloc]
            initWithContentsOfFile:filePath];
        field1.text = [array objectAtIndex:0];
        field2.text = [array objectAtIndex:1];
        field3.text = [array objectAtIndex:2];
        field4.text = [array objectAtIndex:3];
        [array release];
```

```
        NSData *data = [[NSMutableData alloc]
            initWithContentsOfFile:[self dataFilePath]];
        NSKeyedUnarchiver *unarchiver = [[NSKeyedUnarchiver alloc]
            initForReadingWithData:data];
        FourLines *fourLines = [unarchiver decodeObjectForKey:kDataKey];
        [unarchiver finishDecoding];

        field1.text = fourLines.field1;
        field2.text = fourLines.field2;
        field3.text = fourLines.field3;
        field4.text = fourLines.field4;

        [unarchiver release];
        [data release];
    }

    UIApplication *app = [UIApplication sharedApplication];
    [[NSNotificationCenter defaultCenter] addObserver:self
            selector:@selector(applicationWillTerminate:)
            name:UIApplicationWillTerminateNotification
            object:app];
    [super viewDidLoad];
}
...
```

Not very much has changed, really, and this new version takes several more lines of code to implement than property list serialization, so you might be wondering if there really is an advantage to using archiving over just serializing property lists. For this application, the answer is simple: there really isn't. But, think back to the last example in Chapter 9 where we were letting the user edit a list of presidents, and each president had four different fields that could be edited. To handle archiving that list of presidents with a property list would involve iterating through the list of presidents, creating an NSDictionary instance for each president, copying the value from each of their fields over to the NSDictionary instance, and adding that instance to another array, which could then be written to a property list file. That is, of course, assuming that we restricted ourselves to using only serializable properties. If we didn't, using property list serialization wouldn't even be an option without doing a lot of conversion work.

On the other hand, if we had an array of archivable objects, such as the FourLines class that we just built, we could archive the entire array by archiving the array instance itself. Collection classes like NSArray, when archived, archive all of the objects they contain. As long as every object you put into an array or dictionary conforms to NSCoding, you can archive the array or dictionary and restore it, and all the objects that were in it when you archived it will be in the restored array or dictionary. In other words, this approach scales beautifully (in terms of code size, at least), because no matter how many objects you add, the work to write those objects to disk (assuming you're using single-file persistence) is exactly the same. With property lists, the amount of work increases with every object you add.

Using iPhone's Embedded SQLite3

The third persistence option we're going to discuss is the iPhone's embedded SQL database called SQLite3. SQLite3 is very efficient at storing and retrieving large amounts of data. It's also capable of doing complex aggregations on your data, with much faster results than you'd get doing the same thing using objects. For example, if your application needed to calculate the sum of a particular field across all the objects in your application, or if you needed the sum from just the objects that meet certain criteria, SQLite3 would allow you to do that without loading every object into memory. Getting aggregations from SQLite3 is several orders of magnitude faster than loading all the objects into memory and summing up their values. Being a full-fledged embedded database, SQLite3 contains tools to make it even faster by, for example, creating table indexes that can speed up your queries.

TIP

> There are two schools of thought about the pronunciation of "SQL" and "SQLite." Most official documentation says to pronounce "SQL" as "Ess-Queue-Ell" and "SQLite" as "Ess-Queue-Ell-Light." Many people pronounce them, respectively, as "Sequel" and "Sequel Light."

SQLite3 uses the Structured Query Language (SQL). SQL is the standard language used to interact with relational databases, and it is a language with its own syntax and a lot of subtleties that are way beyond the scope of this book. Whole books have been written on the syntax of SQL (dozens of them, in fact), as well as on SQLite itself. So, if you don't already know SQL and you want to use SQLite3 in your application, you're going to have a little work ahead of you. We'll show you how to set up and interact with the SQLite database from your iPhone applications, and you'll see some of the basics of the syntax in this chapter. But to really make the most of SQLite3, you're going to need to do some additional research and exploration.

If you're completely new to SQL, you might want to find out more about SQLite3 and the SQL language before continuing on with this chapter. A couple of good starting points are the *Introduction to the SQLite3 C API* at http://www.sqlite.org/cintro.html and the *SQLite SQL Language Guide* at http://www.sqlite.org/lang.html.

Relational databases, including SQLite3, and object-oriented programming languages use fundamentally different approaches to storing and organizing data. The approaches are different enough that numerous techniques and many libraries and tools for converting between the two have arisen. These different techniques are collectively called object-relational mapping (ORM). There are currently several ORM tools available for Cocoa Touch. In fact, we'll look at one ORM solution provided by Apple called Core Data in the next section. In this chapter, we're going to focus on the basics, including setting up SQLite3, creating a table to hold your data, and saving data to and retrieving values from the database. Obviously, in the real world, such a simple application wouldn't warrant the investment in SQLite3. But its simplicity is exactly what makes it a good learning example.

Creating or Opening the Database

Before you can use SQLite3, you have to open the database. The command that's used to do that, sqlite3_open(), will open an existing database, or if none exists at the specified location, it will create a new one. Here's what the code to open a new database might look like:

```
sqlite3 *database;
int result = sqlite3_open("/path/to/database/file", &database);
```

If result is equal to the constant SQLITE_OK, then the database was successfully opened. One thing you should note here is that the path to the database file has to be passed in as a C string, not as an NSString. SQLite3 was written in portable C, not Objective-C, and it has no idea what an NSString is. Fortunately, there is an NSString method that generates a C-string from an NSString instance:

```
char *stringPath = [pathString UTF8String];
```

When you're all done with an SQLite3 database, you close the database by calling

```
sqlite3_close(database);
```

Databases store all their data in tables. You can create a new table by crafting an SQL CREATE statement and passing it in to an open database using the function sqlite3_exec, like so:

```
char * errorMsg;
const char *createSQL = "CREATE TABLE IF NOT EXISTS PEOPLE ➥
    (ID INTEGER PRIMARY KEY AUTOINCREMENT, FIELD_DATA TEXT)";
int result = sqlite3_exec (database, createSQL, NULL, NULL, &errorMsg;);
```

As you did before, you need to check result for SQLITE_OK to make sure your command ran successfully. If it didn't, errorMsg will contain a description of the problem that occurred. The function sqlite3_exec is used to run any command against SQLite3 that doesn't return data. It's used for updates, inserts, and deletes. Retrieving data from the database is little more involved. You first have to prepare the statement by feeding it your SQL SELECT command:

```
NSString *query = @"SELECT ID, FIELD_DATA FROM FIELDS ORDER BY ROW";
sqlite3_stmt *statement;
int result = (sqlite3_prepare_v2( database, [query UTF8String],
    -1, &statement, nil);
```

NOTE

All of the SQLite3 functions that take strings require an old-fashioned C string. In the create example, we created and passed a C string, but in this example, we created an NSString and derived a C string by using one of NSString's methods called UTF8String. Either method is acceptable. If you need to do manipulation on the string, using NSString or NSMutableString will be easier, but converting from NSString to a C string incurs a tiny bit of extra overhead.

If result equals SQLITE_OK, your statement was successfully prepared, and you can start stepping through the result set. Here is an example of stepping through a result set and retrieving an int and an NSString from the database:

```
while (sqlite3_step(statement) == SQLITE_ROW) {
    int rowNum = sqlite3_column_int(statement, 0);
    char *rowData = (char *)sqlite3_column_text(statement, 1);
    NSString *fieldValue = [[NSString alloc] initWithUTF8String:rowData];
    // Do something with the data here
    [fieldValue release];
}
sqlite3_finalize(statement);
```

Bind Variables

Although it's possible to construct SQL strings to insert values, it is common practice to use something called **bind variables** when inserting into a database. Handling strings correctly, making sure they don't have invalid characters and that quotes are handled property can be quite a chore. With bind variables, those issues are taken care of for us. To insert a value using a bind variable, you create your SQL statement as normal but put a question mark into the SQL string. Each question mark represents one variable that has to be bound before the statement can be executed. Then you prepare the SQL statement, bind a value to each of the variables, and then execute the command.

Here's an example that prepares a SQL statement with two bind variables, binds an int to the first variable and a string to the second variable, and then executes and finalizes the statement:

```
char *sql = "insert into foo values (?, ?);";
sqlite3_stmt *stmt;
if (sqlite3_prepare_v2(database, sql, -1, &stmt, nil) == SQLITE_OK) {
```

```
        sqlite3_bind_int(stmt, 1, 235);
        sqlite3_bind_text(stmt, 2, "Bar", -1, NULL);
    }
    if (sqlite3_step(stmt) != SQLITE_DONE)
        NSLog(@"This should be real error checking!");
    sqlite3_finalize(stmt);
```

There are multiple bind statements available depending on the datatype you wish to use. The first parameter to any bind function, regardless of which datatype it is for, is a pointer to the `sqlite3_stmt` used previously in the `sqlite3_prepare_v2()` call. The second parameter is the index of the variable that you're binding to. This is a one-indexed value, meaning that the first question mark in the SQL statement has index 1, and each one after it is one higher than the one to its left. The third parameter is always the value that should be substituted for the question mark. Most bind functions only take three parameters. A few, such as those for binding text and binary data, have two additional parameters. The first is the length of the data being passed in the third parameter. In the case of C strings, you can pass –1 instead of the string's length, and the function will use the entire string. In all other cases, you have to tell it the length of the data being passed int. The final parameter is an optional function callback in case you need to do any memory cleanup after the statement is executed. Typically, such a function would be used to free memory allocated using `malloc()`.

The syntax that follows the bind statements may seem a little odd, since we're doing an insert. When using bind variables, the same syntax is used for both queries and updates. If the SQL string had a SQL query, rather than an update, we would need to call `sqlite3_step()` called multiple times, until it returns `SQLITE_DONE`. Since this was an update, we call it only once.

Setting Up a Project to Use SQLite3

We've covered the basics, so let's see how this would work in practice. We're going to retrofit our Persistence application one more time, this time storing its data using SQLite3. We're going to use a single table and store the field values in four different rows of that table. We'll give each row a row number that corresponds to its field, so for example, the value from `field1` will get stored in the table with a row number of 1. Let's get started.

SQLite 3 is accessed through a procedural API that provides interfaces to a number of C function calls. To use this API, we'll need to link our application to a dynamic library called *libsqlite3.dylib*, located in */usr/lib* on both Mac OS X and iPhone.

The process of linking a dynamic library into your project is exactly the same as that of linking in a framework.

Go back to Xcode, and open the Persistence project, if it's not still open. Select *Frameworks* in the *Groups & Files* pane. Next, select **Add to Project...** from the **Project** menu now. Then, navigate to */Developer/Platforms/iPhoneSimulator.platform/Developer/SDKs/ iPhoneSimulatorX.Y.sdk/usr/lib*, and find the file called *libsqlite3.dylib*. Note that *X.Y* in *iPhoneSimulatorX.Y* stands for the major and minor release number of the SDK you are currently using. For example, if you are using SDK 3.0, you'd look for *iPhoneSumulator3.0*.

When you are prompted, make sure to uncheck the box labeled *Copy items into destination group's folder (if needed)*. Also, make sure you change *Reference Type* to *Relative to Current SDK*. Note that there may be several other entries in that directory that start with *libsqlite3*. Be sure you select *libsqlite3.dylib*. It is an alias that always points to the latest version of the SQLite3 library.

TIP

You can link directly to */usr/lib/libsqlite3.dylib* if you choose a *Reference Type* of *Absolute Path*. This location is a lot easier to remember, but absolute paths are more fragile and often discouraged. Relative paths are safer and less likely to break in future versions, although in the case of *libsqlite3.dylib*, it's probably safe to link with an absolute path.

Next, make the following changes to *PersistenceViewController.h*:

```
#import <UIKit/UIKit.h>
#import "/usr/include/sqlite3.h"

#define kFilename    @"dataarchive.plist"
#define kDataKey     @"Data"
#define kFilename    @"data.sqlite3"

@interface PersistenceViewController : UIViewController {
    UITextField *field1;
    UITextField *field2;
    UITextField *field3;
    UITextField *field4;

    sqlite3     *database;
}
@property (nonatomic, retain) IBOutlet UITextField *field1;
@property (nonatomic, retain) IBOutlet UITextField *field2;
@property (nonatomic, retain) IBOutlet UITextField *field3;
@property (nonatomic, retain) IBOutlet UITextField *field4;

- (NSString *)dataFilePath;
- (void)applicationWillTerminate:(NSNotification *)notification;
@end
```

Once again, we change the filename so that we won't be using the same file that we used in the previous version and so that the file properly reflects the type of data it holds. We also declare an instance variable, database, which will point to our application's database.

Switch over to *PersistenceViewController.m*, and make the following changes:

```
#import "PersistenceViewController.h"
#import "FourLines.h"

@implementation PersistenceViewController
@synthesize field1;
@synthesize field2;
@synthesize field3;
@synthesize field4;

- (NSString *)dataFilePath {
    NSArray *paths = NSSearchPathForDirectoriesInDomains(
        NSDocumentDirectory, NSUserDomainMask, YES);
    NSString *documentsDirectory = [paths objectAtIndex:0];
    return [documentsDirectory stringByAppendingPathComponent:kFilename];
}

- (void)applicationWillTerminate:(NSNotification *)notification {
        FourLines *fourLines = [[FourLines alloc] init];
        fourLines.field1 = field1.text;
        fourLines.field2 = field2.text;
        fourLines.field3 = field3.text;
        fourLines.field4 = field4.text;

        NSMutableData *data = [[NSMutableData alloc] init];
        NSKeyedArchiver *archiver = [[NSKeyedArchiver alloc]
            initForWritingWithMutableData:data];
        [archiver encodeObject:fourLines forKey:kDataKey];
        [archiver finishEncoding];
        [data writeToFile:[self dataFilePath] atomically:YES];
        [fourLines release];
        [archiver release];
        [data release];

    for (int i = 1; i <= 4; i++) {
        NSString *fieldName = [[NSString alloc]
                            initWithFormat:@"field%d", i];
        UITextField *field = [self valueForKey:fieldName];
        [fieldName release];

        char *errorMsg;
        char *update = "INSERT OR REPLACE INTO FIELDS (ROW, FIELD_DATA) ➥
VALUES (?, ?);";
```

```
        sqlite3_stmt *stmt;
        if (sqlite3_prepare_v2(database, update, -1, &stmt, nil)
                == SQLITE_OK) {
            sqlite3_bind_int(stmt, 1, i);
            sqlite3_bind_text(stmt, 2, [field.text UTF8String], -1, NULL);
        }
        if (sqlite3_step(stmt) != SQLITE_DONE)
            NSAssert1(0, @"Error updating table: %s", errorMsg);
        sqlite3_finalize(stmt);

    }
    sqlite3_close(database);
}
#pragma mark -
- (void)viewDidLoad {

    NSString *filePath = [self dataFilePath];
    if ([[NSFileManager defaultManager] fileExistsAtPath:filePath])
    {
        NSData *data = [[NSMutableData alloc]
            initWithContentsOfFile:[self dataFilePath]];
        NSKeyedUnarchiver *unarchiver =
           [[NSKeyedUnarchiver alloc] initForReadingWithData:data];
        FourLines *fourLines = [unarchiver decodeObjectForKey:kDataKey];
        [unarchiver finishDecoding];

        field1.text = fourLines.field1;
        field2.text = fourLines.field2;
        field3.text = fourLines.field3;
        field4.text = fourLines.field4;

        [unarchiver release];
        [data release];
    }
    if (sqlite3_open([[self dataFilePath] UTF8String], &database)
            != SQLITE_OK) {
        sqlite3_close(database);
        NSAssert(0, @"Failed to open database");
    }

    char *errorMsg;
    NSString *createSQL = @"CREATE TABLE IF NOT EXISTS FIELDS ➥
        (ROW INTEGER PRIMARY KEY, FIELD_DATA TEXT);";
    if (sqlite3_exec (database, [createSQL  UTF8String],
        NULL, NULL, &errorMsg) != SQLITE_OK) {
        sqlite3_close(database);
        NSAssert1(0, @"Error creating table: %s", errorMsg);
    }
```

```
NSString *query = @"SELECT ROW, FIELD_DATA FROM FIELDS ORDER BY ROW";
sqlite3_stmt *statement;
if (sqlite3_prepare_v2(database, [query UTF8String],
    -1, &statement, nil) == SQLITE_OK) {
    while (sqlite3_step(statement) == SQLITE_ROW) {
        int row = sqlite3_column_int(statement, 0);
        char *rowData = (char *)sqlite3_column_text(statement, 1);

        NSString *fieldName = [[NSString alloc]
            initWithFormat:@"field%d", row];
        NSString *fieldValue = [[NSString alloc]
            initWithUTF8String:rowData];
        UITextField *field = [self valueForKey:fieldName];
        field.text = fieldValue;
        [fieldName release];
        [fieldValue release];
    }
    sqlite3_finalize(statement);
}

UIApplication *app = [UIApplication sharedApplication];
[[NSNotificationCenter defaultCenter] addObserver:self
        selector:@selector(applicationWillTerminate:)
        name:UIApplicationWillTerminateNotification
        object:app];
[super viewDidLoad];
}
...
```

Let's take a look at these changes. Hmm?

The first changes we made are in the applicationWillTerminate: method, where we need to save our application data. Because the data in the database is stored in a table, our application's data will look something like Table 11-1 when stored.

To save the data, we loop through all four fields and issue a separate command to update each row of the database. Here's our loop, and the first thing we do in the loop is craft a field name so we can retrieve the correct text field outlet. Remember, valueForKey: allows you to retrieve a property based on its name. We also declare a pointer to be used for the error message if we encounter an error.

Table 11-1. *Data Stored in the FIELDS Table of the Database*

ROW	FIELD_DATA
1	Four score and seven years ago
2	our fathers brought forth on this
3	continent, a new nation, conceived
4	in Liberty, and dedicated to the

```
for (int i = 1; i <= 4; i++)
{
    NSString *fieldName = [[NSString alloc]
        initWithFormat:@"field%d", i];
    UITextField *field = [self valueForKey:fieldName];

    char *errorMsg;
```

We craft an INSERT OR REPLACE SQL statement with two bind variables. The first represents the row that's being stored; the second is for the actual string value to be stored. By using INSERT OR REPLACE instead of the more standard INSERT, we don't have to worry about whether a row already exists or not.

```
    char *update = "INSERT OR REPLACE INTO FIELDS (ROW, FIELD_DATA) ➥
VALUES (?, ?);";
```

Next, we declare a pointer to a statement, then prepare our statement with the bind variables, and bind values to both of the bind variables:

```
    sqlite3_stmt *stmt;
    if (sqlite3_prepare_v2(database, update, -1, &stmt, nil)
            == SQLITE_OK) {
        sqlite3_bind_int(stmt, 1, i);
        sqlite3_bind_text(stmt, 2, [field.text UTF8String], -1, NULL);
    }
```

Then we call sqlite3_step to execute the update, check to make sure it worked, and then finalize the statement and close the database:

```
    if (sqlite3_step(stmt) != SQLITE_DONE)
        NSAssert1(0, @"Error updating table: %s", errorMsg);
    sqlite3_finalize(stmt);
}
sqlite3_close(database);
```

This statement will insert our data into the database if it's not already there, or it will update the existing row whose row number matches if there already is one:

```
    NSString *update = [[NSString alloc] initWithFormat:
        @"INSERT OR REPLACE INTO FIELDS (ROW, FIELD_DATA) ➥
        VALUES (%d, '%@');", i, field.text];
```

Next, we execute the SQL INSERT OR REPLACE against our database:

```
    char *errorMsg;
    char *update = "INSERT OR REPLACE INTO FIELDS (ROW, FIELD_DATA) ➥
VALUES (?, ?);";
```

```
    sqlite3_stmt *stmt;
    if (sqlite3_prepare_v2(database, update, -1, &stmt, nil)
            == SQLITE_OK) {
        sqlite3_bind_int(stmt, 1, i);
        sqlite3_bind_text(stmt, 2, [field.text UTF8String], -1, NULL);
    }
    if (sqlite3_step(stmt) != SQLITE_DONE)
        NSAssert1(0, @"Error updating table: %s", errorMsg);
    sqlite3_finalize(stmt);
```

Notice that we've used an assertion here if we encountered an error. We use assertions rather than exceptions or manual error checking, because this condition should only happen if we, the developers, make a mistake. Using this assertion macro will help us debug our code, and it can be stripped out of our final application. If an error condition is one that a user might reasonably experience, you should probably use some other form of error checking.

Once we're done with the loop, we close the database, and we're finished with this method's changes:

```
    sqlite3_close(database);
```

The only other new code is in the viewDidLoad method. The first thing we do is open the database. If we hit a problem opening the database, we close it and raise an assertion:

```
    if (sqlite3_open([[self dataFilePath] UTF8String], &database)
        != SQLITE_OK) {
        sqlite3_close(database);
        NSAssert(0, @"Failed to open database");
    }
```

Next, we have to make sure that we have a table to hold our data. We can use SQL CREATE TABLE to do that. By specifying IF NOT EXISTS, we prevent the database from overwriting existing data. If there is already a table with the same name, this command quietly exits without doing anything, so it's safe to call every time our application launches without explicitly checking to see if a table exists.

```
    char *errorMsg;
    NSString *createSQL = @"CREATE TABLE IF NOT EXISTS FIELDS ➥
        (ROW INTEGER PRIMARY KEY, FIELD_DATA TEXT);";
    if (sqlite3_exec (database, [createSQL  UTF8String], NULL, NULL,
        &errorMsg) != SQLITE_OK) {
        sqlite3_close(database);
        NSAssert1(0, @"Error creating table: %s", errorMsg);
    }
```

Finally, we need to load our data. We do this using a SQL SELECT statement. In this simple example, we create a SQL SELECT that requests all the rows from the database and ask SQLite3 to prepare our SELECT. We also tell SQLite3 to order the rows by the row number so that we always get them back in the same order. Absent this, SQLite3 will return the rows in the order in which they are stored internally.

```
NSString *query = @"SELECT ROW, FIELD_DATA FROM FIELDS ORDER BY ROW";
sqlite3_stmt *statement;
if (sqlite3_prepare_v2( database, [query UTF8String],
    -1, &statement, nil) == SQLITE_OK) {
```

Then, we step through each of the returned rows:

```
while (sqlite3_step(statement) == SQLITE_ROW) {
```

We grab the row number and store it in an int, and then we grab the field data as a C string:

```
int row = sqlite3_column_int(statement, 0);
char *rowData = (char *)sqlite3_column_text(statement, 1);
```

Next, we create a field name based on the row number (e.g., field1 for row 1), convert the C string to an NSString, and use that to set the appropriate field with the value retrieved from the database:

```
NSString *fieldName = [[NSString alloc]
    initWithFormat:@"field%d", row];
NSString *fieldValue = [[NSString alloc]
    initWithUTF8String:rowData];
UITextField *field = [self valueForKey:fieldName];
field.text = fieldValue;
```

Finally, we do some memory cleanup, and we're all done:

```
        [fieldName release];
        [fieldValue release];
    }
}
```

Why don't you compile and run and try it out? Enter some data, and press the iPhone simulator's home button. Then, relaunch the Persistence application, and on launch, that data should be right where you left it. As far as the user is concerned, there's absolutely no difference between the four different versions of this application, but each version uses a very different persistence mechanism.

Using Core Data

When we wrote the first edition of this book, we included a section in the first chapter listing the things that were available in Cocoa that weren't yet available in Cocoa Touch. One of the more noteworthy absences from the iPhone SDK prior to 3.0 was Core Data, Apple's tool for designing data models visually. When Apple confirmed that iPhone SDK 3 would have full support for Core Data, there was much rejoicing in the iPhone developer community.

Core Data is a robust, full-featured persistence tool, and a full discussion of it is beyond the scope of this chapter. We will, however, show you how to use Core Data to re-create the same persistence you've seen in our Persistence application. For a more comprehensive coverage of Core Data, check out *More iPhone 3 Development* by Dave Mark and Jeff LaMarche (Apress, 2009), which devotes several chapters to Core Data.

In Xcode, create a new project. This time, select the *Window-based Application* template, but don't click the *Choose…* button just yet. If you look in the lower-right pane of the new project assistant, you should see a checkbox labeled *Use Core Data for storage* (see Figure 11-5). There's a certain amount of complexity involved in adding Core Data to an existing project, so Apple has kindly provided this option with some application project templates to do much of the work for you.

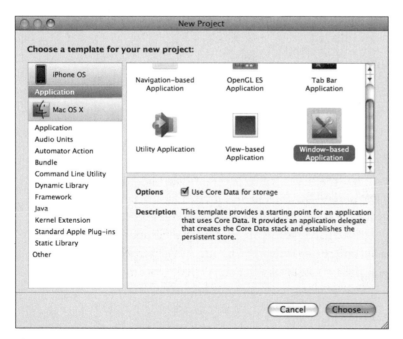

Figure 11-5. *Some project templates, including Window-based Application, offer the option to use Core Data.*

Check that checkbox, and then click the *Choose…* button. When prompted, enter a project name of *Core Data Persistence*. Before we move on to our code, let's take a look at the project window. There's some new stuff here you've not seen before. Expand both the *Classes* and *Resources* folders (see Figure 11-6).

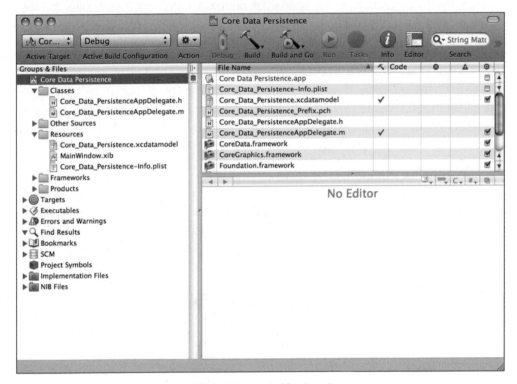

Figure 11-6. *Our project template with the files needed for Core Data*

Entities and Managed Objects

Of course, we have a bunch of files you're already familiar with: an application delegate, a *MainWindow.xib*, and an *info* property list. But, there's another file in the *Resources* folder called *Core_Data_Persistence.xcdatamodel*. That is our data model. Core Data lets us design our data models visually, without writing code. Single-click that file now, and you will be presented with the **data model editor** (see Figure 11-7). You may want to expand your Xcode window and hide the detail pane (⇧⌘E) while working with the data model editor.

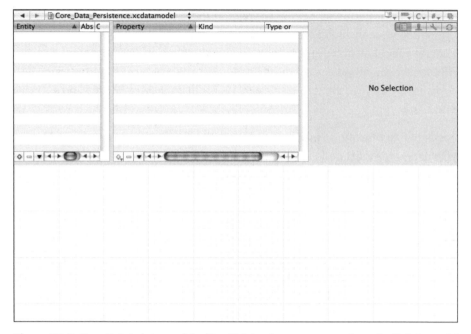

Figure 11-7. *Core Data's data model editor. This is where you an create and edit data models.*

The traditional way to create data models in Cocoa is to create subclasses of NSObject and conform them to NSCoding and NSCopying so that they can be archived, as we did earlier in this chapter. Core Data uses a fundamentally different approach. Instead of classes, you create **entities** here in the data model editor, and then in your code, create **managed objects** from those entities.

TIP

The terms "entity" and "managed object" can be a little confusing, since both refer to data model objects. The term "entity" refers to the description of an object while "managed object" is used to refer to actual concrete instances of that entity created at runtime. So, in the data model editor, you create entities, but in your code, you will create and retrieve managed objects. The distinction between entities and managed objects is similar to the distinction between a class and instances of that class.

An entity is made up of properties. There are four types of properties: attributes, relationships, fetched properties, and fetch requests.

An **attribute** serves the same function in a core data entity as an instance variable does in an objective-C class. They both hold the data.

As the name implies, a **relationship** defines the relationship between entities. For example, suppose you wanted to define a Person entity. You might start by defining a few attributes, like hairColor, eyeColor, height, and weight. You might define address attributes, like state and ZIP code, or you might embed those in a separate, HomeAddress entity. Using this latter approach, you'd then want to create a relationship between a Person and a HomeAddress.

Relationships can be **to one** and **to many**. The relationship from a Person to a HomeAddress is probably "to one," since most people only have a single home address. The relationship from HomeAddress to Person might be "to many," since there may be more than one Person living at that HomeAddress.

A **fetched property** is an alternative to a relationship. The main difference between them is in the way they affect loading. For example, if a Person has a relationship with a HomeAddress, when the Person is loaded, the HomeAddress will be loaded, too. Alternatively, if a Person references HomeAddress as a fetched property, when the Person is loaded, HomeAddress is not loaded, at least not until HomeAddress is accessed. Can you say "lazy loading"?

A **fetch request** is a predefined query. For example, you might say, "Give me every Person whose eyeColor is blue."

Typically, attributes, relationships, and fetched properties are defined using Xcode's data model editor. Fetch requests can be just as easily defined in the data model editor or in your code.

In our Core Data Persistence application, we'll build a simple entity so you can get a sense of how this all works together. For more detail on Core Data, check out the extensive coverage in *More iPhone 3 Development*.

Key-Value Coding

In your code, instead of using accessors and mutators, you will use **key-value coding** to set properties or retrieve their existing values. Key-value coding may sound intimidating, but it's something you've already used quite a bit in this book. Every time we've used NSDictionary, for example, we were using key-value coding because every object in a dictionary is stored under a unique key value. The key-value coding used by Core Data is a bit more complex than that used by NSDictionary, but the basic concept is the same.

When working with a managed object, the key you will use to set or retrieve a property's value is the name of the attribute you wish to set. So, to retrieve the value stored in the attribute called name from a managed object, you would call:

```
NSString *name = [myManagedObject valueForKey:@"name"];
```

Similarly, to set a new value for a managed object's property, you would do this:

```
[myManagedObject setValue:@"Martha Stewart" forKey:@"name"];
```

Putting It All in Context

So, where do these managed objects live? They live in something called a **persistent store**, which is sometimes also referred to as a **backing store**. Persistent stores can take several different forms. By default, a Core Data application implements a backing store as an SQLite database stored in the application's documents directory. Even though your data is stored via SQLite, classes in the Core Data framework do all the work associated with loading and saving your data. If you use Core Data, you won't need to write any SQL statements. You just work with objects, and Core Data figures out what it needs to do behind the scenes. In addition to SQLite, backing stores can also be implemented as binary flat files. There's also a third option to create an in-memory store, which you might use if writing a caching mechanism, but it doesn't save data beyond the end of the current session. In almost all situations, you should just leave it as the default and use SQLite as your persistent store.

Although most applications will have only one persistent store, it is possible to have multiple persistent stores within the same application. If you're curious about how the backing store is created and configured, you can look right in your Xcode project at the file *Core_Data_PersistenceAppDelegate.m*. The Xcode project template, we chose provided us with all the code needed to set up a single persistent store for our application.

Other than creating it (which is handled for us in our application delegate), we generally won't work with our persistent store directly, but rather will use something called a **managed object context**, often just referred to as a **context**. The context intermediates access to the persistent store and maintains information about what properties have changed since the last time an object was saved. The context also registers all changes with the undo manager, meaning that you always have the ability to undo a single change or roll back all the way to the last time data was saved. You can have multiple contexts pointing to the same persistent store, though most iPhone applications will only use one. You can find out more about using multiple contexts and the undo manager in *More iPhone 3 Development* as well.

Many core data calls require an `NSManagedObjectContext` as a parameter, or have to be executed against a context. With the exception of very complicated, multithreaded iPhone applications, you can just use the `managedObjectContext` property from your application delegate, which is a default context that gets created for you automatically, also courtesy of the Xcode project template.

Creating New Managed Objects

Creating a new instance of a managed object is pretty easy, though not quite as straightforward as creating a normal object instance using alloc and init. Instead, you use a factory method on a class called NSEntityDescription. Instances of this class represent a single entity in memory. Remember: entities are like classes. They are a description of an object, and define what properties a particular entity has.

To create a new object, we do this:

```
theLine = [NSEntityDescription
    insertNewObjectForEntityForName:@"EntityName"
            inManagedObjectContext:context];
```

The method is called insertNewObjectForEntityForName:inManagedObjectContext: because, in addition to creating the object, it inserts the newly create object into the context and then returns that object autoreleased. After this call, the object exists in the context but is not yet part of the persistent store. The object will get added to the persistent store the next time the managed object context's save: method is called.

Retrieving Managed Objects

To retrieve managed objects from the persistent store, you create a fetch request and provide that request with an NSEntityDescription that specifies the entity of the object or objects you wish to retrieve. Here is an example that creates a fetch request:

```
NSFetchRequest *request = [[NSFetchRequest alloc] init];
NSEntityDescription *entityDescr = [NSEntityDescription
    entityForName:@"EntityName" inManagedObjectContext:context];
[request setEntity:entityDescr];
```

Optionally, you can also specify criteria for a fetch request using the NSPredicate class. A **predicate** is similar to the SQL where clause and allows you to define the criteria used to determine the results of your fetch request.

NOTE

Learn Objective-C on the Mac by Mark Dalrymple and Scott Knaster (Apress, 2008) has an entire chapter devoted to the use of NSPredicate.

Here is a simple example of a predicate:

```
NSPredicate *pred = [NSPredicate predicateWithFormat:@"(name = %@)",
    nameString];
[request setPredicate: pred];
```

The predicate created by the first line of code would tell a fetch request that, instead of retrieving all managed objects for the specified entity, retrieves just those where the name property is set to the value currently stored in the nameString variable. So, if nameString were an NSString that held the value @"Bob", we would be telling the fetch request to only bring back managed objects that have a name property set to "Bob". This is a simple example, but predicates can be considerably more complex and can use Boolean logic to specify the precise criteria you might need in most any situation.

After you've created your fetch request, provided it with an entity description, and optionally given it a predicate, you **execute** the fetch request using an instance method on NSManagedObjectContext:

```
NSError *error;
NSArray *objects = [context executeFetchRequest:request error:&error];
if (objects == nil) {
    // handle error
}
```

executeFetchRequest:error: will load the specified objects from the persistent store and return them in an array. If an error is encountered, you will get a nil array, and the error pointer you provided will point to an NSError object that describes the specific problem. If there was no error, you will get a valid array, though it may not have any objects in it, since it is possible that there are none that meet the specified criteria. From this point on, any changes you make to the managed objects returned in that array will be tracked by the managed object context you executed the request against and saved when you send that context a save: message.

Let's take Core Data for a spin now.

Designing the Data Model

Let's return our attention to Xcode and create our data model. Single-click *Persistence_Core_Data.xcdatamodel* to open Xcode's data model editor. The upper-left pane of the data model editor is called the **entity pane** because it lists all the entities that are currently in your data model. It's an empty list now, because we haven't created any yet (see Figure 11-8).

Remedy that by clicking the plus icon in the lower-left corner of the entity pane, which will create and select an entity titled *Entity*. If you look in the bottom pane of the data model editor, you'll notice that it's no longer empty (see Figure 11-9)! As you build your data model using the top three panes (collectively called the **browser view**), a graphical representation of your data model is shown in the bottom portion of the screen, which is called the **diagram view**. If you prefer working graphically, you can actually build your entire model in the diagram view. Right-clicking the background of the diagram view will bring up a contextual menu that will allow you to

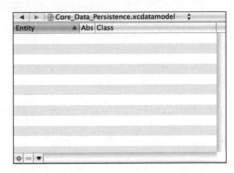

Figure 11-8. *The upper left-pane of the data model editor is the entity pane. Clicking the plus icon in the lower left corner adds an entity*

add entities and change the diagram view's appearance. Right-clicking an entity will bring up a menu that allows you to add properties to the selected entity. We're going to stick with the browser view in this chapter because it's easier to explain, but when you're creating your own data models, feel free to work in the diagram view if that approach suits you better.

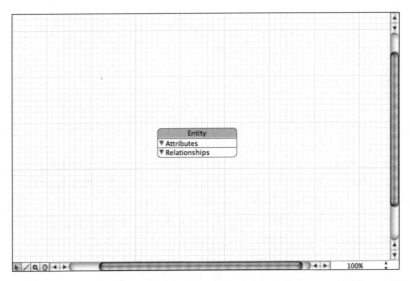

Figure 11-9. *Xcode's data model editor's diagram view shows an editable graphical representation of your data model.*

The upper-right pane of the data model editor is called the **detail pane**. Part of the reason we had you close Xcode's detail pane a minute ago was to avoid confusion caused by having two unrelated detail panes. Throughout the rest of the chapter, when we refer to the detail pane, we'll be referring to the data model editor's detail pane (see Figure 11-10), not Xcode's detail pane. The data model editor's detail pane allows you to edit the currently selected entity or property.

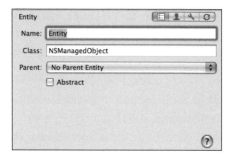

Figure 11-10. *The data model editor's detail pane, not to be confused with Xcode's detail pane*

At the moment, the detail pain shows information about the entity we just added. Change the *Name* field from *Entity* to *Line*. You can ignore the other fields in the detail pane for now. Those other fields will come into play when creating more complex data models, like those discussed in *More iPhone 3 Development*.

The data model editor's upper-middle pane is the **property pane** (see Figure 11-11). As its name implies, the property pane allows you to add new properties to your entity.

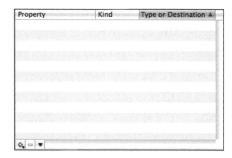

Figure 11-11. *The property pane in Xcode's data model editor. This is where you can add properties to the currently selected entity.*

Notice that plus sign in the lower-left corner of the property pane features a little black triangle. If you click the triangle and hold the mouse button down, a pop-up menu will appear, allowing you to add an attribute, fetched property, relationship, or fetch request to your entity (see Figure 11-12).

Figure 11-12. *Clicking the plus icon in the property pane brings up a menu of options.*

Select **Add Attribute** from the menu that popped up. A new attribute creatively named *newAttribute* should have just been added to your properties pane and selected. In the detail pane, change the new attribute's name from *newAttribute* to *lineNum* and change its *Type* from *Undefined* to *Integer 16*, which turns this attribute into one that will hold an integer value. We will be using this attribute to identify which of the four fields the managed object holds data for. Since we only have four options, we selected the smallest integer type available.

There are three checkboxes below the *Name* field. The leftmost one, *Optional*, should currently be selected. Click it to deselect it; we don't want this attribute to be optional. A line that doesn't correspond to a label on our interface is useless. Don't worry about the other two checkboxes for now. *Transient* attributes are used to store nonstandard objects for which there is no predefined attribute type. Selecting the *Indexed* checkbox will cause an index in the underlying SQL database to get created on the field that holds this attribute's data.

Click the plus-icon, and select *Add Attribute* again, this time creating an attribute with the name *lineText* and changing its *Type* to *String*. This attribute will hold the actual data from the text field. Leave the *Optional* checkbox checked for this one; it is altogether possible that the user won't enter a value for a given field.

When you changed the *Type* to *String*, you'll notice that additional options came up that would let you set a default value or limit the length of the string. We won't be using any of those options for this application, but it's nice to know they're there.

Guess what? Your data model is done. That's all there is to it. Core Data lets you point and click your way to an application data model. Let's finish building the application so we can see how to use our data model from our code.

Creating the Persistence View and Controller

Because we selected the window-based application template, we weren't provided with a view controller. So single-click the *Classes* folder, and press ⌘N or select **New File…** from the **File** menu to bring up the new file assistant. Select *UIViewController subclass* from the *Cocoa Touch Class* heading, and name the file *PersistenceViewController.m*, making sure to have it create *PersistenceViewController.h* as well. Also make sure to check the box that says *With XIB for user interface* to have it create a nib file for you automatically. If *PersistenceViewController.xib* was placed in your *Classes* folder, drag it down to the *Resources* folder so that our project stays nice and organized.

Single-click *PersistenceViewController.h*, and make the following changes, which should look very familiar to you:

```
#import <UIKit/UIKit.h>

@interface PersistenceViewController : UIViewController {
    UITextField *line1;
    UITextField *line2;
    UITextField *line3;
    UITextField *line4;
}
@property (nonatomic, retain) IBOutlet UITextField *line1;
@property (nonatomic, retain) IBOutlet UITextField *line2;
@property (nonatomic, retain) IBOutlet UITextField *line3;
@property (nonatomic, retain) IBOutlet UITextField *line4;
@end
```

Save, and double-click *PersistenceViewController.xib* to open Interface Builder. Design the view, and connect the outlets by following the instructions from earlier in this chapter in the "Designing the Persistence Application View" section. Once you're done, save the nib file, and go back to Xcode.

In *PersistenceViewController.m*, insert the following code at the top of the file:

```
#import "PersistenceViewController.h"
#import "Core_Data_PersistenceAppDelegate.h"

@implementation PersistenceViewController
@synthesize line1;
@synthesize line2;
@synthesize line3;
@synthesize line4;
- (void)applicationWillTerminate:(NSNotification *)notification {
    Core_Data_PersistenceAppDelegate *appDelegate =
        [[UIApplication sharedApplication] delegate];
    NSManagedObjectContext *context = [appDelegate managedObjectContext];
    NSError *error;
    for (int i = 1; i <= 4; i++) {
        NSString *fieldName = [NSString stringWithFormat:@"line%d", i];
        UITextField *theField = [self valueForKey:fieldName];

        NSFetchRequest *request = [[NSFetchRequest alloc] init];

        NSEntityDescription *entityDescription = [NSEntityDescription
            entityForName:@"Line"
            inManagedObjectContext:context];
        [request setEntity:entityDescription];
        NSPredicate *pred = [NSPredicate
            predicateWithFormat:@"(lineNum = %d)", i];
        [request setPredicate:pred];

        NSManagedObject *theLine = nil;

        NSArray *objects = [context executeFetchRequest:request
            error:&error];

        if (objects == nil) {
            NSLog(@"There was an error!");
            // Do whatever error handling is appropriate
        }
        if ([objects count] > 0)
            theLine = [objects objectAtIndex:0];
        else
            theLine = [NSEntityDescription
```

```
                  insertNewObjectForEntityForName:@"Line"
                      inManagedObjectContext:context];

       [theLine setValue:[NSNumber numberWithInt:i] forKey:@"lineNum"];
       [theLine setValue:theField.text forKey:@"lineText"];

       [request release];
    }
    [context save:&error];
}


- (void)viewDidLoad {
    Core_Data_PersistenceAppDelegate *appDelegate =
        [[UIApplication sharedApplication] delegate];
    NSManagedObjectContext *context = [appDelegate managedObjectContext];
    NSEntityDescription *entityDescription = [NSEntityDescription
                entityForName:@"Line"
        inManagedObjectContext:context];
    NSFetchRequest *request = [[NSFetchRequest alloc] init];
    [request setEntity:entityDescription];

    NSError *error;
    NSArray *objects = [context executeFetchRequest:request error:&error];
    if (objects == nil) {
        NSLog(@"There was an error!");
        // Do whatever error handling is appropriate
    }

    for (NSManagedObject *oneObject in objects) {
        NSNumber *lineNum = [oneObject valueForKey:@"lineNum"];
        NSString *lineText = [oneObject valueForKey:@"lineText"];

        NSString *fieldName = [NSString
            stringWithFormat:@"line%@", lineNum];
        UITextField *theField = [self valueForKey:fieldName];
        theField.text = lineText;
    }
    [request release];

    UIApplication *app = [UIApplication sharedApplication];
    [[NSNotificationCenter defaultCenter] addObserver:self
        selector:@selector(applicationWillTerminate:)
           name:UIApplicationWillTerminateNotification
          object:app];
    [super viewDidLoad];
}
...
```

Then, insert the following code into the existing `dealloc` and `viewDidUnload` methods:

```
...
- (void)viewDidUnload {
        // Release any retained subviews of the main view.
    // e.g. self.myOutlet = nil;
    self.line1 = nil;
    self.line2 = nil;
    self.line3 = nil;
    self.line4 = nil;
    [super viewDidUnload];
}

- (void)dealloc {
    [line1 release];
    [line2 release];
    [line3 release];
    [line4 release];
    [super dealloc];
}
...
```

Let's look at `applicationWillTerminate:` first. The first thing we do in that method is to get a reference to our application delegate, which we then use to get the managed object context that was created for us.

```
Core_Data_PersistenceAppDelegate *appDelegate =
    [[UIApplication sharedApplication] delegate];
NSManagedObjectContext *context = [appDelegate managedObjectContext];
```

After that, we go into a loop that executes four times, one for each label.

```
for (int i = 1; i <= 4; i++) {
```

We construct the name of one of the four fields by appending i to the word "line" and use that to get a reference to the correct field using `valueForKey:`.

```
NSString *fieldName = [NSString stringWithFormat:@"line%d", i];
UITextField *theField = [self valueForKey:fieldName];
```

Next, we create our fetch request:

```
NSFetchRequest *request = [[NSFetchRequest alloc] init];
```

After that, we create an entity description that describes the *Line* entity we designed earlier in the data model editor and that uses the context we retrieved from the application delegate. Once we create it, we feed it to the fetch request, so the request knows what type of entity to look for.

```
NSEntityDescription *entityDescription = [NSEntityDescription
            entityForName:@"Line"
    inManagedObjectContext:context];
[request setEntity:entityDescription];
```

Next, we need to find out if there's already a managed object in the persistent store that corresponds to this field, so we create a predicate that identifies the right object for the field:

```
NSPredicate *pred = [NSPredicate
    predicateWithFormat:@"(lineNum = %d)", i];
[request setPredicate:pred];
```

After that, we declare a pointer to an NSManagedObject and set it to nil. We do this because
we don't know yet if we're going to load a managed object from the persistent store or
create a new one. We also declare an NSError that the system will use to notify us of the
specific nature of the problem if we get back a nil array.

```
NSManagedObject *theLine = nil;
NSError *error;
```

Next, we execute the fetch request against the context:

```
NSArray *objects = [context executeFetchRequest:request
    error:&error];
```

Then, we check to make sure that objects is not nil. If it is nil, then there was an error and
we should do whatever error checking is appropriate for our application. For this simple
application, we're just logging the error and moving on.

```
if (objects == nil) {
    NSLog(@"There was an error!");
    // Do whatever error handling is appropriate
}
```

After that, we look to see if an object was returned that matched our criteria, and if there is
one, we load it. If there isn't one, we create a new managed object to hold this field's text.

```
if ([objects count] > 0)
    theLine = [objects objectAtIndex:0];
else
    theLine = [NSEntityDescription
        insertNewObjectForEntityForName:@"Line"
                inManagedObjectContext:context];
```

Then, we use key-value coding to set the line number and text for this managed object:

```
        [theLine setValue:[NSNumber numberWithInt:i] forKey:@"lineNum"];
        [theLine setValue:theField.text forKey:@"lineText"];
        [request release];
    }
```

Finally, once we're done looping, we tell the context to save its changes:

```
    [context save:&error];
}
```

Now, let's look at the `viewDidLoad` method, which needs to see if there is any existing data in the persistent store and, if there is, load the data in and populate the fields with it. We start out the same way as the last method, by getting a reference to the application delegate and using that to get a pointer to our application's default context:

```
    Core_Data_PersistenceAppDelegate *appDelegate =
        [[UIApplication sharedApplication] delegate];
    NSManagedObjectContext *context = [appDelegate managedObjectContext];
```

Next, we create an entity description that describes our entity:

```
    NSEntityDescription *entityDescription = [NSEntityDescription
                entityForName:@"Line"
        inManagedObjectContext:context];
```

The next order of business is to create a fetch request and pass it the entity description so it knows what type of objects to retrieve:

```
    NSFetchRequest *request = [[NSFetchRequest alloc] init];
    [request setEntity:entityDescription];
```

Since we want to retrieve all `Line` objects in the persistent store, we do not create a predicate. By executing a request without a predicate, we're telling the context to give us every `Line` object in the store.

```
    NSError *error;
    NSArray *objects = [context executeFetchRequest:request error:&error];
```

We make sure we got a valid array back, and log it if we didn't.

```
    if (objects == nil) {
        NSLog(@"There was an error!");
        // Do whatever error handling is appropriate
    }
```

Next, we use fast enumeration to loop through the array of retrieved managed objects, pull out the `lineNum` and `lineText` values from it, and use that information to update one of the text fields on our user interface.

```
for (NSManagedObject *oneObject in objects) {
    NSNumber *lineNum = [oneObject valueForKey:@"lineNum"];
    NSString *lineText = [oneObject valueForKey:@"lineText"];

    NSString *fieldName = [NSString stringWithFormat:@"line%@",
        lineNum];
    UITextField *theField = [self valueForKey:fieldName];
    theField.text = lineText;
}
[request release];
```

Then, just like with all the other applications in this chapter, we register to be notified when the application is about to terminate so we can save any changes the user has made to the data:

```
UIApplication *app = [UIApplication sharedApplication];
[[NSNotificationCenter defaultCenter] addObserver:self
    selector:@selector(applicationWillTerminate:)
        name:UIApplicationWillTerminateNotification
      object:app];
[super viewDidLoad];
```

Making Persistence View Controller our Application's Root Controller

Because we used the window-based application template instead of the view-based application template, we have one more step we need to take before our fancy new Core Data application will work: We need to create an instance of `PersistenceViewController` to act as our application's root controller and add its view as a subview of our application's main window. Let's do that now.

The first thing we need is an outlet to the view controller in our application delegate. Single-click *Core_Data_PersistenceAppDelegate.h*, and make the following changes to declare that outlet:

```
@class PersistenceViewController;
@interface Core_Data_PersistenceAppDelegate : NSObject
        <UIApplicationDelegate> {

    NSManagedObjectModel *managedObjectModel;
    NSManagedObjectContext *managedObjectContext;
    NSPersistentStoreCoordinator *persistentStoreCoordinator;

    UIWindow *window;
    PersistenceViewController *rootController;
}
```

```
- (IBAction)saveAction:sender;

@property (nonatomic, retain, readonly) NSManagedObjectModel
    *managedObjectModel;
@property (nonatomic, retain, readonly) NSManagedObjectContext ➥
*managedObjectContext;
@property (nonatomic, retain, readonly) NSPersistentStoreCoordinator ➥
*persistentStoreCoordinator;

@property (nonatomic, readonly) NSString *applicationDocumentsDirectory;

@property (nonatomic, retain) IBOutlet UIWindow *window;
@property (nonatomic, retain) IBOutlet PersistenceViewController
    *rootController;

@end
```

To make the root controller's view a subview of the application's window so that the user can interact with it, single-click *Core_Data_PersistenceAppDelegate.m*, and make the following changes at the top of that file:

```
#import "Core_Data_PersistenceAppDelegate.h"
#import "PersistenceViewController.h"

@implementation Core_Data_PersistenceAppDelegate

@synthesize window;
@synthesize rootController;

#pragma mark -
#pragma mark Application lifecycle

- (void)applicationDidFinishLaunching:(UIApplication *)application {

    // Override point for customization after app launch
    [window addSubview:rootController.view];
    [window makeKeyAndVisible];
}
...
```

Finally, we need to go back to Interface Builder to create the instance of our root controller and connect it to that outlet we just created. Double-click *MainWindow.xib* to launch Interface Builder. Once it's finished launching, drag a *View Controller* from the library, and drop it onto the nib's main window, the one titled *MainWindow.xib*. The new view controller's icon should still be selected (if it's not, just single-click the icon called *View Controller*). Press ⌘4 to bring up the identity inspector, and change the underlying class from *UIViewController* to *PersistenceViewController*, which should cause its label to change from *View Controller* to *Persistence View Controller*. Next, control-drag from the icon labeled *Core_Data_Persistence App Delegate* to the icon labeled *Persistence View Controller*, and select the *rootController* outlet. Save the nib file, and go back to Xcode.

That's it; we're done. Build and run to make sure it works. The Core Data version of your application should behave exactly the same as the previous versions.

And that's all there is to it. It may seem that Core Data entails a lot of work and, for a simple application like this, doesn't offer much of an advantage. But in more complex applications, Core Data can substantially decrease the amount of time you spend designing and writing your data model.

Persistence Rewarded

You should now have a solid handle on four different ways of preserving your application data between sessions—five ways if you include the user defaults that you learned how to use in the previous chapter. We built an application that persisted data using property lists and modified the application to save its data using object archives. We then made a change and used the iPhone's built-in SQLite3 mechanism to save the application data. Finally, we rebuilt the same application using Core Data. These mechanisms are the basic building blocks for saving and loading data in almost all iPhone applications.

Ready for more? Time to drag out your crayons, because in the next chapter, you're going to learn how to draw. Cool!

Drawing with Quartz and OpenGL

*e*very application we've built so far has been constructed from views and controls provided to us as part of the UIKit framework. You can do an awful lot with these stock components, and a great many application interfaces can be constructed using only these stock objects. Some applications, however, can't be fully realized without looking further. For instance, at times, an application needs to be able to do custom drawing. Fortunately for us, we have not one but two separate libraries we can call on for our drawing needs: Quartz 2D, which is part of the Core Graphics framework, and OpenGL ES, which is a cross-platform graphics library. OpenGL ES is a slimmed-down version of another cross-platform graphic library called OpenGL. OpenGL ES is a subset of OpenGL designed specifically for embedded systems such as the iPhone (hence the letters "ES"). In this chapter, we'll explore both of these powerful graphics environments. We'll build sample applications in both and try to get a sense of which environment to use when.

Two Views of a Graphical World

Although Quartz and OpenGL overlap a lot, there are distinct differences between them. Quartz is a set of functions, datatypes, and objects designed to let you draw directly into a view or to an image in memory.

Quartz treats the view or image that is being drawn into as a virtual canvas and follows what's called a **painter's model**, which is just a fancy way to say that that drawing commands are applied in much the same way as paint is applied to a canvas. If a painter paints an entire canvas red, and then paints the bottom half of the canvas blue, the canvas will be half red and half either blue or purple. Blue if the paint is opaque; purple if the paint is semitransparent.

Quartz's virtual canvas works the same way. If you paint the whole view red, and then paint the bottom half of the view blue, you'll have a view that's half red and half either blue or purple, depending on whether the second drawing action was fully opaque or partially transparent. Each drawing action is applied to the canvas on top of any previous drawing actions.

On the other hand, OpenGL ES, is implemented as a **state machine**. This concept is somewhat more difficult a concept to grasp, because it doesn't resolve to a simple metaphor like painting on a virtual canvas. Instead of letting you take actions that directly impact a view, window, or image, OpenGL ES maintains a virtual three-dimensional world. As you add objects to that world, OpenGL keeps track of the state of all objects. Instead of a virtual canvas, OpenGL ES gives you a virtual window into its world. You add objects to the world and define the location of your virtual window with respect to the world. OpenGL then draws what you can see through that window based on the way it is configured and where the various objects are in relation to each other. This concept is a bit abstract, so if you're confused, don't worry; it'll make more sense as we make our way through this chapter's code.

Quartz is relatively easy to use. It provides a variety of line, shape, and image drawing functions. Though easy to use, Quartz 2D is limited to two-dimensional drawing. Although many Quartz functions do result in drawing that takes advantage of hardware acceleration, there is no guarantee that any particular action you take in Quartz will be accelerated.

OpenGL, though considerably more complex and conceptually more difficult, offers a lot more power. It has tools for both two-dimensional and three-dimensional drawing and is specifically designed to take full advantage of hardware acceleration. It's also extremely well suited to writing games and other complex, graphically intensive programs.

This Chapter's Drawing Application

Our next application is a simple drawing program (see Figure 12-1). We're going to build this application twice, once using Quartz 2D and once using OpenGL ES, so you get a real feel for the difference between the two.

Figure 12-1. *Our chapter's simple drawing application in action*

The application features a bar across the top and one across the bottom, each with a seg-mented control. The control at the top lets you change the drawing color, and the one at the bottom lets you change the shape to be drawn. When you touch and drag, the selected shape will be drawn in the selected color. To minimize the application's complexity, only one shape will be drawn at a time.

The Quartz Approach to Drawing

When using Quartz to do your drawing, you'll usually add the drawing code to the view doing the drawing. For example, you might create a subclass of UIView and add Quartz function calls to that class's drawRect: method. The drawRect: method is part of the UIView class definition and gets called every time a view needs to redraw itself. If you insert your Quartz code in drawRect:, that code will get called then the view redraws itself.

Quartz 2D's Graphics Contexts

In Quartz 2D, as in the rest of Core Graphics, drawing happens in a **graphics context**, usually just referred to as a **context**. Every view has an associated context. When you want to draw in a view, you'll retrieve the current context, use that context to make various Quartz draw-ing calls, and let the context worry about rendering your drawing onto the view.

This line of code retrieves the current context:

```
CGContextRef context = UIGraphicsGetCurrentContext();
```

NOTE

> Notice that we're using Core Graphics C functions, rather than Objective-C objects, to do our drawing. Both Core Graphics and OpenGL are C-based APIs, so most of the code we write in this part of the chapter will consist of C function calls.

Once you've defined your graphics context, you can draw into it by passing the context to a variety of Core Graphics drawing functions. For example, this sequence will draw a 2-pixel-wide line in the context:

```
CGContextSetLineWidth(context, 2.0);
CGContextSetStrokeColorWithColor(context, [UIColor redColor].CGColor);
CGContextMoveToPoint(context, 100.0f, 100.0f);
CGContextAddLineToPoint(context, 200.0f, 200.0f);
CGContextStrokePath(context);
```

The first call specifies that any drawing we do should create a line that's 2 pixels wide. We then specify that the stroke color should be red. In Core Graphics, two colors are associated with drawing actions: the stroke color and the fill color. The **stroke color** is used in drawing lines and for the outline of shapes, and the **fill color** is used to fill in shapes.

Contexts have a sort of invisible "pen" associated with them that does the line drawing. When you call `CGContextMoveToPoint()`, you move that invisible pen to a new location, without actually drawing anything. By doing this, we are indicating that the line we are about to draw will start at position (100, 100) (see the explanation of positioning in the next section). The next function actually draws a line from the current pen location to the specified location, which will become the new pen location. When we draw in Core Graphics, we're not drawing anything you can actually see. We're creating a shape, a line, or some other object, but it contains no color or anything to make it visible. It's like writing in invisible ink. Until we do something to make it visible, our line can't be seen. So, the next step is tell Quartz to draw the line using `CGContextStrokePath()`. This function will use the line width and the stroke color we set earlier to actually color (or "paint") the line and make it visible.

The Coordinates System

In the previous chunk of code, we passed a pair of floating-point numbers as parameters to `CGContextMoveToPoint()` and `CGContextLineToPoint()`. These numbers represent positions in the Core Graphics coordinates system. Locations in this coordinate system are denoted by their x and y coordinates, which we usually represent as (x, y). The upper-left corner of the context is (0, 0). As you move down, y increases. As you move to the right, x increases.

In that last code snippet, we drew a diagonal line from (100, 100) to (200, 200), which would draw a line that looked like the one shown in Figure 12-2.

The coordinate system is one of the gotchas in drawing with Quartz, because Quartz's coordinate system is flipped from what many graphics libraries use and from what is usually taught in geometry classes. In OpenGL ES, for example, (0, 0) is in the lower-left corner and as the y coordinate increases, you move toward the top of the context or view, as shown in Figure 12-3. When working with OpenGL, you have to translate the position from the view's coordinate system to OpenGL's coordinate system. That's easy enough to do, and you'll see how it's done when we get into working with OpenGL later in the chapter.

To specify a point in the coordinate system, some Quartz functions require two floating-point numbers as parameters. Other Quartz functions ask for the point to be embedded in a `CGPoint`, a `struct` that holds two floating-point values, x and y. To describe the size of a view or other object, Quartz uses `CGSize`, a `struct` that also holds two floating-point values, `width` and `height`. Quartz also declares a datatype called `CGRect`, which is used to define a rectangle in the coordinate system. A `CGRect` contains two elements, a `CGPoint` called origin that identifies the top left of the rectangle and a CGSize called size that identifies the width and height of the rectangle.

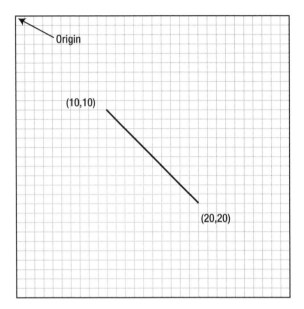

Figure 12-2. *Drawing a line in the view's coordinate system*

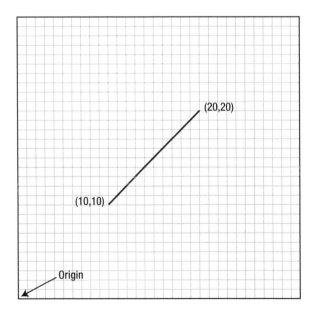

Figure 12-3. *In many graphics libraries, including OpenGL, drawing from (10, 10) to (20, 20) would produce a line that looks like this instead of the line in Figure 12-2.*

Specifying Colors

An important part of drawing is color, so understanding the way colors work on the iPhone is important. This is one of the areas where the UIKit does provide an Objective-C class: UIColor. You can't use a UIColor object directly in Core Graphic calls, but since UIColor is just a wrapper around CGColor (which is what the Core Graphic functions require), you can retrieve a CGColor reference from a UIColor instance by using its CGColor property, something we did earlier in this code snippet:

```
CGContextSetStrokeColorWithColor(context, [UIColor redColor].CGColor);
```

We created a UIColor instance using a convenience method called redColor, and then retrieved its CGColor property and passed that into the function.

A Bit of Color Theory for Your iPhone's Display

In modern computer graphics, a very common way to represent colors is to use four components: red, green, blue, and alpha. In Quartz 2D, these values are of type CGFloat (which, on the iPhone, is a four byte floating-point value, the same as float) and hold a value between 0.0 and 1.0.

> **NOTE**
>
> A floating-point value that is expected to be in the range 0.0 to 1.0 is often referred to as a **clamped floating-point variable**, or sometimes just a **clamp**.

The first three are fairly easy to understand, as they represent the **additive primary colors** or the **RGB color model** (see Figure 12-4). Combining these three colors in different proportions results in different colors. If you add together light of these three shades in equal proportions, the result will appear to the eye as either white or a shade of gray depending on the intensity of the light mixed. Combining the three additive primaries in different proportions, gives you range of different colors, referred to as a **gamut**.

In grade school, you probably learned that the primary colors are red, yellow, and blue. These primaries, which are known as the **historical subtractive primaries** or the **RYB color model**, have little application in modern color theory and are almost never used in computer graphics. The color gamut of the RYB color model is extremely limited, and this model doesn't lend itself easily to mathematical definition. As much as we hate to tell you that your wonderful third grade art teacher, Mrs. Smedlee, was wrong about anything, well, in the context of computer graphics, she was. For our purposes, the primary colors are red, green, and blue, not red, yellow, and blue.

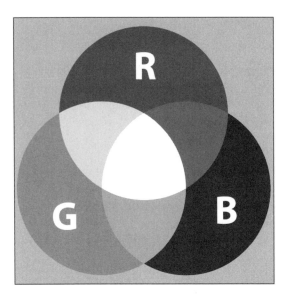

Figure 12-4. *A simple representation of the additive primary colors that make up the RGB color model*

More Than Color Meets the Eye

In addition to red, green, and blue, both Quartz 2D and OpenGL ES use another color component, called **alpha**, which represents how transparent a color is. Alpha is used, when drawing one color on top of another color, to determine the final color that gets drawn. With an alpha of 1.0, the drawn color is 100 percent opaque and obscures any colors beneath it. With any value less than 1.0, the colors below will show through and mix. When an alpha component is used, the color model is sometimes referred to as the **RGBA color model**, although technically speaking, the alpha isn't really part of the color; it just defines how the color will interact with other colors when it is drawn.

Although the RGB model is the most commonly used in computer graphics, it is not the only color model. Several others are in use, including hue, saturation, value (HSV); hue, saturation, lightness (HSL); cyan, magenta, yellow, key (CMYK), which is used in four-color offset printing; and grayscale. To make matters even more confusing, there are different versions of some of these, including several variants of the RGB color space. Fortunately, for most operations, we don't have to worry about the color model that is being used. We can just pass the CGColor from our UIColor object and Core Graphics will handle any necessary conversions. If you use UIColor or CGColor when working with OpenGL ES, it's important to keep in mind that they support other color models, because OpenGL ES requires colors to be specified in RGBA.

UIColor has a large number of convenience methods that return UIColor objects initialized to a specific color. In our previous code sample, we used the redColor method to get a color initialized to red. Fortunately for us, the UIColor instances created by these convenience methods all use the RGBA color model.

If you need more control over color, instead of using one of those convenience methods based on the name of the color, you can create a color by specifying all four of the components. Here's an example:

```
return [UIColor colorWithRed:1.0f green:0.0f blue:0.0f alpha:1.0f];
```

Drawing Images in Context

Quartz 2D allows you to draw images directly into a context. This is another example of an Objective-C class (UIImage) that you can use as an alternative to working with a Core Graphics data structure (CGImage). The UIImage class contains methods to draw its image into the current context. You'll need to identify where the image should appear in the context by specifying either a CGPoint to identify the image's upper-left corner or a CGRect to frame the image—resized, if necessary, to fit the frame. You can draw a UIImage into the current context like so:

```
CGPoint drawPoint = CGPointMake(100.0f, 100.0f);
[image drawAtPoint:drawPoint];
```

Drawing Shapes: Polygons, Lines, and Curves

Quartz 2D provides a number of functions to make it easier to create complex shapes. To draw a rectangle or a polygon, you don't have to calculate angles, draw lines, or do any math at all, really. You can just call a Quartz function to do the work for you. For example, to draw an ellipse, you define the rectangle into which the ellipse needs to fit and let Core Graphics do the work:

```
CGRect theRect = CGMakeRect(0,0,100,100);
CGContextAddEllipseInRect(context, theRect);
CGContextDrawPath(context, kCGPathFillStroke);
```

There are similar methods for rectangles. There are also methods that let you create more complex shapes, such as arcs and Bezier paths. To learn more about arcs and Bezier paths in Quartz, check out the *Quartz 2D Programming Guide* in the iPhone Dev Center at `http://developer.apple.com/documentation/GraphicsImaging/Conceptual/drawingwithquartz2d/` or in Xcode's online documentation.

Quartz 2D Tool Sampler: Patterns, Gradients, and Dash Patterns

Although not as expansive as OpenGL, Quartz 2D does offer quite an impressive array of tools. Though many of these tools are beyond the scope of this book, you should know they exist. For example, Quartz 2D supports the filling of polygons with gradients, not just solid colors, and supports not only solid lines but an assortment of dash patterns. Take a look at the screen shots in Figure 12-5, which are taken from Apple's QuartzDemo sample code, to see a sampling of what Quartz 2D can do for you.

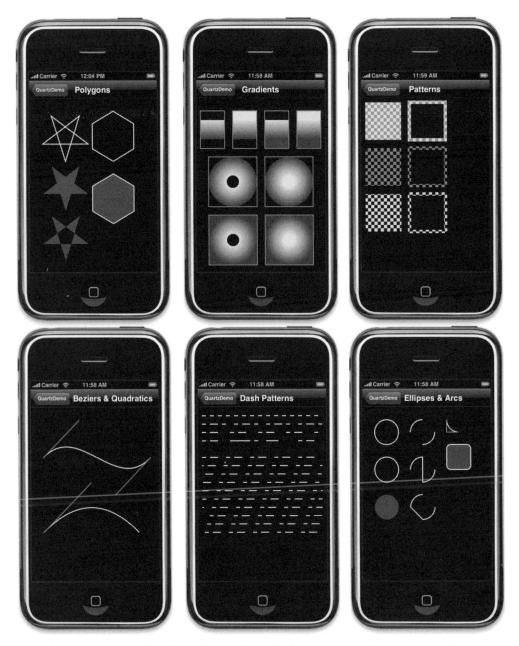

Figure 12-5. *Some examples of what Quartz 2D can do, from the Quartz Demo sample project provided by Apple*

Now that you have a basic understanding of how Quartz 2D works and what it is capable of, let's try it out.

Building the QuartzFun Application

In Xcode, create a new project using the view-based application template, and call it Quartz-Fun. Once it's created, expand the *Classes* and *Resources* folders, and single-click the *Classes* folder so we can add our classes. The template already provided us with an application delegate and a view controller. We're going to be executing our custom drawing in a view, so we need to create a subclass of UIView where we'll do the drawing by overriding the drawRect: method. Create a new *Cocoa Touch Class* file, and select *Objective-C class* and then a *UIView* for *Subclass of*. Just to repeat, use a *Subclass of UIView* and not *NSObject* as we've done in the past. Call the file *QuartzFunView.m*, and be sure to create the header as well.

We're going to define some constants, as we've done several times, but this time, our constants are going to be needed by more than one class and don't relate to one specific class. We're going to create a header file just for the constants, so create a new file, selecting the *Empty File* template from the *Other* heading and calling it *Constants.h*.

We have two more files to go. If you look at Figure 12-1, you can see that we offer an option to select a random color. UIColor doesn't have a method to return a random color, so we'll have to write code to do that. We could, of course, put that code into our controller class, but because we're savvy Objective-C programmers, we're going to put the code into a category on UIColor. Create two more files using the *Empty File* template, calling one *UIColor-Random.h* and the other *UIColor-Random.m*. Alternatively, use the *NSObject subclass* template to create *UIColor-Random.m*, and let the template create *UIColor-Random.h* for you automatically; then, delete the contents of the two files.

Creating a Random Color

Let's tackle the category first. In *UIColor-Random.h*, place the following code:

```
#import <UIKit/UIKit.h>

@interface UIColor(Random)
+(UIColor *)randomColor;
@end
```

Now, switch over to *UIColor-Random.m*, and add this:

```
#import "UIColor-Random.h"

@implementation UIColor(Random)
+(UIColor *)randomColor {
    static BOOL seeded = NO;
```

```
    if (!seeded) {
        seeded = YES;
        srandom(time(NULL));
    }
    CGFloat red =   (CGFloat)random()/(CGFloat)RAND_MAX;
    CGFloat blue = (CGFloat)random()/(CGFloat)RAND_MAX;
    CGFloat green = (CGFloat)random()/(CGFloat)RAND_MAX;
    return [UIColor colorWithRed:red green:green blue:blue alpha:1.0f];
}
@end
```

This is fairly straightforward. We declare a static variable that tells us if this is the first time through the method. The first time this method is called during an application's run, we will seed the random number generator. Doing this here means we don't have to rely on the application doing it somewhere else, and as a result, we can reuse this category in other iPhone projects.

Once we've made sure the random number generator is seeded, we generate three random CGFloats with a value between 0.0 and 1.0, and use those three values to create a new color. We set alpha to 1.0 so that all generated colors will be opaque.

Defining Application Constants

We're going to define constants for each of the options that the user can select using the segmented controllers. Single-click *Constants.h*, and add the following:

```
typedef enum {
    kLineShape  = 0,
    kRectShape,
    kEllipseShape,
    kImageShape
} ShapeType;

typedef enum {
    kRedColorTab = 0,
    kBlueColorTab,
    kYellowColorTab,
    kGreenColorTab,
    kRandomColorTab
} ColorTabIndex;

#define degreesToRadian(x) (M_PI * (x) / 180.0)
```

To make our code more readable, we've declared two enumeration types using typedef. One will represent the available shape options available; the other will represent the various color options available. The values these constants hold will correspond to segments on the two segmented controllers we will create in our application.

Implementing the QuartzFunView Skeleton

Since we're going to do our drawing in a subclass of UIView, let's set up that class with everything it needs except for the actual code to do the drawing, which we'll add later. Single-click *QuartzFunView.h*, and make the following changes:

```
#import <UIKit/UIKit.h>
#import "Constants.h"

@interface QuartzFunView : UIView {
    CGPoint         firstTouch;
    CGPoint         lastTouch;
    UIColor         *currentColor;
    ShapeType       shapeType;
    UIImage         *drawImage;
    BOOL            useRandomColor;
}
@property CGPoint firstTouch;
@property CGPoint lastTouch;
@property (nonatomic, retain) UIColor *currentColor;
@property ShapeType shapeType;
@property (nonatomic, retain) UIImage *drawImage;
@property BOOL useRandomColor;
@end
```

The first thing we do is import the *Constants.h* header we just created so we can make use of our enumerations. We then declare our instance variables. The first two will track the user's finger as it drags across the screen. We'll store the location where the user first touches the screen in firstTouch. We'll store the location of the user's finger while dragging and when the drag ends in lastTouch. Our drawing code will use these two variables to determine where to draw the requested shape.

Next, we define a color to hold the user's color selection and a ShapeType to keep track of the shape the user wants drawn. After that is a UIImage property that will hold the image to be drawn on the screen when the user selects the rightmost toolbar item on the bottom toolbar (see Figure 12-6). The last property is a Boolean that will be used to keep track of whether the user is requesting a random color.

Switch to *QuartzFunView.m*, and make the following changes:

Figure 12-6. *When drawing a UIImage to the screen, notice that the color control disappears.*

```objc
#import "QuartzFunView.h"
#import "UIColor-Random.h"
@implementation QuartzFunView
@synthesize firstTouch;
@synthesize lastTouch;
@synthesize currentColor;
@synthesize shapeType;
@synthesize drawImage;
@synthesize useRandomColor;

- (id)initWithCoder:(NSCoder*)coder
{
    if ( ( self = [super initWithCoder:coder] ) ) {
        self.currentColor = [UIColor redColor];
        self.useRandomColor = NO;
        if (drawImage == nil)
            self.drawImage = [UIImage imageNamed:@"iphone.png"];
    }
    return self;
}
- (id)initWithFrame:(CGRect)frame {
    if (self = [super initWithFrame:frame]) {
        // Initialization code
    }
    return self;
}
- (void)drawRect:(CGRect)rect {

    // Drawing code
}
- (void)touchesBegan:(NSSet *)touches withEvent:(UIEvent *)event {
    if (useRandomColor)
        self.currentColor = [UIColor randomColor];
    UITouch *touch = [touches anyObject];
    firstTouch = [touch locationInView:self];
    lastTouch = [touch locationInView:self];
    [self setNeedsDisplay];
}
- (void)touchesEnded:(NSSet *)touches withEvent:(UIEvent *)event {
    UITouch *touch = [touches anyObject];
    lastTouch = [touch locationInView:self];

    [self setNeedsDisplay];
}
- (void)touchesMoved:(NSSet *)touches withEvent:(UIEvent *)event {
    UITouch *touch = [touches anyObject];
    lastTouch = [touch locationInView:self];
```

```
    [self setNeedsDisplay];

}

- (void)dealloc {
    [currentColor release];
    [drawImage release];
    [super dealloc];
}

@end
```

Because this view is getting loaded from a nib, we first implement initWithCoder:. Keep in mind that object instances in nibs are stored as archived objects, which is the exact same mechanism we used in the previous chapter to archive and load our objects to disk. As a result, when an object instance is loaded from a nib, neither init: nor initWithFrame: ever gets called. Instead, initWithCoder: is used, so this is where we need to add any initialization code. In our case, we set the initial color value to red, initialize useRandomColor to NO and load the image file that we're going to draw. You don't have to fully understand the rest of the code here. We'll get into the details of working with touches and the specifics of the touchesBegan:withEvent:, touchesMoved:withEvent:, and touchesEnded:withEvent: methods in Chapter 13. In a nutshell, these three methods inherited from UIView (but actually declared in UIView's parent UIResponder) can be overridden to find out where the user is touching the iPhone's screen.

touchesBegan:withEvent: gets called when the user's finger first touch the screen. In that method, we change the color if the user has selected a random color using the new randomColor method we added to UIColor earlier. After that, we store the current location so that we know where the user first touched the screen, and we indicate that our view needs to be redrawn by calling setNeedsDisplay on self.

The next method, touchesMoved:withEvent:, gets continuously called while the user is dragging a finger on the screen. All we do here is store off the new location in lastTouch and indicate that the screen needs to be redrawn.

The last one, touchesEnded:withEvent:, gets called when the user lifts that finger off of the screen. Just like in the touchesMoved:withEvent: method, all we do is store off the final location in the lastTouch variable and indicate that the view needs to be redrawn.

Don't worry if you don't fully grok what the three methods that start with touches are doing; we'll be working on these in much greater detail in the next few chapters.

We'll come back to this class once we have our application skeleton up and running. That drawRect: method, which is currently empty except for a comment, is where we will do this application's real work, and we haven't written that yet. Let's finish setting up the application before we add our drawing code.

Adding Outlets and Actions to the View Controller

If you refer to Figure 12-1, you'll see that our interface includes two segmented controllers, one at the top and one at the bottom of the screen. The one on top, which lets the user select color, is applicable to only three of the four options on the bottom, so we're going to need an outlet to that top segmented controller, so we can hide it when it doesn't serve a purpose. We also need two methods, one that will be called when a new color is selected and another that will be called when a new shape is selected.

Single-click *QuartzFunViewController.h*, and make the following changes:

```
#import <UIKit/UIKit.h>

@interface QuartzFunViewController : UIViewController {
    UISegmentedControl *colorControl;
}
@property (nonatomic, retain) IBOutlet UISegmentedControl *colorControl;
- (IBAction)changeColor:(id)sender;
- (IBAction)changeShape:(id)sender;
@end
```

Nothing there should need explanation at this point, so switch over to *QuartzFunView Controller.m*, and make these changes to the top of the file:

```
#import "QuartzFunViewController.h"
#import "QuartzFunView.h"
#import "Constants.h"

@implementation QuartzFunViewController
@synthesize colorControl;

- (IBAction)changeColor:(id)sender {
    UISegmentedControl *control = sender;
    NSInteger index = [control selectedSegmentIndex];

    QuartzFunView *quartzView = (QuartzFunView *)self.view;

    switch (index) {
        case kRedColorTab:
            quartzView.currentColor = [UIColor redColor];
            quartzView.useRandomColor = NO;
            break;
        case kBlueColorTab:
            quartzView.currentColor = [UIColor blueColor];
```

```
                quartzView.useRandomColor = NO;
                break;
        case kYellowColorTab:
                quartzView.currentColor = [UIColor yellowColor];
                quartzView.useRandomColor = NO;
                break;
        case kGreenColorTab:
                quartzView.currentColor = [UIColor greenColor];
                quartzView.useRandomColor = NO;
                break;
        case kRandomColorTab:
                quartzView.useRandomColor = YES;
                break;
        default:
                break;
    }
}
- (IBAction)changeShape:(id)sender {
    UISegmentedControl *control = sender;
    [(QuartzFunView *)self.view setShapeType:[control
        selectedSegmentIndex]];

    if ([control selectedSegmentIndex] == kImageShape)
        colorControl.hidden = YES;
    else
        colorControl.hidden = NO;
}
...
```

Let's also be good memory citizens by adding the following code to the existing viewDidUnload and dealloc methods:

```
...
- (void)viewDidUnload {
    // Release any retained subviews of the main view.
    // e.g. self.myOutlet = nil;
    self.colorControl = nil;
    [super viewDidUnload];
}
- (void)dealloc {
    [colorControl release];
    [super dealloc];
}
...
```

Again, these code changes are pretty straightforward. In the changeColor: method, we look at which segment was selected and create a new color based on that selection. We cast view to QuartzFunView. Next, we set its currentColor property so that it knows what color to use when drawing, except when a random color is selected, in which case, we just set the view's useRandomColor property to YES. Since all the drawing code will be in the view itself, we don't have to do anything else in this method.

In the changeShape: method, we do something similar. However, since we don't need to create an object, we can just set the view's shapeType property to the segment index from sender. Recall the ShapeType enum? The four elements of the enum correspond to the four toolbar segments at the bottom of the application view. We set the shape to be the same as the currently selected segment, and we hide and unhide the colorControl based on whether the *Image* segment was selected.

Updating QuartzFunViewController.xib

Before we can start drawing, we need to add the segmented controls to our nib and then hook up the actions and outlets. Double-click *QuartzFunViewController.xib* to open the file in Interface Builder. The first order of business is to change the class of the view, so single-click the *View* icon in the window labeled *QuartzFunViewController.xib*, and press ⌘4 to open the identity inspector. Change the class from *UIView* to *QuartzFunView*.

Next, look for a *Navigation Bar* in the library. Make sure you are grabbing a *Navigation Bar*— not a *Navigation Controller*. We just want the bar that goes at the top of the view. Place the *Navigation Bar* snugly against the top of the view window, just beneath the status bar.

Next, look for a *Segmented Control* in the library, and drag that right on top of the *Navigation Bar*. Drop it in the center of the nav bar, not on the left or right side. Once you drop it, it should stay selected, so grab one of the resize dots on either side of the segmented control and resize it so that it takes up the entire width of the navigation bar. You won't get any blue guide lines, but Interface Builder won't let you make the bar any bigger than you want it in this case, so just drag until it won't expand any further.

With the segmented control still selected, press ⌘1 to bring up the attributes inspector, and change the number of segments from *2* to *5*. Double-click each segment in turn, changing its label to (from left to right) *Red*, *Blue*, *Yellow*, *Green*, and *Random* in that order. At this point, your *View* window should look like Figure 12-7.

Figure 12-7. *The completed navigation bar*

Control-drag from the *File's Owner* icon to the segmented control, and select the *colorControl* outlet. Make sure you are dragging to the segmented control and *not* the nav bar. Next, make sure the segmented control is selected, and press ⌘2 to bring up the connections inspector. Drag from the *Value Changed* event to *File's Owner*, and select the *changeColor:* action.

Now look for a *Toolbar* in the library, and drag one of those over to the bottom of the window. The *Toolbar* from the library has a button on it that we don't need, so select it and press the delete button on your keyboard. Once it's placed and the button is deleted, grab another *Segmented Control*, and drop it onto the toolbar.

As it turns out, segmented controls are a bit harder to center in a toolbar, so we'll bring in a little help. Drag a *Flexible Space Bar Button Item* from the library onto the toolbar, to the left of our segmented control. Next, drag a second *Flexible Space Bar Button Item* onto the toolbar, to the right of our segmented control. These items will keep the segmented control centered in the toolbar as we resize it. Click the segmented control to select it, and resize it so it fills the toolbar with just a bit of space to the left and right. Interface Builder won't give you guides or stop you from making it wider than the toolbar the way it did with the navigation bar, so you'll have to be a little careful to resize it to the right size.

Next, with the segmented control still selected, press ⌘1 to bring up the attributes inspector, and change the number of segments from *2* to *4*. Change the titles of the four segments to be *Line*, *Rect*, *Ellipse*, and *Image*, in that order. Switch to the connections inspector, and connect *Value Changed* event to *File's Owner's changeShape:* action method. Save and close the nib, and go back to Xcode.

NOTE

> You may have wondered why we put a navigation bar at the top of the view and a toolbar at the bottom of the view. According to the *iPhone Human Interface Guidelines* published by Apple, navigation bars were specifically designed to be placed at the top of the screen and toolbars are designed for the bottom. If you read the descriptions of the *Toolbar* and *Navigation Bar* in Interface Builder's library window, you'll see this design intention spelled out.

Make sure that everything is in order by compiling and running. You won't be able to draw shapes on the screen yet, but the segmented controls should work, and when you tap the *Image* segment in the bottom control, the color controls should disappear. Once you've got everything working, let's do some drawing.

Drawing the Line

Back in Xcode, edit *QuartzFunView.m*, and replace the empty drawRect: method with this one:

```
- (void)drawRect:(CGRect)rect {
    CGContextRef context = UIGraphicsGetCurrentContext();

    CGContextSetLineWidth(context, 2.0);
    CGContextSetStrokeColorWithColor(context, currentColor.CGColor);


    switch (shapeType) {
        case kLineShape:
            CGContextMoveToPoint(context, firstTouch.x, firstTouch.y);
            CGContextAddLineToPoint(context, lastTouch.x, lastTouch.y);
            CGContextStrokePath(context);
            break;
        case kRectShape:
            break;
        case kEllipseShape:
            break;
        case kImageShape:
            break;
        default:
            break;
    }
}
```

We start things off by retrieving a reference to the current context so we know where to draw:

```
    CGContextRef context = UIGraphicsGetCurrentContext();
```

Next, we set the line width to 2.0, which means that any line that we stroke will be 2 pixels wide:

```
    CGContextSetLineWidth(context, 2.0);
```

After that, we set the color for stroking lines. Since UIColor has a CGColor property, which is what this method needs, we use that property of our currentColor instance variable to pass the correct color onto this function:

```
    CGContextSetStrokeColorWithColor(context, currentColor.CGColor);
```

We use a `switch` to jump to the appropriate code for each shape type. We'll start off with the code to handle `kLineShape`, get that working, and then we'll add code for each shape in turn as we make our way through this chapter:

```
switch (shapeType) {
    case kLineShape:
```

To draw a line, we move the invisible pen to the first place the user touched. Remember, we stored that value in the `touchesBegan:` method, so it will always reflect the first spot touched the last time the user did a touch or drag.

```
        CGContextMoveToPoint(context, firstTouch.x, firstTouch.y);
```

Next, we draw a line from that spot to the last spot the user touched. If the user's finger is still in contact with the screen, `lastTouch` contains Mr. Finger's current location. If the user is no longer touching the screen, `lastTouch` contains the location of the user's finger when it was lifted off the screen.

```
        CGContextAddLineToPoint(context, lastTouch.x, lastTouch.y);
```

Then, we just stroke the path. This function will stroke the line we just drew using the color and width we set earlier:

```
        CGContextStrokePath(context);
```

After that, we just finish the `switch` statement, and we're done for now.

```
        break;
    case kRectShape:
        break;
    case kEllipseShape:
        break;
    case kImageShape:
        break;
    default:
        break;
}
```

At this point, you should be able to compile and run. The *Rect*, *Ellipse*, and *Shape* options won't work, but you should be able to draw lines just fine (see Figure 12-8).

Figure 12-8. *The line drawing part of our application is now complete. In this image, we are drawing using a random color.*

Drawing the Rectangle and Ellipse

Let's implement the code to draw the rectangle and the ellipse at the same time, since Quartz 2D implements both of these objects in basically the same way. Make the following changes to your drawRect: method:

- (void)drawRect:(CGRect)rect {

```
    if (currentColor == nil)
        self.currentColor = [UIColor redColor];

    CGContextRef context = UIGraphicsGetCurrentContext();

    CGContextSetLineWidth(context, 2.0);
    CGContextSetStrokeColorWithColor(context, currentColor.CGColor);
```

CGContextSetFillColorWithColor(context, currentColor.CGColor);
CGRect currentRect = CGRectMake (
```
            (firstTouch.x > lastTouch.x) ? lastTouch.x : firstTouch.x,
             (firstTouch.y > lastTouch.y) ? lastTouch.y : firstTouch.y,
             fabsf(firstTouch.x - lastTouch.x),
             fabsf(firstTouch.y - lastTouch.y));
```
```
    switch (shapeType) {
        case kLineShape:
            CGContextMoveToPoint(context, firstTouch.x, firstTouch.y);
            CGContextAddLineToPoint(context, lastTouch.x, lastTouch.y);
            CGContextStrokePath(context);
            break;
        case kRectShape:
```
**   CGContextAddRect(context, currentRect);**
**   CGContextDrawPath(context, kCGPathFillStroke);**
```
            break;
        case kEllipseShape:
```
**   CGContextAddEllipseInRect(context, currentRect);**
**   CGContextDrawPath(context, kCGPathFillStroke);**
```
            break;
        case kImageShape:
            break;
        default:
            break;
    }
}
```

Because we want to paint both the ellipse and the rectangle in a solid color, we add a call to set the fill color using currentColor:

```
CGContextSetFillColorWithColor(context, currentColor.CGColor);
```

Next, we declare a CGRect variable. We'll use `currentRect` to hold the rectangle described by the user's drag. Remember, a CGRect has two members: `size`, and `origin`. A function called `CGRectMake()` lets us create a CGRect by specifying the x, y, width, and height values, so we use that to make our rectangle. The code to make the rectangle may look a little intimidating at first glance, but it's not that complicated. The user could have dragged in any direction, so the origin will vary depending on the drag direction. We use the lower x value from the two points and the lower y value from the two points to create the origin. Then we figure out the size by getting the absolute value of the difference between the two x values and the two y values.

```
CGRect currentRect = CGRectMake (
        (firstTouch.x > lastTouch.x) ? lastTouch.x : firstTouch.x,
        (firstTouch.y > lastTouch.y) ? lastTouch.y : firstTouch.y,
        fabsf(firstTouch.x - lastTouch.x),
        fabsf(firstTouch.y - lastTouch.y));
```

Once we have this rectangle defined, drawing either a rectangle or an ellipse is as easy as calling two functions, one to draw the rectangle or ellipse in the CGRect we defined and the other to stroke and fill it.

```
    case kRectShape:
        CGContextAddRect(context, currentRect);
        CGContextDrawPath(context, kCGPathFillStroke);
        break;
    case kEllipseShape:
        CGContextAddEllipseInRect(context, currentRect);
        CGContextDrawPath(context, kCGPathFillStroke);
        break;
```

Compile and run your application and try out the *Rect* and *Ellipse* tools to see how you like them. Don't forget to change colors now and again and to try out the random color.

Drawing the Image

For our last trick, let's draw an image. There is an image in the *12 QuartzFun* folder called *iphone.png* that you can add to your *Resources* folder, or you can add any *.png* file you want to use as long as you remember to change the filename in your code to point to the image you choose.

Add the following code to your `drawRect:` method:

```
- (void)drawRect:(CGRect)rect {

    if (currentColor == nil)
        self.currentColor = [UIColor redColor];

    CGContextRef context = UIGraphicsGetCurrentContext();
```

```
CGContextSetLineWidth(context, 2.0);
CGContextSetStrokeColorWithColor(context, currentColor.CGColor);

CGContextSetFillColorWithColor(context, currentColor.CGColor);
CGRect currentRect;
currentRect = CGRectMake (
    (firstTouch.x > lastTouch.x) ? lastTouch.x : firstTouch.x,
    (firstTouch.y > lastTouch.y) ? lastTouch.y : firstTouch.y,
    fabsf(firstTouch.x - lastTouch.x),
    fabsf(firstTouch.y - lastTouch.y);

switch (shapeType) {
    case kLineShape:
        CGContextMoveToPoint(context, firstTouch.x, firstTouch.y);
        CGContextAddLineToPoint(context, lastTouch.x, lastTouch.y);
        CGContextStrokePath(context);
        break;
    case kRectShape:
        CGContextAddRect(context, currentRect);
        CGContextDrawPath(context, kCGPathFillStroke);
        break;
    case kEllipseShape:
        CGContextAddEllipseInRect(context, currentRect);
        CGContextDrawPath(context, kCGPathFillStroke);
        break;
    case kImageShape: {
        CGFloat horizontalOffset = drawImage.size.width / 2;
        CGFloat verticalOffset = drawImage.size.height / 2;
        CGPoint drawPoint = CGPointMake(lastTouch.x - horizontalOffset,
                        lastTouch.y - verticalOffset);
        [drawImage drawAtPoint:drawPoint];
        break;
    }
    default:
        break;
    }
}
```

TIP

Notice that, in the `switch` statement, we added curly braces around the code under
case `kImageShape:`. GCC has a problem with variables declared in the first line after a `case` statement. These curly braces are our way of telling GCC to stop complaining. We could also have declared
`horizontalOffset` before the `switch` statement, but this approach keeps the related code
together.

First, we calculate the center of the image, since we want the image drawn centered on the point where the user last touched. Without this adjustment, the image would get drawn with the upper-left corner at the user's finger, also a valid option. We then make a new CGpoint by subtracting these offsets from the x and y values in lastTouch.

```
CGFloat horizontalOffset = drawImage.size.width / 2;
CGFloat verticalOffset = drawImage.size.height / 2;
CGPoint drawPoint = CGPointMake(lastTouch.x - horizontalOffset,
                                lastTouch.y - verticalOffset);
```

Now, we tell the image to draw itself. This line of code will do the trick:

```
[drawImage drawAtPoint:drawPoint];
```

Optimizing the QuartzFun Application

Our application does what we want, but we should consider a bit of optimization. In our application, you won't notice a slowdown, but in a more complex application, running on a slower processor, you might see some lag. The problem occurs in *QuartzFunView.m*, in the methods touchesMoved: and touchesEnded:. Both methods include this line of code:

```
[self setNeedsDisplay];
```

Obviously, this is how we tell our view that something has changed, and it needs to redraw itself. This code works, but it causes the entire view to get erased and redrawn, even if only a tiny little bit changed. We do want to erase the screen when we get ready to drag out a new shape, but we don't want to clear the screen several times a second as we drag out our shape.

Rather than forcing the entire view to be redrawn many times during our drag, we can use setNeedsDisplayInRect: instead. setNeedsDisplayInRect: is an NSView method that marks a just one rectangular portion of a view's region as needing redisplay. By using this, we can be more efficient by marking only the part of the view that is affected by the current drawing operation as needing to be redrawn.

We need to redraw not just the rectangle between firstTouch and lastTouch but any part of the screen encompassed by the current drag. If the user touches the screen and then scribbles all over and we redrew the only section between firstTouch and lastTouch, we'd leave a lot of stuff drawn on the screen that we don't want.

The answer is to keep track of the entire area that's been affected by a particular drag in a CGRect instance variable. In touchesBegan:, we reset that instance variable to just the point where the user touched. Then in touchesMoved: and touchesEnded:, we use a Core Graphics function to get the union of the current rectangle and the stored rectangle, and we store the resulting rectangle. We also use it to specify what part of the view needs to be redrawn. This approach gives us a running total of the area impacted by the current drag.

Right now, we calculate the current rectangle in the drawRect: method for use in drawing the ellipse and rectangle shapes. We'll move that calculation into a new method so that it can be used in all three places without repeating code. Ready? Let's do it. Make the following changes to *QuartzFunView.h*:

```
#import <UIKit/UIKit.h>
#import "Constants.h"

@interface QuartzFunView : UIView {
    CGPoint         firstTouch;
    CGPoint         lastTouch;
    UIColor         *currentColor;
    ShapeType       shapeType;
    UIImage         *drawImage;
    BOOL            useRandomColor;
    CGRect          redrawRect;
}
@property CGPoint firstTouch;
@property CGPoint lastTouch;
@property (nonatomic, retain) UIColor *currentColor;
@property ShapeType shapeType;
@property (nonatomic, retain) UIImage *drawImage;
@property BOOL useRandomColor;
@property (readonly) CGRect currentRect;
@property CGRect redrawRect;
@end
```

We declare a CGRect called redrawRect that we will use to keep track of the area that needs to be redrawn. We also declare a read-only property called currentRect, which will return that rectangle that we were previously calculating in drawRect:. Notice that it is a property with no underlying instance variable, which is okay, as long as we implement the accessor rather than relying on @synthesize to do it for us. We'll still use the @synthesize keyword, but will write the accessor ourselves. @synthesize will create an accessor or mutator only if one doesn't already exist in the class.

Switch over to *QuartzFunView.m*, and insert the following code at the top of the file:

```
#import "QuartzFunView.h"

@implementation QuartzFunView
@synthesize firstTouch;
@synthesize lastTouch;
@synthesize currentColor;
@synthesize shapeType;
```

```
@synthesize drawImage;
@synthesize useRandomColor;
@synthesize redrawRect;
@synthesize currentRect;
- (CGRect)currentRect {
    return CGRectMake (
        (firstTouch.x > lastTouch.x) ? lastTouch.x : firstTouch.x,
        (firstTouch.y > lastTouch.y) ? lastTouch.y : firstTouch.y,
        fabsf(firstTouch.x - lastTouch.x),
        fabsf(firstTouch.y - lastTouch.y));
}
...
```

Now, in the drawRect: method, delete the lines of code where we calculated currentRect, and change all references to currentRect to self.currentRect so that the code uses that new accessor we just created.

```
...
- (void)drawRect:(CGRect)rect {
    if (currentColor == nil)
        self.currentColor = [UIColor redColor];

    CGContextRef context = UIGraphicsGetCurrentContext();

    CGContextSetLineWidth(context, 2.0);
    CGContextSetStrokeColorWithColor(context, currentColor.CGColor);

    CGContextSetFillColorWithColor(context, currentColor.CGColor);

        CGRect currentRect = CGRectMake (
            (firstTouch.x > lastTouch.x) ? lastTouch.x : firstTouch.x,
            (firstTouch.y > lastTouch.y) ? lastTouch.y : firstTouch.y,
            fabsf(firstTouch.x - lastTouch.x),
            fabsf(firstTouch.y - lastTouch.y));

    switch (shapeType) {
        case kLineShape:
            CGContextMoveToPoint(context, firstTouch.x, firstTouch.y);
            CGContextAddLineToPoint(context, lastTouch.x, lastTouch.y);
            CGContextStrokePath(context);
            break;
        case kRectShape:
            CGContextAddRect(context, self.currentRect);
            CGContextDrawPath(context, kCGPathFillStroke);
            break;
        case kEllipseShape:
            CGContextAddEllipseInRect(context, self.currentRect);
```

```
                CGContextDrawPath(context, kCGPathFillStroke);
                break;
        case kImageShape:
            if (drawImage == nil)
                self.drawImage = [UIImage imageNamed:@"iphone.png"];

            CGFloat horizontalOffset = drawImage.size.width / 2;
            CGFloat verticalOffset = drawImage.size.height / 2;
            CGPoint drawPoint = CGPointMake(lastTouch.x - horizontalOffset,
                            lastTouch.y - verticalOffset);
            [drawImage drawAtPoint:drawPoint];
            break;
        default:
            break;
    }
}
...
```

We also need to make some changes to in touchesEnded:withEvent: and
touchesMoved:withEvent:. We need to recalculate the space impacted by the current
operation, and use that to indicate that only portion of our view needs to be redrawn:

```
...
- (void)touchesEnded:(NSSet *)touches withEvent:(UIEvent *)event {
    UITouch *touch = [touches anyObject];
    lastTouch = [touch locationInView:self];

    [self setNeedsDisplay];
    if (shapeType == kImageShape) {
        CGFloat horizontalOffset = drawImage.size.width / 2;
        CGFloat verticalOffset = drawImage.size.height / 2;
        redrawRect = CGRectUnion(redrawRect, CGRectMake(lastTouch.x -
            horizontalOffset, lastTouch.y - verticalOffset,
            drawImage.size.width, drawImage.size.height));
    }
    else
        redrawRect = CGRectUnion(redrawRect, self.currentRect);
    redrawRect = CGRectInset(redrawRect, -2.0, -2.0);
    [self setNeedsDisplayInRect:redrawRect];
}
- (void)touchesMoved:(NSSet *)touches withEvent:(UIEvent *)event {
    UITouch *touch = [touches anyObject];
    lastTouch = [touch locationInView:self];

    [self setNeedsDisplay];
    if (shapeType == kImageShape) {
        CGFloat horizontalOffset = drawImage.size.width / 2;
```

```
        CGFloat verticalOffset = drawImage.size.height / 2;
        redrawRect = CGRectUnion(redrawRect,
            CGRectMake(lastTouch.x - horizontalOffset,
            lastTouch.y - verticalOffset, drawImage.size.width,
            drawImage.size.height));
    }
    redrawRect = CGRectUnion(redrawRect, self.currentRect);
    [self setNeedsDisplayInRect:redrawRect];
}
...
```

With only a few additional lines of code, we reduced the amount of work necessary to
redraw our view by getting rid of the need to erase and redraw any portion of the view that
wasn't been affected by the current drag. Being kind to the iPhone's precious processor
cycles like this can make a big difference in the performance of your applications, especially
as they get more complex.

Some OpenGL ES Basics

As we mentioned earlier in the chapter, OpenGL ES and Quartz 2D take fundamentally different approaches to drawing. A detailed introduction to OpenGL ES would be a book in and
of itself, so we're not going to attempt that here. Instead, we're going to re-create our Quartz
2D application using OpenGL ES, just to give you a sense of the basics and some sample
code you can use to kick start your own OpenGL applications.

NOTE

When you are ready to add OpenGL to your own applications, take a side trip to `http://www.`
`khronos.org/opengles/`, which is the home base of the OpenGL ES standards group. Even better,
visit this page, and search for the word "tutorial": `http://www.khronos.org/developers/`
`resources/opengles/`

Also, be sure to check out the OpenGL tutorial in Jeff LaMarche's iPhone blog:

`http://iphonedevelopment.blogspot.com/2009/05/`➥
`opengl-es-from-ground-up-table-of.html`

Let's get started with our application.

Building the GLFun Application

Create a new view-based application in Xcode, and call it GLFun. To save time, copy the
files *Constants.h*, *UIColor-Random.h*, *UIColor-Random.m*, and *iphone.png* from the Quartz-
Fun project into this new project. Open *GLFunViewController.h*, and make the following

changes. You should recognize them, as they're identical to the changes we made to
QuartzFunViewController.h earlier:

```
#import <UIKit/UIKit.h>

@interface GLFunViewController : UIViewController {
 UISegmentedControl *colorControl;
}
@property (nonatomic, retain) IBOutlet UISegmentedControl *colorControl;
- (IBAction)changeColor:(id)sender;
- (IBAction)changeShape:(id)sender;
@end
```

Switch over to *QuartzFunViewController.m*, and make the following changes at the beginning
of the file. Again, these changes should look very familiar to you:

```
#import "GLFunViewController.h"
#import "Constants.h"
#import "GLFunView.h"
#import "UIColor-Random.h"

@implementation GLFunViewController
@synthesize colorControl;

- (IBAction)changeColor:(id)sender {
    UISegmentedControl *control = sender;
    NSInteger index = [control selectedSegmentIndex];

    GLFunView *glView = (GLFunView *)self.view;

    switch (index) {
        case kRedColorTab:
            glView.currentColor = [UIColor redColor];
            glView.useRandomColor = NO;
            break;
        case kBlueColorTab:
            glView.currentColor = [UIColor blueColor];
            glView.useRandomColor = NO;
            break;
        case kYellowColorTab:
            glView.currentColor = [UIColor yellowColor];
            glView.useRandomColor = NO;
            break;
        case kGreenColorTab:
            glView.currentColor = [UIColor greenColor];
            glView.useRandomColor = NO;
            break;
        case kRandomColorTab:
```

```
                glView.useRandomColor = YES;
                break;
        default:
                break;
    }
}

- (IBAction)changeShape:(id)sender {
    UISegmentedControl *control = sender;
    [(GLFunView *)self.view setShapeType:[control selectedSegmentIndex]];
    if ([control selectedSegmentIndex] == kImageShape)
        [colorControl setHidden:YES];
    else
        [colorControl setHidden:NO];
}
...
```

Let's not forget to deal with memory cleanup:

```
...
- (void)viewDidUnload {
    // Release any retained subviews of the main view.
    // e.g. self.myOutlet = nil;
    self.colorControl = nil;
    [super viewDidUnload];
}
- (void)dealloc {
    [colorControl release];
    [super dealloc];
}
...
```

The only difference between this and *QuartzFunController.m* is that we're referencing a view called GLFunView instead of one called QuartzFunView. The code that does our drawing is contained in a subclass of UIView. Since we're doing the drawing in a completely different way this time, it makes sense to use a new class to contain that drawing code.

Before we proceed, you'll need to add a few more files to your project. In the *12 GLFun* folder, you'll find four files named *Texture2D.h*, *Texture2D.m*, *OpenGLES2DView.h*, and *OpenGLES2DView.m*. The code in the first two files was written by Apple to make drawing images in OpenGL ES much easier than it otherwise would be. The second file is a class we've provided based on sample code from Apple that configures OpenGL to do two-dimensional drawing. OpenGL configuration is a complex topic that entire books have been written on, so we've done that configuration for you. You can feel free to use any of these files in your own programs if you wish.

OpenGL ES doesn't have sprites or images, per se; it has one kind of image called a **texture**. Textures have to be drawn onto a shape or object. The way you draw an image in OpenGL ES is to draw a square (technically speaking, it's two triangles), and then map a texture onto that square so that it exactly matches the square's size. `Texture2D` encapsulates that relatively complex process into a single, easy-to-use class.

`OpenGLES2DView` is a subclass of `UIView` that uses OpenGL to do its drawing. We set up this view so that the coordinate systems of OpenGL ES and the coordinate system of the view are mapped on a one-to-one basis. OpenGL ES is a three-dimensional system. `OpenGLES2DView` maps the OpenGL 3-D world to the pixels of our 2-D view. Note that, despite the one-to-one relationship between the view and the OpenGL context, the y coordinates are still flipped, so we have to translate the y coordinate from the view coordinate system, where increases in y represent moving down, to the OpenGL coordinate system, where increases in y represent moving up.

To use the `OpenGLES2DView` class, first subclass it, and then implement the `draw` method to do your actual drawing, just as we do in the following code. You can also implement any other methods you need in your view, such as the touch-related methods we used in the QuartzFun example.

Create a new file using the *Cocoa Touch Class* template, select *Objective-C class* and *NSObject* for *Subclass of*, and call it *GLFunView.m*, making sure to have it create the header file.

Single-click *GLFunView.h*, and make the following changes:

```
#import <Foundation/Foundation.h>
#import "Constants.h"
#import "OpenGLES2DView.h"

@class Texture2D;

@interface GLFunView : NSObject {
@interface GLFunView : OpenGLES2DView {
    CGPoint         firstTouch;
    CGPoint         lastTouch;
    UIColor         *currentColor;
    BOOL            useRandomColor;

    ShapeType       shapeType;

    Texture2D       *sprite;
}
@property CGPoint firstTouch;
@property CGPoint lastTouch;
@property (nonatomic, retain) UIColor *currentColor;
@property BOOL useRandomColor;
```

```
@property ShapeType shapeType;
@property (nonatomic, retain) Texture2D *sprite;
@end
```

This class is similar to *QuartzFunView.h*, but instead of using UIImage to hold our image, we use a Texture2D to simplify the process of drawing images into an OpenGL ES context. We also change the superclass from UIView to OpenGLES2DView so that our view becomes an OpenGL ES–backed view set up for doing two-dimensional drawing.

Switch over to *GLFunView.m*, and make the following changes.

```
#import "GLFunView.h"
#import "UIColor-Random.h"
#import "Texture2D.h"

@implementation GLFunView
@synthesize firstTouch;
@synthesize lastTouch;
@synthesize currentColor;
@synthesize useRandomColor;
@synthesize shapeType;
@synthesize sprite;

- (id)initWithCoder:(NSCoder*)coder {
    if (self = [super initWithCoder:coder]) {
        self.currentColor = [UIColor redColor];
        self.useRandomColor = NO;
        self.sprite = [[Texture2D alloc] initWithImage:[UIImage
                                        imageNamed:@"iphone.png"]];
        glBindTexture(GL_TEXTURE_2D, sprite.name);
    }
    return self;
}

- (void)draw   {
    glLoadIdentity();

    glClearColor(0.78f, 0.78f, 0.78f, 1.0f);
    glClear(GL_COLOR_BUFFER_BIT);

    CGColorRef color = currentColor.CGColor;
    const CGFloat *components = CGColorGetComponents(color);
    CGFloat red = components[0];
    CGFloat green = components[1];
    CGFloat blue = components[2];

    glColor4f(red,green, blue, 1.0);
```

```
switch (shapeType) {
    case kLineShape: {
        glDisable(GL_TEXTURE_2D);
        GLfloat vertices[4];

        // Convert coordinates
        vertices[0] = firstTouch.x;
        vertices[1] = self.frame.size.height - firstTouch.y;
        vertices[2] = lastTouch.x;
        vertices[3] = self.frame.size.height - lastTouch.y;
        glLineWidth(2.0);
        glVertexPointer(2, GL_FLOAT, 0, vertices);
        glDrawArrays (GL_LINES, 0, 2);
        break;
    }
    case kRectShape: {
        glDisable(GL_TEXTURE_2D);
        // Calculate bounding rect and store in vertices
        GLfloat vertices[8];
        GLfloat minX = (firstTouch.x > lastTouch.x) ?
        lastTouch.x : firstTouch.x;
        GLfloat minY = (self.frame.size.height - firstTouch.y >
                        self.frame.size.height - lastTouch.y) ?
        self.frame.size.height - lastTouch.y :
        self.frame.size.height - firstTouch.y;
        GLfloat maxX = (firstTouch.x > lastTouch.x) ?
        firstTouch.x : lastTouch.x;
        GLfloat maxY = (self.frame.size.height - firstTouch.y >
                        self.frame.size.height - lastTouch.y) ?
        self.frame.size.height - firstTouch.y :
        self.frame.size.height - lastTouch.y;

        vertices[0] = maxX;
        vertices[1] = maxY;
        vertices[2] = minX;
        vertices[3] = maxY;
        vertices[4] = minX;
        vertices[5] = minY;
        vertices[6] = maxX;
        vertices[7] = minY;

        glVertexPointer (2, GL_FLOAT , 0, vertices);
        glDrawArrays (GL_TRIANGLE_FAN, 0, 4);
        break;
    }
    case kEllipseShape: {
        glDisable(GL_TEXTURE_2D);
```

```
            GLfloat vertices[720];
            GLfloat xradius = (firstTouch.x > lastTouch.x) ?
            (firstTouch.x - lastTouch.x)/2 :
            (lastTouch.x - firstTouch.x)/2;
            GLfloat yradius = (self.frame.size.height - firstTouch.y >
                                self.frame.size.height - lastTouch.y) ?
            ((self.frame.size.height - firstTouch.y) -
             (self.frame.size.height - lastTouch.y))/2 :
            ((self.frame.size.height - lastTouch.y) -
             (self.frame.size.height - firstTouch.y))/2;
            for (int i = 0; i < 720; i+=2) {
                GLfloat xOffset = (firstTouch.x > lastTouch.x) ?
                lastTouch.x + xradius
                : firstTouch.x + xradius;
                GLfloat yOffset = (self.frame.size.height - firstTouch.y >
                                    self.frame.size.height - lastTouch.y) ?
                self.frame.size.height - lastTouch.y + yradius :
                self.frame.size.height - firstTouch.y + yradius;
                vertices[i] = (cos(degreesToRadian(i/2))*xradius) + xOffset;
                vertices[i+1] = (sin(degreesToRadian(i/2))*yradius) +
                yOffset;
            }
            glVertexPointer(2, GL_FLOAT , 0, vertices);
            glDrawArrays (GL_TRIANGLE_FAN, 0, 360);
            break;

        }
        case kImageShape:
            glEnable(GL_TEXTURE_2D);
            [sprite drawAtPoint:CGPointMake(lastTouch.x,
                            self.frame.size.height - lastTouch.y)];
            break;
        default:
            break;
    }

    glBindRenderbufferOES(GL_RENDERBUFFER_OES, viewRenderbuffer);
    [context presentRenderbuffer:GL_RENDERBUFFER_OES];
}

- (void)dealloc {
    [currentColor release];
    [sprite release];
    [super dealloc];
}
```

```objc
- (void)touchesBegan:(NSSet *)touches withEvent:(UIEvent *)event {
    if (useRandomColor)
        self.currentColor = [UIColor randomColor];

    UITouch* touch = [[event touchesForView:self] anyObject];
    firstTouch = [touch locationInView:self];
    lastTouch = [touch locationInView:self];
    [self draw];
}

- (void)touchesMoved:(NSSet *)touches withEvent:(UIEvent *)event {

    UITouch *touch = [touches anyObject];
    lastTouch = [touch locationInView:self];

    [self draw];
}

- (void)touchesEnded:(NSSet *)touches withEvent:(UIEvent *)event {
    UITouch *touch = [touches anyObject];
    lastTouch = [touch locationInView:self];

    [self draw];
}
@end
```

You can see that using OpenGL isn't, by any means, easier or more concise than using Quartz 2D. Although it's more powerful than Quartz, you're also closer to the metal, so to speak. OpenGL can be daunting at times.

Because this view is being loaded from a nib, we added an `initWithCoder:` method, and in it, we create and assign a `UIColor` to `currentColor`. We also defaulted `useRandomColor` to NO. and created our `Texture2D` object.

After the `initWithCoder:` method, we have our `draw` method, which is where you can really see the difference in the approaches between the two libraries. Let's take a look at process of drawing a line. Here's how we drew the line in the Quartz version (we've removed the code that's not directly relevant to drawing):

```objc
CGContextRef context = UIGraphicsGetCurrentContext();
CGContextSetLineWidth(context, 2.0);
CGContextSetStrokeColorWithColor(context, currentColor.CGColor);
CGContextMoveToPoint(context, firstTouch.x, firstTouch.y);
CGContextAddLineToPoint(context, lastTouch.x, lastTouch.y);
CGContextStrokePath(context);
```

Here are the steps we had to take in OpenGL to draw that same line. First, we reset the virtual world so that any rotations, translations, or other transforms that might have been applied to it are gone:

```
glLoadIdentity();
```

Next, we clear the background to the same shade of gray that was used in the Quartz version of the application:

```
glClearColor(0.78, 0.78f, 0.78f, 1.0f);
glClear(GL_COLOR_BUFFER_BIT);
```

After that, we have to set the OpenGL drawing color by dissecting a UIColor and pulling the individual RGB components out of it. Fortunately, because we used the convenience class methods, we don't have to worry about which color model the UIColor uses. We can safely assume it will use the RGBA color space:

```
CGColorRef color = currentColor.CGColor;
const CGFloat *components = CGColorGetComponents(color);
CGFloat red = components[0];
CGFloat green = components[1];
CGFloat blue = components[2];
glColor4f(red,green, blue, 1.0);
```

Next, we turn off OpenGL ES's ability to map textures:

```
glDisable(GL_TEXTURE_2D);
```

Any drawing code that fires from the time we make this call until there's a call to glEnable(GL_TEXTURE_2D) will be drawn without a texture, which is what we want. If we allow a texture to be used, the color we just set won't show.

To draw a line, we need two vertices, which means we need an array with four elements. As we've discussed, a point in two-dimensional space is represented by two values, x and y. In Quartz, we used a CGPoint struct to hold these. In OpenGL, points are not embedded in structs. Instead, we pack an array with all the points that make up the shape we need to draw. So, to draw a line from point (100, 150) to point (200, 250) in OpenGL ES, we would create a vertex array that looked like this:

```
vertex[0] = 100;
vertex[1] = 150;
vertex[2] = 200;
vertex[3] = 250;
```

Our array has the format {x1, y1, x2, y2, x3, y3}. The next code in this method converts two CGPoint structs into a vertex array:

```
GLfloat vertices[4];
vertices[0] = firstTouch.x;
vertices[1] = self.frame.size.height - firstTouch.y;
vertices[2] = lastTouch.x;
vertices[3] = self.frame.size.height - lastTouch.y;
```

Once we've defined the vertex array that describes what we want to draw (in this example, a line), we specify the line width, pass the array into OpenGL ES using the method glVertexPointer(), and tell OpenGL ES to draw the arrays:

```
glLineWidth(2.0);
glVertexPointer (2, GL_FLOAT , 0, vertices);
glDrawArrays (GL_LINES, 0, 2);
```

Whenever we finish drawing in OpenGL ES, we have to tell it to render its buffer, and tell our view's context to show the newly rendered buffer:

```
glBindRenderbufferOES(GL_RENDERBUFFER_OES, viewRenderbuffer);
[context presentRenderbuffer:GL_RENDERBUFFER_OES];
```

To clarify, the process of drawing in OpenGL consists of three steps. First, you draw in the context. Second, once all your drawing is done, you render the context into the buffer. And third, you present your render buffer, which is when the pixels actually get drawn onto the screen.

As you can see, the OpenGL example is considerably longer. The difference between Quartz 2D and OpenGL ES becomes even more dramatic when we look at the process of drawing an ellipse. OpenGL ES doesn't know how to draw an ellipse. OpenGL, the big brother and predecessor to OpenGL ES, has a number of convenience functions for generating common two- and three-dimensional shapes, but those convenience functions are some of the functionality that was stripped out of OpenGL ES to make it more streamlined and suitable for use in embedded devices like the iPhone. As a result, a lot more responsibility falls into the developer's lap.

As a reminder, here is how we drew the ellipse using Quartz 2D:

```
CGContextRef context = UIGraphicsGetCurrentContext();
CGContextSetLineWidth(context, 2.0);
CGContextSetStrokeColorWithColor(context, currentColor.CGColor);
CGContextSetFillColorWithColor(context, currentColor.CGColor);
CGRect currentRect;
CGContextAddEllipseInRect(context, self.currentRect);
CGContextDrawPath(context, kCGPathFillStroke);
```

For the OpenGL ES version, we start off with the same steps as before, resetting any move-ment or rotations, clearing the background to white, and setting the draw color based on currentColor:

```
glLoadIdentity();
glClearColor(1.0f, 1.0f, 1.0f, 1.0f);
glClear(GL_COLOR_BUFFER_BIT);
glDisable(GL_TEXTURE_2D);
CGColorRef color = currentColor.CGColor;
const CGFloat *components = CGColorGetComponents(color);
CGFloat red = components[0];
CGFloat green = components[1];
CGFloat blue = components[2];
glColor4f(red,green, blue, 1.0);
```

Since OpenGL ES doesn't know how to draw an ellipse, we have to roll our own, which means dredging up painful memories of Ms. Picklebaum's geometry class. We'll define a vertex array that holds 720 GLfloats, which will hold an x and a y position for 360 points, one for each degree around the circle. We could change the number of points to increase or decrease the smoothness of the circle. This approach looks good on any view that'll fit on the iPhone screen but probably does require more processing than strictly necessary if all you are drawing is smaller circles.

```
GLfloat vertices[720];
```

Next, we'll figure out the horizontal and vertical radii of the ellipse based on the two points stored in firstTouch and lastTouch:

```
GLfloat xradius = (firstTouch.x > lastTouch.x) ?
        (firstTouch.x - lastTouch.x)/2 :
        (lastTouch.x - firstTouch.x)/2;
GLfloat yradius = (self.frame.size.height - firstTouch.y >
        self.frame.size.height - lastTouch.y) ?
        ((self.frame.size.height - firstTouch.y) ñ
        (self.frame.size.height - lastTouch.y))/2 :
        ((self.frame.size.height - lastTouch.y) ñ
        (self.frame.size.height - firstTouch.y))/2;
```

Next, we'll loop around the circle, calculating the correct points around the circle:

```
for (int i = 0; i < 720; i+=2) {
    GLfloat xOffset = (firstTouch.x > lastTouch.x) ?
        lastTouch.x + xradius : firstTouch.x + xradius;
    GLfloat yOffset = (self.frame.size.height - firstTouch.y >
            self.frame.size.height - lastTouch.y) ?
            self.frame.size.height - lastTouch.y + yradius :
            self.frame.size.height - firstTouch.y + yradius;
```

```
    vertices[i] = (cos(degreesToRadian(i/2))*xradius) + xOffset;
    vertices[i+1] = (sin(degreesToRadian(i/2))*yradius) + yOffset;
}
```

Finally, we'll feed the vertex array to OpenGL ES, tell it to draw it and render it, and then tell our context to present the newly rendered image:

```
glVertexPointer (2, GL_FLOAT , 0, vertices);
glDrawArrays (GL_TRIANGLE_FAN, 0, 360);
glBindRenderbufferOES(GL_RENDERBUFFER_OES, viewRenderbuffer);
[context presentRenderbuffer:GL_RENDERBUFFER_OES];
```

We won't review the rectangle method, because it uses the same basic technique; we define a vertex array with the four vertices to define the rectangle, and then we render and present it. There's also not much to talk about with the image drawing, since that lovely Texture2D class from Apple makes drawing a sprite just as easy as it is in Quartz 2D. There is one important thing to notice there, though:

```
glEnable(GL_TEXTURE_2D);
```

Since it is possible that the ability to draw textures was previously disabled, we have to make sure it's enabled before we attempt to use the Texture2D class.

After the draw method, we have the same touch-related methods as the previous version. The only difference is that instead of telling the view that it needs to be displayed, we just the draw method. We don't need to tell OpenGL ES what parts of the screen will be updated; it will figure that out and leverage hardware acceleration to draw in the most efficient manner.

Design the Nib, Add the Frameworks, Run the App

Now, you can double-click *GLFunViewController.xib* and design the interface. We're not going to walk you through it this time, but if you get stuck, you can refer to the earlier section called "Updating QuartzFunViewController.xib" for the specific steps. Be sure to change the class to *GLFunView* instead of *QuartzFunView*.

Once you're done, save and go back to Xcode.

Before we can compile and run this program, you'll need to link in two frameworks to your project. Follow the instruction from Chapter 7 for adding the Audio Toolbox framework but instead of selecting *AudioToolbox.framework*, select *OpenGLES.framework* and *QuartzCore.framework*.

Frameworks added? Good. Go run your project. It should look just like the Quartz version.

You've now seen enough OpenGL ES to get you started. If you're interested in using OpenGL ES in your iPhone applications, you can find the OpenGL ES specification along with links to books, documentation, and forums where OpenGL ES issues are discussed at `http://www.khronos.org/opengles/`.

TIP

If you want to create a full-screen OpenGL ES application, you don't have to build it manually. Xcode has a template you can use. It sets up the screen and the buffers for you and even puts some sample drawing and animation code into the class so you can see where to put your code. Want to try this out? Create a new *iPhone OS* application, and choose the *OpenGL ES Application* template.

Drawing a Blank

In this chapter, we've really just scratched the surface of the iPhone's drawing ability. You should feel pretty comfortable with Quartz 2D now, and with some occasional references to Apple's documentation, you can probably handle most any drawing requirement that comes your way. You should also have a basic understanding of what OpenGL ES is and how it integrates with iPhone's view system.

Next up? You're going to learn how to add gestural support to your applications.

Chapter 13

Taps, Touches, and Gestures

*t*he iPhone screen, with its crisp, bright, 160 pixels per inch, touch-sensitive display, is truly a thing of beauty and a masterpiece of engineering. The iPhone's multitouch screen is one of the key factors in iPhone's tremendous usability. Because the screen can detect multiple touches at the same time and track them independently, applications are able to detect a wide range of gestures, giving the user power that goes beyond the interface.

Suppose you are in the Mail application exploring your inbox, and you decide to delete an e-mail. You could tap the *Edit* button, select the row, and then tap the *Delete* button: that's three steps. Or you could just swipe your finger across the row you want to delete and then tap the *Delete* button that pops up—two steps.

This example is just one of the countless gestures that are made possible by iPhone's multitouch screen. You can pinch your fingers together to zoom into a picture or reverse pinch to zoom out. You can double-tap a frame in Mobile Safari to zoom so that the frame takes up your entire screen. You can swipe two fingers across a scrollable view, such as a long web page or e-mail message, and the view will scroll, up and down, along with your fingers.

In this chapter, we're going to look at the underlying architecture that lets you detect gestures. You'll learn how to detect the most common ones and learn how to create and detect a completely new gesture.

Multitouch Terminology

Before we dive into the architecture, let's go over some basic vocabulary. First, a **gesture** is any sequence of events that happens from the time you touch the screen with one or more fingers until you lift your fingers off the screen. No matter how long it takes, as long as one or more fingers are still against the screen, you are still within a gesture (unless a system event, such as an incoming phone call, interrupts it). A gesture is passed through the system inside an **event**. Events are generated when you interact with the iPhone's multitouch screen and contain information about the touch or touches that occurred.

The term **touch**, obviously, refers to a finger being placed on the iPhone's screen. The number of touches involved in a gesture is equal to the number of fingers on the screen at the same time. You can actually put all five fingers on the screen, and as long as they aren't too close to each other, iPhone can recognize and track them all. Now, there aren't many useful five-finger gestures, but it's nice to know the iPhone can handle one if it needs to.

A **tap** happens when you touch the screen with a single finger and then immediately lift your finger off the screen without moving it around. The iPhone keeps track of the number of taps and can tell you if the user double-tapped or triple-tapped or even 20-tapped. It handles all the timing and other work necessary to differentiate between two single-taps and a double-tap, for example. It's important to note that the iPhone only keeps track of taps when one finger is used. If it detects multiple touches, it resets the tap count to one.

The Responder Chain

Since gestures get passed through the system inside of events, and events get passed through the **responder chain**, you need to have an understanding of how the responder chain works in order to handle gestures properly. If you've worked with Cocoa for Mac OS X, you're probably familiar with the concept of a responder chain, as the same basic mechanism is used in both Cocoa and Cocoa Touch. If this is new material, don't worry; we'll explain how it works.

Several times in this book, we've mentioned the first responder, which is usually the object with which the user is currently interacting. The first responder is the start of the responder chain. There are other responders as well. Any class that has UIResponder as one of its superclasses is a **responder**. UIView is a subclass of UIResponder and UIControl is a subclass of UIView, so all views and all controls are responders. UIViewController is also a subclass of UIResponder, meaning that it is a responder, as are all of its subclasses like UINavigationController and UITabBarController. Responders, then, are so named because they respond to system-generated events, such as screen touches.

If the first responder doesn't handle a particular event, such as a gesture, it passes that event up the responder chain. If the next object in the chain responds to that particular event, it will usually consume the event, which stops the event's progression through the responder chain. In some cases, if a responder only partially handles an event, that responder will take an action and forward the event to the next responder in the chain. That's not usually what happens, though. Normally, when an object responds to an event, that's the end of the line for the event. If the event goes through the entire responder chain and no object handles the event, the event is then discarded.

Here's another, more specific look at the responder chain. The first responder is almost always a view or control and gets the first shot at responding to an event. If the first responder doesn't handle the event, it passes the event to its view controller. If the view controller doesn't consume the event, the event is then passed to the first responder's parent view. If the parent view doesn't respond, the event will go to the parent view's controller, if it has one. The event will proceed up the view hierarchy, with each view and then that view's controller getting a chance to handle the event. If the event makes it all the way up through the view hierarchy, the event is passed to the application's window. If the window doesn't handle the event, it passes that event to our application's `UIApplication` object instance. If `UIApplication` doesn't respond to it, the event goes gently into that good night.

This process is important for a number of reasons. First, it controls the way gestures can be handled. Let's say a user is looking at a table and swipes a finger across a row of that table. What object handles that gesture?

If the swipe is within a view or control that's a subview of the table view cell, that view or control will get a chance to respond. If it doesn't, the table view cell gets a chance. In an application like Mail, where a swipe can be used to delete a message, the table view cell probably needs to look at that event to see if it contains a swipe gesture. Most table view cells don't respond to gestures, however, and if they don't, the event proceeds up to the table view, then up the rest of the responder chain until something responds to that event or it reaches the end of the line.

Forwarding an Event: Keeping the Responder Chain Alive

Let's take a step back to that table view cell in the Mail application. We don't know the internal details of Apple's Mail application, but let's assume, for the nonce, that the table view cell handles the delete swipe and only the delete swipe. That table view cell has to implement the methods related to receiving touch events (which you'll see in a few minutes) so that it can check to see if that event contained a swipe gesture. If the event contains a swipe, then the table view cell takes an action, and that's that; the event goes no further.

If the event doesn't contain a swipe gesture, the table view cell is responsible for forwarding that event manually to the next object in the responder chain. If it doesn't do its forwarding job, the table and other objects up the chain will never get a chance to respond, and the application may not function as the user expects. That table view cell could prevent other views from recognizing a gesture.

Whenever you respond to a touch event, you have to keep in mind that your code doesn't work in a vacuum. If an object intercepts an event that it doesn't handle, it needs to pass it along manually, by calling the same method on the next responder. Here's a bit of fictional code:

```
-(void)respondToFictionalEvent:(UIEvent *)event {
    if (someCondition)
        [self handleEvent:event];
    else
        [self.nextResponder respondToFictionalEvent:event];
}
```

Notice how we call the same method on the next responder. That's how to be a good responder chain citizen. Fortunately, most of the time, methods that respond to an event also consume the event, but it's important to know that if that's not the case, you have to make sure the event gets pushed back into the responder chain.

The Multitouch Architecture

Now that you know a little about the responder chain, let's look at the process of handling gestures. As we've indicated, gestures get passed along the responder chain, embedded in events. That means that the code to handle any kind of interaction with the multitouch screen needs to be contained in an object in the responder chain. Generally, that means we can either choose to embed that code in a subclass of UIView or embed the code in a UIViewController.

So does this code belong in the view or in the view controller?

If the view needs to do something to itself based on the user's touches, the code probably belongs in the class that defines that view. For example, many control classes, such as UISwitch and UISlider, respond to touch-related events. A UISwitch might want to turn itself on or off based on a touch. The folks who created the UISwitch class embedded gesture-handling code in the class so the UISwitch can respond to a touch.

Often, however, when the gesture being processed affects more than the object being touched, the gesture code really belongs in the view's controller class. For example, if the user makes a gesture touching one row that indicates that all rows should be deleted, the gesture should be handled by code in the view controller. The way you respond to touches and gestures in both situations is exactly the same, regardless of the class to which the code belongs.

The Four Gesture Notification Methods

There are four methods used to notify a responder about touches and gestures. When the user first touches the screen, the iPhone looks for a responder that has a method called touchesBegan:withEvent:. To find out when the user first begins a gesture or taps the screen, implement this method in your view or your view controller. Here's an example of what that method might look like:

```
- (void)touchesBegan:(NSSet *)touches withEvent:(UIEvent *)event {

    NSUInteger numTaps = [[touches anyObject] tapCount];
    NSUInteger numTouches = [touches count];

    // Do something here.
}
```

This method, and all of the touch-related methods, gets passed an NSSet instance called touches and an instance of UIEvent. You can determine the number of fingers currently pressed against the screen by getting a count of the objects in touches. Every object in touches is a UITouch event that represents one finger touching the screen. If this touch is part of a series of taps, you can find out the tap count by asking any of the UITouch objects. Of course, if there's more than one object in touches, you know the tap count has to be one, because the system keeps tap counts only as long as just one finger is being used to tap the screen. In the preceding example, if numTouches is 2, you know the user just double-tapped the screen.

All of the objects in touches may not be relevant to the view or view controller where you've implemented this method. A table view cell, for example, probably doesn't care about touches that are in other rows or that are in the navigation bar. You can get a subset of touches that has only those touches that fall within a particular view from the event, like so:

```
NSSet *myTouches = [event touchesForView:self.view];
```

Every UITouch represents a different finger, and each finger is located at a different position on the screen. You can find out the position of a specific finger using the UITouch object. It will even translate the point into the view's local coordinate system if you ask it to, like this:

```
CGPoint point = [touch locationInView:self];
```

You can get notified while the user is moving fingers across the screen by implementing touchesMoved:withEvent:. This method gets called multiple times during a long drag, and each time it gets called, you will get another set of touches and another event. In addition to being able to find out each finger's current position from the UITouch objects, you can also find out the previous location of that touch, which is the finger's position the last time either touchesMoved:withEvent: or touchesBegan:withEvent: was called.

When the user's fingers are removed from the screen, another event, touchesEnded: withEvent:, is invoked. When this method gets called, you know that the user is done with a gesture.

There's one final touch-related method that responders might implement. It's called touchesCancelled:withEvent:, and it gets called if the user is in the middle of a gesture when something happens to interrupt it, like the phone ringing. This is where you can do any cleanup you might need so you can start fresh with a new gesture. When this method is called, touchesEnded:withEvent: will not get called for the current gesture.

OK, enough theory—let's see some of this in action.

The Touch Explorer Application

We're going to build a little application that will give you a better feel for when the four touch-related responder methods get called. In Xcode, create a new project using the view-based application template, and call the new project TouchExplorer. TouchExplorer will print messages to the screen, containing the touch and tap count, every time a touch-related method gets called (see Figure 13-1).

NOTE

> Although the applications in this chapter will run on the simulator, you won't be able to see all of the available multitouch functionality unless you run them on an iPhone or iPod Touch. If you've been accepted into the iPhone Developer Program, you have the ability to run the programs you write on your device of choice. The Apple web site does a great job of walking you through the process of getting everything you need to prepare to connect Xcode to your device.

Figure 13-1. *The Touch Explorer application*

We need three labels for this application: one to indicate which method was last called, another to report the current tap count, and a third to report the number of touches. Single-click *TouchExplorerViewController.h*, and add three outlets and a method declaration. The method will be used to update the labels from multiple places.

```
#import <UIKit/UIKit.h>

@interface TouchExplorerViewController : UIViewController {
    UILabel     *messageLabel;
    UILabel     *tapsLabel;
    UILabel     *touchesLabel;
}
@property (nonatomic, retain) IBOutlet UILabel *messageLabel;
@property (nonatomic, retain) IBOutlet UILabel *tapsLabel;
@property (nonatomic, retain) IBOutlet UILabel *touchesLabel;
- (void)updateLabelsFromTouches:(NSSet *)touches;
@end
```

Now, double-click *TouchExplorerViewController.xib* to open the file in Interface Builder. If the window titled *View* is not open, double-click the *View* icon to open it. Drag three *Labels* from the library to the *View* window. You should resize the labels so that they take up the full width of the view and center the text, but the exact placement of the labels doesn't matter. You can also play with the fonts and colors if you're feeling a bit Picasso. When you're done placing them, double-click each label, and press the delete key to get rid of the text that's in them.

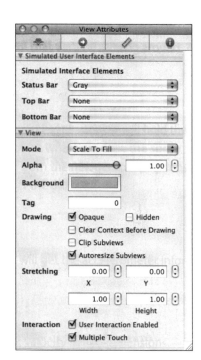

Control-drag from the *File's Owner* icon to each of the three labels, connecting one to the *messageLabel* outlet, another to the *tapsLabel* outlet, and the last one to the *touchesLabel* outlet. Finally, single-click the *View* icon, and press ⌘1 to bring up the attributes inspector (see Figure 13-2). On the inspector, make sure that both *User Interacting Enabled* and *Multiple Touch* are checked. If *Multiple Touch* is not checked, your controller class's touch methods will always receive one and only one touch no matter how many fingers are actually touching the phone's screen.

Figure 13-2. *Making sure that the view is set to receive multitouch events*

When you're done, save and close the nib, and head back to Xcode.

Single-click *TouchExplorerViewController.m*, and add the following code at the beginning of the file:

```
#import "TouchExplorerViewController.h"

@implementation TouchExplorerViewController
@synthesize messageLabel;
@synthesize tapsLabel;
@synthesize touchesLabel;

- (void)updateLabelsFromTouches:(NSSet *)touches {
    NSUInteger numTaps = [[touches anyObject] tapCount];
    NSString *tapsMessage = [[NSString alloc]
        initWithFormat:@"%d taps detected", numTaps];
    tapsLabel.text = tapsMessage;
    [tapsMessage release];

    NSUInteger numTouches = [touches count];
    NSString *touchMsg = [[NSString alloc] initWithFormat:
        @"%d touches detected", numTouches];
    touchesLabel.text = touchMsg;
    [touchMsg release];
}
...
```

Then insert the following lines of code into the existing viewDidUnload and dealloc
methods:

```
...
- (void)viewDidUnload {
    // Release any retained subviews of the main view.
    // e.g. self.myOutlet = nil;
    self.messageLabel = nil;
    self.tapsLabel = nil;
    self.touchesLabel = nil;
    [super viewDidUnload];
}
- (void)dealloc {
    [messageLabel release];
    [tapsLabel release];
    [touchesLabel release];
    [super dealloc];
}
...
```

And add the following new methods at the end of the file:

```
...
#pragma mark -
- (void)touchesBegan:(NSSet *)touches withEvent:(UIEvent *)event {
    messageLabel.text = @"Touches Began";
```

```
    [self updateLabelsFromTouches:touches];

}
- (void)touchesCancelled:(NSSet *)touches withEvent:(UIEvent *)event{
    messageLabel.text = @"Touches Cancelled";
    [self updateLabelsFromTouches:touches];
}
- (void)touchesEnded:(NSSet *)touches withEvent:(UIEvent *)event {
    messageLabel.text = @"Touches Stopped.";
    [self updateLabelsFromTouches:touches];
}
- (void)touchesMoved:(NSSet *)touches withEvent:(UIEvent *)event {
    messageLabel.text = @"Drag Detected";
    [self updateLabelsFromTouches:touches];
}
@end
```

In this controller class, we implement all four of the touch-related methods we discussed earlier. Each one sets messageLabel so the user can see when each method gets called. Next, all four of them call updateLabelsFromTouches: to update the other two labels. The updateLabelsFromTouches: method gets the tap count from one of the touches, figures out the number of touches by looking at the count of the touches set, and updates the labels with that information.

Compile and run the application. If you're running in the simulator, try repeatedly clicking the screen to drive up the tap count, and try clicking and holding down the mouse button while dragging around the view to simulate a touch and drag. You can emulate a two-finger pinch in the iPhone simulator by holding down the option key while you click with the mouse and drag. You can also simulate two-finger swipes by first holding down the option key to simulate a pinch, then moving the mouse so the two dots representing virtual fingers are next to each other, and then holding down the shift key (while still holding down the option key). Pressing the shift key will lock the position of the two fingers relative to each other, and you can do swipes and other two-finger gestures. You won't be able to do gestures that require three or more fingers, but you can do most two-finger gestures on the simulator using combinations of the option and shift keys.

If you're able to run this program on your iPhone or iPod touch, see how many touches you can get to register at the same time. Try dragging with one finger, then two fingers, then three. Try double- and triple-tapping the screen, and see if you can get the tap count to go up by tapping with two fingers.

Play around with the TouchExplorer application until you feel comfortable with what's happening and with the way that the four touch methods work. Once you're ready, let's look at how to detect one of the most common gestures, the swipe.

The Swipes Application

Create a new project in Xcode using the view-based application template again, this time naming the project Swipes.
The application we're about to build does nothing more
than detect swipes, both horizontal and vertical (see Figure
13-3). If you swipe your finger across the screen from left to
right, right to left, top to bottom, or bottom to top, Swipes
will display a message across the top of the screen for a few
seconds informing you that a swipe was detected.

Detecting swipes is relatively easy. We're going to define a
minimum gesture length in pixels, which is how far the user
has to swipe before the gesture counts as a swipe. We'll also
define a variance, which is how far from a straight line our
user can veer and still have the gesture count as a horizontal or vertical swipe. A diagonal line generally won't count
as a swipe, but one that's just a little off from horizontal or
vertical will.

When the user touches the screen, we'll save the location of
the first touch in a variable. Then, we'll check as the user's
finger moves across the screen to see if it reaches a point
where it has gone far enough and straight enough to count
as a swipe. Let's build it.

Figure 13-3. *The Swipes
application*

Click *SwipesViewController.h*, and add the following code:

```
#import <UIKit/UIKit.h>

#define kMinimumGestureLength       25
#define kMaximumVariance            5

@interface SwipesViewController : UIViewController {
    UILabel     *label;
    CGPoint     gestureStartPoint;
}
@property (nonatomic, retain) IBOutlet UILabel *label;
@property CGPoint gestureStartPoint;
- (void)eraseText;
@end
```

We start by defining a minimum gesture length of 25 pixels and a variance of 5. If the user
was doing a horizontal swipe, the gesture could end up 5 pixels above or below the starting
vertical position and still count as a swipe as long as the user moved 25 pixels horizontally.

In a real application, you would probably have to play with these numbers a bit to find what worked best for your application.

We also declare an outlet for our one label and a variable to hold the first spot the user touches. The last thing we do is declare a method that will be used to erase the text after a few seconds.

Double-click *SwipesViewController.xib* to open it in Interface Builder. Make sure that the view is set to receive multiple touches using the attributes inspector, and drag a *Label* from the library and drop it on the *View* window. Set up the label so it takes the entire width of the view from blue line to blue line, and feel free to play with the text attributes to make the label easier to read. Next, double-click the label and delete its text. Control-drag from the *File's Owner* icon to the label, and connect it to the label outlet. Save your nib, close, and go back to Xcode.

Single-click *SwipesViewController.m*, and add the following code at the top:

```
#import "SwipesViewController.h"

@implementation SwipesViewController
@synthesize label;
@synthesize gestureStartPoint;
- (void)eraseText {
    label.text = @"";
}
...
```

Insert the following lines of code into the existing dealloc and viewDidUnload methods:

```
...
- (void)viewDidUnload {
    // Release any retained subviews of the main view.
    // e.g. self.myOutlet = nil;
    self.label = nil;
}
- (void)dealloc {
    [label release];
    [super dealloc];
}
...
```

And add the following methods at the bottom of the class:

```
#pragma mark -
- (void)touchesBegan:(NSSet *)touches withEvent:(UIEvent *)event {

    UITouch *touch = [touches anyObject];
    gestureStartPoint = [touch locationInView:self.view];
```

```
}
- (void)touchesMoved:(NSSet *)touches withEvent:(UIEvent *)event {

    UITouch *touch = [touches anyObject];
    CGPoint currentPosition = [touch locationInView:self.view];

    CGFloat deltaX = fabsf(gestureStartPoint.x - currentPosition.x);
    CGFloat deltaY = fabsf(gestureStartPoint.y - currentPosition.y);

    if (deltaX >= kMinimumGestureLength && deltaY <= kMaximumVariance) {
        label.text = @"Horizontal swipe detected";
        [self performSelector:@selector(eraseText)
            withObject:nil afterDelay:2];
    }
    else if (deltaY >= kMinimumGestureLength &&
            deltaX <= kMaximumVariance){
        label.text = @"Vertical swipe detected";
        [self performSelector:@selector(eraseText) withObject:nil
            afterDelay:2];
    }
}
}
@end
```

Let's start with the touchesBegan:withEvent: method. All we do there is grab any touch from the touches set and store its point. We're primarily interested in single-finger swipes right now, so we don't worry about how many touches there are; we just grab one of them.

```
UITouch *touch = [touches anyObject];
gestureStartPoint = [touch locationInView:self.view];
```

In the next method, touchesMoved:withEvent:, we do the real work. First, we get the current position of the user's finger:

```
UITouch *touch = [touches anyObject];
CGPoint currentPosition = [touch locationInView:self.view];
```

After that, we calculate how far the user's finger has moved both horizontally and vertically from its starting position. The function fabsf() is from the standard C math library that returns the absolute value of a float. This allows us to subtract one from the other without having to worry about which is the higher value:

```
CGFloat deltaX = fabsf(gestureStartPoint.x - currentPosition.x);
CGFloat deltaY = fabsf(gestureStartPoint.y - currentPosition.y);
```

Once we have the two deltas, we check to see if the user has moved far enough in one direction without having moved too far in the other to constitute a swipe. If they have, we set the label's text to indicate whether a horizontal or vertical swipe was detected. We also use performSelector:withObject:afterDelay: to erase the text after it's been on the screen for 2 seconds. That way, the user can practice multiple swipes without having to worry if the label is referring to an earlier attempt or the most recent one:

```
    if (deltaX >= kMinimumGestureLength && deltaY <= kMaximumVariance) {
      label.text = @"Horizontal swipe detected";
      [self performSelector:@selector(eraseText)
          withObject:nil afterDelay:2];
    }
    else if (deltaY >= kMinimumGestureLength &&
          deltaX <= kMaximumVariance){
      label.text = @"Vertical swipe detected";
      [self performSelector:@selector(eraseText)
          withObject:nil afterDelay:2];
    }
```

Go ahead and compile and run. If you find yourself clicking and dragging with no visible results, be patient. Click and drag straight down or straight across until you get the hang of swiping.

Implementing Multiple Swipes

In the Swipes application, we only worried about single-finger swipes, so we just grabbed any object out of the touches set to figure out where the user's finger was during the swipe. This approach is fine if you're only interested in single-finger swipes, which is the most common type of swipe used.

We have a bit of a problem, however, if we want to implement two- or three-finger swipes. That problem is that we are provided the touches as an NSSet, not as an NSArray. Sets are unordered collections, which means that we have no easy way to figure out which finger is which when we do comparison. We can't assume that the first touch in the set, for example, is referring to the same finger that was the first touch in the set back when the gesture started.

To make matters worse, it's completely possible that, when the user does a two- or three-finger gesture, one finger will touch the screen before another, meaning that in the touchesBegan:withEvent: method, we might only get informed about one touch.

We need to find a way to detect a multiple-finger swipe without falsely identifying other gestures, such as pinches, as swipes. The solution is fairly straightforward. When touchesBegan:withEvent: gets notified that a gesture has begun, we save one finger's position just as we did before. No need to save all the finger positions. Any one of them will do.

When we check for swipes, we loop through all the touches provided to the `touchesMoved:` `withEvent:` method, comparing each one to the saved point. If the user did a multiple-finger swipe, when comparing to the saved point, at least one of the touches we get in that method will indicate a swipe. If we find either a horizontal or vertical swipe, we loop through the touches again and make sure that every finger is at least the minimum distance away from the first finger's horizontal or vertical position, depending on the type of swipe. Let's retrofit the Swipes application to detect multiple-finger swipes now.

Next, we need to make a minor change to the header file, so single-click *SwipesView Controller.h*, and add the following code:

```
#define kMinimumGestureLength    25
#define kMaximumVariance          5

typedef enum  {
    kNoSwipe = 0,
    kHorizontalSwipe,
    kVerticalSwipe
} SwipeType;

#import <UIKit/UIKit.h>
...
```

This enumeration will give us an easy way to indicate whether a gesture is a horizontal or vertical swipe or if no swipe was detected at all. Now, switch back to *SwipesViewController.m*, and completely replace the `touchesMoved:withEvent:` method with this new version:

```
- (void)touchesMoved:(NSSet *)touches withEvent:(UIEvent *)event {

    SwipeType swipeType = kNoSwipe;
    for (UITouch *touch in touches) {
            CGPoint currentPosition = [touch locationInView:self.view];

            CGFloat deltaX = fabsf(currentPosition.x-gestureStartPoint.x);
            CGFloat deltaY = fabsf(currentPosition.y-gestureStartPoint.y);

            if (deltaX >= kMinimumGestureLength &&
                deltaY <= kMaximumVariance)
                swipeType = kHorizontalSwipe;
            else if (deltaY >= kMinimumGestureLength &&
                deltaX <= kMaximumVariance)
                swipeType = kVerticalSwipe;
    }

    BOOL allFingersFarEnoughAway = YES;
    if (swipeType != kNoSwipe) {
```

```
        for (UITouch *touch in touches) {
            CGPoint currentPosition = [touch locationInView:self.view];

            CGFloat distance;
            if (swipeType == kHorizontalSwipe)
                distance = fabsf(currentPosition.x - gestureStartPoint.x);
            else
                distance = fabsf(currentPosition.y - gestureStartPoint.y);

            if (distance < kMinimumGestureLength)
                allFingersFarEnoughAway = NO;
        }
    }
    if (allFingersFarEnoughAway && swipeType != kNoSwipe {
        NSString *swipeCountString = nil;
        if ([touches count] == 2)
            swipeCountString = @"Double ";
        else if ([touches count] == 3)
            swipeCountString = @"Triple ";
        else if ([touches count] == 4)
            swipeCountString = @"Quadruple ";
        else if ([touches count] == 5)
            swipeCountString = @"Quintuple ";
        else
            swipeCountString = @"";

        NSString *swipeTypeString = (swipeType == kHorizontalSwipe) ?
            @"Horizontal" : @"Vertical";

        NSString *message = [[NSString alloc] initWithFormat:
            @"%@%@ Swipe Detected.", swipeCountString, swipeTypeString];
        label.text = message;
        [message release];
        [self performSelector:@selector(eraseText)
            withObject:nil afterDelay:2];
    }
}
```

Compile and run. You should be able to trigger double and triple swipes in both directions and should still be able to trigger single swipes. If you have small fingers, you might even be able to trigger a quadruple or quintuple swipe.

With a multiple-finger swipe, one thing to be careful of is that your fingers aren't too close to each other. If two fingers are very close to each other, they may register as only a single touch. Because of this, you shouldn't rely on quadruple or quintuple swipes for any important gestures, because many people will have fingers that are too big to do those swipes effectively.

Detecting Multiple Taps

In the TouchExplorer application, we printed the tap count to the screen, so you've already seen how easy it is to detect multiple taps. It's not quite as straightforward as it seems, however, because often you will want to take different actions based on the number of taps. If the user triple-taps, you get notified three separate times. You get a single-tap, a double-tap, and finally a triple-tap. If you want to do something on a double-tap but something completely different on a triple-tap, having three separate notifications could cause a problem. Let's create another application to illustrate and then solve that problem.

Figure 13-4. *The TapTaps application detecting all tap types simultaneously*

In Xcode, create a new project with the view-based application template. Call this new project TapTaps. This application is going to have four labels, one each that informs us when it has detected a single-tap, double-tap, triple-tap, and quadruple tap. In the first version of the application, all four fields will work independently, so if you tap four times, you'll get notified of all four tap types (see Figure 13-4).

Once we get that first version working, we'll see how to change its behavior so only one label appears when the user stops tapping, showing the total number of user taps.

We need outlets for the four labels, and we also need separate methods for each tap scenario to simulate what you'd have in a real application. We'll also include a method for erasing the text fields. Expand the *Classes* folder, single-click *TapTapsViewController.h*, and make the following changes:

```
#import <UIKit/UIKit.h>

@interface TapTapsViewController : UIViewController {
    UILabel *singleLabel;
    UILabel *doubleLabel;
    UILabel *tripleLabel;
    UILabel *quadrupleLabel;
}
@property (nonatomic, retain) IBOutlet UILabel *singleLabel;
@property (nonatomic, retain) IBOutlet UILabel *doubleLabel;
@property (nonatomic, retain) IBOutlet UILabel *tripleLabel;
@property (nonatomic, retain) IBOutlet UILabel *quadrupleLabel;
- (void)singleTap;
- (void)doubleTap;
```

```
- (void)tripleTap;
- (void)quadrupleTap;
- (void)eraseMe:(UITextField *)textField ;
@end
```

Save it, and then expand the *Resources* folder. Double-click *TapTapsViewController.xib* to open the file in Interface Builder. Once you're there add four *Labels* to the view from the library. Make all four labels stretch from blue guide line to blue guide line, and then format them however you see fit. We chose to make each label a different color but that is, by no means, necessary. When you're done, make sure you double-click each label and press the delete key to get rid of any text. Now, control-drag from the *File's Owner* icon to each label, and connect each one to *singleLabel*, *doubleLabel*, *tripleLabel*, and *quadrupleLabel*, respectively. Once you've done that, you can save and go back to Xcode.

In *TapTapsViewController.m*, add the following code at the top of the file:

```
#import "TapTapsViewController.h"

@implementation TapTapsViewController
@synthesize singleLabel;
@synthesize doubleLabel;
@synthesize tripleLabel;
@synthesize quadrupleLabel;
- (void)singleTap {
    singleLabel.text = @"Single Tap Detected";
    [self performSelector:@selector(eraseMe:)
        withObject:singleLabel afterDelay:1.6f];
}
- (void)doubleTap {
    doubleLabel.text = @"Double Tap Detected";
    [self performSelector:@selector(eraseMe:)
        withObject:doubleLabel afterDelay:1.6f];
}
- (void)tripleTap {
    tripleLabel.text = @"Triple Tap Detected";
    [self performSelector:@selector(eraseMe:)
        withObject:tripleLabel afterDelay:1.6f];
}
- (void)quadrupleTap {
    quadrupleLabel.text = @"Quadruple Tap Detected";
    [self performSelector:@selector(eraseMe:)
        withObject:quadrupleLabel afterDelay:1.6f];
}
- (void)eraseMe:(UITextField *)textField {
    textField.text = @"";
}
...
```

Insert the following lines into the existing dealloc and viewDidUnload methods:

```
...
- (void)viewDidUnload {
     // Release any retained subviews of the main view.
    // e.g. self.myOutlet = nil;
    self.singleLabel = nil;
    self.doubleLabel = nil;
    self.tripleLabel = nil;
    self.quadrupleLabel = nil;
    [super viewDidUnload];
}
- (void)dealloc {
    [singleLabel release];
    [doubleLabel release];
    [tripleLabel release];
    [quadrupleLabel release];
    [super dealloc];
}
```

Now, add the following code at the bottom of the file:

```
...
#pragma mark -
- (void)touchesBegan:(NSSet *)touches withEvent:(UIEvent *)event {
    UITouch *touch = [touches anyObject];
    NSUInteger tapCount = [touch tapCount];
    switch (tapCount) {
        case 1:
            [self singleTap];
            break;
        case 2:
            [self doubleTap];
            break;
        case 3:
            [self tripleTap];
            break;
        case 4:
            [self quadrupleTap];
            break;
        default:
            break;
    }
}
@end
```

The four tap methods do nothing more in this application than set one of the four labels and use `performSelector:withObject:afterDelay:` to erase that same label after 1.6 seconds. The `eraseMe:` method erases any label that is passed into it.

Down in `touchesBegan:withEvent:`, we call the four tap methods whenever we detect the appropriate number of taps. That's easy enough, so compile and run. If you double-tap, you'll see two labels displayed. If you quadruple-tap, you'll see four labels. In some situations, this might be OK, but usually, you want to take actions based on the number of taps that the user ended up doing.

Notice, that we don't implement `touchesEnded:withEvent:` or `touchesMoved:withEvent:` in this program. We don't get notified that the user has stopped tapping, which creates a bit of a conundrum for us. Fortunately, there's an easy way to handle it. You're already familiar with the method `performSelector:withObject:afterDelay:`, which allows us to call a method at some point in the future. There's another method that allows us to cancel those future calls before they execute. It's an NSObject class method called `cancelPreviousPerf ormRequestsWithTarget:selector:object:`. This method will stop any pending perform requests that match the arguments passed into it, and it will help us solve our tap conundrum. In *TapTapsViewController.m*, replace the `touchesBegan:withEvent:` method with this new version:

```
- (void)touchesBegan:(NSSet *)touches withEvent:(UIEvent *)event {
    UITouch *touch = [touches anyObject];
    NSUInteger tapCount = [touch tapCount];

    switch (tapCount) {
        case 1:
            [self performSelector:@selector(singleTap)
                        withObject:nil
                        afterDelay:.4];
            break;
        case 2:
            [NSObject cancelPreviousPerformRequestsWithTarget:self
                        selector:@selector(singleTap)
                        object:nil];
            [self performSelector:@selector(doubleTap)
                        withObject:nil
                        afterDelay:.4];
            break;
        case 3:
            [NSObject cancelPreviousPerformRequestsWithTarget:self
                        selector:@selector(doubleTap)
                        object:nil];
            [self performSelector:@selector(tripleTap)
                        withObject:nil
                        afterDelay:.4];
```

```
                    break;
            case 4:
                [NSObject cancelPreviousPerformRequestsWithTarget:self
                                selector:@selector(tripleTap)
                                object:nil];
                [self quadrupleTap];
                break;
            default:
                break;
        }
    }
}
```

In this version, every time we detect a number of taps, instead of calling the corresponding method immediately, we use `performSelector:withObject:afterDelay:` to call it four-tenths of a second in the future, and we cancel the perform request done by our method when the previous tap count was received. So, when we receive one tap, we call the `singleTap` method four-tenths of a second in the future. When we receive notification of a double-tap, we cancel the call to `singleTap` and call `doubleTap` four-tenths of a second in the future. We do the same thing with triple-taps and quadruple-taps so that only one of the four methods gets called for any particular tap sequence.

Compile and run this version, and when you double-, triple-, or quadruple-tap, you should only see one label displayed.

Detecting Pinches

Another common gesture is the two-finger pinch. It's used in a number of applications, including Mobile Safari, Mail, and Photos to let you zoom in (if you pinch apart) or zoom out (if you pinch together).

Detecting pinches is pretty easy. First, when the gesture begins, we check to make sure there are two touches, because pinches are two-finger gestures. If there are two, we store the distance between them. Then, as the gesture progresses, we keep checking the distance between the user's fingers, and if the distance increases or decreases more than a certain amount, we know there's been a pinch.

Create a new project in Xcode, again using the view-based application template, and call this one *PinchMe*. In this project and the next one, we're going to need to do some fairly standard analytic geometry to calculate such things as the distance between two points (in this project) and later the angle between two lines. Don't worry if you don't remember much geometry, we've provided you with functions that will do the calculations for you. Look in the *13 PinchMe* folder for two files, named *CGPointUtils.h* and *CGPointUtils.c*. Drag both of these to the *Classes* folder of your project. Feel free to use these utility functions in your own applications.

The PinchMe application is only going to need a single outlet for a label, but it also needs an instance variable to hold the starting distance between the fingers and, as with the previous applications, a method for erasing the label. We also will define a constant that identifies the minimum change in distance between the fingers that constitutes a pinch. Expand the *Classes* folder, single-click *PinchMeViewController.h*, and make the following changes:

```
#import <UIKit/UIKit.h>

#define kMinimumPinchDelta 100
@interface PinchMeViewController : UIViewController {
    UILabel *label;
    CGFloat initialDistance;
}
@property (nonatomic, retain) IBOutlet UILabel *label;
@property CGFloat initialDistance;
- (void)eraseLabel;
@end
```

Now that we have our outlet, expand the *Resources* folder, and double-click *PinchMeView-Controller.xib*. In Interface Builder, make sure the view is set to accept multiple touches (check the *Multiple Touch* checkbox on the attributes inspector), and drag a single label over to it. You can place, size, and format the label any way you want. When you're done with it, double-click the label, and delete the text it contains. Next, control-drag from the *File's Owner* icon to the label, and connect it to the *label* outlet. Save and close the nib, and go back to Xcode.

In *PinchMeViewController.m*, add the following code at the top of the file:

```
#import "PinchMeViewController.h"
#import "CGPointUtils.h"

@implementation PinchMeViewController
@synthesize label;
@synthesize initialDistance;
- (void)eraseLabel {
    label.text = @"";
}
...
```

Clean up our outlet in the `dealloc` and `viewDidUnload` methods:

```
...
- (void)viewDidUnload {
    // Release any retained subviews of the main view.
    // e.g. self.myOutlet = nil;
    self.label = nil;
```

```
        [super viewDidUnload];
}

- (void)dealloc {
    [label release];
    [super dealloc];
}
...
```

And add the following method at the end of the file:

```
...
#pragma mark -
- (void)touchesBegan:(NSSet *)touches withEvent:(UIEvent *)event {
    if ([touches count] == 2) {
        NSArray *twoTouches = [touches allObjects];
        UITouch *first = [twoTouches objectAtIndex:0];
        UITouch *second = [twoTouches objectAtIndex:1];
        initialDistance = distanceBetweenPoints(
            [first locationInView:self.view],
            [second locationInView:self.view]);
    }
}

- (void)touchesMoved:(NSSet *)touches withEvent:(UIEvent *)event {

    if ([touches count] == 2) {
        NSArray *twoTouches = [touches allObjects];
        UITouch *first = [twoTouches objectAtIndex:0];
        UITouch *second = [twoTouches objectAtIndex:1];
        CGFloat currentDistance = distanceBetweenPoints(
            [first locationInView:self.view],
            [second locationInView:self.view]);

        if (initialDistance == 0)
            initialDistance = currentDistance;
        else if (currentDistance - initialDistance > kMinimumPinchDelta) {
            label.text = @"Outward Pinch";
            [self performSelector:@selector(eraseLabel)
                        withObject:nil
                        afterDelay:1.6f];
        }
        else if (initialDistance - currentDistance > kMinimumPinchDelta) {
            label.text = @"Inward Pinch";
            [self performSelector:@selector(eraseLabel)
                        withObject:nil
                        afterDelay:1.6f];
        }
```

```
        }
    }

- (void)touchesEnded:(NSSet *)touches withEvent:(UIEvent *)event {
    initialDistance = 0;
}
```

@end

In the `touchesBegan:withEvent:` method, we check to see if this touch involves two fingers. If there are, we figure out the distance between the two points using a method from *CGPointUtils.c* and store the result in the instance variable `initialDistance`.

In `touchesMoved:withEvent:`, we again check to see if we have two touches, and if we do, we calculate the distance between the two touches:

```
    if ([touches count] == 2) {
        NSArray *twoTouches = [touches allObjects];
        UITouch *first = [twoTouches objectAtIndex:0];
        UITouch *second = [twoTouches objectAtIndex:1];
        CGFloat currentDistance = distanceBetweenPoints(
            [first locationInView:self.view],
            [second locationInView:self.view]);
```

The next thing we do is check to see if `initialDistance` is 0. We do this because it is possible for the user's fingers to hit the screen at different times, so it's possible that `touchesBegan:withEvent:` didn't get called with two fingers. If `initialDistance` is 0, this is the first point where both fingers are against the screen, and we store the current distance between the points as the initial distance:

```
    if (initialDistance == 0)
        initialDistance = currentDistance;
```

Otherwise, we check to see if the initial distance subtracted from the current distance is more than the amount we've defined as the minimum change needed to count as a pinch. If so, we have an outward pinch, because the distance now is greater than the initial distance:

```
    else if (currentDistance - initialDistance > kMinimumPinchDelta) {
        label.text = @"Outward Pinch";
        [self performSelector:@selector(eraseLabel)
                    withObject:nil
                    afterDelay:1.6f];
    }
```

If not, we do another check for an inward pinch by looking to see if initial distance minus the current distance is enough to qualify as a pinch:

```
    else if (initialDistance - currentDistance > kMinimumPinchDelta) {
        label.text = @"Inward Pinch";
        [self performSelector:@selector(eraseLabel)
                        withObject:nil
                        afterDelay:1.6f];
    }
```

And that's all there is to pinch detection. Compile and run to give it a try. If you're on the simulator, remember that you can simulate a pinch by holding down the option key and clicking and dragging in the simulator window using your mouse.

Defining Custom Gestures

You've now seen how to detect the most commonly used iPhone gestures. The real fun begins when you start defining your own, custom gestures!

Defining a custom gesture is tricky. You've already mastered the basic mechanism, and that wasn't too difficult. The tricky part is being flexible when defining what constitutes a gesture. Most people are not precise when they use gestures. Remember the variance we used when we implemented the swipe so that even a swipe that wasn't perfectly horizontal or vertical still counted? That's a perfect example of the subtlety you need to add to your own gesture definitions. If you define your gesture too strictly, it will be useless. If you define it too generically, you'll get too many false positives, which will frustrate the user. In a sense, defining a custom gesture can be hard because you have to be precise about a gesture's imprecision. If you try to capture a complex gesture like, say, a figure eight, the math behind detecting the gesture is also going to get quite complex.

In our sample, we're going to define a gesture shaped like a checkmark (see Figure 13-5).

Figure 13-5. *An illustration of our checkmark gesture*

What are the defining properties of this checkmark gesture? Well, the principal one is that sharp change in angle between the two lines. We also want to make sure that the user's finger has traveled a little distance in a straight line before it makes that sharp angle. In Figure 13-5, the legs of the checkmark meet at an acute angle, just under 90 degrees. A gesture that required exactly an 85-degree angle would be awfully hard to get right, so we'll define a range of acceptable angles.

Create a new project in Xcode using the view-based application template, and call the project CheckPlease. We're going to need a function from CGPointUtils, so add *CGPointUtils.h* and *CGPointUtils.c* to this project's *Classes* folder.

Expand the *Classes* folder, single-click *CheckPleaseViewController.h*, and make the following changes:

```
#import <UIKit/UIKit.h>

#define kMinimumCheckMarkAngle    50
#define kMaximumCheckMarkAngle    135
#define kMinimumCheckMarkLength    10

@interface CheckPleaseViewController : UIViewController {
    UILabel      *label;
    CGPoint      lastPreviousPoint;
    CGPoint      lastCurrentPoint;
    CGFloat      lineLengthSoFar;
}
@property (nonatomic, retain) IBOutlet UILabel *label;
- (void)eraseLabel;
@end
```

You can see that we've defined a minimum angle of 50 degrees and a maximum angle of 135 degrees. This is a pretty broad range, and depending on your needs, you might decide to restrict the angle. We experimented a bit with this and found that our practice checkmark gestures fell into a fairly broad range, which is why we chose a relatively large tolerance here. We were somewhat sloppy with our checkmark gestures, and so we expect that at least some of our users will be as well.

Next, we define an outlet to a label that we'll use to inform the user when we've detected a checkmark gesture. We also declare three variables, lastPreviousPoint, lastCurrentPoint, and lineLengthSoFar. Each time we're notified of a touch, we're given the previous touch point and the current touch point. Those two points define a line segment. The next touch adds another segment. We store the previous touch's previous and current points in lastPreviousPoint and lastCurrentPoint, which gives us the previous line segment. We can then compare that line segment to the current touch's line segment. Comparing these two line segments can tell us if we're still drawing a single line or if there's a sharp enough angle between the two segments that we're actually drawing a checkmark.

Remember, every UITouch object knows its current position in the view, as well as its previous position in the view. In order to compare angles, however, we need to know the line that the previous two points made, so we need to store the current and previous points from the last time the user touched the screen. We'll use these two variables to store those two values each time this method gets called, so that we have the ability to compare the current line to the previous line and check the angle.

We also declare a variable to keep a running count of how far the user has dragged the finger. If the finger hasn't traveled at least 10 pixels (the value in kMinimumCheckMarkLength), whether the angle falls in the correct range doesn't matter. If we didn't require this distance, we would receive a lot of false positives.

Expand the *Resources* folder, and double-click *CheckPleaseViewController.xib* to open Interface Builder. Since this is a single-finger gesture, you don't need to turn on multitouch support for the view, just add a *Label* from the library and set it up the way you want it to look. Double-click the label to delete its text, and control-drag from the *File's Owner* icon to that label to connect it to the *label* outlet. Save the nib file. Now go back to Xcode, single-click *CheckPleaseViewController.m*, and add the following code to the top of the file:

```
#import "CheckPleaseViewController.h"
#import "CGPointUtils.h"

@implementation CheckPleaseViewController
@synthesize label;
- (void)eraseLabel {
    label.text = @"";
}
...
```

Add the following code to the existing viewDidUnload and dealloc methods:

```
...
- (void)viewDidUnload {
    // Release any retained subviews of the main view.
    // e.g. self.myOutlet = nil;
    self.label = nil;
    [super viewDidUnload];
}

- (void)dealloc {
    [label release];
    [super dealloc];
}
...
```

And add the following new methods at the bottom of the file:

```
...
#pragma mark -
- (void)touchesBegan:(NSSet *)touches withEvent:(UIEvent *)event {
    UITouch *touch = [touches anyObject];
```

```
        CGPoint point = [touch locationInView:self.view];
        lastPreviousPoint = point;
        lastCurrentPoint = point;
        lineLengthSoFar = 0.0f;
}
- (void)touchesMoved:(NSSet *)touches withEvent:(UIEvent *)event {

        UITouch *touch = [touches anyObject];
        CGPoint previousPoint = [touch previousLocationInView:self.view];
        CGPoint currentPoint = [touch locationInView:self.view];
        CGFloat angle = angleBetweenLines(lastPreviousPoint,
                                          lastCurrentPoint,
                                          previousPoint,
                                          currentPoint);

        if (angle >= kMinimumCheckMarkAngle&& angle <= kMaximumCheckMarkAngle
               && lineLengthSoFar > kMinimumCheckMarkLength) {
            label.text = @"Checkmark";
            [self performSelector:@selector(eraseLabel)
                withObject:nil afterDelay:1.6];
        }

        lineLengthSoFar += distanceBetweenPoints(previousPoint, currentPoint);
        lastPreviousPoint = previousPoint;
        lastCurrentPoint = currentPoint;
}
@end
```

The CheckPlease Touch Methods

Let's take a look at the touch methods. First, in touchesBegan:withEvent:, we determine
the point that the user is currently touching and store that value in lastPreviousPoint and
lastCurrentPoint. Since this method is called when a gesture begins, we know there is no
previous point to worry about, so we store the current point in both. We also reset the running line length count to 0.

Then, in touchesMoved:withEvent:, we calculate the angle between the line from the
current touch's previous position to its current position, and the line between the two
points stored in the lastPreviousPoint and lastCurrentPoint instance variables. Once
we have that angle, we check to see if it falls within our range of acceptable angles and
check to make sure that the user's finger has traveled far enough before making that sharp
turn. If both of those are true, we set the label to show that we've identified a checkmark
gesture. Next, we calculate the distance between the touch's position and its previous position, add that to lineLengthSoFar, and replace the values in lastPreviousPoint and

`lastCurrentPoint` with the two points from the current touch so we'll have them next time through this method.

Compile and run, and try out the gesture.

When defining new gestures for your own applications, make sure you test them thoroughly, and if you can, have other people test them for you as well. You want to make sure that your gesture is easy for the user to do, but not so easy that it gets triggered unintentionally. You also need to make sure that you don't conflict with other gestures used in your application. A single gesture should not count, for example, as both a custom gesture and a pinch.

Garçon? Check, Please!

Well, you should now understand the mechanism the iPhone uses to tell your application about touches, taps, and gestures. You also know how to detect the most commonly used iPhone gestures and even got a taste of how you might go about defining your own custom gestures. The iPhone's interface relies on gestures for much of its ease of use, so you'll want to have these techniques at the ready for most of your iPhone development.

When you're ready to move on, turn the page, and we'll tell you how to figure out where in the world you are using Core Location.

Chapter 14

Where Am I? Finding Your Way with Core Location

Your iPhone has the ability to determine where in the world it is using a framework called Core Location. There are actually three technologies that Core Location can leverage to do this: GPS, cell tower triangulation, and Wi-Fi Positioning Service (WPS). GPS is the most accurate of the three but is not available on first-generation iPhones. GPS reads microwave signals from multiple satellites to determine the current location. Cell tower triangulation determines the current location by doing a calculation based on the locations of the cell towers in the phone's range. Cell tower triangulation can be fairly accurate in cities and other areas with a high cell tower density but becomes less accurate in areas where there is a greater distance between towers. The last option, WPS, uses the IP address from iPhone's Wi-Fi connection to make a guess at your location by referencing a large database of known service providers and the areas they service. WPS is imprecise and can be off by many miles.

All three methods put a noticeable drain on iPhone's battery, so keep that in mind when using Core Location. Your application shouldn't poll for location any more often than is absolutely necessary. When using Core Location, you have the option of specifying a desired accuracy. By carefully specifying the absolute minimum accuracy level you need, you can prevent unnecessary battery drain.

The technologies that Core Location depends on are hidden from your application. We don't tell Core Location whether to use GPS, triangulation, or WPS.

We just tell it how accurate we would like it to be, and it will decide from the technologies available to it which is best for fulfilling your request.

The Location Manager

The Core Location API is actually fairly easy to work with. The main class we'll work with is `CLLocationManager`, usually referred to as the **Location Manager**. In order to interact with Core Location, we need to create an instance of the Location Manager, like this:

```
CLLocationManager *locationManager = [[CLLocationManager alloc] init];
```

This creates an instance of the Location Manager for us, but it doesn't actually start polling for our location. We have to assign a delegate to the Location Manager. The Location Manager will call delegate methods when location information becomes available or changes. The process of determining location may take some time, even a few seconds. The delegate must conform to the `CLLocationManagerDelegate` protocol.

Setting the Desired Accuracy

After you set the delegate, you also want to set the requested accuracy. As we said before, don't specify a degree of accuracy any greater than you absolutely need. If you're writing an application that just needs to know which state or country the phone is in, don't specify a high level of precision. Remember, the more accuracy you demand of Core Location, the more juice you're likely to use. Also, keep in mind that there is no guarantee that you will get the level of accuracy that you have requested.

Here's an example of setting the delegate and requesting a specific level of accuracy:

```
locationManager.delegate = self;
locationManager.desiredAccuracy = kCLLocationAccuracyBest;
```

The accuracy is set using a `CLLocationAccuracy` value, a type that's defined as a `double`. The value is in meters, so if you specify a `desiredAccuracy` of 10, you're telling Core Location that you want it to try to determine the current location within 10 meters, if possible. Specifying `kCLLocationAccuracyBest`, as we did previously, tells Core Location to use the most accurate method that's currently available. In addition to `kCLLocationAccuracyBest`, you can also use `kCLLocationAccuracyNearestTenMeters`, `kCLLocationAccuracyHundredMeters`, `kCLLocationAccuracyKilometer`, and `kCLLocationAccuracyThreeKilometers`.

Setting the Distance Filter

By default, the Location Manager will notify the delegate of any detected change in location. By specifying a **distance filter**, you are telling Location Manager not to notify you for every change and to notify you only when the location changes more than a certain amount. Setting up a distance filter can reduce the amount of polling that your application does. Distance filters are also set in meters. Specifying a distance filter of 1000 tells the Location Manager not to notify its delegate until the iPhone has moved at least 1,000 meters from its previously reported position. Here's an example:

```
locationManager.distanceFilter = 1000.0f;
```

If you ever want to return the Location Manager to the default setting of no filter, you can use the constant kCLDistanceFilterNone, like this:

```
locationManager.distanceFilter = kCLDistanceFilterNone;
```

Starting the Location Manager

When you're ready to start polling for location, you tell the Location Manager to start, and it will then go off and do its thing and then call a delegate method when it has determined the current location. Until you tell it to stop, it will continue to call your delegate method whenever it senses a change that exceeds the current distance filter. Here's how you start the Location Manager:

```
[locationManager startUpdatingLocation];
```

Using the Location Manager Wisely

If you need to determine the current location only and have no need to continuously poll for location, you should have your location delegate stop the Location Manager as soon as it gets the information your application needs. If you need to continuously poll, make sure you stop polling as soon as you possibly can. Remember, as long as you are getting updates from the Location Manager, you are putting a strain on the user's battery. To tell the Location Manager to stop sending updates to its delegate, call stopUpdatingLocation, like this:

```
[locationManager stopUpdatingLocation];
```

The Location Manager Delegate

The Location Manager delegate must conform to the CLLocationManagerDelegate proto-col, which defines two methods, both of which are optional. One of these methods is called by the Location Manager when it has determined the current location or when it detects a change in location. The other method is called when the Location Manager encounters an error.

Getting Location Updates

When the Location Manager wants to inform its delegate of the current location, it calls the `locationManager:didUpdateToLocation:fromLocation:` method. This method has three parameters. The first parameter is the Location Manager that called the method. The second is a `CLLocation` object that defines the current location of the iPhone, and the third is a `CLLocation` object that defines the previous location from the last update. The first time this method is called, the previous location object will be `nil`.

Getting Latitude and Longitude Using CLLocation

Location information is passed from the Location Manager using instances of the `CLLocation` class. This class has five properties that might be of interest to your application. The latitude and longitude are stored in a property called `coordinate`. To get the latitude and longitude in degrees, do this:

```
CLLocationDegrees latitude = theLocation.coordinate.latitude;
CLLocationDegrees longitude = theLocation.coordinate.longitude;
```

The `CLLocation` object can also tell you how confident the Location Manager is in its latitude and longitude calculations. The `horizontalAccuracy` property describes the radius of a circle with the `coordinate` as its center. The larger the value in `horizontalAccuracy`, the less certain Core Location is of the location. A very small radius indicates a high level of confidence in the determined location.

You can see a graphic representation of `horizontalAccuracy` in the Maps application (see Figure 14-1). The blue circle shown in Maps uses `horizontalAccuracy` for its radius when it detects your location. The Location Manager thinks you are at the center of that circle. If you're not, you're almost certainly somewhere inside the blue circle. A negative value in `horizontalAccuracy` is an indication that you cannot rely on the values in `coordinate` for some reason.

The `CLLocation` object also has a property called `altitude` that can tell you how many meters above or below sea level you are:

```
CLLocationDistance altitude = theLocation.➥
altitude;
```

Figure 14-1. *The Maps application uses Core Location to determine your current location. The blue circle is a visual representation of the horizontal accuracy.*

Each CLLocation object maintains a property called verticalAccuracy that is an indication of how confident Core Location is in its determination of altitude. The value in altitude could be off by as many meters as the value in verticalAccuracy, and if the verticalAccuracy value is negative, Core Location is telling you it could not determine a valid altitude.

CLLocation objects also have a timestamp that tells when the Location Manager made the location determination.

In addition to these properties, CLLocation also has a useful instance method that will let you determine the distance between two CLLocation objects. The method is called getDistanceFrom:, and it works like this:

```
CLLocationDistance distance = [fromLocation getDistanceFrom:toLocation];
```

The preceding line of code will return the distance between two CLLocation objects, fromLocation and toLocation. This distance value returned will be the result of a great-circle distance calculation that ignores the altitude property and calculates the distance as if both points were at sea level. For most purposes, a great-circle calculation will be more than sufficient, but if you do need to take altitude into account when calculating distances, you'll have to write your own code to do it.

Error Notifications

If Core Location is not able to determine your current location, it will call a second delegate method named locationManager:didFailWithError:. The most likely cause of an error is that the user denies access. Location Manager use has to be authorized by the user, so the first time your application goes to determine the location, an alert will pop up on the screen asking the user if it's OK for the current program to access your location (see Figure 14-2).

If the user clicks the *Don't Allow* button, your delegate will be notified of the fact by the Location Manager using the locationManager:didFailWithError: with an error code of kCLErrorDenied. At the time of this writing, the only other error code supported by Location Manager is kCLErrorLocationUnknown, which indicates that Core Location was unable to determine the location but that it will keep trying. The kCLErrorDenied error generally indicates that your application will not be able to access

Figure 14-2. *Location Manager access has to be approved by the user.*

Core Location any time during the remainder of the current session. On the other hand, kCLErrorLocationUnknown errors indicate a problem that may be temporary.

NOTE

> When working in the simulator, you will not be prompted for access to Core Location, and location will be determined using a super secret algorithm kept in a locked vault buried deep beneath Apple headquarters in Cupertino.

Trying Out Core Location

Let's build a small application to detect the iPhone's current location and the total distance traveled while the program has been running. You can see what our final application will look like in Figure 14-3.

Latitude:	37.3317°
Longitude:	-122.031°
Horizontal Accuracy:	100m
Altitude:	0m
Vertical Accuracy:	-1m
Distance Traveled:	0m

Figure 14-3. *The WhereAmI application in action. This screenshot was taken in the simulator. Notice that the vertical accuracy is a negative number, which tells us it couldn't determine the altitude.*

In Xcode, create a new project using the view-based application template, and call the project WhereAmI. Expand the *Classes* and *Resources* folders, and single-click *WhereAmIViewController.h*. Make the following changes, which we'll discuss in a moment:

```
#import <UIKit/UIKit.h>
#import <CoreLocation/CoreLocation.h>

@interface WhereAmIViewController :
    UIViewController <CLLocationManagerDelegate> {
    CLLocationManager      *locationManager;

    CLLocation             *startingPoint;

    UILabel *latitudeLabel;
    UILabel *longitudeLabel;
    UILabel *horizontalAccuracyLabel;
    UILabel *altitudeLabel;
    UILabel *verticalAccuracyLabel;
    UILabel *distanceTraveledLabel;
}
@property (retain, nonatomic) CLLocationManager *locationManager;
@property (retain, nonatomic) CLLocation *startingPoint;
@property (retain, nonatomic) IBOutlet UILabel *latitudeLabel;
@property (retain, nonatomic) IBOutlet UILabel *longitudeLabel;
@property (retain, nonatomic) IBOutlet UILabel *horizontalAccuracyLabel;
@property (retain, nonatomic) IBOutlet UILabel *altitudeLabel;
@property (retain, nonatomic) IBOutlet UILabel *verticalAccuracyLabel;
@property (retain, nonatomic) IBOutlet UILabel *distanceTraveledLabel;
@end
```

The first thing to notice is that we've included the Core Location header files. Core Location is not part of the UIKit, so we need to include the header files manually. Next, we conform this class to the CLLocationManagerDelegate method so that we can receive location information from the Location Manager.

After that, we declare a CLLocationManager pointer, which will be used to hold the instance of the Core Location we create. We also declare a pointer to a CLLocation, which we will set to the location we receive in the first update from the Location Manager. This way, if the user has our program running and moves far enough to trigger updates, we'll be able to calculate how far our user moved. Our delegate will be notified of the previous location with each call, but not the original starting location, which is why we store it.

The remaining instance variables are all outlets that will be used to update labels on the user interface.

Double-click *WhereAmIViewController.xib* to open Interface Builder. Using Figure 14-3 as your guide, drag 12 *Labels* from the library to the *View* window. Six of them should be placed on the left side of the screen, right justified, and made bold. Give the six bold labels the values *Latitude:*, *Longitude:*, *Horizontal Accuracy:*, *Altitude:*, *Vertical Accuracy:*, and *Distance Traveled:*. The other six should be left justified and placed next to each of the bold labels. Each of the labels on the right side should be connected to the appropriate outlet we defined in the header file earlier. Once you have all six attached to outlets, double-click each one in turn, and delete the text it holds. Save and go back to Xcode.

Single-click *WhereAmIViewController.m*, and make the following changes at the top of the file:

```
#import "WhereAmIViewController.h"

@implementation WhereAmIViewController
@synthesize locationManager;
@synthesize startingPoint;
@synthesize latitudeLabel;
@synthesize longitudeLabel;
@synthesize horizontalAccuracyLabel;
@synthesize altitudeLabel;
@synthesize verticalAccuracyLabel;
@synthesize distanceTraveledLabel;

#pragma mark -
- (void)viewDidLoad {
    self.locationManager = [[CLLocationManager alloc] init];
    locationManager.delegate = self;
    locationManager.desiredAccuracy = kCLLocationAccuracyBest;
    [locationManager startUpdatingLocation];
}
...
```

Insert the following lines in `viewDidUnload` and `dealloc` to clean up our outlets:

```
...
- (void)viewDidUnload {
    // Release any retained subviews of the main view.
    // e.g. self.myOutlet = nil;
    self.locationManager = nil;
    self.latitudeLabel = nil;
    self.longitudeLabel = nil;
    self.horizontalAccuracyLabel = nil;
    self.altitudeLabel = nil;
    self.verticalAccuracyLabel = nil;
    self.distanceTraveledLabel= nil;
    [super viewDidUnload];
}
- (void)dealloc {
    [locationManager release];
    [startingPoint release];
    [latitudeLabel release];
    [longitudeLabel release];
```

```
    [horizontalAccuracyLabel release];
    [altitudeLabel release];
    [verticalAccuracyLabel release];
    [distanceTraveledLabel release];
    [super dealloc];
}
...
```

And insert the following new methods at the end of the file:

```
...
#pragma mark -
#pragma mark CLLocationManagerDelegate Methods
- (void)locationManager:(CLLocationManager *)manager
        didUpdateToLocation:(CLLocation *)newLocation
        fromLocation:(CLLocation *)oldLocation {

    if (startingPoint == nil)
        self.startingPoint = newLocation;

    NSString *latitudeString = [[NSString alloc] initWithFormat:@"%g°",
            newLocation.coordinate.latitude];
    latitudeLabel.text = latitudeString;
    [latitudeString release];

    NSString *longitudeString = [[NSString alloc] initWithFormat:@"%g°",
            newLocation.coordinate.longitude];
    longitudeLabel.text = longitudeString;
    [longitudeString release];

    NSString *horizontalAccuracyString = [[NSString alloc]
        initWithFormat:@"%gm",
        newLocation.horizontalAccuracy];
    horizontalAccuracyLabel.text = horizontalAccuracyString;
    [horizontalAccuracyString release];

    NSString *altitudeString = [[NSString alloc] initWithFormat:@"%gm",
            newLocation.altitude];
    altitudeLabel.text = altitudeString;
    [altitudeString release];

    NSString *verticalAccuracyString = [[NSString alloc]
        initWithFormat:@"%gm",
        newLocation.verticalAccuracy];
    verticalAccuracyLabel.text = verticalAccuracyString;
    [verticalAccuracyString release];
```

```
        CLLocationDistance distance = [newLocation
            getDistanceFrom:startingPoint];
        NSString *distanceString = [[NSString alloc]
            initWithFormat:@"%gm", distance];
        distanceTraveledLabel.text = distanceString;
        [distanceString release];
    }


- (void)locationManager:(CLLocationManager *)manager
        didFailWithError:(NSError *)error {

        NSString *errorType = (error.code == kCLErrorDenied) ?
                @"Access Denied" : @"Unknown Error";
        UIAlertView *alert = [[UIAlertView alloc]
            initWithTitle:@"Error getting Location"
                  message:errorType
                 delegate:nil
        cancelButtonTitle:@"Okay"
        otherButtonTitles:nil];
        [alert show];
        [alert release];


    }
@end
```

In the `viewDidLoad` method, we allocate and initialize a `CLLocationManager` instance, assign our controller class as the delegate, set the desired accuracy to the best available, and then tell our Location Manager instance to start giving us location updates:

```
- (void)viewDidLoad {
    self.locationManager = [[CLLocationManager alloc] init];
    locationManager.delegate = self;
    locationManager.desiredAccuracy = kCLLocationAccuracyBest;
    [locationManager startUpdatingLocation];
}
```

Updating Location Manager

Since this class designated itself as the Location Manager's delegate, we know that location updates will come in to this class if we implement the delegate method `locationmanager:didUpdateToLocation:fromLocation:`, so let's look at our implementation of that method. The first thing we do in that method is check to see whether `startingPoint` is `nil`. If it is, then this update is the first one from the Location Manager, and we assign the current location to our `startingPoint` property.

```
    if (startingPoint == nil)
        self.startingPoint = newLocation;
```

After that, we update the first six labels with values from the CLLocation object passed in the newLocation argument:

```
NSString *latitudeString = [[NSString alloc] initWithFormat:@"%g°",
    newLocation.coordinate.latitude];
latitudeLabel.text = latitudeString;
[latitudeString release];

NSString *longitudeString = [[NSString alloc] initWithFormat:@"%g°",
    newLocation.coordinate.longitude];
longitudeLabel.text = longitudeString;
[longitudeString release];

NSString *horizontalAccuracyString = [[NSString alloc]
    initWithFormat:@"%gm",
    newLocation.horizontalAccuracy];
horizontalAccuracyLabel.text = horizontalAccuracyString;
[horizontalAccuracyString release];

NSString *altitudeString = [[NSString alloc] initWithFormat:@"%gm",
    newLocation.altitude];
altitudeLabel.text = altitudeString;
[altitudeString release];

NSString *verticalAccuracyString = [[NSString alloc]
    initWithFormat:@"%gm",
    newLocation.verticalAccuracy];
verticalAccuracyLabel.text = verticalAccuracyString;
[verticalAccuracyString release];
```

TIP

You can type the degree symbol (°) by pressing ⇧ ⌥8.

Determining Distance Traveled

Finally, we determine the distance between the current location and the location stored in startingPoint and display the distance. While this application runs, if the user moves far enough for the Location Manager to detect the change, the *Distance Traveled:* field will get continually updated with the distance away from where the user's were when the application was started.

```
CLLocationDistance distance = [newLocation
    getDistanceFrom:startingPoint];
NSString *distanceString = [[NSString alloc]
```

```
        initWithFormat:@"%gm", distance];
    distanceTraveledLabel.text = distanceString;
    [distanceString release];
```

And there you have it. Core Location is fairly straightforward and easy to use. Before you can compile this program, you have to add *CoreLocation.framework* to your project. You do this exactly the same as you did in Chapter 7 when you added the *AudioToolbox.framework*, except you choose *CoreLocation.framework* instead of *CoreGraphics.framework* after navigating to the appropriate *Frameworks* folder. Compile and run the application, and try it. If you have the ability to run the application on your iPhone, try going for a drive with the application running and watch the values change as you drive. Um, actually, better have someone else do the driving!

Wherever You Go, There You Are

You've now seen pretty much all there is to Core Location. Although the underlying technology is quite complex, Apple has provided a simple interface that hides most of the complexity, making it quite easy to add location-related features to your applications, so you can tell where the users are and identify when they move.

And speaking of moving, when you're ready, proceed directly to the next chapter so we can play with iPhone's built-in accelerometer.

Chapter 15

Whee!
Accelerometer!

O ne of the coolest features of the iPhone and iPod Touch is the built-in accelerometer, the tiny device that lets the iPhone know how it's being held and if it's
being moved. The iPhone OS uses the accelerometer to handle autorotation,
and many games use it as a control mechanism. It can also be used to detect
shakes and other sudden movement.

Accelerometer Physics

An accelerometer measures both acceleration and gravity by sensing the
amount of inertial force in a given direction. The accelerometer inside iPhone
is a three-axis accelerometer, meaning that it is capable of detecting either
movement or the pull of gravity in three-dimensional space. As a result, you
can use the accelerometer to tell not only how the phone is currently being
held (as autorotation does) but also if it's laying on a table and even whether
it's face down or face up.

Accelerometers give measurements in g-forces ("g" for gravity), so a value of
1.0 returned by the accelerometer means that 1 g is sensed in a particular
direction. If the iPhone is being held still with no movement, there will be
approximately 1 g of force exerted on it by the pull of the earth. If the iPhone
is being held perfectly upright, in portrait orientation, the iPhone will detect
and report about 1 g of force exerted on its y axis. If the iPhone is being held
at an angle, that 1 g of force will be distributed along different axes depending
on how the iPhone is being held. When held at a 45-degree angle, that 1 g of
force will be split roughly equally between two of the axes.

Sudden movement can be detected by looking for accelerometer values considerably larger than 1 g. In normal usage, the accelerometer does not detect significantly more than 1 g on any axis. If you shake, drop, or throw your iPhone, the accelerometer will detect a greater amount of force on one or more axes. Please do not drop or throw your own iPhone to test this theory.

You can see a graphic representation of the three axes used by iPhone's accelerometer in Figure 15-1. One thing to notice is that the accelerometer uses the more standard convention for the y coordinate, with increases in y indicating upward force, which is the opposite of Quartz 2D's coordinate system. When you are using the accelerometer as a control mechanism with Quartz 2D, you have to translate the y coordinate. When working with OpenGL ES, which you are more likely to be using if you are using the accelerometer to control animation, no translation is required.

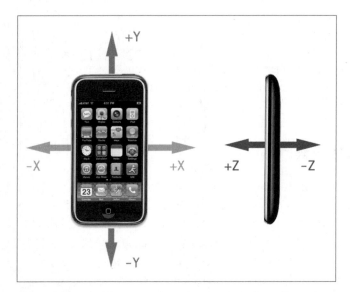

Figure 15-1. *The iPhone accelerometer's axes in three dimensions*

Accessing the Accelerometer

The UIAccelerometer class exists as a singleton. To retrieve a reference to the class, call the method sharedAccelerometer, like so:

```
UIAccelerometer *accelerometer = [UIAccelerometer sharedAccelerometer];
```

Getting information from the accelerometer is similar to getting information from Core Location. You create a class that conforms to the UIAccelerometerDelegate protocol, implement a method to which the accelerometer will provide information, and specify an instance of that class to be the accelerometer's delegate.

When you assign a delegate, you need to specify an update interval in seconds. iPhone's accelerometer supports polling at a rate of up to 100 times per second, although there is no guarantee that it will actually update you that many times or that those updates will be exactly evenly spaced. To assign a delegate and specify a polling interval of 60 times per second, you would do this:

```
accelerometer.delegate = self;
accelerometer.updateInterval =  1.0f/60.0f;
```

Once you've done that, all that's left is to implement the method that the accelerometer uses to update its delegate, `accelerometer:didAccelerate:`. This method takes two arguments. The first is a reference to the shared `UIAccelerometer` instance. The second contains the actual data from the accelerometer, embedded in an object of the class `UIAcceleration`. Before we look at the delegate method, let's talk about the `UIAcceleration` object that's used to pass the information to the delegate.

UIAcceleration

We mentioned earlier that the iPhone's accelerometer detects acceleration along three axes, and it provides this information to the delegate using instances of the `UIAcceleration` class. Each `UIAcceleration` instance has an x, y, and z property, each of which holds a signed floating point value. A value of 0 means that the accelerometer detects no movement on that particular axis. A positive or negative value indicates force in one direction. For example, a negative value for y indicates that downward pull is sensed, which is probably an indication that the phone is being held upright in portrait orientation. A positive value for y indicates some force is being exerted in the opposite direction, which could mean the phone is being held upside down or that the phone is being moved in an upward direction.

Keeping the diagram in Figure 15-1 in mind, let's look at some accelerometer results. Note that, in real life, you will almost never get values this precise, as the accelerometer is sensitive enough to pick up even tiny amounts of motion, and you will usually pick up at least

Figure 15-2. *Idealized acceleration values for different device orientations*

some tiny amount of force on all three axes. This is real-world physics and not high school physics lab.

Implementing the accelerometer:didAccelerate: Method

In order to receive accelerometer information, the class you specify as the accelerometer's delegate needs to implement the `accelerometer:didAccelerate:` method. If you wanted to display the acceleration values in a `UILabel`, you might implement that method like this:

```
- (void)accelerometer:(UIAccelerometer *)accelerometer
      didAccelerate:(UIAcceleration *)acceleration {
   NSString *newText = [[NSString alloc]
      initWithFormat:@"x: %g\ty:%g\tz:%g", acceleration.x,
      acceleration.y, acceleration.z];
   label.text = newText;
   [newText release];
}
```

This method would update a label on the interface every time it was called. How frequently this method gets called is based on the `updateInterval` value you specified earlier.

Detecting Shakes

One fairly common use of the accelerometer in applications is to detect a shake. Like a gesture, a shake can be used as a form of input to your application. For example, the drawing program GLPaint, which is one of the iPhone sample code projects, lets the user erase drawings by shaking the iPhone, sort of like an Etch-a-Sketch.

Detecting shakes is relatively trivial; all it requires is checking for an absolute value on one of the axes that is greater than a set threshold. During normal usage, it's not uncommon for one of the three axes to register values up to around 1.3 gs, but much higher than that generally requires intentional force. The accelerometer seems to be unable to register values higher than around 2.3 gs (at least on first-generation iPhones), so you don't want to set your threshold any higher than that.

To detect a shake, you could check for an absolute value greater than 1.5 for a slight shake and 2.0 for a strong shake, like this:

```
- (void)accelerometer:(UIAccelerometer *)accelerometer
     didAccelerate:(UIAcceleration *)acceleration {

     if (fabsf(acceleration.x) > 2.0
         || fabsf(acceleration.y) > 2.0
         || fabsf(acceleration.z) > 2.0) {
         // Do something here...
     }
}
```

The preceding method would detect any movement on any axis that exceeded two g-forces. You could implement more sophisticated shake detection by requiring the user to shake back and forth a certain number of times to register as a shake, like so:

```objc
- (void)accelerometer:(UIAccelerometer *)accelerometer
    didAccelerate:(UIAcceleration *)acceleration {

    static NSInteger shakeCount = 0;
    static NSDate *shakeStart;

    NSDate *now = [[NSDate alloc] init];
    NSDate *checkDate = [[NSDate alloc] initWithTimeInterval:1.5f
        sinceDate:shakeStart];
    if ([now compare:checkDate] ==
        NSOrderedDescending || shakeStart == nil) {
        shakeCount = 0;
        [shakeStart release];
        shakeStart = [[NSDate alloc] init];
    }
    [now release];
    [checkDate release];

    if (fabsf(acceleration.x) > 2.0
        || fabsf(acceleration.y) > 2.0
        ||  fabsf(2.0.z) > 2.0) {
        shakeCount++;
        if (shakeCount > 4) {
            // Do something
            shakeCount = 0;
            [shakeStart release];
            shakeStart = [[NSDate alloc] init];
        }
    }
}
```

This method keeps track of the number of times the accelerometer reports a value above 2.0, and if it happens four times within a second and a half span of time, it registers as a shake.

BAKED-IN SHAKING

There's actually another way to check for shakes, one that's baked right into the responder chain. Remember back in Chapter 13, how we implemented methods like `touchesBegan:withEvent:` to detect touches? Well, starting with SDK3, there are now three similar responder methods for detecting motion. When motion begins, the `motionBegan:withEvent:` method gets sent to the first responder and then on through the responder chain as discussed in Chapter 13. When the motion ends, the `motionEnded:withEvent:` method gets sent to the first responder. If the phone rings, or some other interrupting action happens during the shake, the `motionCancelled:withEvent:` message gets sent to the first responder.

This means that you can actually detect a shake without using `UIAccelerometer` directly. All you have to do is override the appropriate motion-sensing methods in your view or view controller, and they will get automatically called when the user shakes their phone. Unless you specifically need more control over the shake gesture, you should use the baked-in motion detection rather than manual method in this chapter, but we thought we'd show you the manual method in case you ever do need more control.

Accelerometer as Directional Controller

Probably the most common usage of the accelerometer in third-party applications is as a controller for games. Instead of using buttons to control the movement of a character or object in a game, the accelerometer is used. In a car racing game, for example, twisting the iPhone like a steering wheel might steer your car, while tipping it forward might accelerate and tipping back might brake.

Exactly how you use the accelerometer as a controller is going to vary greatly depending on the specific mechanics of the game. In the simplest cases, you might just take the value from one of the axes, multiply it by a number, and tack that on to the coordinates of the controlled objects. In more complex games where physics are modeled more realistically, you would have to make adjustments to the velocity of the controlled object based on the values returned from the accelerometer.

The one tricky aspect of using the accelerometer as a controller is that the delegate method is not guaranteed to call back at the interval you specify. If you tell the accelerometer to update your delegate class 60 times a second, all that you can say for sure is that it won't update you more than 60 times a second. You're not guaranteed to get 60 evenly spaced updates every second, so if you're doing animation based on input from the accelerometer, you have to keep track of the time that passes between delegate method calls and factor that into your equations to determine how far objects have moved.

We'll create a program that uses the accelerometer for input a little later in the chapter, but first, we're going to break your phone.

NOTE

The applications in this chapter do not function on the simulator because the simulator has no accelerometer. Aw, shucks.

Shake and Break

OK, we're not really going to break your phone, but we're going to write an application that detects shakes and then makes your phone look and sound like it broke as a result of the shake. When you launch the application, the program will display a picture that looks like the iPhone home screen (see Figure 15-3).

Shake the phone hard enough, though, and your poor phone will make a sound that you never want to hear coming out of a consumer electronics device. What's more, your screen will look like the one shown in Figure 15-4. Why do we do these evil things?

Not to worry. You can reset the iPhone to its previously pristine state by touching the screen.

Figure 15-3. *The ShakeAndBreak application looks innocuous enough. . .*

Figure 15-4. *. . . but handle it too roughly and—oh no!*

The Code That Breaks

Create a new project in Xcode using the view-based application template. Call the new project ShakeAndBreak. In the *15 ShakeAndBreak* folder of the project archive, we've provided you the two images and the sound file you need for this application, so drag *home.png*, *homebroken.png*, and *glass.wav* to the *Resources* folder of your project. There's also an *icon. png* in that folder. Add that to the *Resources* folder as well.

NOTE

> Just for completeness, we've included a modified version of Shake and Break in the project archives based on the 3.0 shake detection method. You'll find it in the project archive in a folder named *15 ShakeAndBreak - Motion Methods*. The magic is in `ShakeAndBreakViewController`'s `motionEnded:withEvent:` method.

Next, expand the *Resources* folder, and single-click *ShakeAndBreak-Info.plist*. We need to add an entry to the property list to tell our application not to use a status bar, so single-click the row that says *Information Property List*, and click the button that appears at the end of the row to add a new child. Change the new row's *Key* to *UIStatusBarHidden*. After you change the key, the *Value* column should change to a checkbox. If it doesn't change automatically, control-click (or right-click if you have a two-button mouse) the empty *Value* column in the row you just added. A contextual menu should appear (see Figure 15-5). From that menu, select the **Value Type** submenu, and then select **Boolean**. Now, click the checkbox so that it is checked. Finally, type *icon.png* in the *Value* column next to the *Icon file* key.

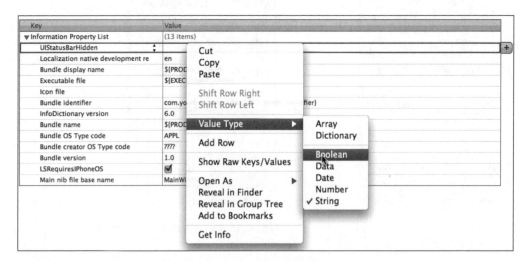

Figure 15-5. *Changing the Value Type for UIStatusBarHidden*

Now, expand the *Classes* folder. We're going to need to create an outlet to point to an image view so that we can change the displayed image. We'll also need a couple of UIImage instances to hold the two pictures, a sound ID to refer to the sound, and a Boolean to keep track of whether the screen needs to be reset. Single-click *ShakeAndBreakViewController.h*, and add the following code:

```
#import <UIKit/UIKit.h>
#import <AudioToolbox/AudioToolbox.h>

#define kAccelerationThreshold      2.2
#define kUpdateInterval             (1.0f/10.0f)

@interface ShakeAndBreakViewController :
    UIViewController <UIAccelerometerDelegate> {
    UIImageView     *imageView;

    BOOL            brokenScreenShowing;
    SystemSoundID   soundID;
    UIImage         *fixed;
    UIImage         *broken;
}
@property (nonatomic, retain) IBOutlet UIImageView *imageView;
@property (nonatomic, retain) UIImage *fixed;
@property (nonatomic, retain) UIImage *broken;
@end
```

Save the header file, and double-click *ShakeAndBreakViewController.xib* to open the file in Interface Builder. Single-click the *View* icon. First, press ⌘1 to bring up the attribute inspector, and change the *Status Bar* pop-up under *Simulated User Interface Elements* from *Gray* to *None*. Now, drag an *Image View* over from the library to the window labeled *View*. The image view should automatically resize to take up the full window, so just place it so that it sits perfectly within the window.

Control-drag from the *File's Owner* icon to the image view, and select the *imageView* outlet. Now, save and close the nib file, and go back to Xcode. When you get there, single-click the *ShakeAndBreakController.m* file, and add the following code at the top of the file:

```
#import "ShakeAndBreakViewController.h"

@implementation ShakeAndBreakViewController
@synthesize imageView;
@synthesize fixed;
@synthesize broken;
- (void) viewDidLoad {
    UIAccelerometer *accel = [UIAccelerometer sharedAccelerometer];
    accel.delegate = self;
    accel.updateInterval = kUpdateInterval;
```

```
    NSString *path = [[NSBundle mainBundle] pathForResource:@"glass"
        ofType:@"wav"];
    AudioServicesCreateSystemSoundID((CFURLRef)[NSURL
        fileURLWithPath:path], &soundID);

    self.fixed = [UIImage imageNamed:@"home.png"];
    self.broken = [UIImage imageNamed:@"homebroken.png"];

    imageView.image = fixed;
}
...
```

Insert the following lines of code into the existing dealloc and viewDidUnload methods:

```
...
- (void)viewDidUnload {
    // Release any retained subviews of the main view.
    // e.g. self.myOutlet = nil;
    self.imageView = nil;
    self.fixed = nil;
    self.broken = nil;
    [super viewDidUnload];
}

- (void)dealloc {
    [imageView release];
    [fixed release];
    [broken release];
    [super dealloc];
}
...
```

And add the following new methods at the bottom of the file:

```
...
#pragma mark -
- (void)accelerometer:(UIAccelerometer *)accelerometer
    didAccelerate:(UIAcceleration *)acceleration {
    if (!brokenScreenShowing) {
        if (acceleration.x > kAccelerationThreshold
            || acceleration.y > kAccelerationThreshold
            || acceleration.z > kAccelerationThreshold) {
            imageView.image = broken;
            AudioServicesPlaySystemSound(soundID);
            brokenScreenShowing = YES;
        }
    }
}
```

```
- (void)touchesBegan:(NSSet *)touches withEvent:(UIEvent *)event {
    imageView.image = fixed;
    brokenScreenShowing = NO;
}

@end
```

The first method we implement is `viewDidLoad`, where we get a reference to the shared accelerometer instance, set `self` to be the accelerometer's delegate, and then set the update frequency using the constant we defined earlier:

```
UIAccelerometer *accel = [UIAccelerometer sharedAccelerometer];
accel.delegate = self;
accel.updateInterval = kUpdateInterval;
```

Load the Simulation Files

Next, we load the glass sound file into memory and save the assigned identifier in the soundID instance variable:

```
NSString *path = [[NSBundle mainBundle] pathForResource:@"glass"
    ofType:@"wav"];
AudioServicesCreateSystemSoundID((CFURLRef)[NSURL
    fileURLWithPath:path], &soundID);
```

We then load the two images into memory:

```
self.fixed = [UIImage imageNamed:@"home.png"];
self.broken = [UIImage imageNamed:@"homebroken.png"];
```

Finally, we set `imageView` to show the unbroken screenshot and set `brokenScreenShowing` to NO to indicate that the screen does not currently need to be reset:

```
imageView.image = fixed;
brokenScreenShowing = NO;
```

The next new method is the accelerometer delegate method. In it, we check `brokenScreenShowing`. If it is NO, we know the screen is already showing the broken image, so we don't want to do anything.

```
if (! brokenScreenShowing) {
```

Otherwise, we check all three of the axes passed in and see if any of them exceed the acceleration threshold we defined earlier. If any of the three axes do, we set the image view to show the broken image, play the sound, and set `brokenScreenShowing` to YES so that we don't do this again until the user has reset the screen:

```
    if (acceleration.x > kAccelerationThreshold || acceleration.y >
        kAccelerationThreshold || acceleration.z >
        kAccelerationThreshold) {
        imageView.image = broken;
        AudioServicesPlaySystemSound (soundID);
        brokenScreenShowing = YES;
    }
}
```

All Better—The Healing Touch

The last method is one you should be quite familiar with by now. It's called when the screen is touched. All we do in that method is to set the image back to the unbroken screen and set brokenScreenShowing back to NO:

```
    imageView.image = fixed;
    brokenScreenShowing = NO;
```

Finally, add the *AudioToolbox.framework* so that we can play the sound file. You can link *AudioToolbox.framework* into your application by following the instructions from Chapter 7 that start on page 190.

Compile and run the application, and take it for a test drive. For those of you who don't have the ability to run this application on your iPhone or iPod touch, you might want to give the 3.0 version a try. The simulator does not simulate the accelerometer hardware, but it does simulate the 3.0 shake gesture, so the version of the application in *15 ShakeAndBreak - Motion Method* will work with the simulator.

Go have some fun with it. When you're done, come on back, and you'll see how to use the accelerometer as a controller for games and other programs.

The Rolling Marble Program

For our next trick, we're going to let you move a sprite around iPhone's screen by tilting the phone. This is going to be a very simple example of using the accelerometer to receive input. We're going to use Quartz 2D to handle our animation. As a general rule, when you're working with games and other programs that need smooth animation, you'll probably want to use OpenGL ES. We're using Quartz 2D in this application for the sake of simplicity and to reduce the amount of code that's unrelated to using the accelerometer. The animation won't be quite as smooth as if we were using OpenGL, but it will be a lot less work.

In this application, as you tilt your iPhone, the marble will roll around as if it were on the surface of a table (see Figure 15-6). Tip it to the left, and the ball will roll to the left. Tip it further, and it will move faster. Tip it back, and it will slow down and then start going the other direction.

In Xcode, create a new project using the view-based application template, and call this one Ball. Expand the *Classes* and *Resource* folders, so you can see the files we will be working with. In the *15 Ball* folder in the project archive, you'll find an image called *ball.png*. Drag that to the *Resources* folder of your project.

Now, single-click the *Classes* folder, and select **New File...** from the **File** menu. Select *Objective-C class* from the *Cocoa Touch Class* category, and then select *UIView* in the *Subclass of* pop-up. Name the new file *BallView.m*, making sure to have it create the header class for you as well.

Double-click *BallViewController.xib* to open the file in Interface Builder. Single-click the *View* icon, and use the identity inspector to change the view's class from *UIView* to *BallView*. Next, switch to the attribute inspector, and change the view's background color to black. After that, control-drag from the *File's Owner* icon to the *Ball View* icon, and select the *view* outlet to reestablish the link between the controller and the view. Save the nib, close it, and go back to Xcode.

Figure 15-6. *The Rolling Marble application lets you do just that—roll a marble around the screen.*

Implementing the Ball View Controller

Single-click *BallViewController.h*. All we need to do here is conform the class to the `UIAccelerometerDelegate` protocol, so make the following change:

```
#import <UIKit/UIKit.h>

#define kUpdateInterval     (1.0f/60.0f)

@interface BallViewController :
    UIViewController <UIAccelerometerDelegate> {

}

@end
```

Next, switch to *BallViewController.m*, and make the following changes at the top of the file these changes:

```
#import "BallViewController.h"
#import "BallView.h"

@implementation BallViewController

- (void)viewDidLoad {
    UIAccelerometer *accelerometer = [UIAccelerometer sharedAccelerometer];
    accelerometer.delegate = self;
    accelerometer.updateInterval =  kUpdateInterval;
    [super viewDidLoad];
}
...
```

And add the following new method at the bottom of the file:

```
...
#pragma mark -
- (void)accelerometer:(UIAccelerometer *)accelerometer
    didAccelerate:(UIAcceleration *)acceleration {

    [(BallView *)self.view setAcceleration:acceleration];
    [(BallView *)self.view draw];
}
@end
```

The `viewDidLoad` method here is nearly identical to the previous one. The main difference is that we are declaring a much higher update interval of 60 times per second. Down in the `accelerometer:didAccelerate:` method, we pass the acceleration object into our view and then call a method named `draw`, which updates the position of the ball in the view based on acceleration and the amount of time that has passed since the last update.

Writing the Ball View

Since we're doing the bulk of our work in the `BallView` class, we'd better write it, huh? Single-click *BallView.h*, and make the following changes:

```
#define kVelocityMultiplier    500
#import <UIKit/UIKit.h>

@interface BallView : UIView {
    UIImage        *image;

    CGPoint        currentPoint;
    CGPoint        previousPoint;
```

```
    UIAcceleration *acceleration;
    CGFloat         ballXVelocity;
    CGFloat         ballYVelocity;
}
@property (nonatomic, retain) UIImage *image;
@property CGPoint currentPoint;
@property CGPoint previousPoint;
@property (nonatomic, retain) UIAcceleration *acceleration;
@property CGFloat ballXVelocity;
@property CGFloat ballYVelocity;
- (void)draw;
@end
```

Let's look at the instance variables and talk about what we're doing with each of them. The first instance variable is a `UIImage` that will point to the sprite that we'll be moving around the screen:

```
    UIImage *image;
```

After that, we keep track of two `CGPoint` variables. The `currentPoint` variable will hold the current position of the ball. We'll also keep track of the last point where we drew the sprite so that we can build an update rectangle that encompasses both the new and old positions of the ball so that it gets drawn at the new spot and erased at the old one:

```
    CGPoint     currentPoint;
    CGPoint     previousPoint;
```

Next is a pointer to an acceleration object, which is how we will get the accelerometer information from our controller:

```
    UIAcceleration *acceleration;
```

We also have two variables to keep track of the ball's current velocity in two dimensions. Although this isn't going to be a very complex simulation, we do want the ball to move in a manner similar to a real ball, so we'll calculate velocity using the formula `velocity = velocity + acceleration`. We'll get acceleration from the accelerometer and keep track of velocity on two axes with these variables.

```
    CGFloat ballXVelocity;
    CGFloat ballYVelocity;
```

Let's switch over to *BallView.m* and write the code to draw and move the ball around the screen. First, make the following changes at the top of *BallView.m*:

```
#import "BallView.h"

@implementation BallView
@synthesize image;
@synthesize currentPoint;
@synthesize previousPoint;
@synthesize acceleration;
@synthesize ballXVelocity;
@synthesize ballYVelocity;

- (id)initWithCoder:(NSCoder *)coder {

    if (self = [super initWithCoder:coder]) {
        self.image = [UIImage imageNamed:@"ball.png"];
        self.currentPoint = CGPointMake((self.bounds.size.width / 2.0f) +
            (image.size.width / 2.0f),
            (self.bounds.size.height / 2.0f) + (image.size.height / 2.0f));

        ballXVelocity = 0.0f;
        ballYVelocity = 0.0f;
    }
    return self;
}
...
```

Now, insert the following lines of code into the existing drawRect: and dealloc methods:

```
...
- (void)drawRect:(CGRect)rect {
    // Drawing code
    [image drawAtPoint:currentPoint];
}
- (void)dealloc {
    [image release];
    [acceleration release];
    [super dealloc];
}
...
```

And we have a few new methods to add at the end of the class:

```
...
#pragma mark -
- (CGPoint)currentPoint {
    return currentPoint;
}
- (void)setCurrentPoint:(CGPoint)newPoint {
```

```
    previousPoint = currentPoint;
    currentPoint = newPoint;

    if (currentPoint.x < 0) {
        currentPoint.x = 0;
        ballXVelocity = 0;
    }
    if (currentPoint.y < 0){
        currentPoint.y = 0;
        ballYVelocity = 0;
    }
    if (currentPoint.x > self.bounds.size.width - image.size.width) {
        currentPoint.x = self.bounds.size.width  - image.size.width;
        ballXVelocity = 0;
    }
    if (currentPoint.y > self.bounds.size.height - image.size.height) {
        currentPoint.y = self.bounds.size.height - image.size.height;
        ballYVelocity = 0;
    }

    CGRect currentImageRect = CGRectMake(currentPoint.x, currentPoint.y,
            currentPoint.x + image.size.width,
            currentPoint.y + image.size.height);
    CGRect previousImageRect = CGRectMake(previousPoint.x, previousPoint.y,
            previousPoint.x + image.size.width,
            currentPoint.y + image.size.width);
    [self setNeedsDisplayInRect:CGRectUnion(currentImageRect,
        previousImageRect)];
}

- (void)draw {
    static NSDate *lastDrawTime;

    if (lastDrawTime != nil) {
        NSTimeInterval secondsSinceLastDraw =
            -([lastDrawTime timeIntervalSinceNow]);

        ballYVelocity = ballYVelocity + -(acceleration.y *
            secondsSinceLastDraw);
        ballXVelocity = ballXVelocity + acceleration.x *
            secondsSinceLastDraw;

        CGFloat xAcceleration = secondsSinceLastDraw * ballXVelocity * 500;
        CGFloat yAcceleration = secondsSinceLastDraw * ballYVelocity * 500;

        self.currentPoint = CGPointMake(self.currentPoint.x +
            xAcceleration, self.currentPoint.y + yAcceleration);
```

```
        }
        // Update last time with current time
        [lastDrawTime release];
        lastDrawTime = [[NSDate alloc] init];
    }
@end
```

The first thing to notice is that one of our properties is declared as @synthesize, yet we have implemented the mutator method for that property in our code. That's OK. The @synthesize directive will not overwrite accessor or mutator methods that you write; it will just fill in the blanks and provide any ones that you do not.

Calculating Ball Movement

We are handling the currentPoint property manually, since, when the currentPoint changes, we need to do a bit of housekeeping, such as making sure that the ball hasn't rolled off of the screen. We'll look at that method in a moment. For now, let's look at the first method in the class, initWithCoder:. Recall that when you load a view from a nib, that class's init or initWithFrame: methods will never get called. Nib files contain archived objects, so any instances loaded from nib will get initialized using the initWithCoder: method. If we need to do any additional initialization, we need to do it in that method.

In this view, we do have some additional initialization, so we've overridden initWithCoder:. First, we load the *ball.png* image. Second, we calculate the middle of the view and set that as our ball's starting point, and we set the velocity on both axes to 0.

```
self.image = [UIImage imageNamed:@"ball.png"];
        self.currentPoint = CGPointMake((self.bounds.size.width / 2.0f) +
            (image.size.width / 2.0f), (self.bounds.size.height / 2.0f) +
            (image.size.height / 2.0f));

        ballXVelocity = 0.0f;
        ballYVelocity = 0.0f;
```

Our drawRect: method couldn't be much simpler. We simply draw the image we loaded in initWithCoder: at the position stored in currentPoint. The currentPoint accessor is a standard accessor method. The setCurrentPoint: mutator is another story, however.

The first things we do in setCurrentPoint: is to store the old currentPoint value in previousPoint and assign the new value to currentPoint:

```
    previousPoint = currentPoint;
    currentPoint = newPoint;
```

The next thing we do is a boundary check. If either the x or y position of the ball is less than 0 or greater than the width or height of the screen (accounting for the width and height of the image), then the acceleration in that direction is stopped.

```
if (currentPoint.x < 0) {
    currentPoint.x = 0;
    ballXVelocity = 0;
}
if (currentPoint.y < 0){
    currentPoint.y = 0;
    ballYVelocity = 0;
}
if (currentPoint.x > self.bounds.size.width - image.size.width) {
    currentPoint.x = self.bounds.size.width  - image.size.width;
    ballXVelocity = 0;
}
if (currentPoint.y > self.bounds.size.height - image.size.height) {
    currentPoint.y = self.bounds.size.height - image.size.height;
    ballYVelocity = 0;
}
```

BOUNCY BOUNCY

Want to make the ball bounce off the walls more naturally, instead of just stopping? It's easy enough to do. Just change the two lines `setCurrentPoint:` that currently read

```
        ballXVelocity = 0;
```

to

```
        ballXVelocity = - (ballXVelocity / 2.0);
```

And change the two lines that currently read

```
        ballYVelocity = 0;
```

to

```
        ballYVelocity = - (ballYVelocity / 2.0);
```

With this change, instead of killing the ball's velocity, we reduce it in half and set it to the inverse so that the ball now has half the velocity in the opposite direction.

After that, we calculate two CGRects based on the size of the image. One rectangle encompasses the area where the new image will be drawn, and the other encompasses the area where it was last drawn. We'll use these two rectangles to ensure that the old ball gets erased at the same time the new one gets drawn.

```
CGRect currentImageRect = CGRectMake(currentPoint.x, currentPoint.y,
        currentPoint.x + image.size.width,
        currentPoint.y + image.size.height);
CGRect previousImageRect = CGRectMake(previousPoint.x, previousPoint.y,
        previousPoint.x + image.size.width,
        currentPoint.y + image.size.width);
```

Finally, we create a new rectangle that is the union of the two rectangles we just calculated and feed that to `setNeedsDisplayInRect:` to indicate the part of our view that needs to be redrawn:

```
[self setNeedsDisplayInRect:CGRectUnion(currentImageRect,
        previousImageRect)];
```

The last substantive method in our class is `draw`, which is used to figure the correct new location of the ball. This method is called in the accelerometer method of its controller class after it feeds the view the new acceleration object. The first thing this method does is declare a static `NSDate` variable that will be used to keep track of how long it has been since the last time the `draw` method was called.

The first time through this method, when `lastDrawTime` is `nil`, we don't do anything because there's no point of reference. Because the updates are happening about 60 times a second, nobody will ever notice a single missing frame:

```
static NSDate *lastDrawTime;

if (lastDrawTime != nil) {
```

Every other time through this method, we calculate how long it has been since the last time this method was called. We negate the value returned by `timeIntervalSinceNow` because `lastDrawTime` is in the past, so the value returned will be a negative number representing the number of seconds between the current time and `lastDrawTime`:

```
NSTimeInterval secondsSinceLastDraw =
        -([lastDrawTime timeIntervalSinceNow]);
```

Next, we calculate the new velocity in both directions by adding the current acceleration to the current velocity. We multiply acceleration by `secondsSinceLastDraw` so that our acceleration is consistent across time. Tipping the phone at the same angle will always cause the same amount of acceleration.

```
ballYVelocity = ballYVelocity + -(acceleration.y *
    secondsSinceLastDraw);
ballXVelocity = ballXVelocity + acceleration.x *
    secondsSinceLastDraw;
```

After that, we figure out the actual change in pixels since the last time the method was called based on the velocity. The product of velocity and elapsed time is multiplied by 500 to create movement that looks natural. If we didn't multiple it by some value, the acceleration would be extraordinarily slow, as if the ball were stuck in molasses.

```
CGFloat xAcceleration = secondsSinceLastDraw * ballXVelocity *
    kVelocityMultiplier;
CGFloat yAcceleration = secondsSinceLastDraw * ballYVelocity *
    kVelocityMultiplier;
```

Once we know the change in pixels, we create a new point by adding the current location to the calculated acceleration and assign that to currentPoint. By using self.currentPoint, we use that accessor method we wrote earlier rather than assigning the value directly to the instance variable.

```
self.currentPoint = CGPointMake(self.currentPoint.x +
    xAcceleration, self.currentPoint.y +yAcceleration);
```

That ends our calculations, so all that's left is to update lastDrawTime with the current time:

```
[lastDrawTime release];
lastDrawTime = [[NSDate alloc] init];
```

Go ahead and build and run.

NOTE

Unfortunately, Ball just will not do much on the simulator. If you want to experience Ball in all its gravity-obeying grooviness, you'll have to join the for-pay iPhone developer program and install it on your own device.

If all went well, the application will launch, and you should be able to control the movement of the ball by tilting the phone. When the ball gets to an edge of the screen, it should stop. Tip back the other way, and it should start rolling in the other direction. Whee!

Rolling On

Well, we've certainly had some fun in this chapter with physics and the amazing iPhone acceler-o-meter. We wrote a great April Fools' prank, and you got to see the basics of using the accelerometer as a control device. The possibilities for applications using the accelerometer are as nearly endless as the universe. So now that you've got the basics down, go create something cool and surprise us!

When you feel up to it, we're going to get into using another bit of iPhone hardware: the built-in camera.

iPhone Camera and Photo Library

By now, it should come as no surprise to you that the iPhone has a built-in camera (which the current iPod touch unfortunately lacks) and a nifty application called Photos to help you manage all those awesome pictures you've taken. What you may not know is that your programs can use the built-in camera to take pictures and that your programs can also allow the user to select pictures from among the photos already on the iPhone.

Because of the way iPhone applications are sandboxed, applications ordinarily can't get to photographs or other data that lives outside of their own sandboxes. Fortunately, both the camera and the image library are made available to your application by way of an **image picker**. As the name implies, an image picker is a mechanism that lets you select an image from a specified source. Typically, an image picker will use a list of images as its source (see the picture on the left of Figure 16-1). You can, however, specify that the picker use the camera as its source (see the picture on the right of Figure 16-1).

Figure 16-1. *An image picker in action using a list of images (left) and the camera (right)*

Using the Image Picker and UIImagePickerController

The image picker interface is implemented by way of a modal controller class called UIImagePickerController. You create an instance of this class, specify a delegate (as if you didn't see that coming), specify its image source, and then launch it modally. The image picker will then take control of the iPhone to let the user either select a picture from an existing set of images or take a new picture with the camera. Once the user takes or selects the image, you can allow an opportunity to do some basic editing, such as scaling or cropping, on the selected image. Assuming the user doesn't press cancel, the image the user takes or selects from the library will be delivered to your delegate.

Regardless of whether an image is selected or canceled, your delegate has the responsibility to dismiss the UIImagePickerController so that the user can return to your application.

Creating a UIImagePickerController is extremely straightforward. You just allocate and initialize an instance the way you would with most classes. There is one catch, however. Not every device that runs the iPhone OS has a camera. The iPod touch is the first example of this, but more such devices may roll off Apple's assembly lines in the future. Before you create an instance of `UIImagePickerController`, you need to check to see whether the device your program is currently running on supports the image source you want to use. For example, before letting the user take a picture with the camera, you should make sure the program is running on a device that has a camera. You can check that by using a class method on `UIImagePickerController`, like this:

```
if ([UIImagePickerController isSourceTypeAvailable:
    UIImagePickerControllerSourceTypePhotoLibrary]) {
```

In this example, we're passing `UIImagePickerControllerSourceTypePhotoLibrary` to indicate that we want to let the user pick one of the images out of the library of existing photographs. The method `isSourceTypeAvailable:` will return `YES` if the specified source is currently available. There are two other values you can specify, in addition to `UIImagePickerControllerSourceTypePhotoLibrary`:

- `UIImagePickerControllerSourceTypeCamera` specifies that the user will take a picture using the built-in camera. That image will be returned to your delegate.

- `UIImagePickerControllerSourceTypeSavedPhotosAlbum` specifies that the user will select the image from the library of existing photographs but that the selection will be limited to the most recent camera roll. This option will run on an iPod touch but does not do anything useful.

After making sure that the device your program is running on supports the image source you want to use, launching the image picker is relatively easy:

```
UIImagePickerController *picker = [[UIImagePickerController alloc] init];
picker.delegate = self;
picker.sourceType = UIImagePickerControllerSourceTypePhotoLibrary;
[self presentModalViewController:picker animated:YES];
[picker release];
```

After we've created and configured the `UIImagePickerController`, we use a method that our class inherited from `UIView` called `presentModalViewController:animated:` to present the image picker to the user.

TIP

The `presentModalViewController:animated:` method is not limited to just presenting image pickers; you can present any view controller to the user, modally, by calling this method on the view controller for a currently visible view.

Implementing the Image Picker Controller Delegate

The object that you want to be notified when the user has finished using the image picker interface needs to conform to the `UIImagePickerControllerDelegate` protocol, which defines two methods, `imagePickerController:didFinishPickingImage:editingInfo:` and `imagePickerControllerDidCancel:`.

The first of these methods, `imagePickerController:didFinishPickingImage:editingInfo:`, gets called when the user has successfully taken a photo or selected one from the photo library. The first argument is a pointer to the `UIImagePickerController` that you created earlier. The second argument is a `UIImage` instance containing the actual photo the user selected. The last argument is an `NSDictionary` instance that will be passed in if you enabled editing and the user cropped or scaled the image. That dictionary will contain the original, unedited image stored under the key `UIImagePickerControllerOriginalImage`. Here's an example delegate method that retrieves the original image:

```
- (void)imagePickerController:(UIImagePickerController *)picker
        didFinishPickingImage:(UIImage *)image
        editingInfo:(NSDictionary *)editingInfo {

    UIImage *selectedImage = image;
    UIImage *originalImage = [editingInfo objectForKey:
    UIImagePickerControllerOriginalImage];

    // do something with selectedImage and originalImage

    [picker dismissModalViewControllerAnimated:YES];
}
```

The `editingInfo` dictionary will also tell you which portion of the entire image was chosen during editing by way of an `NSValue` object stored under the key `UIImagePickerControllerCropRect`. You can convert this string into a `CGRect` like so:

```
    NSValue *cropRect = [editingInfo
        objectForKey:UIImagePickerControllerCropRect];
    CGRect theRect = [cropRect CGRectValue];
```

After this conversion, `theRect` will specify the portion of the original image that was selected during the editing process. If you do not need this information, you can just ignore it.

CAUTION

If the image returned to your delegate comes from the camera, that image will not get stored in the photo library. It is your application's responsibility to save the image if necessary.

The other delegate method, `imagePickerControllerDidCancel:`, gets called if the user decides to cancel the process without taking or selecting a picture. When the image picker calls this delegate method, it's just notifying you that the user is finished with the picker and did not choose an image.

Both of the methods in the `UIImagePickerControllerDelegate` protocol are marked as optional, but they really aren't, and here is why: modal views like the image picker have to be told to dismiss themselves. As a result, even if you don't need to take any application-specific actions when the user cancels an image picker, you still need to dismiss the picker. At a bare minimum, your `imagePickerControllerDidCancel:` method will need to look like this in order for your program to function correctly:

```
- (void)imagePickerControllerDidCancel:(UIImagePickerController *)picker {

    [picker dismissModalViewControllerAnimated:YES];
}
```

Road Testing the Camera and Library

In this chapter, we're going to build an application that lets the user take a picture with the camera or select one from their photo library and then display the selected picture in an image view (see Figure 16-2). If the user is on a device without a camera, we will hide the *Take Picture* button and the *Pick from Library* button and only allow selection from the photo library.

Create a new project in Xcode using the view-based application template, naming the application Camera. We'll need a couple of outlets in this application. We need one to point to the image view so that we can update it with the image returned from the image picker, and we'll also need outlets to point to the *Take New Picture* button and the *Select from Camera Roll* button, so we can hide both of these buttons if the device doesn't have a camera. We also need two action

Figure 16-2. *The Camera application in action*

methods, one that will be used for both the *Take New Picture* and *Select from Camera Roll* buttons and a separate one for letting the user select an existing picture from the photo library. Expand the *Classes* and *Resources* folders so that you can get to all the relevant files.

Single-click *CameraViewController.h*, and make the following changes:

```
#import <UIKit/UIKit.h>

@interface CameraViewController : UIViewController
       <UIImagePickerControllerDelegate, UINavigationControllerDelegate> {
    UIImageView *imageView;
    UIButton *takePictureButton;
    UIButton *selectFromCameraRollButton;
}
@property (nonatomic, retain) IBOutlet UIImageView *imageView;
@property (nonatomic, retain) IBOutlet UIButton *takePictureButton;
@property (nonatomic, retain) IBOutlet UIButton
    *selectFromCameraRollButton;
- (IBAction)getCameraPicture:(id)sender;
- (IBAction)selectExistingPicture;
@end
```

The first thing you might notice is that we've actually conformed our class to two different protocols: `UIImagePickerControllerDelegate` and `UINavigationControllerDelegate`. Because `UIImagePickerController` is a subclass of `UINavigationController`, we have to conform our class to both of these protocols. The methods in `UINavigation ControllerDelegate` are both optional, and we don't need either of them to use the image picker, but we need to conform to the protocol or the compiler will give us a warning. Everything else here is pretty straightforward, so save it. Now, double-click *CameraViewController. xib* to open the file in Interface Builder.

Designing the Interface

Drag three *Round Rect Buttons* from the library over to the window labeled *View*. Place them one above the next. Double-click the top one, and give it a title of *Take New Picture*. Double-click the middle one, and give it a title of *Pick from Camera Roll*. Then double-click the bottom button, and give it a title of *Pick from Library*. Next, drag an *Image View* from the library, and place it above the buttons. Expand it to take the entire space of the view above the buttons, as shown in Figure 16-2.

Now, control-drag from the *File's Owner* icon to the image view, and select the *imageView* outlet. Drag again from *File's Owner* to the *Take New Picture* button, and select the *takePictureButton* outlet. Finally, drag from *File's Owner* to the *Pick from Camera Roll* button, and select the *selectFromCameraRollButton* outlet.

Next, select the *Take New Picture* button, and press ⌘**2** to bring up the connections inspector. Drag from the *Touch Up Inside* event to *File's Owner*, and select the *getCameraPicture:* action. Next, single-click the *Pick from Camera Roll* button, drag from the *Touch Up Inside* event on the connections inspector to *File's Owner*, and select the *getCameraPicture:* action. Then, select the *Pick from Library* button. Drag from the *Touch Up Inside* event on the connections inspector to *File's Owner*, and select the *selectExistingPicture* action. Once you've made those connections, save and close the nib, and go back to Xcode.

Implementing the Camera View Controller

Single-click *CameraViewController.m*, and make the following changes at the beginning of the file:

```
#import "CameraViewController.h"

@implementation CameraViewController
@synthesize imageView;
@synthesize takePictureButton;
@synthesize selectFromCameraRollButton;
- (void)viewDidLoad {
    if (![UIImagePickerController isSourceTypeAvailable:
        UIImagePickerControllerSourceTypeCamera]) {
        takePictureButton.hidden = YES;
        selectFromCameraRollButton.hidden = YES;
    }
}
...
```

Next, insert the following lines of code into the existing viewDidUnload and dealloc methods:

```
...
- (void)viewDidUnload {
    // Release any retained subviews of the main view.
    // e.g. self.myOutlet = nil;
    self.imageView = nil;
    self.takePictureButton = nil;
    self.selectFromCameraRollButton = nil;
    [super viewDidUnload];
}

- (void)dealloc {
    [imageView release];
    [takePictureButton release];
    [selectFromCameraRollButton release];
    [super dealloc];
}
...
```

Now insert the following methods at the end of the file:

```
...
#pragma mark -
- (IBAction)getCameraPicture:(id)sender {
    UIImagePickerController *picker =
        [[UIImagePickerController alloc] init];
    picker.delegate = self;
    picker.allowsImageEditing = YES;
    picker.sourceType = (sender == takePictureButton) ?
        UIImagePickerControllerSourceTypeCamera :
        UIImagePickerControllerSourceTypeSavedPhotosAlbum;
    [self presentModalViewController:picker animated:YES];
    [picker release];

}


- (IBAction)selectExistingPicture {
    if ([UIImagePickerController isSourceTypeAvailable:
        UIImagePickerControllerSourceTypePhotoLibrary]) {
        UIImagePickerController *picker =
            [[UIImagePickerController alloc] init];
        picker.delegate = self;
        picker.sourceType = UIImagePickerControllerSourceTypePhotoLibrary;
        [self presentModalViewController:picker animated:YES];
        [picker release];
    }
    else {
        UIAlertView *alert = [[UIAlertView alloc]
            initWithTitle:@"Error accessing photo library"
                message:@"Device does not support a photo library"
                delegate:nil
        cancelButtonTitle:@"Drat!"
        otherButtonTitles:nil];
        [alert show];
        [alert release];
    }
}

#pragma mark  -
- (void)imagePickerController:(UIImagePickerController *)picker
        didFinishPickingImage:(UIImage *)image
        editingInfo:(NSDictionary *)editingInfo {
    imageView.image = image;
    [picker dismissModalViewControllerAnimated:YES];

}
```

```
- (void)imagePickerControllerDidCancel:(UIImagePickerController *)picker {
    [picker dismissModalViewControllerAnimated:YES];
}
```

@end

The first method we wrote was `viewDidLoad:`, and all we do there is check to see whether we're running on a device that has a camera:

```
if (![UIImagePickerController isSourceTypeAvailable:
            UIImagePickerControllerSourceTypeCamera]){
```

If we're running a device without a camera, we hide the two camera-dependent buttons:

```
        takePictureButton.hidden = YES;
        selectFromCameraRollButton.hidden = YES;
    }
```

In our first action method, `getCameraPicture:`, we allocate and initialize a `UIImagePickerController` instance:

```
UIImagePickerController *picker =
        [[UIImagePickerController alloc] init];
```

We then assign `self` as the image picker's delegate and specify that the user is allowed to edit the image after taking it:

```
    picker.delegate = self;
    picker.allowsImageEditing = YES;
```

Next, we set the `sourceType` based on which button was pressed. If the user tapped the *Take New Picture* button, we tell the picker to allow use of the camera. If the user tapped the *Pick from Camera Roll* button, we use `UIImagePickerControllerSourceTypeSavedPhoto-sAlbum`, which, on a device with a camera, lets the user choose from the current camera roll.

```
    picker.sourceType = (sender == takePictureButton) ?
            UIImagePickerControllerSourceTypeCamera :
            UIImagePickerControllerSourceTypeSavedPhotosAlbum;
```

Finally, we present the image picker modally and release the instance:

```
    [self presentModalViewController:picker animated:YES];
    [picker release];
```

We didn't bother to check again to see whether this device supports the camera, because we know that the buttons that trigger this action method will not be visible if it doesn't. This method should never get called on a device that doesn't have a camera.

Our second action method is similar to the first one. This is where we allow the user to select an image from a photo library. If the photo library exists, we create an image picker with a sourceType of UIImagePickerControllerSourceTypePhotoLibrary.

```
if ([UIImagePickerController isSourceTypeAvailable:
    UIImagePickerControllerSourceTypePhotoLibrary]) {
    UIImagePickerController *picker =
        [[UIImagePickerController alloc] init];
    picker.delegate = self;
    picker.sourceType = UIImagePickerControllerSourceTypePhotoLibrary;
    [self presentModalViewController:picker animated:YES];
    [picker release];
}
```

If the device doesn't have a photo library, we show an error alert. Note that having an empty photo library is not the same as having no photo library. All current iPhone OS devices support a photo library, so this code should never fire, but it's a good idea to code defensively like this, since showing an alert is much kinder than crashing unexpectedly.

```
else {
    UIAlertView *alert = [[UIAlertView alloc]
    initWithTitle:@"Error accessing photo library"
        message:@"Device does not support a photo library"
        delegate:nil
cancelButtonTitle:@"Drat!"
otherButtonTitles:nil];
    [alert show];
    [alert release];
}
```

Next up are our two delegate methods. Let's look first at imagePickerController: didFinishPickingImage:editingInfo, which gets called when the user is done using the image picker. This same method will get called when the user has selected a picture, regardless of which source type was used. All we do in this method is set our imageView to display the returned image:

```
imageView.image = image;
```

After that, we tell the picker to dismiss itself so that the user is returned to our application view:

```
[picker dismissModalViewControllerAnimated:YES];
```

This last step of dismissing the modal view controller is repeated in `imagePickerControllerDidCancel:`. We don't need to do anything else if the user cancels, but we do need the image picker to go away, or the image picker will just sit there getting in the way of our application's view.

That's all we need to do. We don't even need to link in any additional libraries this time. Compile and run. If you're running on the simulator, you won't have the option to take a new picture. If you have the opportunity to run on a real device, go ahead and try it. You should be able to take a new picture and zoom in and out of the picture using the pinch gestures (see Figure 16-3).

If you zoom in before hitting the *Use Photo* button, the image that gets returned to our application in the delegate method will be the cropped image.

Figure 16-3. *If you set allowsEditing to YES, the user will be able to zoom and crop images before returning to our application.*

It's a Snap!

Believe it or not, that's all there is to letting your users take pictures with the iPhone's camera so that the pictures can be used by your application. You can even let the user do a small amount of editing on that image if you so choose.

In the next chapter, we're going to look at reaching a larger audience for your iPhone applications by making them oh so easy to translate into other languages. *Êtes-vous prêt? Tournez la page et allez directement. Allez, allez!*

Chapter 17

Application Localization

*a*t the time of this writing, the iPhone is available in 84 different countries and that number will continue to increase over time. You can now buy and use an iPhone on every continent except Antarctica. If you plan on releasing applications through the iPhone App Store, your potential market is considerably larger than just people in your own country who speak your own language. Fortunately, iPhone has a robust **localization** architecture that lets you easily translate your application (or have it translated by others) into not only multiple languages but even into multiple dialects of the same language. Want to provide different terminology to English speakers in the United Kingdom than you do to English speakers in the United States? No problem.

That is, no problem at all if you've written your code correctly. Retrofitting an existing application to support localization is much harder than writing your application that way from the start. In this chapter, we'll show you how to write your code so it is easy to localize, and then we'll go about localizing a sample application.

Localization Architecture

When a nonlocalized application is run, all of the application's text will be presented in the developer's own language, also known as the **development base language**.

When developers decide to localize their application, they create a subdirectory in their application bundle for each supported language. Each language's subdirectory contains a subset of the application's resources that were translated into that language. Each subdirectory is called a **localization project**,

also called a **localization folder**. Localization folder names always end with the extension
.lproj.

In the Settings application, the user has the ability to set the language and region format.
For example, if the user's language is English, available regions might be United States,
Australia, or Hong Kong—all regions in which English is spoken.

When a localized application needs to load a resource, such as an image, property list, or nib,
the application checks the user's language and region and looks for a localization folder that
matches that setting. If it finds one, it will load the localized version of the resource instead
of the base version.

For users who selected French as their iPhones' language and France as their region, the
application will look first for a localization folder named *fr_FR.lproj*. The first two letters of the
folder name are the ISO country code that represents the French language. The two letters
following the underscore are the ISO two-digit code that represents France.

If the application cannot find a match using the two-digit code, it will look for a match using
the language's three-digit ISO code. All languages have three-digit codes. Only some have
two-digit codes.

NOTE

You can find a list of the current ISO country codes on the ISO web site. Both the two- and three-digit
codes are part of the ISO 3166 standard (`http://www.iso.org/iso/country_codes.htm`).

In our previous example, if the application was unable to find the folder named *fr_FR.lproj*,
it will look for a localization folder named *fre_FR* or *fra_FR*. All languages have at least one
three-digit code; some have two three-digit codes, one for the English spelling of the language and one for the native spelling. When a language has both a two-digit code and a
three-digit code, the two-digit code is preferred.

If the application cannot find a folder that is an exact match, it will then look for a localization folder in the application bundle that matches just the language code without the
region code. So, staying with our French-speaking person from France, the application
would next look for a localization project called *fr.lproj*. If it didn't find a language project
with that name, it would try looking for *fre.lproj*, then *fra.lproj*. If none of those was found, it
would look for *French.lproj*. The last construct exists to support legacy Mac OS X applications,
and generally speaking, you should avoid it (though there is an exception to that rule that
we'll look at later in this chapter).

If the application doesn't find a language project that matches either the language/region
combination or just the language, it will use the resources from the development base
language. If it does find an appropriate localization project, it will always look there first for

any resources that it needs. If you load a UIImage using imageNamed:, for example, it will look first for an image with the specified name in the localization project. If it finds one, it will use it. If it doesn't, it will fall back to the base language resource.

If an application has more than one localization project that matches, for example, a project called *fr_FR.lproj* and one called *fr.lproj*, it will look first in the more specific match, in this case *fr_FR.lproj*. If it doesn't find the resource there, it will look in the *fr.lproj*. This gives you the ability to provide resources common to all speakers of a language in one language project, localizing only those resources that are impacted by differences in dialect or geographic region.

You only have to localize resources that are affected by language or country. If an image in your application has no words and its meaning is universal, there's no need to localize that image.

Using String Files

What do we do about string literals and string constants in your source code? Consider this source code from the previous chapter:

```
UIAlertView *alert = [[UIAlertView alloc]
    initWithTitle:@"Error accessing photo library"
         message:@"Device does not support a photo library"
        delegate:nil
cancelButtonTitle:@"Drat!"
otherButtonTitles:nil];
[alert show];
[alert release];
```

If we've gone through the effort of localizing our application for a particular audience, we certainly don't want to be presenting alerts written in the development base language.

The answer is to store these strings in special text files call **string files**. String files are nothing more than Unicode (UTF-16) text files that contain a list of string pairs, each identified by a comment.

Here is an example of what a strings file might look like in your application:

```
/* Used to ask the user his/her first name */
"First Name" = "First Name";

/* Used to get the user's last name */
"Last Name" = "Last Name";

/* Used to ask the user's birth date */
"Birthday" = "Birthday";
```

The values between the /* and the */ characters are just comments for the translator. They are not used in the application and can safely be excluded, though they're a good idea. They give context, showing how a particular string is being used in the application.

You'll notice that each line lists the same string twice. The string on the left side of the equals sign acts as a key, and it will always contain the same value regardless of language. The value on the right side of the equals sign is the one that gets translated to the local language. So, the preceding strings file, localized into French, might look like this:

```
/* Used to ask the user his/her first name */
"First Name " = "Prénom";

/* Used to get the user's last name */
"Last Name " = "Nom de famille";

/* Used to ask the user's birth date */
"Birthday" = "Anniversaire";
```

Creating the Strings File

You won't actually create the strings file by hand. Instead, you'll embed all localizable text strings in a special macro in your code. Once your source code is final and ready for localization, you'll run a command-line program, named genstrings, which will search all your code files for occurrences of the macro, pulling out all the unique strings and embedding them in a localizable strings file.

Here's how the macro works. Let's start with a traditional string declaration:

```
NSString *myString = @"First Name";
```

To make this string localizable, you'll do this instead:

```
NSString *myString = NSLocalizedString(@"First Name",
    @"Used to ask the user his/her first name");
```

The NSLocalizedString macro takes two parameters. The first is the string value in the base language. If there is no localization, the application will use this string. The second parameter will be used as a comment in the strings file.

NSLocalizedString looks in the application bundle, inside the appropriate localization project, for a strings file named *localizable.strings*. If it does not find the file, it returns its first parameter, and the string will appear in the development base language. Strings are typically displayed only in the base language during development, since the application will not yet be localized.

If NSLocalizedString finds the strings file, it searches the file for a line that matches the first parameter. In the preceding example, NSLocalizedString will search the strings file for the string "First Name". If it doesn't find a match in the localization project that matches the user's language settings, it will then look for a strings file in the base language and use the value there. If there is no strings file, it will just use the first parameter you passed to the NSLocalizedString macro.

Let's take a look at this process in action.

Real-World iPhone: Localizing Your Application

We're going to create a small application that displays the user's current **locale**. A locale (an instance of NSLocale) represents both the user's language and region. It is used by the system to determine what language to use when interacting with the user and to determine how to display dates, currency, and time information, among other things. After we create the application, we will then localize it into other languages. You'll learn how to localize nib files, string files, images, and even your application's icon. You can see what our application is going to look like in Figure 17-1. The name across the top comes from the user's locale. The words down the left side of the view are static labels that are set in the nib file. The words down the right side are set programmatically using outlets. The flag image at the bottom of the screen is a static UIImageView.

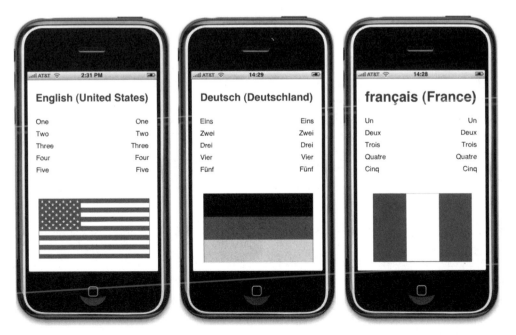

Figure 17-1. *The LocalizeMe application shown with three different language/region settings*

Let's hop right into it. Create a new project in Xcode using the view-based application template, and call it LocalizeMe. If you look in the *17 LocalizeMe* folder, you'll see a subfolder named *Resources*. Inside *Resources*, you'll find a directory named *Base Language*. In that folder, you'll find two images, *icon.png* and *flag.png*. Drag both of those to the *Resources* folder of your project. Now, single-click *LocalizeMe-Info.plist*, and set the *Icon file* value to *icon.png* so that the icon image will be used as your application's icon.

We need to create outlets to a total of six labels: one for the blue label across the top of the view and five for the words down the right-hand side. Expand the *Classes* folder, single-click *LocalizeMeViewController.h*, and make the following changes:

```
#import <UIKit/UIKit.h>

@interface LocalizeMeViewController : UIViewController {
    UILabel *localeLabel;
    UILabel *label1;
    UILabel *label2;
    UILabel *label3;
    UILabel *label4;
    UILabel *label5;
}
@property (nonatomic, retain) IBOutlet UILabel *localeLabel;
@property (nonatomic, retain) IBOutlet UILabel *label1;
@property (nonatomic, retain) IBOutlet UILabel *label2;
@property (nonatomic, retain) IBOutlet UILabel *label3;
@property (nonatomic, retain) IBOutlet UILabel *label4;
@property (nonatomic, retain) IBOutlet UILabel *label5;
@end
```

Now double-click the *LocalizeMeViewController.xib* file to open the file in Interface Builder. Once it's open, drag a *Label* from the library, and drop it at the top of the window. Resize it so that it takes the entire width of the view from blue guide line to blue guide line. With the label selected, make the text bold using ⌘B, and change the text alignment to centered and the text color to a bright blue using the attributes inspector.

You can also make the font size larger if you wish. To do that, select **Show Fonts** from the **Font** menu. Make the font as large as you like. As long as *Adjust to fit* is selected in the attributes inspector, the text will be resized if it gets too long to fit.

With your label in place, control-drag from the *File's Owner* icon to this new label, and select the *localeLabel* outlet.

Next, drag five more *Labels* from the library, and put them against the left margin using the blue guide line, one above the other, as shown in Figure 17-1. Double-click the top one, and change it from *Label* to *One*. Repeat that step with the other four labels you just added so that they contain the numbers from one to five spelled out.

Drag five more *Labels* from the library, this time placing them against the right margin. Change the text alignment using the attributes inspector so that they are right aligned, and increase the size of the label so that it stretches from the right blue guide line to about the middle of the view. Control-drag from *File's Owner* to each of the five new labels, connecting each one to a different numbered label outlet. Now, double-click each one of the new labels, and delete its text. We will be setting these values programmatically.

Finally, drag an *Image View* from the library over to the bottom part of the view. In the attributes inspector, select *flag.png* for the view's *Image* attribute, and resize the image to stretch from blue guide line to blue guide line. Next, on the attributes inspector, change the *Mode* attribute from *Center* to *Aspect Fit*. Not all flags have the same aspect ratio, and we want to make sure the localized versions of the image look right. Selecting this option will cause the image view to resize any other images put in this image view so they fit, but it will maintain the correct aspect ratio (ratio of height to width). If you like, make the flag taller, until the sides of the flag touch the blue guide lines.

Save and close the nib file, and head back to Xcode. Single-click *LocalizeMeViewController.m*, and insert the following code at the top of the file:

```
#import "LocalizeMeViewController.h"

@implementation LocalizeMeViewController
@synthesize localeLabel;
@synthesize label1;
@synthesize label2;
@synthesize label3;
@synthesize label4;
@synthesize label5;

- (void)viewDidLoad {

    NSLocale *locale = [NSLocale currentLocale];
    NSString *displayNameString = [locale
        displayNameForKey:NSLocaleIdentifier
        value:[locale localeIdentifier]];
    localeLabel.text = displayNameString;

    label1.text = NSLocalizedString(@"One", @"The number 1");
    label2.text = NSLocalizedString(@"Two", @"The number 2");
    label3.text = NSLocalizedString(@"Three", @"The number 3");
    label4.text = NSLocalizedString(@"Four", @"The number 4");
    label5.text = NSLocalizedString(@"Five", @"The number 5");
    [super viewDidLoad];
}
...
```

Also, add the following code to the existing `viewDidUnload` and `dealloc` methods:

```
...
- (void)viewDidUnload {
    // Release any retained subviews of the main view.
    // e.g. self.myOutlet = nil;
    self.localeLabel = nil;
    self.label1 = nil;
    self.label2 = nil;
    self.label3 = nil;
    self.label4 = nil;
    self.label5 = nil;
    [super viewDidUnload];
}

- (void)dealloc {
    [localeLabel release];
    [label1 release];
    [label2 release];
    [label3 release];
    [label4 release];
    [label5 release];
    [super dealloc];
}
@end
```

The only thing we need to look at in this class is the `viewDidLoad` method. The first thing we do there is get an `NSLocale` instance that represents the users' current locale, which can tell us both their language and their region preferences, as set in their iPhone's Settings application.

```
NSLocale *locale = [NSLocale currentLocale];
```

Looking at the Current Locale

The next line of code might need a little bit of explanation. `NSLocale` works somewhat like a dictionary. There is a whole bunch of information that it can give us about the current users' preferences, including the name of the currency they use and the date format they expect. You can find a complete list of the information that you can retrieve in the `NSLocale` API reference.

In this next line of code, we're retrieving the **locale identifier**, which is the name of the language and/or region that this locale represents. We're using a function called `displayNameForKey:value:`. The purpose of this method is to return the value of the item we've requested in a specific language.

The display name for the French language, for example, would be *Français* in French, but *French* in English. This method gives us the ability to retrieve data about any locale so that it can be displayed appropriately to any users. In this case, we're getting the display name for the locale in the language of that locale, which is why we pass in [locale localeIdentifier] in the second argument. The localeIdentifier is a string in the format we used earlier to create our language projects. For an American English speaker, it would be *en_US* and for a French speaker from France, it would be *fr_FR*.

```
NSString *displayNameString = [locale
            displayNameForKey:NSLocaleIdentifier
            value:[locale localeIdentifier]];
```

Once we have the display name, we use it to set the top label in the view:

```
localeLabel.text = displayNameString;
```

Next, we set the five other labels to the numbers one through five spelled out in our development base language. We also provide a comment telling what each word is. You can just pass an empty string if the words are obvious, as they are here, but any string you pass in the second argument will be turned into a comment in the strings file, so you can use this comment to communicate with the person doing your translations.

```
label1.text = NSLocalizedString(@"One", @"The number 1");
label2.text = NSLocalizedString(@"Two", @"The number 2");
label3.text = NSLocalizedString(@"Three", @"The number 3");
label4.text = NSLocalizedString(@"Four", @"The number 4");
label5.text = NSLocalizedString(@"Five", @"The number 5");
```

Trying Out LocalizeMe

Let's run our application now. You can use either the simulator or a device to test this. The simulator does seem to cache some language and region settings, so you may want to do this on the device if you have that option. Once the application launches, it should look like Figure 17-2.

By using the NSLocalizedString macros instead of static strings, we are all ready for localization. But we are not localized yet. If you use the Settings application on the simulator or on your iPhone to change to another language or region, the results would look essentially the same, except for the label at the top of the view (see Figure 17-3).

Figure 17-2. *The language running under the authors' base language. Our application is set up for localization but is not yet localized.*

Figure 17-3. *The nonlocalized application run on an iPhone set to use the French language*

Localizing the Nib

Now, let's localize the nib file. The basic process for localizing any file is the same. In Xcode, single-click *LocalizeMeViewController.xib*, and then press ⌘I to open the *Info* window for that file. If the window is not currently showing the *General* tab, select the *General* tab. Click the button that says *Make File Localizable* in the lower-left part of the window (see Figure 17-4).

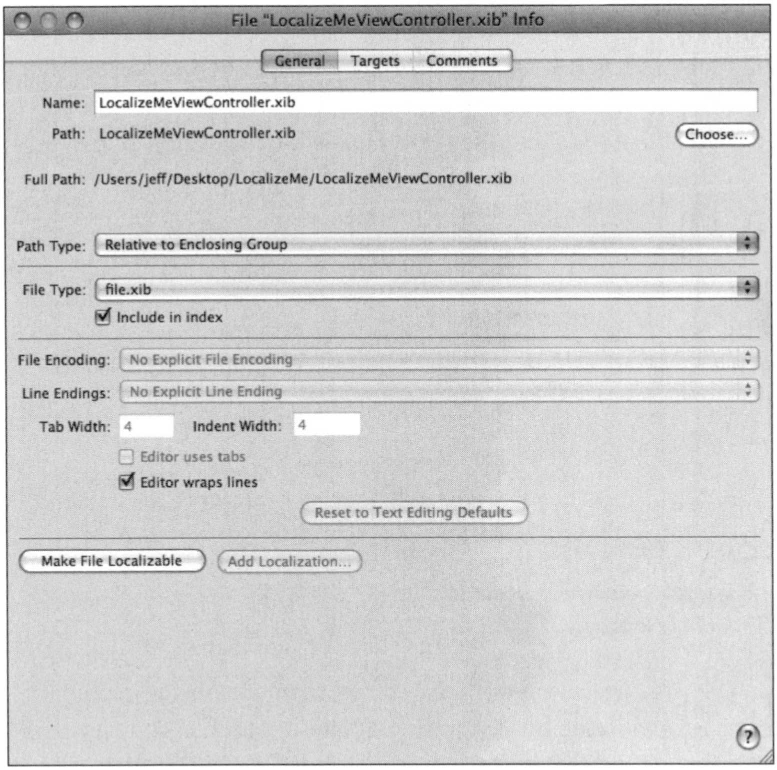

Figure 17-4. *The LocalizeMeViewController.xib Info window*

When you click the *Make File Localizable* button, the window will switch to the *Targets* tab. Close the *Info* window, and look at the *Groups & Files* pane in Xcode. Notice that the *LocalizeMeViewController.xib* file now has a disclosure triangle next to it, as if it were a group or folder. Expand it, and take a look (see Figure 17-5).

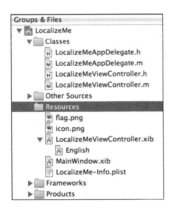

Figure 17-5. *Localizable files have a disclosure triangle and a child value for each language or region you add.*

Looking at the Localized Project Structure

In our project, *LocalizeMeViewController.xib* has one child, *English*. This one was created automatically, and it represents your development base language. Go to the Finder, and open your *LocalizeMe* project folder. You should see a new folder named *English.lproj* (see Figure 17-6).

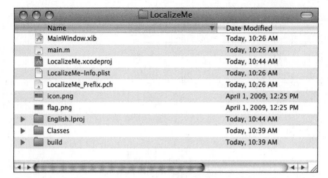

Figure 17-6. *By making a file localizable, Xcode created a language project folder for our base language.*

At the time of this writing, Xcode is still using the legacy project name for the development base language project, *English.lproj*, rather than following Apple's localization convention of using the ISO two-letter language code, which would have resulted in a folder called *en.lproj* instead. This is listed in the Xcode 3.1 release notes as a known issue. You don't need to change this folder name, as it will work just fine, but use the ISO codes for any new localizations you add.

Single-click *LocalizeMeViewController.xib* in the *Groups & Files* pane again, and press ⌘I to bring the *Info* window back up. Go back to the *General* tab if you're not on it, and click the *Add Localization* button. A sheet will drop down and ask you to enter the name of the new localization. Let's add localization for the French language, so type *fr*. Don't select **French** from the drop-down menu, as that will use the legacy name of *French*.

TIP

When dealing with locales, language codes are lowercase, but country codes are uppercase. So, the correct name for the French language project is *fr.lproj*, but the project for Parisian French (French as spoken by people in France) is *fr_FR.lproj*, not *fr_fr.lproj* or *FR_fr.lproj*. The iPhone's file system is case sensitive, so it is important to match case correctly.

After you press return, Xcode will create a new localization project in your project folder called *fr.lproj* and copy *LocalizeMeViewController.xib* there. In the *Groups & Files* pane,

LocalizeMeViewController.xib should now have two children, *English* and *fr*. Double-click *fr* to open the nib file that will be shown to French speakers.

CAUTION

Xcode will allow you to localize pretty much any file in the *Groups & Files* pane. Just because you can, doesn't mean you should. Do not ever localize a source code file. Doing so will cause compile errors, as multiple object files with the same name will be created.

The nib file that opens in Interface Builder will look exactly like the one you built earlier, because the nib file you just created is a copy of the earlier one. Any changes you make to this one will be shown to people who speak French, so double-click each of the labels on the left side and change them from *One, Two, Three, Four, Five* to *Un, Deux, Trois, Quatre, Cinq*. Once you have changed them, save the nib, and go back to Xcode. Your nib is now localized in to French. Compile and run the program. After it launches, tap the home button.

iPhone caches settings, so if we were to just go and run the application now, there's a very good chance we would see exactly what we saw before. In order to make sure we see the correct thing, we need to go reset the simulator and do a clean build of our application.

On the simulator, there's a menu option under the **iPhone Simulator** menu to **Reset Content and Settings…**. Select that now. After you select it, you should be presented with the home screen. From there, go to the Settings application, and select the *General* row and then the row labeled *International*. From here, you'll be able to change your language and region preferences (see Figure 17-7).

Change the *Region Format* from *United States* to *France* (which is under the row for *French*), and then change *Language* from *English* to *Français*. Now click the *Done* button. And finally, quit the simulator, and go to Xcode. You want to change the *Region Format* first, because once you change the language, your iPhone will reset and go back to the home screen. Now, your phone is set to use French.

Back in Xcode, and select **Clean** from the **Build** menu. Make sure all the checkboxes on the presented sheet are checked, and then click the *Clean* button. This will remove all traces of the previous build. Once the clean operation is done, build and run LocalizeMe again. This time, the words down the left-hand side should show up in French (see Figure 17-8).

Figure 17-7. *Changing the language and region, the two settings that affect the user's locale*

The problem is that the flag and right column of text are still wrong. We'll take care of the flag first. Now, we could have changed the flag image right in the nib by just selecting a different image for the image view in the French localized nib file. Instead of doing that, we'll actually localize the flag image itself. When an image or other resource used by a nib is localized, the nib will automatically show the correct version for the language, though not for the dialect, at the time of this writing. If we localize the *flag.png* file itself with a French version, the nib will automatically show the correct flag when appropriate.

Localizing an Image

Let's localize the flag image now. Single-click *flag.png* in Xcode's *Groups & Files* pane. Next, press ⌘I to bring up the *Info* window for that file, and click the *Make File Localizable* button. Once you do that, Xcode is going to copy *flag.png* into the *English.lproj* folder (or from your base language folder, if it's different). Switch back to the *General* tab, and click the *Add Localization* button. When prompted for a language, type *fr*. There should now be another file in your

Figure 17-8. *The application is partially translated into French now.*

fr.lproj folder inside of your *LocalizeMe* project folder, called *flag.png*; it is a copy of the *flag.png* file from the base language. Obviously, that's not the correct image. Since Xcode doesn't let you edit image files, the easiest way get the right image into the localization project is to just copy the correct image into the project using the Finder. In the *Resources* folder of the *17 LocalizeMe* folder, you'll find a folder called *fr*. In that subfolder, you'll find a *flag.png* file that contains the French flag rather than the American one. Copy the *flag.png* file from there to your project's *fr.lproj* subfolder, overwriting the file that's there.

That's it. You're done. If you are running in the simulator, reset the simulator and do a clean build, as you did earlier before rerunning the program. Once you rerun, you'll need to reset the region and language to get the French flag to appear.

If you're running on the device, your iPhone has probably cached the American flag from the last time you ran the application, let's remove the old application from your iPhone using the *Organizer* window in Xcode.

Select **Organizer** from the **Window** menu, or press ^⌘O to bring it up (see Figure 17-9).

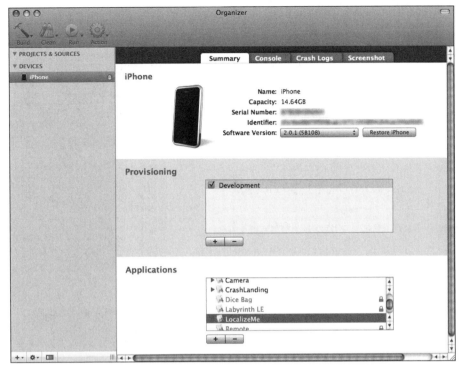

Figure 17-9. *The Xcode Organizer window lets you manually remove applications.*

On the *Summary* tab, you'll see three sections. The bottommost section is labeled *Applications*. In the list of applications, look for *LocalizeMe*; select it, and click the minus button to remove the old version of that application and the caches associated with it.

Now, select **Clean** from the **Build** menu, and build and run the application again. Once the application launches, you'll need to reset the region then the language and the French flag should now come up in addition to the French words down the left-hand side (see Figure 17-10).

Localizing the Application Icon

You can localize the application's icon image in exactly the same way that you localized *flag.png*. Single-click *icon.png* in the *Groups & Files* pane's *Resources* group. Bring up the *Info* window, and switch to the *General* tab if you're not already there. Click the *Make File Localizable* button, and

Figure 17-10. *The image and nib are both localized now.*

switch back to the *General* tab. Click the *Add Localization* button, and when prompted for the language, type *fr*.

In the *fr* folder in the *Resources* folder of *17 LocalizeMe*, where you just copied the *flag.png* file, you'll also find a localized version of *icon.png*. Copy that into your *fr.lproj* folder using the Finder, overwriting the version that's there. Now, the iPhone will automatically detect and show this icon to users who speak French, though you'll probably need to delete the application from your phone again, or reset the simulator to get the change to show up.

Generating and Localizing a Strings File

If you look at Figure 17-10, you'll see that the words on the right-hand side of the view are still in English. In order to translate those, we need to generate our base language strings file and then localize that. In order to accomplish this, we'll need to leave the comfy confines of Xcode for a few minutes.

Launch *Terminal.app*, which is in */Applications/Utilities/*. When the terminal window opens, type *cd* followed by a space. Don't press return.

Figure 17-11. *We localized our application icon!*

Now, go to the Finder, and drag your LocalizeMe project folder to the terminal window. As soon as you drop the folder onto the terminal window, the path to the project folder should appear on the command line. Now, press return.

The cd command is Unix-speak for "change directory," so what you've just done is steer your terminal session from its default directory over to your project directory.

Our next step is to run the program genstrings and tell it to find all the occurrences of NSLocalizedString in our *.m* files in the *Classes* folder. To do this, type the following command, and then press return:

```
genstrings ./Classes/*.m
```

When the command is done executing (it just takes a second on a project this small) you'll be returned to the command line. In the Finder, look in the project folder for a new file called *Localizable.strings*. Drag that to the *Resources* folder in Xcode's *Groups & Files* pane, but when it prompts you, don't click the *Add* button just yet.

TIP

You can rerun `genstrings` at any time to re-create your base language file, but once you have had your strings file localized into another language, it's important that you don't change the text used in any of the `NSLocalizedString()` macros. That base-language version of the string is used as a key to retrieve the translations, so if you change them, the translated version will no longer be found, and you will either have to update the localized strings file or have it retranslated.

Localizable.strings files are encoded in UTF-16, which is a two-byte version of Unicode. Most of us are probably using UTF-8 or a language-local encoding scheme as our default encoding in Xcode. When we import the *Localizable.strings* file into our project, we need to take that into account. First, uncheck the box that says *Copy items into destination group's folder (if needed)*, because the file is already in our project folder. More importantly, change the text encoding to *Unicode (UTF-16)* (see Figure 17-12). If you don't do that, the file will look like gibberish when you try to edit it in Xcode.

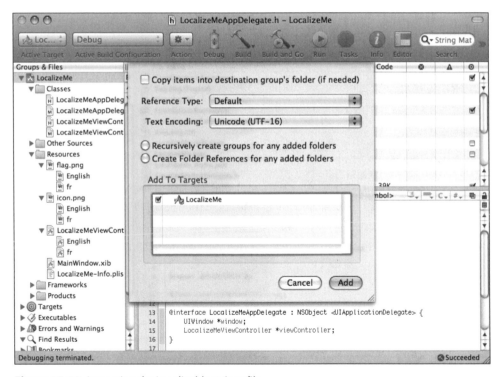

Figure 17-12. *Importing the Localizable.strings file*

Now, go ahead and click the *Add* button. Once the file is imported, single-click *Localizable. strings* in *Resources*, and take a look at it. It should contain five entries, because we use NSLocalizableString five times with five distinct values. The values that we passed in as the second argument have become the comments for each of the strings.

The strings were generated in alphabetical order, which is a nice feature. In this case, since we're dealing with numbers, alphabetical order is not the most intuitive way to present them, but in most cases, having them in alphabetical order will be helpful.

```
/* The number 5 */
"Five" = "Five";

/* The number 4 */
"Four" = "Four";

/* The number 1 */
"One" = "One";

/* The number 3 */
"Three" = "Three";

/* The number 2 */
"Two" = "Two";
```

Let's localize this sucker.

Single-click *Localizable.strings*, and press ⌘I to bring up the *Info* window. If you switch to the *General* tab, you'll find that same *Make File Localizable* button that we used to make the images and the nib file localizable. Click it now.

Switch back to the *General* tab, and click *Add Localization*. When prompted for a language, type *fr* to indicate that we are localizing for all dialects of the French language. Back in the *Groups & Files* pane of Xcode, click the disclosure triangle next to *Localizable.strings*. Single-click *fr*, and in the editor pane of Xcode, make the following changes:

```
/* The number 5 */
"Five" = "Cinq";

/* The number 4 */
"Four" = "Quatre";

/* The number 1 */
"One" = "Un";

/* The number 3 */
"Three" = "Trois";
```

```
/* The number 2 */
"Two" = "Deux";
```

In real life (unless you're multilingual), you would ordinarily send this file out to a translation service to translate the values on the right of the equals signs. In this simple example, armed with knowledge that came from years of watching *Sesame Street*, we can do the translation ourselves.

Now save, compile, and run—our application is now fully localized for the French language. We've provided you with the information in the *Resources* subfolder of *17 LocalizeMe* to do the German and Canadian French localizations if you want some more practice. You'll find two more copies of the *icon.png*, *flag.png*, and *Localizable.strings* file if you want to try adding support for additional languages.

Auf Wiedersehen

If you want to maximize sales of your iPhone application, localize it as much as possible. Fortunately, iPhone's localization architecture makes easy work of supporting multiple languages, and even multiple dialects of the same language, within your application. As you saw in this chapter, nearly any type of file that you add to your application can be localized, as needed.

Even if you don't plan on localizing your application, get in the habit of using `NSLocalizedString` instead of just using static strings in your code. With Xcode's Code Sense feature, the difference in typing time is negligible, and should you ever want to translate your application, your life will be much, much easier.

At this point, our journey is nearly done. We're almost to the end of our travels together. After the next chapter, we'll be saying *sayonara, au revoir, auf wiedersehen, αντίο, arrivederci,* and *adiós*. You now have a solid foundation you can use to build your own cool iPhone applications. Stick around for the going-away party though, as we've still got a few helpful bits of information for you.

Chapter 18

Where to Next?

Well, wow! You're still with us, huh? Great! It sure has been a long journey since that very first iPhone application we built together. You've certainly come a long way. We'd love to tell you that you now know it all, but when it comes to technology, and especially when it comes to programming, you never know it all. The programming language and frameworks we've been working with for the last 17 chapters are the end result of more than 20 years of evolution. And Apple engineers are feverishly working round the clock, thinking of that next cool new thing. The iPhone platform has just begun to blossom. There is so much more to come.

By making it through this book, you've built yourself a sturdy foundation. You've got a solid knowledge of Objective-C, Cocoa Touch, and the tools that bring these technologies together to create incredible new iPhone applications. You understand the iPhone software architecture, the design patterns that make Cocoa Touch sing. In short, you are ready to chart your own course. We are so proud! So where to next?

Getting Unstuck

At its core, programming is about problem solving, about figuring things out. It's fun, and it's rewarding like few things are. But, at times, you will run up against a puzzle that just seems insurmountable, a problem that just does not seem to have a solution.

Sometimes, the answer just appears if you take a bit of time away from the problem. A good night's sleep or a few hours of doing something different can often be all that is needed to get you through it. Believe us; you can stare at the same problem for hours, overanalyzing and getting yourself so worked up that you miss an obvious solution.

And then there are times when even a change of scenery doesn't help. And in those situations, it's good to have friends in high places. The following sections outline some resources you can turn to when you're in a bind.

Apple's Documentation

Become one with Xcode's documentation browser, grasshopper. The documentation browser is a front end to a wealth of incredibly valuable sample source code, concept guides, API references, video tutorials, and a whole lot more. There are few areas of the iPhone that you won't be able to learn more about by making your way through Apple's documentation. And if you get comfortable with Apple's documentation, making your way through uncharted territories and new technologies as Apple rolls them out will be easier.

NOTE

> Xcode's documentation browser takes you to the same information you can get to by going to Apple's Developer Connection web site at `http://developer.apple.com`.

Mailing Lists

You might also want to sign up for these handy mailing lists:

`http://lists.apple.com/mailman/listinfo/cocoa-dev` — This moderately high-volume list run by Apple is primarily about Cocoa for Mac OS X. Because of the common heritage shared by Cocoa and Cocoa Touch, however, many of the people on this list may be able to help you. Make sure to search the list archives before asking your question, though.

`http://lists.apple.com/mailman/listinfo/xcode-users` — Another list maintained by Apple, this one is specific to questions and problems related to Xcode.

`http://lists.apple.com/mailman/listinfo/quartz-dev` — This is an Apple-maintained mailing list for discussion of the Quartz 2D and Core Graphics technologies.

Discussion Forums

These discussion forums allow you to post your questions to a wide range of forum readers:

`http://devforums.apple.com` — This is a web forum set up by Apple specifically for discussing iPhone and Mac software development. Many iPhone programmers, both new and experienced, including many of Apple's engineers and evangelists, contribute to these forums. It's also the only place you can legally discuss issues with pre-release versions of the SDK that are under nondisclosure agreements.

`http://www.iphonedevsdk.com` — On this web forum, iPhone programmers, both new and experienced, help each other out with problems and advice.

`http://discussions.apple.com/category.jspa?categoryID=164` — This link connects you to Apple's community forums for Mac and iPhone software developers.

`http://discussions.apple.com/category.jspa?categoryID=201` — This one connects to Apple's community forums for discussing the iPhone.

Web Sites

Visit these web sites for helpful coding advice:

`http://www.iphonedevbook.com` — This is the official web site for this book. We will post errata as people report bugs and typos to us and maintain the most current version of all book projects. We'll also tell you what we've been working on lately and what we've got in the works.

`http://www.cocoadevcentral.com` — This portal contains links to a great many Cocoa-related web sites and tutorials.

`http://cocoaheads.org` — CocoaHeads is a group dedicated to peer support and promotion of Cocoa. It focuses on local groups with regular meetings where Cocoa developers can get together, help each other out, and even socialize a little bit. There's nothing better than knowing a real person who can help you out, so if there's a Cocoa-Heads group in your area, check it out. If there's not, why not start one?

`http://nscodernight.com` — NSCoder Nights are weekly, organized meetings where Cocoa programmers get together to code and socialize. Like CocoaHeads meetings, NSCoder Nights are independently organized local events.

`http://cocoablogs.com` — This portal contains links to a great many blogs related to Cocoa programming.

`http://www.iphonedevcentral.org` — This web site is devoted to iPhone programming tutorials.

`http://www.iphonesdkarticles.com/` — This site is also devoted to iPhone SDK tutorials.

`http://stackoverflow.com/` — A community site targeted at programmers. Many experienced iPhone programmers hang out here and answer questions.

Blogs

If you still haven't found a solution to your coding dilemma, you might want to read these blogs:

`http://theocacao.com` — This blog is maintained by Scott Stevenson, an experienced Cocoa programmer.

`http://www.wilshipley.com/blog/` — Wil Shipley is one of the most experienced Objective-C programmers on the planet. His *Pimp My Code* series of blog postings should be required reading for any Objective-C programmer.

`http://rentzsch.com` — Wolf Rentzsch is an experienced, independent Cocoa programmer and the founder of the C4 independent developers' conference.

`http://eschatologist.net/blog/` — Chris Hanson works at Apple on the Xcode team, and his blog is filled with great insight and information about Xcode and related topics.

`http://cocoacast.com/` — A blog and podcast about various Cocoa programming topics, available in both English and French.

Dave and Jeff Blogs and Twitter

Dave and Jeff are both active Twitter users. You can follow them via `http://twitter.com/davemark` and `http://twitter.com/jeff_lamarche`. Dave and Jeff have blogs, too:

`http://iphonedevelopment.blogspot.com` — This is Jeff's iPhone development blog. It contains lots of great technical material. Be sure to check out the ongoing series on OpenGL ES.

`http://www.davemark.com` — This is Dave's little slice of everything under the sun. There's some technical material, but mostly just stuff that catches his attention.

More iPhone 3 Development

If you're serious about diving more deeply into the iPhone SDK, especially if you're interested in all the great new functionality introduced with the iPhone 3 SDK, of which we only scratched the surface in this book, you should check out *More iPhone 3 Development*, also by Dave Mark and Jeff LaMarche (Apress, 2009).

And If All Else Fails. . .

Drop Dave and Jeff an e-mail at daveandjeff@iphonedevbook.com. This is the perfect place to send e-mails about typos in the book or bugs in *our* code. We can't promise to respond to every e-mail, but we will read all of them. Be sure to read the errata before clicking send. And please *do* write and tell us about the cool applications you develop.

Farewell

We sure are glad you came along on this journey with us. We wish you the best of luck and hope that you enjoy programming the iPhone as much as we do.

Index

You Need the Companion eBook